*other books by Brenda Sternquist...*

*International Retailing* (In Japanese)  Tokyo, Japan: Shin-Hyoron Publisher (2009)

*International Retailing 2ed*  New York:  Fairchild Press (2007)

*International Retailing*  New York: Fairchild Books and Visuals. (1998)

*European Retailing's Vanishing Borders*  Westport, Connecticut: Quorum Publishers. (1994)

# Retail Strategic International Expansion (SIRE²)
# Theory and Cases

*Edited by:*
*Brenda Sternquist, Professor*
*Michigan State University*
*East Lansing, MI  48824*

Retail Strategic International Expansion (SIRE²) Theory and Cases

Copyright 2011 Brenda Sternquist
Gavin Witter Assistant Editor
Samantha Wax Technical Assistant
Molly Brown Production Assistant

Library of Congress Cataloging-in-Publication Data

Brenda Sternquist
Retail Strategic International Expansion (SIRE²) Theory and Cases/Brenda Sternquist.
Haslett, MI: BSC Publisher

ISBN 9780982726006
1. Retail trade-international retailing-global retailers-multinational retailers
HD38.5.F57 2011

# Brenda Sternquist

Brenda Sternquist, Professor at Michigan State University, is a specialist in International Retailing. She has conducted research throughout the world, but particularly focuses on China, India and Japan. She has done research in China since 1986. This research is summarized in her most recent book, International Retailing 2nd edition published by Fairchild Press, New York in 2007. This book has also been published in Japanese. Her first book focused on the European transition, this book European Retailing's Borderless World was published by Greenwood Press. She has also published more than one hundred research articles. She was selected as the first Outstanding National Retail Educator in 2004. The award is presented by the National Retail Federation, Center for Retail Studies Texas A&M and JC Penney. In 1999 she received the Michigan State University Distinguished Faculty Award, the highest award given at Michigan State University in recognition of an outstanding career in research, teaching and service, and was selected for the Alumnae Club of Mid-Michigan Quality in Undergraduate Teaching Award in 1997. She teaches undergraduate and graduate classes in International Retailing and graduate courses on Theories and Retail Strategy and Meta-theory and Retailing.

Sternquist's achievements span three decades. She received recognition as a Centennial Leader Award from the University of Tennessee, where she earned her doctorate. She received recognition from the College of Human Ecology at Michigan State University as an Outstanding Faculty Member. She has been recognized in 1996 receiving the All-University Excellence in Diversity Award, cited by Phi Kappa Phi in 1994 for scholarly achievement, and was named Michigan State University CASE outstanding Professor in 1992. She was named the 1991 Outstanding Researcher by the College of Human Ecology at Michigan State University.

Dr. Sternquist is on the board of Tsinghua University, China Retail Research Center.

She has received external research funding from USDA National Research Initiative, USDA Challenge Grant, Hoso Bunko Foundation, Japanese Telecommunication Advancement Foundation and Isetan and Mauri Department Stores.

She is interested in retail structure throughout the world, but is particularly interested in how retail systems change with economic development, or with political changes such as those occurring in China and India. She has done research for over 20 years in Japan and China, and ten years in India. A sub-interest is in commercial buyer-supplier relationships in various international settings. Retail buyers are gate-keepers of consumer choice and therefore play a major role in how products are distributed in various countries. Understanding the buying system used in a country...and company, can answer many other questions.

## Selected Consulting Experiences
Government of Egypt-USAID: Review of 500 state owned department stores for development of privatization packages:
Elopak International: Seminar on Current Trends in Retail Internationalization,
Tsinghua University: Seminar on Retail Buying Strategy,
Daimler-Chrysler: Seminar to top 200 executives on doing business in China,
Reebok International: Consulting project on retail internationalization,
Central Department Store-Thailand: Seminar on retail strategy to top corporate executives.

## Specialties
Commercial buyer-supplier relationships, retail internationalization, channel development and change, retailing in transitional economies like China and India. Cultural issues for understanding retailing in countries like Japan.

# Acknowledgements

The 91 authors of this book and I have shared a journey. We were enrolled together in a semester of RET 465, International Retailing. The authors all read my book *International Retailing* and applied its concepts to analyze international retailer's strategies. They gathered information about companies and put it into the cases. They also analyzed research propositions to determine if a given theory fit a retailer. Through this process the authors have emerged as true researchers. All the cases in this book received a 4.0. I am very proud of these students.

My journey started over 25 years ago when the retailing faculty at Michigan State University decided the future was international retailing. We spent several years looking for a faculty member in this area. After several unsuccessful attempts, I chose to retool into this area. It has been a long and fascinating journey.

Accompanying me on this journey are my friends and colleagues in the Retailing faculty. I greatly appreciate their support. Our graduate students have provided us with sparkling intellect to keep us excited. Judy Osbun provided support by establishing the design of this book. Her retirement in February causes us to miss her in more ways than we can say. I must thank her for the work she did on this project and for everything during my 33 years at Michigan State University.

Samantha Wax, Technical Assistant, worked on publishing and coordinating issues for the initial organization of the cases. Molly Brown, Production Assistant, edited the files and coordinated the author contacts. I thank them both for their support.

Lastly, I would like to thank Gavin Witter, Assistant Editor, for editing all the chapters, designing the cover and essentially putting this baby to bed.

# Table of Contents

# Retail Strategic International Expansion (SIRE²) Theory and Cases

*Brenda Sternquist*

## SIRE²

Are retailers really different from manufacturers when they internationalize? And is there a model that will predict who, what, when, where and why retailers will internationalize? This chapter will explore what I think I know about retailer internationalization, and then the rest of the book will focus on case studies of international retailers. I highly recommend that you read my book, International Retailing, for a more detailed description of the concepts in this case book.[1]

Retailers sell directly to consumers, requiring a physical presence in a country. Unlike manufacturers, retailers do not have an export option. This means that many theories of internationalization simply do not fit retailers. In International Retailing I develop a theory for predicting retailer's international expansion. The SIRE2 model connects a variety of theoretical perspectives.

I think there are two major problems with theories related to retailer internationalization. The first is that most researchers have lumped all retailers together. I think that there are two distinctive types of international retailers, global and multinational. If you lump them together you get mud, separating them out provides a clearer picture of their international activities. The second problem is that until very recently all the studies of retail internationalization have focused on successful expansion. When we do something and we are successful, we just celebrate. But if we are not successful we analyze why we weren't successful, we learn a great deal by an international expansion that isn't successful. Very recently some research attention has focused on this phenomena.[2]

These cases were written by students in my International Retailing class. These cases are similar in that they will start with a timeframe showing when and where the retailers internationalized, whether they are still in the country and how many stores they have today. Then a narrative case study is presented. Four questions are answered and finally they analyze the propositions designated for their type of retailer. Let's start with the four questions because they set the stage for which propositions will be analyzed.

## Four Questions

1. **Is the retailer classified as a global retailer or a multinational retailer? Explain its pattern of expansion. What expansion strategy did/is the retailer use/using?**

2. **Based on Dunning's eclectic theory, how do ownership, locational and internalization factors play in your retailers' international expansion?**

3. **What role does cultural proximity and geographical proximity play in the retailers' international moves?**

4. **Can you predict the retailer's future international expansion?**

# Model of Strategic International Retail Expansion (SIRE)

| | Result of International Activity | Predicted Expansion Pattern | Low Risk Alternative |
|---|---|---|---|

**Ownership**
Asset Based
**Transaction Based**

Global Expansion → Little Learning ⬆

**Own Store**
**Rapid Expansion**
*Small Size Stores-Hard Discounters,*
*Convenience*
*Operating Experience*
*International Orientation*
*Tolerance for Risk*
*Competitive Advantage-AB*

**Franchising**
*Small Size*
*Limited Operating Experienc*
*Limited International Orientation*
*Low Tolerance for Risk*
*Little Competitive Advantage*

⬅ **Internalization** ➡

**Locational**
**Cultural Proximity**
**Market Size**
**Competitor's Moves**
**Geographic Proximity**
**Low Cost Land & Labor**

Multinational Expansion → Much Learning ⬆

**Own Store**
**Expansion in Stages**
*Countries with attractive locational advantages*
*Large Size Stores-Hypermarkets*
*Cash and Carry*
*International Orientation*
*Tolerance for Risk*
*Competitive Advantage-TB*

**Licensing**
*Large Size Stores*
*Limited Operating Experienc*
*Limited International Orientation*
*Low Tolerance for Risk*
*Little Competitive Advantage*

## Question 1 - Global versus Multinational

Previously many authors have treated all retailers the same, but I believe that there are two types of retailers that strategically internationalize, global and multinational.[3] I have read many fine articles about retail internationalization, and time and again I have thought, if they just separated out the two types of retailers they would get much clearer results. So in this book whenever you see the term global or multinational, we are applying this hard definition. Many studies use the term international, global and multinational interchangeably, but in this book we will stick to a hard definition. Global retailers are centralized and expand in a standard format, multinational retailers are decentralized and adapt to new cultures/locations. Also many studies intermix the meaning of licensing and franchising, in this book whenever we discuss franchising we will mean business format franchising. Only global retailers are able to franchise because to franchise you need to be able to codify all the operations that the retailer will undertake. It is possible to do this with a very standard operating system, so global retailers can franchise. It would be impossible to do this for a retailer that is so large scale and one that changes their offering for different locations, so multinational retailers can not franchise, but can opt for licensing.

Global. These retailers are centrally managed, they use a standard retail format whereever they go and they are often backwards vertically integrated, meaning that they often have 100% private label. They are typically a smaller scale retailer. Because they are smaller scale retailers they have the potential to codify their operations, essentially to write down everything someone needs to know to operate the business, and this leads to the ability to franchise. Zara and Mango are two retailers that fit this profile. Because they operate a standard retail format they can expand at a very rapid rate. For some global retailers with very unique offerings it might be important for them to colonize a concept, meaning to expand rapidly so that other retailers do not have a chance to mimic their concept. There are two theoretical explanations for franchising. One is agency theory, which maintains that since it is so difficult to oversee stores in other countries, rather than having their own stores and oversee managers they should make them owner/operators, or franchisees. The other explanation is resource based theory which maintains that a retailer may franchise because they cannot afford to operate their own stores, but at a later date when they have additional cash they will reacquire those franchised units. A detailed discussion of the international expansion of global retailers is presented in Park and Sternquist.[4]

Multinational. This type of retailer customizes their offerings when they go into a new country, for this reason they typically expand to countries that are the closest cultural match to their home market. They are decentralized and are generally large scale stores. These retailers expand using stages theory, they will expand to a country culturally closest to their home market and then expand throughout that country and region before jumping to a new location. Multinational retailers generally do not expand outside their home market until they have saturated that market, or have reached growth impediments at home. Europe has some of the most restrictive laws barring the growth of large scale retailers, if European retailers wanted to continue to grow they need to internationalize very early, as a result, European Retailers are the most international of any of the top 250 retailers.[5] Because they are adapting to each new culture they enter they end up with a portfolio of knowledge about how to do business in various parts of the world. So there is a great deal of learning for multinational retailers. Wal-Mart, Carrefour and Tesco are international retailers that fit this description.

There are two other types of retail internationalization methods, acquisition and pure franchising. Acquisition is when a company purchases a firm that is well managed, and they essentially just leave the acquisition alone. This is the strategy used by Ahold in their international expansion. Rather than deciding strategically on a country to expand to they waited until the gem retail company within a country was available and then they purchase the gem and enter the market. Pure franchising is using only franchise operations in the international expansion. Both of these represent dormant types of management, and essentially are opportunistic, not strategic. You cannot model random events, or events that are opportunistic, so I have not included them in this analysis.

## Question 2 - Dunning's Ecletic Theory/Paradign[6]

Dunning maintained that a firm needed three types of advantages to successfully expand to a foreign market: Ownership, Internalization and Locational.

Ownership advantages include those factors that provide value for the firm. There are two types of ownership advantages, asset based and transaction based. Asset based are tangible things like the company name, unique private label and buildings/facilities. Transaction based advantages are based on knowing how to do something. Wal-Mart's logistic system would be a transaction based ownership advantage. Although Zara's private label products would be considered an asset based advantage their ability to produce the products so quickly would be a transaction based ownership advantage, in other words, knowing how to get the design, produce the products and get it into retail stores in two weeks would be based on knowing how to do something.

Internalization refers to keeping secrets inside the company. The more transaction based the ownership advantages the more important it is to keep those within the governance of the firm. Some types of expansion like licensing and franchising requires that the firm give their ownership advantages to others. These would be low on internalization. On the other hand operating only wholly owned subsidiaries would keep company secrets within the company.

Locational advantages refer to factors that would make expansion to another country look attractive. There are two basic kinds of locational factors: push and pull. Push factors are those things within a retailer's home country that make international expansion favorable. Many governments, particularly those in Europe, make it difficult for large scale stores to expand, therefore if they want to expand it means that they need to find new markets. Likewise if a retailer has saturated their home market they will need to look for new countries to continue expansion. An economic downturn in the home market might force retailers to look elsewhere. Pull factors are things that make a new market attractive. Cultural similarity to the home market might make expansion to this area seem relatively easy. Low cost land and labor, are two of the most important enticements for multinational retailers. Multinational retailers' major value added is in the training of employees to meet customer's needs, a type of vocational training. Locational advantages are really only important for multinational retailers since global retailers do not change much about how they operate.

## Question 3 - Cultural and Geographic Proximity

My observation has been that cultural and geographic proximity is not important for a global retailer. I believe that global retailers expand to world class cities where a relatively indistinguishable segment of consumers are the same throughout the world.

Multinational retailers seem to select countries for their initial expansion that are similar to their home country, but this becomes less important as they get greater international experience. However Evan's et. al[7] found that retailers expanding to culturally different locations did better than those selecting culturally similar areas. They hypothesize that if retailers do not think the cultural difference is great they may fail to adapt when adaptation is needed. They call this the cultural distance paradox.

## Question 4 - Prediction of Future International Expansion

Based on the expansion pattern of your retailer predict where they might go next. The student authors were told to not base this on statements made by the company, but rather what they predict.

The next stage is for the authors to analyze these propositions. The propositions are presented followed by a reasoning behind the proposition.

## Propositions for Retailer's Strategic International Expansion

After gathering information about the company the authors of the cases analyze these propositions. Everyone answers Propositions 1-4. Propositions 5-12 are answered if the company is a multinational company and only Propositions 13-19 if the company is a global company.

## Propositions Related to Ownership Advantages

**P1: The greater the ownership advantages for retailers, the less likely they will franchise or license.**

*Reason: Companies with significant ownership advantages do not want to give their secrets away. They would rather use wholly owned investment to allow them to control these ownership advantages.*

*In the case of international expansion, the availability of slack resources, defined as a cushion of excess resources that can be used in a discretionary manner.*[8] *Organization slack (has three components- available, recoverable and potential) it refers to excess resources that can be used in a discretionary manner.*

*Once you get the ratio's: eg. P3- Year 1 = a Year 2=b, Year 3=c. Then if a < (less than) b < c then you would support the proposition. E.g. of three year average, if a firm established its first manufacturing facility in a given country in 1980, the ratios regarding slack at 1977 (t-3), 1978 (t-2) and 1979 (t-1) were computed and averaged.*

**P2: The greater the available organizational slack the greater the likelihood of expanding internationally.**

**[Ratio of Current Assets to Current Liabilities (3 year average before their first international expansion)]**

*Reason: This is the current ratio. The more excess liquid cash they have, the more they need to invest this capital in themselves.*[8] *If they have saturated the home market, it is likely they will use these resources for international expansion.*

**P3:The greater the recoverable slack the greater the likelihood of expanding internationally.**

**[Ratio of General and Administrative Expenses to Sales (3 year average before their first international expansion)]**

*Reason: A company can use excess resources (general and administrative expenses) for an expanded operation. Some expenses become less as a percent of larger sales volume. If the company expands, this expense becomes a smaller percent of their overall sales.*

**P4:The greater the potential slack the greater the likelihood of expanding internationally.**

**[Ratio of Equity to Capital (3 year average before their first international expansion)]**

*Reason: Ratio of Equity to Capital is the best financial measure of performance on behalf of the owners. Companies who have excess capital may be punished by the investment community (stock market) if they do not expand internationally. The stock market rewards companies that reinvests in themselves. The quest for growth is continual, and if the home market is saturated the logical next step is international expansion.*

## Propositions for Locational Advantages

In the propositions I am using the term multinational and global on a continuum that you would use for establishing the actual conceptual relations it would be adaptive ---→standardized. Adaptive would be the multinational retailers and standardized would be the global retailers.

## Multinational Companies (High adaptive-Decentralized)

**P5:Multinational retailers will move to countries with lower disposable income than their home country.**

*Reason: Multinational retailers will seek low cost locations for their offerings. As mentioned earlier, multinational retailers will seek locations with low cost land and labor, they will find this resource in countries less economically developed than their home market.*

**P6:Multinational retailers will move to countries that have a high positive change in Gross Domestic Product (GDP)**

**(GDP at the time of expansion -GDP 5 years before expansion)**

_____

**GDP 5 years before expansion**

_Reason: A high positive change in GDP indicates positive economic development. Retailers moving into countries undergoing rapid economic development will generally find less competition in those market and can expect a higher growth rate. In developing markets the growth rate is very stable and relatively low. To achieve double digit growth rates the company needs to seek countries with high growth potential._

_The Q ratio is the ratio of a publicly traded company's market capitalization to the value of its tangible assets. A ratio of more than 1 is an indication that financial market participants believe that part of a company's value comes from intangible assets such as brand equity, differentiation, innovation, market dominance and customer loyalty. Retailers in emerging markets have done very well, the composite for emerging market retailers is 1.932 compared to US based retailers (1.406) and European retailers (.99). South Africa countries performed the best, five retailers on the top 250 list of the Global Powers in Retailing have a composite Q ratio of 2.931._

**P7:Multinational retailers will move to countries that have a high positive change in service-value added as % of GDP.**

**(Service% of GDP at the time of Expansion - Service% of GDP 5 years before expansion)**

_____

**Service% of GDP 5 years before expansion**

_Reason: Service-value as a % of GDP is an indicator of economic development. As countries become richer, consumers hire others to take care of them. Retailing is a service industry. Part of retailing is a hard service (where the product and the service can be separated, but the other part of retail service is a soft service (where production and consumption can not be separated). So the products that a retailer sells could be considered hard service, but the retail environment, sales service and retail experience are soft service._

**P8:Multinational retailers will first move to countries that are culturally the most similar to their home country. (Hofstede's indicators Home country-Host country for four factors, MvsFHuvsLU; IndvsCol; HPDvsLPD)**

*Reason:Multinational retailers will alter their offering when they move to a new country so it is important for them to understand culture. Although Hofstede's dimensions of difference are not very strong indicators of culture, they are a starting point for understanding these differences. A retailer needs to be careful not to fall into the cultural distance paradox where they do not make adaptations that are necessary because they believe the cultures to be so similar.*

**P9:Multinational retailers will expand within the country and then will expand regionally within that area (for example expanding to Brazil and then Argentina and Chile)**

*Reason: Stages theory explains this proposition. Once they have expanded to a new country they need to set up a company infrastructure that will support their logistics and warehouse system. They expand within the region for the same reason, they are amassing a knowledge about the culture in the region.*

**P10: Periodically the multinational retailers will "jump" to a new geographic area and begin the stages form of expansion.**

*Reason: The multinational retailer will eventually seek a new regional area and begin the process all over again. Wal-Mart expanded to Mexico and then South America, regions that are related. Later they jumped to Asia and began the expansion process there. In this new location they could use some of the lessons learned in Mexico and South America, but largely they would need to develop a new perspective for the Asian market. Over time the multinational retailer will have a broad perspective about how to do business in various parts of the world.*

**P11: Multinational retailers will move to countries that are geographically close to the home country initially, then expand to more distant countries (Miles from Home Country to Host country).**

*Reason: Although geographic proximity is not nearly as important for multinational retailers as cultural proximity, it is still a consideration. Geographic proximity becomes less important with greater experience.*

**P12: Multinational retailers will move to countries with large population bases.**

*Reason: Multinational retailers are generally mass merchandisers so they seek areas with a large population base to support their operations.*

## Global Companies (Standard format-centralized)

**P13: Global companies will move to the largest/capital cities in a country.**

*Reason: Global retailers seek a universal target customer. This customer exists quite universally in world class cities such as New York, London, Paris. Zara executives say that they are looking for the Zara girl.*

**P14: Global companies will not be attracted by population size, income, cultural proximity or geographical proximity. (Support using figures wherever appropriate: population size, income, use Hofstede's indicators: Home country-Host country for four factors, MvsFHuvsLU; IndvsCol; HPDvsLPD for cultural proximity and use Miles from Home Country to Host country for geographical proximity)**

*Reason: Unlike multinational retailers who will adapting their offering for various cultural and economic difference, the global retailer will not consider any of these factors.*

**P15: The greater the asset based ownership advantages of a global retailer, the more likely they are to franchise.**

*Reason: Global retailer's most important asset based advantage is likely to be their private label line. If this is their most important ownership advantage then getting the product distributed as widely as possible would be advantageous so they will welcome franchising as a way of colonizing their concept. Nothing can stop other retailers from copying a private label line, so aggressively expanding through franchising will not deplete the advantage.*

**P16: The greater the transaction based ownership advantages of a global retailer, the less likely they are to franchise.**

*Reason: If their most important ownership advantage is knowing how to do something then they will resist franchising because that would amount to giving away their secrets.*

*The reasons for these three propositions are provided earlier but here I am predicting an outcome of reacquiring the franchised outlets. This would support the resource based view of explaining why retailers franchise.*

P17: The greater the available organizational slack the greater the likelihood that global retailers will reacquire international franchisees.

[Ratio of Current Assets to Current Liabilities (3 year average before they begin reacquisition)]

P18: The greater the recoverable slack the greater the likelihood that global retailers will reacquire international franchisees.

[Ratio of General and Administrative Expenses to Sales (3 year average before they begin reacquisition)]

P19: The greater the potential slack the greater the likelihood that global retailers will reacquire international franchisees.

[Ratio of Equity to Capital (3 year average before they begin reacquisition)]

## Formats

Retail formats include small scale operations such as convenience stores and hard discount operations. Large scale formats include hypermarkets, warehouse clubs and department stores.

In terms of theory development, our underlying assumption is that more practical experience in managing different formats is better and should lead to higher performance. However research findings suggest that as the number of formats increase, performance decreases. The outcome of this study is also consistent with the concentrated strategy in other areas such as management and international marketing literature. Examples of retailers that concentrate in one retail format are Couche-Tard from Canada (55.4% sales growth), Amazon.com from U.S. (53.9% sales growth), Starbucks from U.S. (25.6% sales growth), and Carrefour from France (20.8% sales growth). These examples show that retailers who concentrate in specific sector have gained an advantage over multi-format retailers. One explanation is that by combining many business models within the portfolio dilutes the firm's ability to share information and experience.[9]

# Ownership

Ownership types range from a wholly owned subsidiary to licensing. From the standpoint of retailing information (secrets) within the firm it ranges from:

Licensing---Franchising---Joint Venture---Wholly Owned Subsidiary

Wholly owned subsidiaries offer the most control, but also cost the most.

As countries open to FDI they often require retail joint ventures. Even if joint ventures are not required by the government they are usually short term. To gain local knowledge, Tesco invested heavily at the beginning of the joint venture in Korea with Samsung Corporation at a time when Korean retailers were suffering from the Asian financial crisis in 1997. Later, Tesco focused on local customers' needs and wants through its joint venture to gain knowledge. Tesco started to realize that Korean consumers care about their shopping environment. Tesco, which is called "Homeplus" in Korea, opened a big discount store as a multiple complex at Jamsil, Seoul, Korea centered on an art and wellbeing concept. It includes social centers and art, health, techno service facilities, and 700 lectures with 160 instructors as its customer service in 2007. Moreover, Tesco made a gym, a sauna, a golf practice area, and a wine bar in Korea.[10] Therefore, Tesco was able to accomplish customer information acquisition through multiple channels, and Tesco's transaction cost at the beginning has paid off through knowledge acquisition in Korea. After Tesco gained the local customer knowledge through the joint venture, Tesco gained most of shares in the joint venture.[11][12]

# Summary and Conclusions

There are many books with retail cases, however I believe this is the first book to provide a theoretical explanation for strategic international expansion. Like all theories, it is important to analyze how well reality fits the theory that has been presented, and if it doesn't fit, rethinking the theory is a necessary consequence.

# Endnotes

1.  Sternquist, B. (2008) International Retailing. New York: Fairchild Books

2.  Alexander, N. & B. Quinn (2002) International retail divestment. International Journal of Retail & Distribution Management, 30 (2'3) 112-125.

3.  Salmon, W. & Tordjman, A. (1989). The internationalization of retailing, International Journal of Retailing, 4(2): 3-16.

4.  Park, Y. and B. Sternquist (2008). The global retailer's strategic proposition

and choice of entry mode. International Journal of Retail & Distribution Management.36, (4) 281-299.

5.   Global Powers of Retailing 2011. (2011) Deloitte. www.deloitte.com/consumer business.

6.   Dunning, J.H. (1981). International Production and the Multinational Enterprise. London: Allen & Unwin.

7.   Evans, J. & F. Mavondo (2002) Psychic distance and organizational performance: An empirical examination of international retailing operations. Journal of International Business Studies, 33, 3, 515-532.

8.   Rhee, Jay and L.C. Cheng (2002). Foreign market uncertainty and incremental international expansion: The moderating effect of firm industry and host country factors. Management International Review. Vol. 42, 419-439.

9.   Chan, P., C. Finnegan and B. Sternquist (forthcoming) Country and firm level factors in international retail expansion. European Journal of Marketing.

10.  Kim, D. "Samsung Tesco Homeplus.." hankuk kyungjai, September 27, 2007, via hankyung.com, http://www.hankyung.com/news/app/newsview.php?aid=200709 2679951&sid=01040105&nid=102&type=0.

11.  Suh, Y. and Howard, E. (2009). Restructuring retailing in Korea: the case of Samsung-Tesco. Asia Pacific Business Review 15(1): 29-40.

12.  Sung, E. and B. Sternquist (2010) Strategic international joint venture: Opportunity, expansion and longevity for retailers' internationalization. Journal of Euromarketing. 19(1): 55-66.

# Amazon.com

*Angelique Gangnier, Stephany Meekhoff, Katy Barkell,*
*Otha Hardeman, Andrew Erspamer, Jacquelyn Karwoski,*
*Rachael Koscielny, Lindsey Potterpin, Kayse Smith, Lindsay Yruma*

## Amazon.com

With the focus on building a customer community, Amazon.com is the first major bookseller on the web to offer consumers an immediate approach to browse millions of titles. Beginning in 1995, Amazon has progressed further becoming a Fortune 500 company with a vision for continuous expansion, innovation, and technology. Based in Seattle, Washington Amazon.com is now a global leader in e-commerce retailing. Founder and CEO, Jeff Bezos, unconventionally turned Amazon.com into the number one retailer of music and toys and the most visited retailer site on the Web. Word-of-mouth, clever marketing, and a hefty sum in advertising costs has made Amazon.com a billion dollar global retailer.[1]

After Amazon became a publicly traded company in 1997, they expanded their product offerings, expanded warehouses into seven countries around the world, and dedicated themselves to customer service and fulfillment.[2] Amazon's goal is to be able to give their customers whatever products they desire as soon as possible from international websites in the United Kingdom, Denmark, Japan, France, Canada, and China. Massive international expansion has resulted in Amazon's alignment with their vision, "to be earth's most customer-centric company in the world, to build a place where people can come to find and discover anything they might want to buy online."[3]

Focusing primarily on their customers and the importance of their business, this site has grown globally and continues to expand. As a pioneer of the web and leader of online shopping, Amazon's website is designed to be a simple, functional, and easy customer shopping experience based on speed and convenience. Partnering up with companies such as Target, Shutterfly, Office Depot, and Fidelity has helped Amazon provide a deeper product offering. Amazon offers top 10 charts which categorize books, videos, and movies to help customers find the best selling products that are on the market.[4]

## Amazon.Com Flow Chart on Expansion

| | |
|---|---|
| United Kingdom | 1998 |
| Germany | 1998 |
| France | 2000 |
| Japan | 2000 |
| Canada | 2002 |
| China | 2004 |

## Mission Statement

Amazon.com has a mission statement that encompasses their vision. Their statement is as follows, "Our vision is to be earth's most customer centric company; to build a place where people can come to find and discover anything they might want to buy online."[5] This stresses the array of different products that people can find in one place.

## Products Offered

Amazon began as an online bookstore and started offering other products such as videotapes and DVDs, music CDs, kitchen items, consumer electronics, tools, lawn and garden items, software, toys and games, baby products, sporting goods, gourmet food, apparel jewelry, watches, health and personal-care items, musical instruments, industrial and scientific supplies, beauty products, groceries, and the list continues. Forty percent of Amazon's sales come from "Associates," which is an independent business or seller that receives a commission for referring customers to the Amazon.com site.[6]

## Target Market

Amazon has two segments, North American and International consumers. Their wide variety of products allows Internet users to shop online from home. The company is attempting to reach every single internet user by moving into countries that are expanding Internet usage. Amazon also has Amazon Marketplace which targets individuals and small businesses. Amazon's Merchant program is marketed toward larger businesses.[7] Currently Amazon occupies 13% of the market share in Internet retailing against Wal-Mart, Target, and Overstock.com.[8]

Amazon markets its site as friendly and low priced, from middle to high income consumers. Amazon's target consumer is willing to shop online and technologically literate, and looking for affordable merchandise. The target consumer is typically 25-45, single or married, with young children. Amazon's segmentation strategy is mass marketing, and uses demographics and behavior to determine segmentation strategy.[9]

## SWOT Analysis

### Strengths

- Expansion of brick and mortar warehouses gives Amazon.com total control over distribution of most of their products, allowing for a unique experience for its customers with 20 fulfillment centers world-wide.[10]

- Recent expansion in the United Kingdom and Germany will significantly reduce shipping costs and reduce delivery time. Amazon.com is increasing its inventory overseas.[11]

- In 1999, Amazon reported a 73% growth in repeat customers, in addition to its already strong customers base.[12]

- Amazon.com has a strong brand image that allows them to expand into different product segments. This also allows for a competitive advantage in the online retailing industry since Amazon.com's global brand name has created mindspace to consumers worldwide.[13]

- Amazon.com International paves the way for category domination in books, music, and toys. Amazon.com currently offers the "earth's biggest selection".[14]

- International net sales growth is currently 27%, up from the previous quarter.[15]

- Amazon Prime, their first ever membership program, uniquely offers customers a flat fee, and in return customers receive a free unlimited two-day shipping offer for free with a bundle of other great deals.[16]

- International expansion gives Amazon.com a great way to provide customers with everything they need from anywhere in the world.

- Amazon.de just launched its new sporting goods store on July, 11, 2006.[17]

**Weaknesses**

- Since 1995, boosting sales have been very costly for the company. Discounted shipping, diversity in merchandise, and creating "earth's biggest selection" had cost the company well over the amount investors expected.[18]

- Amazon could be stretching its brand too thin. With everything that Amazon.com offers from books, movies, and toys to gardening tools and jewelry, the goal of having every product can create high inventory expenses and poses a risk to the company.

**Opportunities**

- In recent years, Amazon.com has created alliances with many popular bricks-and-mortar retailers such as Target, Office Depot, and Toys-R-Us; all of which have gained considerable momentum.

- With the rapid growth of China's economy, expansion into Chinese markets increase consumer demand for retailing services provided by online retailers.

- First-mover advantage over bricks-and-mortar retailers when expanding into developing countries with the continuous expansion of the Internet and computer technology.

- Another opportunity for Amazon is to expand into Australia; Amazon has touched base in Asia and Europe, now they need to open in Australia.

**Threats**

- Competition is fierce due to the growing popularity of the Internet. Pure online retailers such as overstock.com and ebay.com also control a great portion of the market share.

- Online virtual shops currently used by e-bay offer a fixed-price webpage for the sale of new goods.[18]

- Only one fulfillment center receives a majority of the online orders for the international sites. This could cause an increase in net shipping costs especially at the holiday season when orders are more frequent.[19]

- With the current fluctuations in foreign exchange rates, net sales could be negatively impacted.[14]

## Competition

Ever since Amazon sued Barnesandnoble.com in 1999 for replicating their patented "one-click" shopping online feature, these two companies have been in close competition.[20] Borders Books is another source of competition for Amazon. Although all three of these competitors have almost identical product offerings related to books, DVDs, CDs, textbooks and gifts, Amazon has a competitive advantage by carrying a more extensive product line. Along with additional merchandise, Amazon strives to differentiate their customer service and easy accessibility online to become the most preferred Internet retailer. Even though Amazon's quarterly profit continues to drop, sales continue to rise. These results mean that Amazon is reinvesting in their business, expanding and remaining a fierce competitor. Offering free shipping on eligible items and lowered prices helps Amazon to compete against Barnes and Noble and Borders Books. One main difference between Amazon and its two competitors is the fact that Amazon is an online retail sector only, and has no franchised stores. Borders, the second largest bookstore chain has 1200 locations worldwide; 475 stores throughout the U.S, with an additional presence in the United Kingdom and Pacific Rim. Their Books etc. division has 31 stores in Great Britain and they are also teaming with Walden Books, which has helped spur annual sales.[21] Barnes and Noble takes pride in having 799 stores as of July 2006 in the U.S. and does not expand stores internationally; only the online sector is international serving over 200 countries.[22]

Amazon.com's continuous innovation has resulted in an increase of spending on technology causing their budget to take a hit. Amazon reported that third-quarter earnings have fallen by more than a third, because of heavy spending on new projects, even as sales rose 24 percent.[23] "Profit at Amazon dropped 58%, to 22 million, or 5 cents a share, in the second quarter, down from 52 million, or 12 cents a share, in the period a year earlier when analysts had forecasted a profit of 7 cents a share".[24] Amazon.com has also spent heavily on incentives to attract customers which in-turn cuts into any money the company would have gained. Incentives such as their subscription shipping program doubled from November to December in 2005.[25] The incentives have been attracting new customers by 19 percent in the fourth quarter from a year ago to 48.6 million, according to Nielsen/NetRatings. Purchases grew 31 percent to more than 8.2 million from January to November 2005.[25]

Amazon.com stays on top of competition by offering several services online that are advantageous for not only sellers of products but buyers as well. These services consist of advantage programs, corporate accounts, paid placements, and ways to sell the items. Amazon.com also promotes their name in the community by Amazon Connect, Amazon Fishbowl, Amazon Wire Podcast, email subscriptions, and Giving at Amazon. For developers, Amazon offers web services, for advertisers they offer Advertise with us, and for partner services there is Broadband, Financial and Travel Services.[26] All of these online links help Amazon users. Services that users appreciate are rewarding to Amazon, because they create loyalty and help to increase sales.

Although the international retail e-commerce continues to grow, competition will intensify. Local businesses in foreign countries also compete with Amazon.com as private labels and customer loyalties are already established with local retailers. Also, governments in foreign countries have tougher restrictions on internet retailing when compared to the United States.

## Expansion

Expanding into new markets will propel Amazon into a market of unlimited possibilities. Amazon.com continues to update merchandise and customer services to appeal to all markets. Amazon's Unibox, a new development of music, video, and book downloads, is set to take them a step further in the future. Heavy spending and potential profit losses are mainly attributed to new technologies. Recent sales have seen a 22% increase, but the 58% profit loss in the second quarter this year is said to have been directly impacted by Unibox. Jeff Bezos acknowledges this project is forecasted for the long term, meaning that what is not profitable in the short run, will hope to strengthen future sales along with customer satisfaction and loyalty. Although Amazon remains secretive about its plans, the online retailer is expected to launch its new service for downloading movies and television shows which will compete with Netflix and Apple's new I-movies.[27]

Expectations are high for the coming holiday season. Amazon.com expects sales to increase up to 33% or $3.95 billion. The company also expects an operating income of up to $235 million which would demonstrate a 43% increase from the previous year.[28]

## Presence in the Industry

Although the internet retailing industry is fairly new, Amazon and competitors have become successful in recent years. In fact, Internet retailing sales have totaled over 34 billion dollars to date. Not expecting to earn a profit for at least five years has made Amazon's business strategy much more unusual than other online company business models. Although out of the ordinary, the strategy was effective. As many other Internet companies grew at a blindingly fast pace, Amazon grew steadily throughout the 90's. When the Dot-com bubble exploded causing several e-companies to go out of business, Amazon had a profit in the fourth quarter of 2002: although it was only $5 million dollars (one cent per share), it was very representational. Profit continued to grow due to product diversification and international presence: $3.9 billion in 2002, $5.3 billion in 2003, $6.9 billion in 2004 and $8.5 billion 2005.[29]

Several different divisions reside within this global retailer, including a North American division along with an International division. The North American segment includes www.amazon.com and www.amazon.ca. The International segment includes www.amazon.co.uk, www.amazon.de, www.amazon.fr, www.amazon.co.jp, and www.joyo.com. Amazon has www.a9.com and www.alexa.com operating as search engines, www.imdb.com which is a comprehensive movie database, and www.mturk.com acting as a web service that provides the sharing of networks. Although Amazon is a direct product retailer, the company also has auction components called zShop and Amazon Marketplace which are for individuals, small businesses, while the larger scale Merchants is for larger businesses. These include both new and used products and the company derives revenues through fixed fees, sales commissions, and per-unit activity fees. Amazon differentiates themselves from other websites by attempting to offer anything a consumer may desire, all in one place. Amazon is the only Internet retailer allowing customers to shop for anything they want and only concern themselves with one owner of merchandise, one payment system, one secured web site, and the least amount of privacy concern.[30]

## International Expansion

Amazon.com. Inc's expansion strategy and Service Oriented Architecture, which is their platform for growing Amazon's Web services, is to constantly have exposure and keep it simple. Amazon's solution to the problem of making decisions not conducive to flexibility in growth and expansion was to first cut ties with their earliest hardware system and build a website that could handle online business transactions, while harboring the retailer's databases. To keep track of every Web service, they each have one team of workers and developers to keep track of and be responsible for their own Web service.[31]

In 1995, Amazon started with a single server providing a simple web ordering system, they have now evolved through technological development to become a platform in online services throughout the world.[31]

## Amazon.com and Dunning's Theory of International Expansion

Amazon.com has expanded internationally to attract the Internet users world wide. Expanding internationally has provided a convenient way of shopping online to purchase that item that is hard to find. Dunning's theory of International Expansion consists of ownership advantage, internalization advantage, and location advantage.[33] Amazon.com has many ownership advantages. They have both asset based ownership advantages and transaction based advantages. Amazon.com offers well known brand names because of their partnerships with companies such as Chico's, Macy's, Foot Locker, and Lands' End. They have transaction based advantages because of their specific way they run their online business that makes them successful. They have distribution centers all over the world that makes it convenient to get their merchandise out to their customers. Amazon.com has internalization advantage because they are an Internet company that will not franchise because they do not have physical locations to spread across the world. They internalize their company structure, format, and success so their online competitors will not have an advantage. Amazon has locational advantage because their headquarters is in the United States but they also built sites in the United Kingdom, Austria, and Japan to make it accessible to their customers for selling and trading purposes.

Amazon has expanded internationally because of their possession as a unique market format.[33] Amazon's format has created a new way of shopping online at home. When they expand they want to introduce their business to a new market before online imitators take advantage of their market.[33] Amazon expands to developed countries because those are the established consumers that have access to the internet and Amazon. Amazon is a market share leader in its industry because of its strong presence in each country that it enters. They have a recognizable name and positive shopping experience that makes international customers want to be involved. Another reason Amazon expanded is because of first-mover advantages.[33] They want to be the first ones in a country to have a distribution center and headquarters so they will not lose their market share to a competitor. It is important for Amazon to retain their current customers and gain new ones so they can increase their sales and growth.

## International Expansion Analysis

"We are rapidly and significantly expanding our operations both domestically and internationally and will continue to expand further to pursue growth of our product and service offerings and customer base."[46]  The international segment of Amazon.com is a significant asset to the company.  Amazon.com will continue to expand into international markets as they are an important component to both revenues and profits.  Amazon.com predicts that their international segment will make up over 50% of their net sales over time.  However, currently, international revenue growth rates have declined 20%.  The decrease is due to changes in currency exchange rates which had a negative impact on revenue growth by $78 million, a major decrease from the previous two years.  By offering lower prices and better convenience, the company aspires to increase sales over time.  Amazon.com will also continue to accumulate additional product lines to their mix to increase sales.[46]

Amazon.com continues to grow with an annual revenue growth of 59% a year, and total asset growth of 44.5% a year.  Their annual earnings per share growth is 33% a year.  Forecasters expect an average growth rate of 20.6%.  Unfortunately, the expected growth rate would be a decrease when compared to the company's history.  Amazon.com's current assets are $2,929 million and asset turnover is very strong at 3.0 times.  The companies return on assets has skyrocketed in the past few years to 12% in 2006 from 1% in 2003, although there has been a recent decline.[47]

## Germany

Amazon.com entered Germany in 1998 when it added a German language website.  This occurred when Amazon.com partnered with Yahoo.com.  Yahoo.com provided links on its international Yahoo.de website to Amazon.com where Germans could find German language books from Amazon.de.  David Risher, senior Vice President at Amazon.com, said "This agreement with Yahoo!, combined with our local presence in Germany and the United Kingdom, strengthens our position around the world as a leading global book merchant."  Amazon.de opened it virtual doors on October 15th, 1998.  It replaced ABC Bucherdienst in Germany and Bookpages, LTD in the U.K. after Amazon.com purchased both companies in April of 1998.[48]  Special features such as personalized recommendations, book services, hundreds of browsing lists, professional and customer book reviews and single click ordering capabilities were added to the new German and U.K. sites.[11]

Upon opening in 1998 Amazon.com only had 1,600 employees, all of which were in the United States.  In 2006 there are over 12,000 employees all over the world.  German Amazon headquarters are located in Regensburg, a site in Bad Hersfeld, and editorial marketing offices in Munich where Amazon.com employees work to better the International website.[11]  When Amazon.com entered Germany and many other European countries this was an example of organic expansion and a hands-on acquisition since they did acquire a few companies before entering and they wanted to improve their international sales by providing websites for non-English speaking customers. Amazon.com is the largest pure internet retailer in Germany, second only to AOL. Since Austria is a German language speaking country, Amazon.de also ships its products there. In Germany they expanded their product lines to include kitchen and home items. (GMID) International sales, including German sales, were up 29% from third quarter reports in 2005.

Currently, Amazon.de has a 5.7% market share due to the fact that there are seven other leading Internet retailers in Germany. All together they have 29.9% of the total market share. Amazon.de comes in second to KarstadtQuelle in German Internet sales.[49] According to the World Development Report in 2003 Germany's Service percentage of GDP was 69.4% totaling $2,714.4 billion U.S dollars. This is due to a large high income group that is spending more than in the past.

## United Kingdom

Amazon.co.uk is the trading name for Amazon EU Sarl and Amazon Services Europe S.a.r.l., which are both subsidiaries of Amazon.com. In 1998, Amazon.com acquired three online bookstores including an independent online store called Bookpages, which was established in 1996 and from there Amazon.co.uk was established. Amazon.co.uk has gained its fame from selling mostly books, but offers millions of other new and used products as carried on the United States site from music to household items.[50]

They also offer other sites such as Amazon Marketplace, zShops, and Auctions, which allow small businesses or customers to buy and sell new and used merchandise to United Kingdom customers. Amazon.co.uk can now also be accessed through mobile phones with WAP technology.[51]

In 1998, along with the launch of the site, Amazon.co.uk opened a fulfillment center in Marston Gate, United Kingdom followed by launch of the Music Store, Auctions and zShops in 1999, launch of the DVD/Video Store, a new customer service center in Slough, United Kingdom, a Software/Video game Store in 2000, launch of Electronics Store, Kids Store, and Travel Store in 2001, launch of Marketplace in 2002, launch Kitchen Store and Outdoor Store in 2003, opened new fulfillment center in Inverclyde, Scotland, started Alliance with Borders Limited, launched DVD Rental service in 2004, opened a final fulfillment center in Glenrothes, Scotland in 2005.[52]

The UK has the second most developed on-line retail market in the world after the US. United Kingdom grosses a GDP of $1,782,000 and a 73 percent of GDP. Market share is 0.6%. However, there is still plenty of room to grow in this industry. Consumers are still unaware of many aspects of the Internet and its benefits, so as consumers learn more, the industry is predicted to grow. Internet retail sales are predicted to grow over the next few years by 75%.[49]

It seems Amazon.co.uk is staying on top of its competitors in the United Kingdom, from a 2006 statistics poll by hitwise of the top 50 online retailers in the UK grossing $50 billion in sales through online channels, Amazon.co.uk was number one.[53]

## France

Amazon.com launched the French version of the website on August 31st, 2000. The long awaited site was greeted with a variety of different opinions as some thought that it compromised France's cultural exception and was bringing something too main-stream to the country. Others however viewed Amazon and its creator Jeff Bezos as a "new economy exemplar of the American dream."[54] Despite all of this, Amazon arrived with full force in France. On the day of its launch Amazon had a full offering of books, music, videos, and DVDs; this was the first time that they had launched all four types of media together. Amazon saw the threat and great competition in smaller local book sellers, so developed a plan to be equally competitive.[55] Focusing on low prices, as they do in the US, was not an option because of France's book pricing laws which state that books cannot be discounted by more than 5%.[54] Bezos then decided to focus on speed, reliability, choice, and service instead. Amazon then became the first retailer in France to introduce a unique level of service and made it available 24 hours a day, seven days a week.

Amazon's decision to enter into France went along with the goal to increase foreign sales by at least 50% and to make at least 60% of their sales come from the foreign market. Another motivation to expand into France was the extremely high population density which makes shipping much cheaper than in the US.[54] Amazon's market share in France has also been rising since their introduction into France and now is at a solid 6.3%, comparable to other new Internet retailers. Amazon's entry into France has proved to be successful and the business has taken well to the French economy.

## Japan

In late October 2000, Amazon.com Inc. developed Amazon.co.jp, to expand their online retailer to Japanese speakers around the world. The website is designed and written in the Japanese language in order to serve Amazon's largest export market more efficiently. At the time of expansion in 2000, Amazon had 193,000 Japanese customers who spent over $34 million (U.S.) a year. The company has also been consistently named the top e-commerce site in Japan. Amazon.co.jp was the company's first Asian-language site and fourth international site, after Germany, France, and the United Kingdom. Amazon has set up offices in Tokyo, a distribution center in Ichikawa, Chiba, and a customer service building in Sapporo, Hokkaido.[56]

Although East Asia is one of the most well developed areas in the world, the over-populated market of Japan had analysts questioning the expansion. Softbank Corporation and major Japan retailer Kinokuniya held high percentages in the online book market. Kinokuniya is an 87-store retail chain that does about $3.3 million of business a month on its Internet site.[57] Also, legal restrictions that prohibit large discounts and any bypassing of the sales tax, undercut one of Amazon's biggest strength, competitive prices. The average price of a paperback in Japan was $4.50 at the time of expansion in 2000.[58]

Another problem Amazon faced was that Japanese consumers were reluctant to use credit cards online. Other Internet booksellers introduced a format to order the book online and purchase it at convenience stores. Amazon.co.jp promised a 30 percent discount on foreign books, which would give them an advantage over other Japanese retailers. Although Japan's market is near its overflow point, Amazon still believes they can succeed in their largest export market by giving their 193,000 customers an easier access to their products.[58]

## Canada

Although Amazon.com's Canadian customers could easily purchase products through their main site, Amazon wanted to better accommodate Canadian consumers, so Amazon launched their Canadian site on June 25, 2002.[59] The new branch of Amazon made for Canada, offers the convenience of shopping with Amazon with prices in Canadian dollars and local shipping from Canada Post Corporation as well as operating as a bilingual site for the Canadian market.[60] This expansion was said to be well over due, it was the first international expansion in over 18 months. This expansion was also to help Amazon achieve its goal of raising sales derived from outside its domestic market from one third to by half by 2005.[61]

With the new Amazon.ca, Canada customers can find and discover over a million English and French books, CDs, videos and DVDs. Amazon.ca sources products directly from Canadian publishers and distributors, ensuring a great offering of Canadian titles and content. Features such as original editorial reviews in English and French and product recommendations help Amazon.ca customers find the right products for them among the site's broad selection just as they would with any of Amazons other special country websites.[62]

## China

Amazon.com Inc. decided to expand into China in late August of 2004 by acquiring Joyo.com, China's largest online retailer of books, music, and videos. Amazon.com agreed to pay $75 million (U.S.) to gain access to the 27.7 million Chinese consumers who shop online. Joyo.com owns and operates three "fulfillment centers" in Beijing, Shanghai, and Guangzhou that use 30 delivery centers to distribute their goods. Amazon's international sales growth was on the decline dropping 31% from the second quarter a year earlier. Out of the world's 20 largest economies, China is the fastest growing among them.[63]

E-commerce, or online spending, is also growing rapidly in China. Market researcher IDC showed that Chinese consumers spent $4.8 billion online in 2004 and also predicted that number to increase to $14.6 billion by 2005.[64] China is Amazon's sixth international website, where users can search for their purchases using the same format as the American website, but focused primarily on Chinese interests. According to International Data Corporation, Internet retailers would have sold $8.59 billion worth of products to China in 2004, enticing Amazon.com to expand. Also, Chinese Internet users are rapidly increasing by 28 percent in one year from 2003.[63]

The intense competition of the U.S. market along with the decrease of international sales growth helped aid the decision to expand into China. The growth potential in Internet users and the success of Joyo.com indicated to Amazon that this would be an ideal location to sell. Although Yahoo and Ebay have expanded to China before Amazon, the company still holds a first-mover advantage over any other Internet retailer to follow. Amazon.com holds a strong portion of the e-commerce market, and when partnered with a unique selling format and wide variety of products, will continue to bring success to the company.

## Questions

**1. Is the retailer classified as a global or multinational retailer? Explain its pattern of expansion. What expansion did/is the retailer using?**

*Amazon.com is classified as a global retailer. With this format they have been able to reach several different countries without altering the format of their webpage although they have altered the language and color scheme of a few websites. This is due to the fact that different colors have different meanings in certain countries. For example in some cultures green may have a different meaning than red so Amazon has to take this into consideration. Amazon.Joyo, Germany, France and*

China do have different languages on their website as well, yet people can still distinguish this website from other online retailers. If you are looking at Amazon. de, a shopper can tell that the website is a branch that belongs to Amazon.com with the same typology and products.

## 2. Based on Dunning's eclectic theory, how do ownership, locational, and internalization factors play in your retailers' international expansion?

Dunning's Theory of the Eclectic Firm tries to explain why a company would attempt to expand into a country outside its own. Three components a company must have to be successful in its international expansion are ownership, internalization, and location advantages. Amazon.com Inc. ranks high on both asset based and transaction based ownership advantages. Their strong brand recognition remains the top asset based advantage they have. The company has also patented a shopping process that lets returning customers buy items without having to reenter credit card and shipping information.[34] In addition to this, they also hold many transaction based advantages including pioneering the online shopping technique. Amazon.com created one of the most sophisticated supply chain systems in the world, spending $200 million a year on business technology.[35]

Amazon.com runs every website they create the same as the first, by having a good human resource culture, intelligent branding by offering customers great value for their money, and applying an excellent logistics system.[36] The company does not enter franchising agreements therefore their internal affairs are never given out to potential competitors. Amazon's internalization advantage holds strong among other international franchising companies.

Locational advantages represent the suitability a potential host country has in respect to how the company wants to run its business. The following question portrays a more in depth analysis on this portion of Dunning's Theory. Amazon. com enters countries with a high-developed economy where their host customers would purchase their products more frequently. Alas, the company does hold a locational advantage since it is accessible from anywhere in the world as long as an internet connection is nearby.[36]

## 3. What role does cultural proximity or geographical proximity play in the retailer's international moves?

Cultural proximity and geographical proximity play no role in this competitor's international advances. With expansion to Canada, France, Germany, Japan and China, it is evident that this retailer is not attempting to maintain ties with just one distinct culture or offer products to countries with similar patterns of life. Geographical proximity also shows no importance to this company; they are *located all over the world with thousands of miles in between.*

**4.  Can you predict the retailer's future international expansion?**

*Amazon's future international expansion will include creating Amazon Australia. Currently there is no Amazon Australia but they have a wide customer base that is ordering products from Amazon UK. There is such a high demand for Amazon to enter their market and Australians are ordering from other Amazon sites. With Amazon's previous success entering different countries, it is likely that Amazon Australia will flourish. This will allow Australian customers to purchase from each other through Amazon.com and also save on international shipping prices.*

## Propositions

**P1:  The greater the ownership advantages for retailers, the less likely they will franchise or license.**

*Amazon has been able to expand internationally due to strong ownership advantages. Amazon has primarily transaction based ownership advantages, possessing a unique market format. Amazon is the only Internet retailer to offer a vast assortment of products in one place, maximizing consumer satisfaction. An online retail environment makes it possible for Amazon to carry many products and it improves logistics, because extensive warehousing is not required for merchandise as opposed to a physical retail store.*

**P2:  The greater the available organizational slack the greater the likelihood of expanding internationally.**

Current assets/ Current liabilities= Organizational slack

| | |
|---|---|
| 1,820,809,000 / 1,252,701,000 | 1.4535 |
| 2,539,396,000/ 1,620,400,000 | 1.5671 |
| 2,929,000,000/ 1,929,000,000 | 1.5184 |

Information Retrieved from: Amazon.com Inc., Mergent Online Database.

*Amazon's organizational slack increased from 2003 to 2004, concurring with the international expansion of the company. After 2004, the company aimed to expand in an alternative way by offering more products and a wider variation of merchandise.*

**P3:  The greater the recoverable slack the greater the likelihood of expanding Internationally**

1995: 35,000/511,000 = .068

1996: 1,035,000/15,746,000 = .066
1997: 6,573,000/147,758,000 = .044
Information Retrieved from:
Amazon.com Inc., Mergent Online Database

*No, the recoverable slack does not consistently increase each year, but fluctuates from year to year. This fluctuation shows that while Amazon.com has indeed worked to decrease expenses they still do not have a large amount of recoverable slack available to aid in international expansion. If expenses were to continually decrease, and a pattern of this decrease was shown in future ratios, the likelihood of expanding internationally would be much greater.*

**P4:The greater the potential slack the greater the likelihood of expanding internationally.**

1995: 977,000/1,084,000 = .9013
1996: 3,401,000/8,271,000 = .4112
1997: 28,486,000/149,000,000 = .1912
Information Retrieved from:
Amazon.com, Inc., Mergent Online Database

*The results illustrate that with each additional year the potential slack decreases. Although Amazon's assets increased from year to year, their equity did as well, along with their assets being far below equity each year. This proves that the potential slack the company had should not have indicated the further likelihood of expanding internationally.*

**P 13: Global companies will move to the largest/capital cities in the country.**

*When global companies expand into a foreign market they are bringing the knowledge of a previously successful retail format with them. Global companies such as Amazon.com have proven throughout the years that their format on entrepreneurial practices has excelled and that they have excelled in the category as an Internet retailer. If this global company had decided to become multinational, they would have pursued different online formats. Each countries individual website would have incorporated different ordering processes for their individuality and cultural preferences, along with vast differences in product offerings. However, communication barriers do exist within the different borders, so in response to this, Amazon.com has adapted their market structure to include different languages. As a global retailer the fundamental format remains unchanged. Amazon.com didn't take the route of expanding multi-nationally because their retail offerings alone have brought continual success to the company.*

Global companies will move to the largest capital cities in a country. Amazon. com has strategically positioned seven headquarters in high traffic cities worldwide along with six software development centers. With Seattle Washington as the global leader in ecommerce sites are also operated in the United Kingdom, Germany, France, Japan, Canada, and China (Joyo) along with maintaining 20 fulfillment centers around the world encompassing more than ten million square feet."[38]

Amazon.com's domestic expansion has had a positive effect on its value with the aid of their domestic customer service center, distribution centers and regional expansion. Amazon.com's strategies in these areas consist of continual domestic expansion which helps cut shipping times to serve non-English speaking customers.

**P14: Global Companies will not be attracted by population size, income, cultural proximity, or geographical proximity.**

Global companies do indeed need high traffic areas to begin their internationalization process, however, once established in the worldwide market they look to other outlets for future growth. One example of Amazon.com's competitive advantages over Barnes and Nobles online sector is their free super saver shipping on select items over 25 dollars. By doing this, shoppers who can not afford or do not want to pay the additional shipping can enjoy their items being shipped for free, overall enhancing sales for Amazon.

Established global companies can be attracted to expand in areas outside of large populations and high geographical locations. For example, as of 2005, India's estimated population was 1,095,351,995. There is a greater population of people living in this country than any of Amazon's seven countries .The United Kingdoms population for 2005 was approximated to be around 60,609,153 and Germanys was 82,422,299 which are two of the countries that Amazon.com has a website for.[39] If this global retailer was interested in expanding towards high population countries, India would be a prime location to base a website.[40] The concept of not locating their headquarters in the largest populated city is also true. Take the United States for example: Seattle Washington is the e-commerce leader for Amazon.com with an overall population in 2005 of approximately 573,911 people. Compared the United States' largest cities such as Los Angeles and New York, Seattle's population is not large. In 2005 alone the approximated population for Los Angeles was 3,844,829 and in New York it was approximated to be 8,143,197.[41] High income areas are not important for Amazon.com to consider in expansion, seeing as not all of their retail offerings are high priced. Although a country's purchasing power does contribute and help to buy the higher priced items, this is not Amazon's primary focus in their international expansion. The 25 cent miracle which is a hardcover book written by Teresa Nelson is sold used on the website for 30 cents, along with

*several other low cost items such as candy bars and small household necessities.*[42]
*The country does need a somewhat stable income per household though seeing as in order to receive free shipping on eligible items, at least 25 dollars must be spent. Amazon.com has based their strategy on success of their sales rather than focusing these sales in the wealthiest areas.*

*Below is a chart listing the Per Capita incomes of several of the wealthiest countries in 1998, the year this retailer was founded. As you can see, Norway, Switzerland and Denmark bring home the highest average annual income per household but these countries are also three that have no access to Amazon.com.*[43] *This concludes that Amazon.com does not focus on the wealthiest countries for their strategic expansion.*

**Per Capita Income in US. Dollars - 1998** [43]

| | |
|---|---|
| Switzerland | 39,980 |
| Norway | 34,310 |
| Denmark | 33,040 |
| Japan | 32,350 |
| Singapore | 30,170 |
| United States | 29,240 |
| Austria | 26,830 |
| Germany | 26,570 |
| Sweedon | 25,580 |
| Belgium | 25,380 |
| Netherlands | 24,780 |
| Finland | 24,280 |
| France | 24,210 |
| HongKong | 23,660 |
| United Kingdom | 21,410 |
| Canada | 19,170 |

*Proximity to the host country does not play a factor for Amazon.com either. The countries that Amazon have expanded to are in no way positioned close to the host country of the United States, or host city for that matter, in Seattle.*

*Amazon.com does not follow cultural proximity either. As you can see they have expanded to Germany, Japan, France and China which all adhere to different cultures and languages.*

*According to Hofstede's Dimensional Model, the culture in the expanded countries* revolves around low uncertainty avoidance due to the risk of ordering a product online. The purchaser is taking a chance of having to send back the product if they are dissatisfied which in-turn, costs time and money on the purchasers' behalf.

**P15: The greater the asset based ownership advantages of a global retailer, the more likely they are to franchise.**

Asset based ownership advantages are possessions of the company such as well known brand names.[44] Amazon.com is an asset based ownership global retailer that has allowed other companies to use their systems such as Target and Borders. By partnering up with Borders, Amazon is able to sell Borders books on their website. As an online retailer it is difficult for them to franchise because they are a web based company and do not have standing businesses.

**P16: The greater the transaction based ownership advantages of a global retailer, the less likely they are to franchise.**

Transaction based ownership advantages deal with how a company carries out their business. Examples of these transaction based ownership advantages include specific knowledge of a logistics system, method for producing private labels, sophisticated merchandising information systems, or a just-in-time inventory system.[33] Although Amazon does not provide private labels, superior knowledge of logistics systems is important to Amazon's success as a global retailer. Amazon owns many fulfillment centers world-wide, and prides itself on its sophistication in technology. Transaction based advantages are important to Amazon because they continue to learn how to run their business by perfecting their strategies over time. Tactical learning plays an important role in these advantages. Amazon can not purchase these advantages; rather, they are to be learned through trial and error. As a franchisor, a company will give up their rights or trade secrets to a franchisee. The company name and other transaction based ownerships are then adopted by the franchisee. The franchisee will then have to learn the assets in order to efficiently run their business. Amazon.com is a global e-tailer and therefore gives up its rights to franchise. They do, however, take part in acquisitions with other retailers that do franchise.

**P17: The greater the available organizational slack the greater the likelihood that global retailers will reacquire international franchisees.**

The 2004 ratio of current assets to current liabilities (3,248/ 3,248) is 1. The 2003 ratio of current assets to current liabilities (2,162/ 2,162) is 1. The 2002 ratio of current assets to current liabilities (1,990/ 1,990) is 1. Since Amazon.com is an internet retailer they will never franchise regardless of what the available organizational slack may be.

**P19: The greater the potential slack the greater the likelihood that global retailers will reacquire international franchisees.**

*[Ratio of Equity to Capital (3 year average before they begin reacquisition)]*

*Amazon.com does not enter franchise agreements therefore the proposition does not apply to our company. Although after researching, it seems that if the proposition was altered slightly, it could easily be connected with Amazon.com. The greater the potential slack, the greater the likelihood that global retailers would acquire property. If an organization has excess resources, there is a greater chance for them to expand than a company with a less equity to capital ratio. In the past three years, Amazon.com's gross profit has risen by nearly $800 million. Their potential slack, consequently, is higher, persuading them to continue to expand internationally.*[45]

## Endnotes

1. Dodge, 1999

2. Amazon, 2006

3. Amazon.com, 2006

4. Amazon.com, 2006

5. Amazon.com, 2006

6. Amazon.com, 2006

7. CNNMoney, 2006

8. Adamson, 2006

9. echeat, 2005

10. Amazon.com, 2006

11. Nicholls, Paul. (1998, October 15). Ecommerce. Amazon.com goes global. Retrieved on October 25, 2006, from www.internetnews.com/ec-news/article.php/31351

12. CNNMoney.com, 2000

13. Dbic.datamonitor.com

14. Amazon.com. (n.d.). Wikipedia. Retrieved October 30, 2006, from Answers Website http://www.answers.com/topic/amazon-com

15. BusinessWire, 2006

16. BusinessWire, 2006

17. JPMorgan, 2006

18. Economist, the. (2006, August 17). Click to download. The Economist. Retrieved on October 4, 2006, from www.economist.com/business/displaystory. cfm?story_id=7791530

19. Amazon.com, 2006

20. Ginty, Maura. (1999, October 22). Amazon.com Sues barnesandnoble Over Patent. Retrieved November 11, 2006, from http://www.internetnews.com/ec-news/print.php/4_223991

21. Bordersgroupinc.com. (2006). Overview About Us. Retrieved November 11, 2006, from http://www.bordersgroupinc.com/about/index.html

22. Barnesandnoble.com. (2006). About Barnes and Noble.com. Retrieved November 14, 2006, from http://www.barnesandnoble.com/help/cds2.asp?PID=8 184&z=y&cds2Pid=9481&linkid=760969

23. Flynn, Laurie J. (2006, October 25). Amazon to Curtail Its Spending. The New York Times, Technology. Retrieved Novemeber 14, 2006, from http://www. nytimes.com/2006/10/25/technology/25amazon.html?ex=1319432400&en=8f6a6 ebd5e924436&ei=5089&partner=rssyahoo&emc=rss

24. Flynn, Laurie J. (2006, July 26). Costs of Competition Send Amazon Profit Down 58%. The New York Times,Technology. Retrieved November 11, 2006, from http://www.nytimes.com/2006/07/26/technology/26amazon.html?ex=1311 566400&en=9f28af0fd05bb9df&ei=5088&partner=rssnyt&emc=rss

25. Gonsalves, Antone. (2006, February 2). Amazon. Profits Fall. Tech Web Technology News. Retrieved October 20, 2006, from http://www.techweb.com/ showArticle.jhtml?articleID=178601145

26. Amazon.com, 2006

27. Wall Street Journal, 2006

28. wsj.com, 2006

29. Wikipedia. (2006). Amazon.com. Retrieved October 30, 2006, from http:// en.wikipedia.org/wiki/Amazon.com

30. Mergent Online, 2006

31. Seely, Rich. (2006). SOA creates order out of chaos @ Amazon. Retrieved

October 10, 2006, from http://searchwebservices.techtarget.com/
originalContent/0,289142,sid26_gci1195702,00.html

32. Basis Technology Corp. (2006, February). Basis Technology Announces
Strategic Alliance With And Minority Investment From Amazon.com. Retrieved
September 25, 2006, from http://www.basistech.com/press-releases/2000/
amazon-0002.html

33. Sternquist, 1997

34. Preston, Rob. (2004, May 13). Patently Absurd. Down to Business. Retrieved
November 3, 2006, from Lexis-Nexis database.

35. Bacheldor, Beth. (2004, March 8). From Scratch: Amazon keeps supply
chainclose to home. Information Week – Supply Chain. Retrieved November 3,
2006, from Lexis-Nexis database.

36. Shankar, S. Jai. (May 16, 2002). An Amazonian tale. New Straits Times
Press(Malaysia) Berhad Malaysian Business. Retrieved November 3, 2006, from
Lexis-Nexis database.

37. Yee, 2006

38. Amazon.com, 2006

39. World Factbook, The. (July 2006). Retrieved November 14, 2006 fromhttps://
www.cia.gov/cia/publications/factbook/geos/gm.html

40. Wikipedia. (2006). India. Retrieved November 1, 2006, from http://
en.wikipedia.org/wiki/India

41. U.S. Census Bureau. (2005). American Community Survey Data Profile
Highlights. Los Angeles. Retrieved November 3, 2006, from http://factfinder.
census.gov/servlet/ACSSAFFFacts?_event=ChangeGeoContext&geo_
id=16000US0644000&_geoContext=&_street=&_county=los+angeles&_
cityTown=los+angeles&_state=&_zip=&_lang=en&_
sse=on&ActiveGeoDiv=geoSelect&_useEV=&pctxt=fph&pgsl=010&_
submenuId=factsheet_1&ds_name=ACS_2005_SAFF&_ci_nbr=null&qr_
name=null&reg=null%3Anull&_keyword=&_industry=

42. Amazon.com, 2006

43. World Bank, The. (1998). All Regions, Whole World Per Capita. Retrieved
November 1, 2006, from http://www.worldbank.org/depweb/english/modules/
economic/gnp/datanot.html

44. Sternquist, 2006

45. Amazon.com, 2006

46. Amazon Annual Report, 2006

47. Price Target Research. (2006, October 15). Amazon.com Inc. Retrieved on October 21, 2006 from Investtext.

48. Anonymous. Oct. 15, 1998.

49. Global Market Information Database. (2004, April 1) Retailing in Germany, Country Report, Retrieved October 30,2006, from Global Market Information Database.

50. Amazon.com, 1996-2006

51. Amazon.com, 2006

52. Amazon, 2006

53. Enclick. (2006, May). Top Online Retailers in the UK. Retrieved October 20, 2006, from http://blog.enclick.com/ecommerce/top_online_retailers_in_the_uk.html

54. Barrett, A. (2000, August 30). Amazon.com to Launch French Web Site With Four Product Lines Simultaneously. The Wall Street Journal, p.B12.

55. Nawotka, Edward (2000). Amazon to Conquer France. Publishers Weekly, 247(35), 21.The World Bank Group. (2006). Data Query. Retrieved November 1, 2006, from http://devdata.worldbank.org/data-query/

56. Business Editors/Technology Writers. (2000). Amazon.com Launches Amazon.co.jp With a Comprehensive Catalog of Japanese and Foreign Books for Japan and Japanese Speakers Worldwide. Business Wire. Retrieved November 3, 2006, from Lexis-Nexis database.

57. Brophy, Barry. (2000). Japan' publishing industry just got a powerful new player. Metropolis Magazine, Article 357. Retrieved November 3, 2006, from http://metropolis.co.jp/tokyofeaturestories/357/tokyofeaturestoriesinc.htm

58. Sakurai, Joji. (November 1, 2000). Amazon.com opens shop in a land of avid readers, risks wait ahead. The Associated Press State & Local Wire. Retrieved November 2, 2006, from Lexis-Nexis database.

59. Amazon.ca, 2006

60. Answers.com, 2006

61. Hunt, Ben. (2002). Amazon Launches site in Canada. News Digest.. The financial times Limited. Retrieved October 29,2006, from: Lexis, Nexis.

62. Amazon.com, 2006

63. Ouchi, Monica. (2004, August 20). Amazon to buy online Chinese bookstore.

64.    Seattle Times. Retrieved November 2, 2006, from Lexis-Nexis database.

65. Xingdang, Fang. (August 30, 2004). DangDang slips good chance to join Amazon. Global News Wire - Asia Africa Intelligence Wire. Retreved November 3, 2006, from Lexis-Nexis database.

# Blockbuster Inc.

*Jordan Berman, Elizabeth DeJonge, Yuenming Kwan, Matt Lewis*
*Douglas Rabaut, John Raven, Emily Sandelands, Andrew Wirth*

## Blockbuster Inc.

B lockbuster Inc. is a primary retailer of home and movie entertainment around the globe. Founded in 1985, Blockbuster currently has over 7,400 stores throughout America, Asia, Australia, and Europe. Blockbuster is continuing to broaden its presence both domestically and internationally. They are the only company that provides their customers with complete access to entertainment throughout multiple channels.[1] Via mail, vending machines, digital downloads, or in-store sales, Blockbuster has managed to increase their reach and target new market segments. Blockbuster is able to cater to many different lifestyles by offering a wide variety of entertainment genres and also by customizing merchandise, quantity, and layout at the store level to meet the needs of local customers. With the ever changing entertainment industry Blockbuster has continued to adapt to consumer wants and needs, and plans to stay at the top of the entertainment industry.

Blockbuster was first operated by Blockbuster Entertainment Corporation, which was incorporated in Delaware in 1982 and penetrated the movie industry in 1985. Blockbuster Inc., formerly a subsidiary of Viacom was incorporated in Delaware on October 16, 1989. On September 29, 1994 Blockbuster Entertainment Corporation merged with Viacom. Subsequently, business operations were conducted by indirect subsidiaries of Viacom. In 1999 Blockbuster announced their Initial Public Offering, and business operations were merged with Blockbuster Inc. As of October 2004, Blockbuster Inc. divested from Viacom and became an independent company.

The company founder is David Cook, who operated the business and introduced it to public. Blockbuster is a chain store which provides rental and retail movies as well as game entertainment. The company provides its customers access to media entertainment delivery though distribution channels such as in store, via mail, vending and kiosks, and online. In addition, Blockbuster provides an Internet rental and retail service where customers can acquire their media entertainment through mail or digital copy online.

Blockbuster has a strong international presence that increases market share and develops increased revenue. Currently, Blockbuster has over 7,400 stores in United States including its territories and 20 other international markets. There are a total of 2,820 international stores; of these stores, 1,928 of them are directly operated by Blockbuster and 892 are operated through franchisees.[2] However, all these stores are under Blockbuster Brand. In Italy, Denmark, Mexico and Canada, company operated store–in-store game locations exist. All these stores are under GAME RUSH brand. In the Republic of Ireland and Northern Ireland Blockbuster operated under the XTRA-VISION brand until they divested in 2009.[2]

## FLOW CHART

1985:   United States (3,878 company-owned stores & 707 franchises)
1989:   Canada (459 company-owned stores)
1989:   Great Britain (663 company-owned stores)
1991:   Australia (333 franchises)
1991:   Chile (69 franchises)
1991:   Mexico (320 company-owned stores & 4 franchises)
1991:   Spain (withdrew in 2006)
1991:   Venezuela (20 franchises)
1991:   Japan (withdrew in 1999)
1992:   Ireland (Republic) & Northern Ireland (186 company-owned stores)
1994:   Italy (157 company-owned stores & 55 franchises)
1994:   Argentina (70 company-owned stores)
1994:   New Zealand (30 franchises)
1995:   Germany (withdrew in 1996)
1995:   Israel (10 company-owned franchises)
1995:   Brazil (175 franchises)
1995:   Peru (withdrew in 2006)
1995:   Colombia (22 franchises)
1995:   Thailand (3 franchises)
1996:   Denmark (70 company-owned stores)
1996:   Ecuador (withdrew in 2004)

1996:   Portugal (19 franchises)
1996:   El Salvador (withdrew in 2008)
1996:   Panama (15 franchises)
1997:   Ireland (withdrew in 2009)
1997:   Taiwan (132 franchises)
1997:   Uruguay (3 company-owned stores)
1999:   Hong Kong (withdrew in 2004)
1999:   Philippines (withdrew in 2001)
2001:   Costa Rica (withdrew in 2003)
2001:   Guatemala (5 franchises)
2002:   Norway (withdrew in 2004)

## Industry Analysis

The global video and retail industry is constantly forced to reinvent and differentiate its offerings in order to meet economic and technological shifts in the market. In order of market share, global industry leaders are Blockbuster Inc., Movie Gallery Inc., Netflix and Tatsuya.[3] Movie Gallery and Netflix currently operate exclusively within the United States (and combined with Blockbuster held over 50% of the U.S. rental market as of 2003).[3] While Tatsuya leads the market in Southeast Asia (holding 31.5 percent of the Japanese market as of 2003). Blockbuster has without a doubt defined industry standards since the birth of its international expansion efforts. Prior to Blockbuster's expansion into foreign markets, many video rental retailers operated within unorganized, dingy and cramped spaces with insufficient copies of new and in-demand releases.[4]

Blockbuster's organized, well-lit and well-stocked retail format has since been sufficiently adopted by domestic and international competitors, and market leaders now compete in service diversification to stay afloat in a declining market.

Brick and mortar outlets have been forced to differentiate to survive. Owing their success to the adoption of a smaller, light-weight DVD format, Netflix pioneered online rental in 1999, also eliminating late-fees; Blockbuster was quick to follow suit, launching its own online rental service in the UK and US in 2004.[3] Up until this point, late fees had accounted for 10 percent of the fees collected by movie studios and 15 percent of store revenue[3] and this in turn decreased DVD prices, hoping to push consumers towards purchasing units. In developed countries, the rental industry is facing competition from Video-On-Demand services and Internet outlets while in many other parts of the world, piracy has greatly affected the decline. Pirated videos make up a large portion in many Latin American markets; accompanied with little regulation, this has made it extremely hard for companies to merely break even.[3] Operations in China have also faced many piracy-related obstacles. Despite the fact that piracy is technically illegal in mainland China, fines assessed to counterfeiters are so low that it is well worth the risk.[3]

In order to stay ahead of the curve, rental retailers have chosen to diversify by offering trade-ins, operating computerized rental kiosks and streamlining selection offerings by eliminating niche titles in favor of stocking higher quantities of popular units. Fortune magazine reported that a typical Blockbuster store devoted only 65 percent of its space to rentals and the other 35 percent to services like the sale of new and used DVDs, point of purchase items and gaming centers.[5] The industry is not focused so much on which markets seem to provide fertile grounds for expansion, but how to stabilize and align its offerings with consumer trends in established markets.

## Competitor's Analysis

The competition for movie and video game rentals has changed dramatically in the market over the past decade. The ideas behind watching movies online and having rentals mailed to a consumer's house have changed the make-up of the industry. Today, Blockbuster's biggest rivals are companies such as Netflix. Other new competing companies include Hastings Entertainment, Movie Gallery and Wal-Mart. These newly developed competitors have taken a lot of market share away from Blockbuster over the past years. This has forced Blockbuster to restructure their business so they can compete with these rivals.

Netflix is by far Blockbusters biggest competitor, they have been able to create a market demand for having rentals mailed to customers' homes and have increased the amount of movies streamed online. By having movies available through these channels this particular company has a lot more viewing traffic than Blockbuster. Micheal Olsen, an analyst of the Piper Jaffney firm, says that Blockbuster's online traffic has decreased 9% while Netflix has increased their traffic 17 percent.[5] Recently, Blockbuster has tried to structure a service similar to Netflix so that they can directly compete with them. In 2005, they developed an online subscription service known as Total Access; however, the service has incurred high startup and operational costs.[5] Netflix does not, that is actual stores. This competitive advantage has allowed Blockbuster to stay in competition with Netflix. Companies like Netflix have struggled to retain customers because they do not have any physical locations.[5]

The recent economic downturn has allowed hypermarket retailers such as Wal-Mart to direct their services to price-conscious consumers who are watching their discretional spending. Blockbuster has started slashing prices relative to what places like Wal-Mart offer so they can continue to retain their loyal customers.

Blockbuster Canada has slashed prices to $3.99 for two night rentals on new releases.[7] This is a 30% total decrease in the prices that they were charging before.[7] This is important for Blockbuster Canada in terms of competing against discount hypermarkets because Blockbuster is currently Canada's largest video retail chain and one of Blockbuster's larger international markets.[7] Losing consumers in international markets such as this is not good since they have already lost a strong presence in their parent country, the United States.

It is important for Blockbuster's International expansion to enable customers to not only rent from physical locations but to be able to access movies online as well. Many countries simply do not have the resources and space available for locations to be established, so creating a strong Internet presence can be beneficial to Blockbuster's global effort. If they are to continue to build strong relationships with their customers overseas they need to develop an understanding of cultural similarities and differences as well as developing an understanding of how competitors do business in these diverse cultures. Not all countries use the Internet as prevalently as others so it is important to understand what the reach is in gaining customer awareness.

## Business Strategy

With the company's introduction in the United States in 1985, rapid domestic expansion led to strong national success and brand recognition. Blockbuster's retailing growth paralleled the demand for VHS and DVD home entertainment. In the US, many markets became saturated due to the high level of business acceptance. The company's convenient, community-friendly format and overall worldwide demand for their business opened the door to enter other countries and pursue profitability in additional markets. Taking expansion risk factors into heavy consideration, their international expansion strategy revolved around the utilization of foreign partners and fast business introduction. Purchasing other companies with closely related business formats was another widely used company tactic in building market share and international presence.

International franchising and joint ventures were the chosen forms of expansion for the majority of Blockbuster's international entrances. The introduction of the Blockbuster business format, many times through other forms of company titles, had proven to be a successful route for creating their international presence. The purchasing of various smaller product-related companies followed. In foreign countries, the implementation of master franchisors took much of the stress and responsibility off the shoulders of company executives.[8] The practice of a dormant management style was also chosen during many of their international endeavors.

Much of Blockbuster's international achievement was because of the solid management of their partnering companies. Lowered cultural risks through the use of these international management companies proved to be invaluable during the formation of company offerings. This often meant including and excluding items, resulting in small portions of their stores adapting to their cultural environments — while keeping the video rental format unchanged.

In many cases, Blockbuster owned the minority share of their international companies. During company expansion, the reacquisition of certain international entities was sought.[9] The reacquisition of franchises implies the company's strategy was designed on the resource-based theory of international expansion — growing with the help of additional companies and management, only until future resources become available to buy the majority of their international outlets from their owners.[9] Pursuing a majority and wholly-owned company structure was partially because of company growth, but also because of internal company management ability. Many of the investing groups Blockbuster targeted during expansion had become less of a necessity due to the company's success later in their international movement.

The increasing popularity of their retail format and overall brand awareness led the company into markets that proved uninviting. The entrance and exit from some countries, due to various conflicting economic, cultural and normative circumstances, showed the company's ability to cut their losses and search for more enticing locations. Even though the company has been faced with the decision to leave targeted countries in the past, many of their early decisions have become international benchmark outlets. The United Kingdom, Blockbuster's first international country, still operates the company's largest international outlet. Brazil's debut led to the most productive opening month in company history, including US outlets.[10] Blockbuster has shown that successful investments are protected and enhanced. The sucessful investments are either taken over by Blockbuster management or shut down. Optimizing productive outlets while limiting minimal contributors has not only played a large part in the company strategy, but the company's success — domestically and internationally.

## Retail Culture

Blockbuster has established themselves as the leader in home video entertainment since 1989. In 2004, Blockbuster realized the potential of expanding its services online. Shane Evangelist, Vice President and General Manager of Blockbuster Online, noted that the new online presence "will enable us to provide our customers - old and new alike - with unmatched convenience, service, selection and value".[11] On August 11, 2004, the web site was launched, and offered Blockbuster customers access "for a low monthly fee of $19.99, giving customers unlimited DVD rentals, up to three out at a time, plus two free in-store movie rental coupons per month".[11]

Today, the company offers movie and game rentals, new and traded movie products, a game store-in-store called GAME RUSH brand and also operates an online service providing rental and sale of movies delivered by mail and digital delivery through blockbuster.com.[12]

The future of DVD rentals is through Blockbuster Express Kiosks as well as their digital offerings.[13] Thomas Kasey, Blockbuster's financial officer, says that these kiosks won't have an effect on company revenue until at least the second half of 2010, because NCR, the maker of these kiosks, will pay Blockbuster only after they have made a certain number of sales transactions.[13] Blockbuster also offers a pay-per-view feature through about 30 Samsung products such as HDTVs and Blu-ray Disc players as well as Tivo digital video recorders.[13]

## Blockbuster Country Summaries

### United States

First Store Opened: 1985                    Number of Locations: 4,585

Blockbuster's first opened in 1985 in Dallas, Texas and they now operate in all 50 states as well as over 20 countries globally. According to the 2009 Blockbuster Annual Report, as of January 4, 2009 Blockbuster had 4,585 stores operating in the United States and its territories. Most recently, Blockbuster has noticed a change in demand for DVD rentals and has shifted distribution across five channels including in-store, by mail, vending and kiosks, online, and at home.[14] Along with changing the focus of distribution and adapting to current demand, the company is also implementing plans of enhancing retailing and merchandising opportunities, leveraging growth and leadership position, developing digital solutions, and implementing cost controls.[14] Currently, due to the economy, Blockbuster is expecting lower revenues compared to that of the past and is planning to close many locations.

### Canada

First Store Opened: 1989                    Number of Locations: 459

Canada has a strong economy, similar to that of the United States. Canada has enjoyed solid economic growth, and prudent fiscal management has produced consecutive balanced budgets from 1997 to 2007.[15] Canada relies on its high-tech society for growth and currently has a $1.3 trillion GDP.[15] Blockbuster entered Canada in 1989 with 19 stores and currently has over 360 stores operating in over 10 provinces under the name Blockbuster Canada Co.[16] It is a wholly-owned subsidiary of Blockbuster Inc. and currently employs over 5000 associates.[17]

## United Kingdom

First Store Opened: 1989                    Number of Locations: 700+

Blockbuster Inc. entered the United Kingdom in 1989. The UK was targeted because it was the largest video market in Europe. The UK had a large population of households with VCRs, with an estimated penetration of 62 percent, totaling roughly 12.5 million houses.[18] The first Blockbuster was opened on Walworth Road in London. Currently the store on Walworth Road is the largest Blockbuster outlet outside the United States. There are over 700 stores in the UK and approximately five million member accounts due to an early investment that placed Blockbuster as the leader in the video rental market.[19] In the UK Blockbuster Inc. is the largest movie chain. In October 2002, Blockbuster Inc. began providing a version of online video rental. At the same time, Blockbuster Inc. acquired the UK-based games retail Gamestation to increase product variety but sold the company in 2007 to Game Group PLC.[20] In May 2004, Blockbuster UK developed a conventional online subscription service. This unlimited 3-disc plan is £14.99 per month with no in-store disc exchange. Against competition, Blockbuster UK was awarded the Best DVD rental service in a head-to-head test by UK magazine *Web User*.

## Australia

First Store Opened: 1991                    Number of Locations: 333

Blockbuster Australia set up in 1991 and is a wholly owned subsidiary of the American parent company. There are approximately 45 stores in Australia. A 29 store acquisition took place between 1993 and 1994 increasing the total to approximately 45.[21] John Mlyniski, Blockbuster vice president for the Asia-Pacific region, describes the region as vast and full of opportunity.[21] The company wants to continue to have a strong presence in Australia and believes that its future is bright there. There are 333 franchised outlets in Australia today.[22]

## Chile

First Store Opened: 1991                    Number of Locations: 69

Blockbuster and Video Chile entered into a licensing agreement in 1991. Video Chile was the active management of the company's presence in Chile until 1996 when Blockbuster acquired all 50 retail operations under license agreement in the country. Along with this purchase, Blockbuster also obtained ownership of Video Chile's Argentina outlets, Video Argentina.[23] The purchase of the Chilean outlets was a strategic move for Blockbuster that allowed the further expansion in Chile and Argentina under company control and management. The company is currently under ownership and management of Blockbuster Video International Corporation (Chile) Ltda. and is a wholly owned subsidiary of Blockbuster Video.

## Japan

First Store Opened: 1991, withdrew in 1999          Number of Locations: 38

In 1991, Blockbuster partnered with Fujita & Co. Ltd. (franchisor of McDonald's in Japan) to develop an aggressive program of Blockbuster retail outlets in Japan, planning over 1000 outlets by 2001.[24] Blockbuster was the first foreign-owned rental chain in Japan, making changes to the traditional video rental landscape in Japan such as offering store spaces twice as large as average Japanese video shops and refusing to carry pornographic content (which at the time accounted for 16 percent of total video rentals in Japan).[24] Expansion was steady as opposed to astronomical through the mid-nineties as Blockbuster faced competition from other retailers attempting to go after the family market and also ran into problems finding affordable retail space in popular locations. By the end of 1998, Blockbuster Japan operated only 38 stores; citing disappointing sales and the high cost of operating large outlets in prime commercial areas, Blockbuster Inc. sold its remaining shares for an undisclosed sum to Fujita & Co., who subsequently rebranded all locations.[25]

## Mexico

First Store Opened: 1991          Number of Locations: 324

Mexico operates a free market economy in the trillion-dollar class.[26] It is continually becoming more modernized and relies heavily on the industry's private sector. Blockbuster entered the Mexican market in 1991 by franchising and operates under the name Blockbuster de Mexico, SA de CV. As of 2001, Mexico's VCR penetration was growing with 55 percent currently owning VCR's and 250,000 households owning DVD players.[27] These numbers made the Mexican market a large opportunity for Blockbuster Inc. Mexico, which continues to operate over 300 stores.

## Spain

First Store Opened: 1991                    Number of Locations: 94

In 1991, Blockbuster Inc. opened its first Spanish store. Blockbuster stores in Spain were operated strictly through franchising until 1997 when they reacquired all of their Spanish franchises, formerly Video Invest Espanola S.A. (VIESA).[28] In 2006, Blockbuster announced that they planned to close all Spanish stores. These closings affected 688 employees. These store closings resulted from economic reasons, competition with piracy, and digital TV providers in Spain.[29] Also, changes in consumers' discretionary spending aided in exit from Spain for Blockbuster.

## Venezuela

First Store Opened: 1991                    Number of Locations: 20

Hugo Chavez, President of Venezuela since 1999, has been on a mission to promote what he calls 21st Century Socialism, which ultimately purports to alleviate social ills while at the same time attacking globalization and undermining regional stability.[30] A consumption boom in 2007 due to an increase in domestic credit has come with costs – inflation levels rose over 30% in 2008.[30] After opening its first location in Venezuela in 1991, Blockbuster furthered its franchise presence in Venezuela, and by 1995, the company had over 2,000 locations in nine countries outside of the United States.[31]

## Italy

First Store Opened: 1993                    Number of Locations: 212

Italy has a largely diversified industrial economy, Northern Italy is industrial, whereas Southern Italy is impoverished and shows high rates of unemployment. In recent years the economy has shown direct impacts of the global economic crisis and is expected to contract for the next couple years. Italy has a GDP of $1.823 trillion.[32] Blockbuster and Standa S.p.A, an Italian retailer, created a joint venture to develop Blockbuster video stores in Italy. This press release was announced on December 17, 1993. The joint venture called for the establishment of 200 stores in five years; initial development began in Milan and other parts of Northern Italy.[33]

## Argentina

First Store Opened: 1994                    Number of Locations: 70

Video Chile S.A., Blockbuster's neighboring operations in Chile, was granted development rights by Blockbuster Video to expand locations to Argentina in 1994. Argentina was selected for international expansion because of its affluent and dynamic economy. Buenos Aires was targeted because of the high population, nearly 11 million people, representing potential growth for the company. An economy of scale was the basis of the expansion into Argentina for Blockbuster. Company efficiency in the region was another major priority for the company when deciding to enter Argentina with Video Chile. The original contract with Video Argentina called for 75 retail outlets in the country, but was later changed to a target of 125 outlets by Video Chile. Due to slow growth in the country, Blockbuster purchased the majority of the company for an undisclosed sum. Company operations in Argentina are now under management of Blockbuster Video.[35] The company is currently Blockbuster Argentina, S.A.

## Brazil

First Store Opened: 1995                                    Number of Locations: 175

Blockbuster Entertainment Corporation announced the exclusive development rights to a Brazilian company in 1994 which would allow the company's expansion into Brazil. The Moreira Salles Group was awarded the rights to open up to 250 Blockbuster stores over a seven-year period. The Group agreed to invest $20 million in the franchise deal with Blockbuster and Brazilian company Uniao de Bancos.[35] The first Brazilian Blockbuster store was opened in 1995 in South America's largest city, Sao Paolo. The company planned to expand to as many as 20 additional Blockbusters that year in Sao Paulo. Success for the company was based on the small, individually owned retail market of Sao Paulo in the early 90's. The high level of VCR penetration in Brazil made Sao Paulo the ideal location to saturate, with nearly eight million homes owning a VCR at the time.[36] After the March opening in 1995, Blockbuster sales exceeded $300,000 for the opening month. The sales performance of the Sao Paulo outlet for that month was the highest level of sales for any location in company history. Outside of the United States, Blockbuster in Brazil was the most successful foreign market.[37] Blockbuster grew to 175 stores in Brazil before the company was purchased by Lojas Americanas, a Brazilian retailer, for $87.5 million. Blockbuster agreed to license the Blockbuster trademark to Lojas Americanas for a term of 20 years following the deal.[38] The company is currently under management of Lojas Americanas S.A.

## Colombia

First Store Opened: 1995                    Number of Locations: 22

In 1995, with an already palpable presence in South America, Blockbuster opened its first Colombian retail outlet in Bogota, making Colombia Blockbuster's 16th international market. Exclusive development rights were granted to a group of prominent retailers lead by Miami real estate developer Bernardo Batievsky.[39] Within the first seven weeks of operation, Blockbuster had already signed up 25,000 members at its three Bogota locations.[40]

## Germany

First Store Opened: 1995, Withdrew in 1996        Number of Locations: 17

Blockbuster entered into a joint venture agreement with successful German publishing house Burda Verlag in 1995 to expand operations into Germany, with 20 stores planned to open by the end of 1996.[41] However, Blockbuster's poor decisions to rapidly establish a myriad of stores (20 stores at its height in 1996) in the saturated markets of Berlin and Munich and refusal to stock pornographic films (which accounted for 1/3 of the German rental market)[42] led Burda to sell its 49 percent stake back to Blockbuster in April 1996; Blockbuster subsequently halted operations on December 31, 1996.[43]

## Israel

First Store Opened: 1995                    Number of Locations: 15

Blockbuster Inc. first entered Israel in August 1995 through a master franchise contract between Canadian investor Leon Koffler and Viacom, the owner of Blockbuster at the time. Israel was considered for a franchise agreement due to the large percentage of Israelis who preferred selective viewing instead of the vast amount of dated programming.[44] Two Blockbuster Locations were opened in 1995. The first was in Ramat Gan and the second location was located in the Ron Cinema Complex in Jerusalem.[45] As of 2009, Blockbuster has a total of 10 franchised stores.[46]

## Thailand

First Store Opened: 1995                    Number of Locations: 3

Blockbuster granted Sun-Master Entertainment of Thailand exclusive rights to open up to 105 Blockbuster video stores in Thailand. Blockbuster wanted to establish locations in main cities like Bangkok and then "roll out" 6 to 12 stores in the years after first entering the country in 1995.[47] Blockbuster had trouble dealing with design space for this specific region due to the less than normal space quarters. Today, Thailand currently has three stores open and they seem to be struggling in the market.[48]

## Denmark

First Store Opened: 1996                    Number of Locations: 70

Denmark displayed a viable opportunity for market expansion. Denmark has a stable currency, a stable political system and a large dependence on foreign trade. Denmark's financial position is among the strongest in the EU. Denmark has a GDP with a relatively steady growth rate at $203.6 billion.[49] Blockbuster entered Denmark on May 15, 1996 by acquiring Christianshavn Video. The 31-store chain acquisition marks Blockbuster's entrance in the Scandanavian market. Blockbuster's CEO stated "Aggressive international expansion is one of our primary growth strategies, and this action represents a significant step in our European initiative". Blockbuster is implementing strategic tactics by servicing clients with an expansive collection, an emphasis on cleanly lit interiors, as well as outstanding customer service.[50]

## El Salvador

First Store Opened: 1996, withdrew in 2008          Number of Locations: 5

Blockbuster Entertainment commenced operations in El Salvador in 1996, awarding exclusive development rights to Corporation Centroamericana de Entretenimiento, a local El Salvadoran corporation.[51] Citing El Salvador's economic and political stability, Blockbuster planned nine superstores to be built throughout the country, however, the expansion efforts soon lost steam.[51] Store numbers dwindled through the 2000's and Blockbuster eventually pulled out in 2008 citing piracy concerns.[52]

## New Zealand

First Store Opened: 1996                    Number of Locations: 30

Blockbuster entered Christchurch, New Zealand in 1991 and later franchised two stores into the north island in 1996 through franchisee Steve Dobbs.[53] Currently, Blockbuster franchises 30 stores in New Zealand, which include some stores operated by Blockbuster Australia.[54] Blockbuster was well received by New Zealand residents, but with increasing technology, these stores are not experiencing the same customer flow as before. By the end of 2005, there were 39 Blockbuster stores. The decrease in stores between 2005 and 2009 really shows the difficulty that Blockbuster International has been experiencing.

## Panama

First Store Opened: 1996                      Number of Locations: 15

With its impressive economic performance in 2008, which reduced its national poverty level to 29%, Panama hopes to lower high unemployment rates and counter its reputation of having "the second most unequal income distribution in Latin America".[55] Blockbuster entered Panama in early 1996 and was the company's 20th international market.[56] Panama was the company's "first entry into Central America and offered one of the greatest opportunities in the region due to the high number of VCR households".[56] Today, the company operates 15 franchised locations throughout the country.

## Portugal

First Store Opened: 1996                      Number of Locations: 19

Blockbuster Entertainment Group gave exclusive rights to develop Blockbuster in Portugal in 1996 to the franchisee Lano Video S.A.[57] "The Blockbuster Video superstore concept has great potential in Portugal, a market in which superstores are almost non-existent. The creation of the franchisee partnership with Lano Video S.A. represents an important step in the execution of our strategy to continue expanding Blockbuster's International home video operations in Europe and other world markets" claims Blockbuster's International President Mike Murray. The company planned to open 20 franchised stores in the first three years of operation and currently operates 19.[58]

## Ireland

First Store Opened: 1997, withdrew in 2009    Number of Locations: 186

Blockbuster acquired Xtra-Vision stores, previously owned by a consortium, in 1997. Xtra-Vision achieved rampant success throughout Ireland, so Blockbuster operated under the existing Xtra-Vision name. On August 28, 2009 Blockbuster announced the divesture of its 186 store Xtra-Vision entertainment retailer to Birchall Investments Limited for proceeds of up to $45 million, subject to certain adjustments.[59] Birchall Investments is an NBC Venture and one of

Ireland's largest independent securities firms. Jim Keyes, Blockbuster Chairman and Chief Executive Officer, said, "Today's announcement furthers our goal of improving liquidity and underscores our intent to advance the sale and licensing of our international assets as we focus on transformation of our North American business".[59]

## Taiwan

First Store Opened: 1997                    Number of Locations: 132

Blockbuster in Taiwan has been fading along with many of the Blockbusters globally due to a faltering economy and increased competition. Blockbuster BEI Taiwan Ltd. opened five stores in March 1997, just before an announcement that earnings had dropped by 20%.[60] The first franchise store in Taiwan was located in Taipei, which was a 2500-square-foot store.[61] Taiwan Blockbuster said they are financially independent from United States Blockbuster.[62] Blockbuster's push into the global market then became relentless because this was a key business strategy for them and they were willing to pursue it. Currently, Taiwan Blockbuster has introduced a Life Warehouse in store which means they are also selling other convenience products such as pet food, toys and snacks.[62] These programs help Blockbuster gain more profit and a competitive position in the Taiwan market. Taiwan has opened 132 stores and is thriving more in the market than other countries in the region such as Thailand.[63]

## Uruguay

First Store Opened: 1997                    Number of Locations: 3

Shortly after Blockbuster opened its first Uruguay location in 1997, the country's economy suffered a major downturn, the unemployment rate rose, inflation surged, and the burden of external debt doubled.[64] Thankfully, the economy has since begun to turn around, and has been on the rise by nearly eight percent per-year since 2004.[64] Uruguay's population shows promise as a market, and Thibault de Chatellus, Division Vice President of Latin America for Blockbuster International, adds that consumers in Uruguay appreciate our expansive selection of video titles, the emphasis on family entertainment products, and our outstanding customer service.[65] Today, the company owns three locations country-wide in Carasco, Malvin, and Punta Carretas.

## Hong Kong

First Store Opened: 1999, withdrew in 2004        Number of Locations: 24

Blockbuster first entered Hong Kong in 1999 with hopes of using it as a springboard into launching operations into mainland China.[66] The company was short lived in Hong Kong closing all stores in 2004, a mere five years later. Blockbuster initially focused on video compact discs as an alternative to VHS. They planned on using one-third of the floor space for VCD rentals which was a significant shift in the company policy which originally set VHS rentals a priority.[67] Although Blockbuster claimed the reason for removing themselves from the country was due to high operating costs and escalating rent payments, customers of Blockbuster Hong Kong blame rampant piracy for the company's withdrawal.[68] According to one customer, Eddie Jim Kwok-sang, "The store has a large supply but the prices are not so attractive when compared with the pirated versions," said Mr. Jim.[68] The company was unable to compete with the counterfeiting of VCDs and allowed all stores to expire.

## Phillippines

First Store Opened: 1999, Withdrew in 2001        Number of Locations: 2

Fresh off the failure of a nine-year investment in the Japanese market, Blockbuster planned expansion throughout the rest of Asia. In 1999, Blockbuster entered into a franchise development agreement with Arcon Video Corporation to open stores around Manila, citing the popularity of the entertainment industry in the Philippines as a major decision factor.[69] However, with only two stores open by the end of 2000, operations dissolved in 2001.[70]

## Guatemala

First Store Opened: 2001        Number of Locations: 5

Blockbuster announced expansion into Guatemala and Costa Rica in late 2000, rounding out the heavy South and Central American expansion program that had gained steam in the mid-nineties. Franchise rights were granted to the Corporacion de Entretenimiento de Guatemala, an affiliate of Blockbuster's El Salvadoran franchisee, who opened three stores by the end of 2001.[71] Guatemalan operations currently stand strong against the threat of piracy, responsible for waves of store closings throughout South and Central America between 2003 and 2008.

## Norway

First Store Opened: 2002, Withdrew in 2004       Number of Locations: 2

Citing the steady success of Blockbuster's format in the Danish market, Blockbuster opened a company operated store In Oslo during 2002. In early 2003, plans were announced for a 40-store expansion;[72] however, within six months of operations, Blockbuster stated that it would pull out of Norway by early 2004, closing its two Oslo locations.[72]

## Country Summary: Conclusion

Blockbuster Inc. uses a variety of internationalization strategies and patterns of expansion. Additionally, Blockbuster has had many successes and failures in their international markets. They have acquired many replacement acquisitions. Their main methods of expansion into foreign countries includes joint ventures, franchising, and licensing. The development of online multimedia has provided a variety of channels to reach consumers, which has enabled Blockbuster to expand its reach.

## Questions

**1. Is the retailer classified as a global retailer or a multinational retailer? Explain its pattern of expansion. What expansion strategy did/is the retailer use/using?**

*Blockbuster Inc. is a global retailer located in 20+ countries. Blockbuster's pattern of expansion consists of foreign market acquisitions and joint ventures to create presence in foreign markets. Blockbuster generally franchises. Of Blockbuster's 7,400+ stores, 4,585 stores are operating under the Blockbuster brand in the United States and its territories, of which 707 stores are operating through their franchises. Previously, Blockbuster's expansion strategy consists of acquiring a controlling share in existing movie chains, creating new enterprises, or franchising locations. Presently, Blockbuster is in a state of reorganization and has divested some locations to improve their financial situation.*

**2. Based on Dunning's Eclectic Theory, how do ownership, locational and internalization factors play in your retailers' international expansion?**

*Dunning's Eclectic Paradigm is a mix of three various theories of FDI, or foreign direct investment. The three elements include ownership, locational, and internalization advantages. Ownership advantages refer to the development of a competitive advantage resulting from efficient utilization of company resources. Locational advantages are derived from the ability to develop more profits in* foreign markets than in domestic markets. Internalization results from exclusive company knowledge which enables firms to compete competitively – usually a result of tacit knowledge, or learning from experience.

These factors have directly influenced Blockbuster's international expansion. Ownership advantages have been impacted by the ever-changing technological environment. The advancement of online media, pirating, and mail-order videos have had negative impacts on Blockbuster's proven way of doing business. Locational advantages for Blockbuster refer to their efficient distribution systems throughout the world and the geographic proximity involved in their logistics. Their locational advantages have enabled Blockbuster to develop a strong international presence and to significantly increase their market share. Internalization at Blockbuster is not as significant of a factor as ownership and location; however, it does play a crucial role in the success of Blockbuster's foreign markets. The movie/video game industries are fairly standardized and Blockbuster's internalization would consist of their methods of distribution and factors in evaluating potential foreign markets.

### 3. What role does cultural proximity and geographical proximity play in the retailers' international moves?

Research has shown that patterns of international expansion are significantly determined by geographical and cultural proximity, depending on the orientation of the company. Multinational corporations follow a pattern of international development where they first enter countries with high cultural proximity and potentially high geographical proximity. In terms of global retailers such as Blockbuster, these factors are not relevant. Global retailers generally have the tacit knowledge and brand recognition to expand into foreign markets without similar cultures.

Blockbuster competes in a specialty market which is perceived differently in many countries. However, with the presence of large global retailers it seems that American culture has been widely disseminated around the world decreasing cultural proximities. Many foreign countries watch American movies and play American video games. In China, nearly any American movie may be found at your local video store. These factors have acted as a pull strategy to entice Blockbuster to penetrate these foreign markets. Additionally, Blockbuster has achieved standardization across multiple countries even with the cultural proximity factor. Their international websites appear identical from country to country.

### 4. Can you predict the retailer's future international expansion?

From 2007 – 2008 Blockbuster's net profit has decreased by 7.075 percent and their revenue has decreased by $227,400,000. *Blockbuster has also divested their Ireland subsidiary Xtra-Vision to Birchall Invetments. In light of the suffering global economy, the changes in channels of distribution, and the financial damages Blockbuster will not be considering any additional expansion into new foreign markets. They will use their capital to invest in their most successful and growing markets as well as focus on improving their distribution services. When the economy is in a steady growth phase Blockbuster will continue to use capital to strengthen their current markets and begin reconsidering new countries for potential expansion.*

## Propositions

**P1:The greater the ownership advantages for retailers, the less likely they will franchise or license.**

*We believe that this proposition is true in relation to Blockbuster Inc. Blockbuster has a large international presence in 20 different markets located outside of the United States. Out of the total 2,820 international stores, 892 are either franchised or licensed.*[73] *Overall, Blockbuster has extremely weak ownership advantages. Mainly, this is because of the products they offer. In the movie rental business, there are no tangible, unique products in which retailers can sell to create a competitive advantage. The more prevalent advantages are locational and first mover.*

**P2: The greater the available organizational slack the greater the likelihood of expanding internationally.**

1997:  Current Assets = $627,900,000.[00]
Current Liabilities = $713,100,000.[00]
Ratio = .88

1998:  Current Assets = $631,700,000.[00]
Current Liabilities = $846,200,000.[00]
Ratio = .75

**OR**

1999:  Current Assets = $712,600,000.[00]
Current Liabilities = $1,131,400,000.[00]
Ratio = .63

2000:  Current Assets = $799,500,000.[00]
Current Liabilities = $1,123,200,000.[00]
Ratio = .71

2001:   Current Assets = $716,400,000.$^{00}$
        Current Liabilities = $1,268,800,000.$^{00}$
        Ratio = .56

*References for Ratios*[74]

*Upon computing the ratios, we found that they do not support the proposition. In Blockbuster's case, the ratios showed no continuous positive increase; comparatively, they showed both an increase and decrease between the three years. In 1997 the ratio was .88. In 1998 the ratio decrease to .75 and decreased again to .63 in 1999.*

**P3:The greater the recoverable slack the greater the likelihood of expanding internationally.**

1997:   General & Administrative Expense = $1,605,700,000.$^{00}$
        Sales (Revenue) = $3,313,600,000.$^{00}$
        Ratio = .48

1998:   General & Administrative Expense = $1,732,300,000.$^{00}$
        Sales (Revenue) = $3,893,400,000.$^{00}$
        Ratio = .45

1999:   General & Administrative Expense = $1,953,200,000.$^{00}$
        Sales (Revenue) = $4,463,500,000.$^{00}$
        Ratio = .44

2000:   General & Administrative Expense = $2,174,000,000.$^{00}$
        Sales (Revenue) = $4,960,100,000.$^{00}$
        Ratio = .44

2001:   General & Administrative Expense = $2,311,500,000.$^{00}$
        Sales (Revenue) = $5,156,700,000.$^{00}$
        Ratio = .45

*These ratios measuring recoverable slack do not led us to accept the proposition.*

**P4:The greater the potential slack the greater the likelihood of expanding internationally.**

1997:   Stockholders Equity = $7,617,600,000.$^{00}$
        Total Assets = $8,731,000,000.$^{00}$
        Ratio = .87

1998:   Stockholders Equity = $5,637,900,000.$^{00}$
        Total Assets = $8,274,800,000.$^{00}$
        Ratio = .68

1999:   Stockholders Equity = $6,125,000,000.$^{00}$
        Total Assets = $8,540,800,000.$^{00}$
        Ratio = .72

2000:   Stockholders Equity = $6,008,400,000.$^{00}$
        Total Assets = $8,548,900,000.$^{00}$
        Ratio =.70

2001:   Stockholders Equity = $5,748,700,000.$^{00}$
        Total Assets = $7,752,400,000.$^{00}$
        Ratio = .74

*We must disagree with this proposition because the ratios do not support this theory. From 1997 to 1999, the ratios of equity to capital fluctuated greatly, showing a significant decrease from 1997 to 1998 and then showing a small increase from 1998 to 1999.*

**P13: Global companies will move to the largest/capital cities in a country.**

*We agree with this proposition. One of the main international strategies utilized by Blockbuster is to have a store for every 40,000 people and some Blockbuster chains have increased this number to 80,000 people.*[75] *For example, when Blockbuster expanded internationally into Brazil, their first store was located in Sao Paulo. Sao Paulo is the largest city with a population over 11 million people.*

**P14: Global companies will not be attracted by population size, income, cultural proximity or geographical proximity.**

*Blockbuster Inc. has a history of internationally expanding to countries of close geographic proximity and high levels of population, cultural proximity and income levels. As an example of geographic proximity, the company entered Argentina, Paraguay and Chile — which all share country borders. Saturating successful areas was a priority for the company during early international franchising. Blockbuster found that by occupying countries with minimal geographic distance they could increase distribution efficiency. Another example in South America is Brazil. Sao Paulo was targeted in Brazil based on their large population and high levels of income and cultural similarity to countries previously entered. Based on the company's track record of international expansion, this proposition would be refuted due to conflicting company actions.*

## P15: The greater the asset based ownership advantages of a global retailer, the more likely they are to franchise.

*Asset based ownership advantages for Blockbuster could be viewed as physical store ownership, monetary assets or product ownership. The company has a presence in multiple international countries, but many of these are through franchising, not wholly owned subsidiaries which limits their physical store asset value. The company has been known for reacquiring franchises in international markets, which would support the resource based theory — franchising because of minimal resources (money), rather than franchising because of trust within other companies or owners.*

*When considering the decisions the company would face based on asset based ownership advantages, Blockbuster would need to make these decisions based on the products they own or could produce, not necessarily the value of their physical presence. The selection of products the company offers are nationally popular videos and video games, not private label products. Even without private label implementation, the company's video rental format was widely successful with the introduction of VHS tapes and even on through DVD technology. Although the rental industry was internationally popular and successful, these products could be purchased from other retail outlets as a permanent expenditure by the consumer which was constantly a threat. Only recently has the company faced decreased asset value and consumer demand due to digital video downloading and the outdating of their current product offerings.*

*In the case of Blockbuster, their asset based ownership advantages are minimal and would not be the means in which they would decide to strictly franchise. This proposition would be denied due to lack of asset value evidence.*

## P16: The greater the transaction based ownership advantages of a global retailer, the less likely they are to franchise.

*Blockbuster Inc.'s ownership advantages lie within their large selection of products and mainly their ease of product rental. Although the large number of movie and video game titles could be considered an asset based advantage, it is not sustainable because of the low level of competitive effort needed to copy the selection. Regional video chains often stock the same selection as Blockbuster, only with less reach through number of outlets.*

*By having a company that offers products available through other channels, increased revenue would be most attractive through franchising. The lack of asset based ownership advantages has a large effect on the company's strategy for expansion, meaning profitability would be most attainable through a large number of outlets, rather than optimizing their margin levels. By introducing as many outlets as possible, the company competed with local chains and individual "mom and pop" stores, decreasing competition and increasing brand value through transaction based reputation. In response to the proposition, Blockbuster's strategy does not agree with the idea that transaction based ownership advantages of a global retailer would lead the company to be less likely to franchise. In fact, their strategy was the opposite. Transaction based ownership advantages and high levels of franchising lead to the company's international success and overall company growth.*

**P17: The greater the available organizational slack the greater the likelihood that global retailers will reacquire international franchisees.**

1997:  Current Asserts = $627,900,000.$^{00}$
Current Liabilities = $713,100,000.$^{00}$
Ratio = .88

1998:  Current Assets = $631,700,000.$^{00}$
Current Liabilities = $846,200,000.$^{00}$
Ratio = .75

**OR**

1999:  Current Assets = $712,600,000.$^{00}$
Current Liabilities = $1,131,400,000.$^{00}$
Ratio = .63

2000:  Current Assets = $799,500,000.$^{00}$
Current Liabilities = $1,123,200,000.$^{00}$
Ratio = .71

2001:  Current Assets = $716,400,000.$^{00}$
Current Liabilities = $1,268,800,000.$^{00}$
Ratio = .56

*Due to the number of franchises and licensing agreements Blockbuster allowed, the company began to collect international revenue with low associated costs, which made reacquisition possible in certain markets. Franchising was initially a means of creating a presence within a country while collecting fees from the franchisees.*

*After countries had proven the format was successful in their market, Blockbuster Inc. often entered the country with the purchase of these companies. The reacquisition increased their level of generated revenue from franchising income to ownership profits, but also significantly increased their liabilities. In many cases, the money earned from franchising agreements was used to buy the companies from the owners that had previously been paying Blockbuster their dues. Although the company was profitable through franchising, the ratios from their annual reports go against this proposition.*

**P18: The greater the recoverable slack the greater the likelihood that global retailers will reacquire international franchisees.**

    1997:   General & Administrative Expense = $1,605,700,000.$^{00}$
              Sales (Revenue) = $3,313,600,000.$^{00}$
              Ratio = .48

    1998:   General & Administrative Expense = $1,732,300,000.$^{00}$
              Sales (Revenue) = $3,893,400,000.$^{00}$
              Ratio = .45

    1999:   General & Administrative Expense = $1,953,200,000.$^{00}$
              Sales (Revenue) = $4,463,500,000.$^{00}$
              Ratio = .44

    2000:   General & Administrative Expense = $2,174,000,000.$^{00}$
              Sales (Revenue) = $4,960,100,000.$^{00}$
              Ratio = .44

    2001:   General & Administrative Expense = $2,311,500,000.$^{00}$
              Sales (Revenue) = $5,156,700,000.$^{00}$
              Ratio = .45

*Annual reports support this proposition although the ratios do not. Due to their international success, the company found themselves with revenues increasing at a faster rate than their expenses. Economies of scale impacted the company positively and allowed them to optimize their operations — leading to higher earnings and the ability to pursue international reacquisitions.*

**P19: The greater the potential slack the likelier that global retailers will reacquire international franchisees.**

1997: Stockholders Equity = $7,617,600,000.[00]
Total Assets = $8,731,000,000.[00]
Ratio = .87

1998: Stockholders Equity = $5,637,900,000.[00]
Total Assets = $8,274,800,000.[00]
Ratio = .68

1999: Stockholders Equity = $6,125,000,000.[00]
Total Assets = $8,540,800,000.[00]
Ratio = .72

2000: Stockholders Equity = $6,008,400,000.[00]
Total Assets = $8,548,900,000.[00]
Ratio =.70

2001: Stockholders Equity = $5,748,700,000.[00]
Total Assets = $7,752,400,000.[00]
Ratio = .74

*Blockbuster's international effectiveness was because of the company's overall level of introduction success. The video rental format was historically widely accepted by cultures all over the world and profitably competed with the various other consumer options of video distribution — movie theaters, retail stores and individual video rental outlets. The operational effectiveness the company had seen in other countries led to the rapid international expansion Blockbuster had in the 1990's and early 2000's. Unfortunately, stockholder's equity did not reflect the rapid expansion. With the increase of international success, in terms of revenue, came a greater international push to reacquire outlets which in-turn led to many of Blockbuster's international franchises being re-named with the Blockbuster trademark. The radios based on the information from corporate anual reports refute this proposition.*

## Endnotes

1. Company Overview. (2009) Blockbuster. Retrieved November 11, 2009 from http://www.blockbuster.com/corporate/news

2. Blockbuster - Mergent Report. (2009) Retrieved November 9, 2009 from Mergent Academic database

3.  Video Tape Rental & Retail. (2008) Gale Group – Encyclopedia of Global Industries (Online Edition). Retrieved November 11, 2009 from [Business & Company Resource Center Database]

4.  Kageyama, Y., & Writer, A. P. (1996) U.S. Video – Rental Chain Making Aggressive Push in Japan. Associated Press

5.  Boyle, Matthew. Blockbuster Takes on the Entire Block. (2005) Fortune. Retrieved November 8, 2009 from [Factiva]

6.  Anderson, T. Netflix: The Comeback Kid, (2007) Kiplinger.com. Retrieved November 16, 2009 from LexisNexis Academic database

7.  Flavelle, D. $3.99 Rentals Escalate Video Wars; Blockbuster Lops 30% off Price for New Releases, Undercutting Rival as Online Movie-Watching Grows. (2009) The Toronto Star. Pg. B01

8.  Sternquist, B. International Retailing, Second Edition. (2007) New York: Fairchild Publications.

9.  Blockbuster Acquires Franchise in Argentina. (1996) Retrieved November 7, 2009 from, LexisNexis Academic database

10.  Blockbuster Opens Brazil Outlet. (1995) Retrieved November 7, 2009, from LexisNexis Academic database

11.  Blockbuster, Inc. Blockbuster Launches New Online DVD Rental Service. (2004) Blockbuster Corporate, News Releases. Retrieved: November 16, 2009, from, http://www.blockbuster.com/corporate/news

12.  Synopsis. (2005) Blockbuster, Inc. (NYS:BBI). Retrieved November 16, 2009 from, Mergent Academic database

13.  King, Danny. Blockbuster to Build on Inventory. (2009) Video Business, 29(44), 1. Retrieved: November 18, 2009, from, Proquest Academic database

14.  Blockbuster Annual Report. (2009) Mergent Online. Retrieved November 9, 2009 from, Mergent Academic database

15.  Canada. (2009) The CIA – World Fact Book. Retrieved November 9, 2009 from, https://www.cia.gov/library/publications/the-world-factbook/geos/ca.html

16.  Blockbuster Canada Co. (2009) Retrieved November 9, 2009 from, http://www.shopintoronto.com/Blockbuster-Canada-Co---Head-Office/343454.htm

17.  Blockbuster Merger Ok'd by Shareholders/of Major Video. (1989) The Journal Record. Retrieved November 9, 2009 from, http://www.highbeam.com/doc/1P2-5467555.html

18. United Kingdom Site of Blockbuster's 1,000th Store. (1989) Retrieved November 8, 2009 from, LexisNexis Academic database

19. Entertainment Giant to Make £62 Million Investment in UK. (1995) Retrieved on November 8, 2009 from, LexisNexis Academic database

20. Game Group PLC Acquisition. (2007) Retrieved November 8, 2009 from, LexisNexis Academic database

21. Blockbuster Set to Expand in Asia. (1994) Billboard. Retrieved November 9, 2009 from, LexisNexis Academic database

22. Australia. (2009) The CIA – World Fact Book. Retrieved November 9, 2009 from, https://www.cia.gov/library/publications/the-world-factbook/geos/as.html

23. Blockbuster Acquires 50 Retail Outlets of Chilean Franchisee. (1996) Retrieved November 7, 2009 from, LexisNexis Academic database

24. Holland, L., & Writer, J. S. (1991) Blockbuster Move into Japan Video Rental is Planned; 1,000 Stores Pictured in Decade; Venture Linked to McDonald's. The Japan Economic Journal, pp. 10. Retrieved November 8, 2009 from LexisNexis Academic database

25. Blockbuster Sells Japan Video Business To Fujita - Nikkei. (1999) Dow Jones International News. Retrieved  November 8, 2009 from Factiva Academic database

26. 4Mexico. (2009) The CIA – World Fact Book. Retrieved November 9, 2009 from, https://www.cia.gov/library/publications/the-world-factbook/geos/mx.html

27. Blockbuster Mexico Poised to Acquire Rival Outfit. Screen Daily. Retrieved November 9, 2009 from, http://www.screendaily.com/blockbuster-mexico-poised-to-acquire-rival-outfit/406186.article

28. Blockbuster Acquires Video Franchise in Spain. (1997) Retrieved November 8, 2009 from, LexisNexis Academic database

29. Blockbuster Exits Spain. (2006) Retrieved November 8, 2009 from, LexisNexis Academic database

30. Venezuela. (2009) The CIA – World Fact Book. Retrieved November 4, 2009 from https://www.cia.gov/library/publications/the-world-factbook/geos/ve.html

31. Hill, Charles & W.L., Jones, Gareth R. Blockbuster's Emerging Strategies.(2009) Essentials of Strategic Management, Second Edition. Retrieved November 5, 2009 from http://books.google.com/books?id=Sy8vejqbcocC&pg=PT312&lpg=PT312&dq=blockbuster+and+venezuela&source=bl&ots=lHG2_7aqRV&sig=JIUWl_aY9kbysdfAMkD6apZBl_Y&hl=en&ei=GR3zSoixGYGV8Abez9XiAQ&sa=

X&oi=book_result&ct=result&resnum=3&ved=0CBEQ6AEwAjgK#v=onepage&
q=bloc&f=false

32. Italy. (2009) The CIA – World Fact Book. Retrieved November 2, 2009 from
https://www.cia.gov/library/publications/the-world-factbook/geos/it.html

33. Company News; Blockbuster in Joint Venture to Expand into Italy. (1993)
The New York Times. Retrieved November 2, 2009 from http://www.nytimes.
com/1993/12/17/business/company-news-blockbuster-in-joint-venture-to-
expand-into-italy.html

34. Blockbuster Acquires Franchise in Argentina. (1996) Retrieved November 7,
2009 from, LexisNexis Academic database

35. Blockbuster Video Enters Brazilian Market with Moreira Salles Group as
Developer. (1994) Retrieved November 7, 2009 from, Lexis Nexis Academic
database

36. Blockbuster Planning New Stores in Latin America. (1994) Retrieved November
7, 2009 from, Lexis Nexis Academic database

37. Blockbuster Opens Brazil Outlet. (1995) Retrieved November 7, 2009, from
LexisNexis Academic database

38. Retailer Lojas Americanas Buys BWU and will use Blockbuster Trademark in
Brazil. (2007) Retrieved November 7, 2009 from, Lexis Nexis Academic database

39. Blockbuster Video Awards Development Rights for Colombia, Peru; 16th & 17th
International Markets. (1995) PR Newswire . Retrieved November 8, 2009 from
Factiva database

40. Customers Flock to Bogota Blockbusters. (1995) The San-Diego Union Tribune ,
p. C2. Retrieved November 8, 2009 from Factiva database

41. Blockbuster, Burda Form Joint Venture to develop Video Stores in Germany.
(1995) PR Newswire. Retrieved November 10, 2009 from Factiva Academic
database

42. Hansen, E. (1998) Blockbuster's out of Germany. The Hollywood Reporter.
Retrieved November 10, 2009 from LexisNexis Academic database

43. Rohwedder, C. (1998) Blockbuster Hits Eject Button on Stores in Germany as
Video - Rental Sales Sag. Wall Street Journal, pp. 6B. Retrieved November 10,
2009 from LexisNexis Academic database

44. Neiman, Rachel. (1994) Koffler to Represent Blockbuster. The Jerusalem Post.
Retrieved November 9, 2009 from, Lexis Nexis Academic database

45. Cashman, Greer, Fay. (1995). Déjà vu that Comes with a Generous Dollop of Nostalgia. The Jerusalem Post. Retrieved November 9, 2009 from, Lexis Nexis Academic database

46. Company Overview. (2009) Blockbuster. Retrieved November 11, 2009 from http://www.blockbuster.com/corporate/news

47. News: Blockbuster Grants Rights in Thailand. (1995) Music and Copyright. Retrieved November 9, 2009 from, Lexis Nexis Academic database

48. Thailand. (2009) The CIA – World Fact Book. Retrieved November 9, 2009 from, https://www.cia.gov/library/publications/the-world-factbook/geos/th.html

49. Denmark. (2009) The CIA – World Fact Book. Retrieved November 2, 2009 from https://www.cia.gov/library/publications/the-world-factbook/geos/da.html

50. Blockbuster Video Enters Scandinavian Market with Denmark Acquisition. (1996) PR Newswire Europe Ltd. Retrieved November 2, 2009 from http://www.prnewswire.co.uk/cgi/news/release?id=42182

51. Blockbuster Video Awards Development Rights for El Salvador, 21st International Market. (1995) PR Newswire. Retrieved November 8, 2009 from, Factiva database.

52. 2009 Investment Climate Statement - El Salvador. (2009) Retrieved November 10, 2009, from U.S. Department Of State: http://www.state.gov/e/eeb/rls/othr/ics/2009/117666.htm

53. Blockbuster Arrives. (1996) The Evening Post (Wellington). Retrieved November 9, 2009 from, LexisNexis Academic database

54. Blockbuster Annual Report. (2009) Mergent Online. Retrieved November 9, 2009 from, Mergent Academic database

55. Panama. (2009) The CIA – World Fact Book. Retrieved November 4, 2009 from https://www.cia.gov/library/publications/the-world-factbook/geos/pm.html

56. Blockbuster Video Awards Development Rights for Panama, 20th International Market. (1995) PRNewswire. Retrieved November 9, 2009 from, http://www.highbeam.com/doc/1G1-17252437.html

57. Blockbuster Award Development Rights for Portugal. (1996) PR Newswire Europe. Retrieved November 9, 2009 from LexisNexis Academic database

58. Viacom's Blockbuster to Open 20 Stores in Portugal. (1996) AFX News. Retrieved November 9, 2009 from, LexisNexis Academic database

59. Blockbuster Announces Sale of Ireland Entertainment Retailer Xtra-vision

Limited to Birchhall Investments Limited. (2009) Blockbuster Inc. Retrieved November 16, 2009 from http://www.marketwatch.com/story/blockbuster-announces-sale-of-ireland-entertainment-retailer-xtra-vision-limited-to-birchhall-investments-limited-2009-08-28

60. South China Morning Post (1999) Hong Kong. Retrieved November 9, 2009 from, Lexis Nexis Academic database

61. Blockbuster Opens First Store in Taiwan. (1997) PRNewswire. Retrieved November 4, 2009 fromhttp://www.encyclopedia.com/doc/1G1-19203132.html

62. Blockbuster Stores in Taiwan and Sell Toys, Blu-ray Machine. (2009) ZDnet. Retrieved November 4, 2009 fromhttp://www.zdnet.com.tw/news/software/0,2000085678,20113254,00.htm

63. Taiwan. (2009) The CIA – World Fact Book. Retrieved November 9, 2009 from, https://www.cia.gov/library/publications/the-world-factbook/geos/tw.html

64. Uruguay. (2009) The CIA – World Fact Book. Retrieved November 4, 2009 from https://www.cia.gov/library/publications/the-world-factbook/geos/uy.html

65. Blockbuster Entertainment Group. Blockbuster Expands Into Uruguay; Video Retailer Now Operates in 28 Countries. (1997) Blockbuster Media Room. Retrieved November 4, 2009 from http://blockbuster.mediaroom.com/index.php?s=press_releases&item=34

66. Blockbuster Drops Expansion Plan in China. (2004) Financial Times. Retrieved November 18, 2009 from Factiva database

67. VCDs Put New Focus on Rental Chain. (1999) South China Morning Post. Retrieved November 18, 2009 from, Factiva database

68. Blockbuster Sunk by Pirates, say Patrons. (2004) South China Morning Post. Retrieved November 18, 2009 from, Factiva Academic database

69. Blockbuster® Enters the Philippines; Global Leader in Rentable Home Entertainment Announces Development Agreement. (1999) PR Newswire. Retrieved November 10, 2009 from, Factiva Academic database

70. Blockbuster, Inc. (2002) 2001 Annual Report. Retrieved November 1, 2009, from Blockbuster Inc.: http://www.blockbuster.com).

71. Blockbuster Inc. Expands Presence in Central America; Opens Stores in Costa Rica and Guatemala. (2001) PR Newswire . Retrieved November 8, 2009 from Factiva database

72. Blockbuster Cancels Norwegian plans. (2004) Nordic Business Report. Retreived November 10, 2009 from, LexisNexis Academic database

73.	Global Markets Direct – SWOT Analysis. (2009) Retrieved November 9, 2009 from, Mergent Academic database Balance Sheet. (2009) Blockbuster Inc. Retrieved November 9, 2009 from, Mergent Academic database

74.	Sommer, Allison. Kaplan: The Jerusalem Post. (1995) Retrieved November 9, 2009 from, http://www.highbeam.com/doc/1P1-5993812.

# Carrefour

*Jill Flaugher, Colleen Nickles, Kayla Deming, Alison Mair*

## Carrefour

A s one of the world's largest retailers, second only to Wal-Mart, Carrefour operates over 15,661 stores under a variety of retail formats, but is most known for its hypermarket concept. In addition to the hypermarket concept, Carrefour also operates supermarkets, convenience stores, discount stores, cash and carry outlets, and gas stations in over 34 countries in Europe, Latin America and Asia, employing approximately 475,976 employees. Striving only to exist in countries where they will be one of the top three retailers, Carrefour has encountered both success as well as failure throughout their international expansion.

This case study starts with an overview of Carrefour, moving then into the company's expansion strategies and concluding with the various countries of the world when the company has expanded.

# FLOW CHART

1959: France (5,440 stores including 92 in French overseas territories)
1969: Belgium (withdrew in 1978, reentered in 2000, 627 stores)
1969: UK (withdrew in 1983)
1972: Italy (1,545 stores)
1973: Spain (667 stores)
1975: Brazil (605 stores)
1976: Austria (withdrew in 1979)
1977: Germany (withdrew in 1979)
1982: Argentina (601 stores)
1988: U.S. (withdrew in 1993)
1989: Taiwan (65 stores)
1991: Greece (including Cyprus there are 919 stores)
1992: Portugal (524 stores)
1993: Malaysia (19 stores)
1993: Turkey (866 stores)
1995: Mexico (withdrew in 2005)
1995: China (516 stores)
1996: United Arabe Emirates (23 stores)
1996: South Korea (withdrew in 2006)
1996: Thailand (40 stores)
1996: Hong Kong (withdrew in 2000)
1997: Singapore (2 stores)
1997: Poland (312 stores)
1998: Indonesia (76 stores)
1998: Chile (withdrew in 2004)
1998: Columbia (69 stores)
1998: Czech Republic (withdrew in 2005)
2000: Slovakia (4 stores)
2000: Japan (withdrew stores in 2005 but 6 partner licenses remain)
2000: Qatar (2 stores)
2000: Oman (2 stores)
2000: Domincan Republic (1 store)
2001: Romania (47 stores)
2001: Tunisia (44 stores)
2001: Switzerland (withdrew in 2007)
2002: Egypt (5 stores)
2004: Saudi Arabia (11 stores)
2004: Norway (n/a)

2007: Algeria (withdrew in 2009)
2007: Kuwait (1 store)
2007: Jordan (1 store)
2008: Bahrain (1 store)
2009: Iran (1 store)
2009: Syria (1 store)
2009: Morocco (23 stores)
2009: Monaco (1 store)
2009: Bulgaria (4 stores)
2009: Russia (2 stores)
2010: Azerbaijan (1 store)

## Overview

Carrefour originated in France in 1959, when the Fournier and Defforey families made a decision to collaborate on owning and operating a supermarket. One year later, the two families opened their first store in Annecy, Haute-Savoie, France. Soon after in 1963, Carrefour opened an oversized supermarket later labeled as a hypermarket offering various product lines including food, clothing, electronics, and household appliances at a lower, discounted price.[1]

Carrefour's hypermarket concept, most prominent in France, operating around 5,400 stores and accounting for about 40% of retail sales, has rapidly expanded internationally since its first successes in the 1960's. Carrefour became the number one retailer in Europe upon its merger with Promodes, another food retailer, which extended the Carrefour banner over their stores as well. With the additional purchases and mergers of retailers GB, Marinopolous and Gruppo GS Spa, the company has intensified its grip in the European market.[2] With the imminent popularity of free service and the supermarket concept, Carrefour combined the two ideas with a different approach, offering low prices, a variety of food and nonfood items and less aesthetically pleasing store designs, an innovative idea for the time, which proved to be a vast success. As a competitor, Wal-Mart has derived its retail format from Carrefour.

Carrefour has operated for over 35 years outside France, its home market. Employing one of the most productive retailing strategies, the company utilizes its hypermarket as drawing power for its other stores, hoping to achieve total market share in consumers by drawing them into numerous types of shopping experiences.[3] Carrefour's approach is to target consumers to the hypermarket bi weekly, draw them to their supermarket weekly, to the hard discounters for price, and the convenience stores for fill-ins or late night purchases.

"Think global, act local" a philosophy that Carrefour applies to their retail formats, most predominately, their hypermarkets and supermarkets. Carrefour's hypermarket concept has historically been the most thriving of the retail formats, but has seen a decrease in sales over the past several years due to competition from hard discounters. Products and store characteristics are tailored to the country and offer consumers value-based pricing in a convenient one stop shopping environment.

## Competitor's Analysis

Even with Carrefour's multiple retail formats and significant size the company still faces competition. Carrefour's top competitors, are Auchan, Metro AG, Tesco and Wal-Mart.[4] These competitors, mainly European based, also operate multiple store formats including hypermarkets, grocery stores, discount retail stores and specialty or convenience stores. Recently, particularly in France, consumers have been more attracted to shopping at discounters and specialty stores, and shopping less frequently at large scale stores, such as the hypermarkets.[4] With the elevated competition challenging domestic growth in its home market, Carrefour has begun to lose market share to competitors. This is serious because Carrefour gets more than forty percent of its revenue from its home market's stores.[5]

Carrefour has achieved success against its competitors by discounting prices and adapting its store formats. Carrefour was forced to expand internationally because government regulations limited their domestic expansions, Carrefour expands internationally through acquisitions, joint ventures and organic expansion.[6] Carrefour had an early mover advantage by expanding to countries where the completion was low and the hypermarket concept was recently introduced. Carrefour was the first foreign retailer to establish a presence in many countries such as Spain, Brazil, Argentina, Taiwan, China, and Japan.[7]

Looking only to stay in countries that the retailer will have a top three presence, Carrefour's four-point growth strategy consists of better competing with hard discounters by creating a lower price image in its French hypermarkets, as well as increasing their market share in their home country. Carrefour is also improving the profitability of its international stores as well as increasing store expansion.[8] Carrefour is known to withdraw from markets where they are not successful. An advantage the retailer has developed is the vast amount of information it has gathered from successes and failures in foreign markets, allowing them to eventually re-enter countries with a different approach in order to be successful.[9] This gives Carrefour a sustainable advantage over other competitors who are also entering into new markets or who have recently tried and proven unsuccessful.[10]

A crucial aspect to Carrefour's success is its ability to attract an internationally motivated management team. Carrefour has been known to employ some of the best and most experienced managers, which one could suggest attributes to the company's success and competitive advantage.[11] Carrefour as a company is determined to expand internationally and in some markets has developed a presence so strong, that it is thought of as a national organization by some local populations.[12] Carrefour's management team understands the importance of adapting to local markets when utilizing a first mover advantage technique.

Concentrating on putting more of an emphasis on local business, Carrefour group is typically one of the leading private employers in any country it operates, recruiting, and hiring management, as well as offering on the job training. For private label food brands, Carrefour sources and gives priority to local suppliers, striving to boost business, create jobs and stimulate the local economy. Around ninety to ninety-five percent of the products on a Carrefour store's shelves are most often locally sourced, varying in assortment depending on the country.[13] Carrefour seeks to understand the market, its consumers and their culture before expanding, regardless of how attractive the market is at that time. This allows them to tailor their product mix in order to appeal to the local culture.

## Expansion Strategy

Carrefour expanded internationally quickly before the governmental regulations of store size were implemented. Initially expanding through joint ventures and partnerships with local retailers, Carrefour later acquired full interest in the stores and expanded organically when capital and market potential was available.[14] When expanding, Carrefour concentrates expansion efforts to countries where modern retailing systems have not been previously established, making the hypermarket an attractive new concept to consumers. Offering low prices and a vast amount of SKUs in both food and non food product lines, Carrefour focused on food items as their main draw. The spatial expansion has been based upon preliminary development through joint subsidiary companies combined with local or regional retailers eventually resulting in the acquisition of the joint ventures. Carrefour's dominant mind set of international expansion has increased their market share, but caused their home market sales to suffer due to a variety of factors including; competition from hard discounters, weak economies and government pricing regulations. Carrefour has recently responded by launching a private label line, called Number One, in order to compete with the hard discounters' low prices.

Among other characteristics, the French retailer's expansion success can be attributed to its ability to tailor its format and offerings to local tastes. By diversifying themselves, Carrefour is able to operate in multiple countries in multiple formats where other retailers have not fared so well.[15] Generally operating a joint venture when first moving to a new country, Carrefour uses the other company's knowledge as a resource to connect with local companies and research consumer behavior, culture and tastes.[17] In China, for example, they adopted elements of a traditional outdoor markets for their fish and produce section in order to attract Chinese shoppers who have habitually shopped in traditional retail formats for these items.[17] The retailer expands internationally under the belief that they can succeed anywhere if cultural characteristics and norms are learned, before expansion this has not always been a proven true. Carrefour expands anticipating long term success, never looking for short term.

Through their rapid expansion, Carrefour typically first opens a hypermarket in foreign countries; Carrefour seeks markets where modern retailing concepts are not currently employed. Through the knowledge gained from the joint venture, Carrefour is able to find out if a different retail format would better fit the country. Focusing on being client and consumer focused while also offering a low price, Carrefour expands into foreign markets with the anticipation of the eventual opening of various retail formats, in order to better appeal to numerous types of consumers. The retailer conducts business, having one sole ambition, to make Carrefour the preferred retailer wherever it operates.[18]

No longer looking to expand into foreign markets with such speed, due to past failures and globally poor economies, Carrefour has adopted the strategy: strengthen at home, then either dominate or withdraw abroad. Withdrawing from Mexico and other countries whose market place did not emulate a market without a modern retail system, Carrefour has recently put its focus on increasing market share in the countries it currently occupies.[19]

## France

The company's home market, France, has 5,440 stores but has encountered governmental regulations in its home country limiting the size of stores, and inhibiting the retailer from opening large store formats, such as hypermarkets.[20] Accounting for over half of the company's sales, Carrefour is suffering in its home market due to hard discounter's stiff competition and governmental regulations.[21]

Carrefour has recently begun adopting their discount formats and transitioning newly acquired convenience stores and supermarkets to more modern formats under the Carrefour banner. Emphasising their focus on their home market and countries where they have a more dominant presence, the French retailer has recently seen an increase in sales.[30] Lowering prices, keeping up with current trends, and creating more private labeled Carrefour products has allowed the retailer to begin to gain back their market share.

## Europe

Having a powerful presence and operating in ten European countries, Carrefour has over 13,000 stores across Europe. The group's four main markets are France, Spain, Belgium and Italy, together accounting for over 72% of the company's sales.[23] The retailer has gained market share and consumer mind share while expanding across Western Europe in their different retail formats. With the merger with Promodes, Carrefour initially had a difficult time consolidating the corporate culture of the two companies.[24] With such a large size, Carrefour has been questioned in regions across the markets about whether or not their market position is too great. The government may force them to sell some of their retail stores to encourage healthy competition has been rumored.[25] In addition to its large store presence, Carrefour's Europe operations account for sixty four percent of the company's total staff, around 317,000 employees. Carrefour heavily recruits in Europe and is known as a leader in human resources.[26]

Still in the process of transferring recently acquired stores to the Carrefour banner in Italy, Carrefour plans to focuse its investments in areas of the country where it is has been most profitable in the past. In 2009, during Spain's tough economic time, Carrefour executed a massive amount of price cuts, the largest series of price cuts in the country's retail history, keeping Carrefour as the country's leading retailer.[27] In Eastern Europe Carrefour has remained successful since its first expansion, capitalizing on formats that have produced a positive response, the retailer has recently opened stores in Poland, Bulgaria, Romania and Greece.

## Latin America

The Carrefour stores located in Latin America in 2009 reported a 17.1% growth rate, therefore making Latin America one of Carrefour's top growth engines. Opening hypermarkets and acquiring new existing stores in Brazil further expanded the retailer's presence where hypermarkets were proven to be a great success. In Argentina, Carrefour has expanded into opening hypermarkets, supermarkets and hard discount stores upon their entrance into the market. Emphasizing their private label products Carrefour has been successful in offering low prices in each of their store formats.[28]

## Asia

As the first international retailer to enter into the Asian market in 1989, Carrefour entered into Taiwan by joint venture, in order to ensure its success. Using the knowledge of native business concepts and ideas, with Carrefour's success the company was able to further expand throughout Asia. Carrefour used the same entry mode when they expanded to China, where they now operate over five hundred stores with hard discount being the primary format. Carrefour has a sustainable advantage over its competitors due to the knowledge they have acquired through their previous joint ventures and their ability to tailor store formats to local culture. Asia represents eight percent of the company's sales and the company is number one, operating 140 hypermarkets in Asia, 29 in Taiwan, the country it initially entered. The company also has a purchasing office in Bangkok to service the regions hypermarkets.[29] Carrefour was forced to adapt their store format in order to comply with governmental regulations and cultural norms.

## Sustainability and Social Responsibility Efforts

Over the past few years, global efforts to become more sustainable and environmentally friendly have pushed their way to the forefront of importance for many companies, Carrefour has become part of this going green movement. In their own effort to become more sustainable, Carrefour has reduced energy consumption over the past three years throughout its stores and as a result, Carrefour's greenhouse gas emissions have also been reduced. Carrefour has also made a conscious effort to add organic and free trade products to their assortment, which showcases Carrefour's social responsibility efforts. Carrefour also plans to completely eliminate the use of plastic grocery bags by 2012 and instead replace them with free, reusable grocery bags.[34] Carrefour recently announced that over 300 of their food items are labeled reared without GMO's, which means these items have not been genetically modified.[35] Table 1-1 provides a timeline of Carrefour's efforts to become more socially responsible.

**Table 1-1**

**Sustainability and Social Responsibility Timeline**[30, 31, 32, 33]:

| 1992 | Carrefour Quality Line introduced to promote high quality standards to customers |
|------|------|
| 1996 | Applied for precautionary principle when choosing products with no GMO's |
| 1997 | Launch of Carrefour-Bio: Carrefour's own organic brand |
| 2000 | Developed a supplier social charter with International Federation of Human Rights (FIDH) |
| 2001 | Carrefour becomes a member of the UN Global Compact in agreement with Union Network International (UNI) |
| 2004 | Carrefour signed Diversity Charter and adopted a Code of Ethics |
| 2005 | Launch of Responsible Fishing Range, combating illegal fishing and making sure products come from sustainable sources |
| 2006 | Launched Carrefour AGIR, participation in creation of the Global Social Compliance Program |
| 2007 | Committed to cut Group energy consumption by 20% |
| 2008 | Became a member of Social Accountability International (SAI) |
| 2009 | Energy efficiency commitment raised to 30%, commitment to use 100% palm oil in all brand products by 2015, and first Sustainable Development Awards for suppliers in France |

## Private Label

In order to better compete in France, as well as other areas Carrefour has recently refocused its strategy, putting less emphasis on rapid expansion and more focus on the branding of stores and their private label lines. Originally having more of a fragmented private label, the company is implementing a three tier strategy of good, better, best.[36] Carrefour competes with the hard discounters and manufacturer brands by appealing to three different types of consumers, price based, category based and the less price sensitive, more benefit based consumer by offering three levels of products a generic, a copy cat product and a premium product.[36] The Number One discount brand and products Carrefour International can be found in the retail outlets in France, Belgium, Italy and Spain, and Carrefour's most mature markets in Europe. These private label brands are around sixteen to twenty percent cheaper than its own standard label.[37] Carrefour Discount, released in May of

2009 offers a selection of everyday essentials at low prices but also at a high quality that is consistent with the brand's image. The entry level product line consisting of 83% food items and 17% household items, is a compliment to Carrefour's existing products in order to provide consumers a trusted alternative to hard discounters. The line is available in over 1,200 stores including the company's hypermarkets, Champion stores, Carrefour Market supermarkets, as well as Carrefour City.[38]

## Questions

**1.   Is the retailer classified as a global retailer or a multinational retailer? Explain its pattern of expansion.  What expansion strategy did/is the retailer use/using?**

*Carrefour would be classified as a multinational retailer due to the fact that they have decentralized management. The Carrefour Group has many retail formats including hypermarket, supermarket, cash and carry, and hard discount stores. Each of these formats has a different product offering and the company will drastically alter their offerings based on cultures and consumer buying behaviors for each country. The company concentrated its expansion within a geographic area in early stages and changed its retail offering based on customer and cultural differences. Although Carrefour had not yet saturated their home market, they chose to expand internationally, which seemed like a good move for them at the time. Carrefour used first move advantage by introducing the first hypermarket in many countries. When first entering a new market, Carrefour often merged with companies using joint ventures, which was their most common form of entry mode. By entering a joint venture, Carrefour invests less risk if the company fails. Joint ventures force the company to share their secrets, but in return they will gain information on how to open and run their business in an unfamiliar market. Carrefour also chose to license in over ten of the fifty countries they expanded to. By licensing, the company has no monetary risk invested; however, they lose some control over those stores. In markets where the company did not see the success they hoped for, Carrefour will immediately withdraw which was a wise move on their part because they can reduce the amount of loss they suffer. Some of these withdrawals resulted in the company successfully re-entering several years later.*

**2.   Based on Dunning's Eclectic Theory, how do ownership, locational and internalization factors play in your retailers' international expansion?**

*Dunning's eclectic theory is split into three concepts: ownership, location, and internalization; all of these play a role in Carrefour's planning and execution of* international expansion. Ownership advantages will be the first area of focus. Carrefour's expansion is influenced more by transaction-based advantages, rather than asset-based advantages. While Carrefour does carry a private label, which would be an asset-based advantage, the company focuses more on the concept and the way things are done. Typically an unfamiliar private label will not be well received in a foreign country; it is more beneficial to expose the private label once the company has been well established in the area. Therefore, Carrefour must focus more on tacit learning, which is one reason why the company is less likely to franchise. Customer service and operations are important to the business and it is crucial that Carrefour's employees are well trained on the company's standards and expectations. Licensing makes it more difficult for the company to control those factors. Carrefour most often uses joint ventures for expansion because they will have more control over these concepts and it allows for an active management role from the company. Secondly, location advantages play an important role in Carrefour's expansions. The company used cultural proximity as their first method for international moves. Cultural proximity allows Carrefour to copy their current format without having to make drastic changes and it is a less risky move. As stated before, if the countries are geographically close they also may have many overlapping aspects of their cultures. Therefore, cultural and geographical proximity are Carrefour's focus as far as location advantages. Things the company must also keep in mind are market size, low cost land and labor, and competitors' moves. For example, Metro AG is one of Carrefour's biggest competitors. Metro AG's home country is Germany and Carrefour's early international move to Germany ended in failure. Had the company taken more consideration in competition when selecting the location for their next move they probably would not have suffered the loss. Finally, internalization is an important focus for international expansion. Carrefour knows they need to keep their secrets within the company if they don't want their successful ideas and formats to be copied. Wholly owned subsidiaries are a great way for the company to do this; however, this is very expensive for Carrefour to do which is one reason why they often opted for a joint venture. Joint ventures force the company to share their secrets, but in return they learn the cultures and business practices of the country they're expanding to. All in all, each of these three aspects plays a huge role in the planning and execution of international expansion for Carrefour, but the company has focused more on ownership advantages than location and internalization.

### 3. What role does cultural proximity and geographical proximity play in the retailers' international moves?

Cultural proximity plays an important role in a retailer's international expansion. In the early stages of Carrefour's expansions they relied heavily on cultural proximity. Using cultural proximity as a basis for the beginning of the company's *international moves was a huge factor in their success. Carrefour had a much lower risk factor moving into countries that shared cultural attributes with their home country of France. The company focused mainly on cultural proximity as they would have to make fewer changes to their format and retail offering in the countries that had overlapping cultural dimension with Carrefour. After the retailer began establishing themselves in more countries the locational advantages became less of a factor when considering new countries for expansion.*

#### 4.   Can you predict the retailer's future international expansion?

*Predicting expansion for Carrefour is relatively easy at the time because they are putting all of their focus back into France (their home market) and its surrounding geographic region (Europe). While Carrefour seemed to be expanding frequently, sales have suffered in France and because France is their home market, it is Carrefour's most important market. Knowing Carrefour has expanded quite rapidly could be a predictor for the future, but because hard discounters are gaining momentum against Carrefour's hypermarket strategy in France, Carrefour is likely to slow down expansion efforts. While focusing on improving business in France, they would like to "reinvent" the hypermarket in the European countries they are present in. This includes more efficient supply chain to redesigning stores. Carrefour after all is the original hypermarket and therefore should be the most efficient. Carrefour however is getting ready to expand into the Balkan countries (Albania, Bosnia, Croatia, Macedonia, Montenegro, Serbia, and Slovenia) as part of a joint venture with the Greek company Marinopoulous. Carrefour is also in the early stages of centralizing their operations, which creates many potential benefits, including enhanced logistics. This relates back to Carrefour's focus on their hypermarkets in their home market and surrounding region.*

### Propositions

**P1:The greater the ownership advantages for retailers, the less likely they will franchise or license.**

*Carrefour does support this proposition. Carrefour does not use licensing or franchising due to the fact that they use stakeholders in their company. The Carrefour Group created two boards: The Executive Board and the Executive Committee. Each were designed to create overall company standards, goals, plans, alignment of management and leadership principles, and the execution of all these. Carrefour's success in many retail formats, including the first hypermarket is intellectual property that the group would not want to share with others. This ownership advantage eliminates the need for franchising as a primary source of international expansion. However, Carrefour does use licensing as a way to enter into markets with governmental barriers to entry, such as the Middle East, before expanding with their own independent stores.*

**P2: The greater the available organizational slack the greater the likelihood of expanding internationally.**

| Year | Current Assets (in millions) | Current Liabilities (in millions) | Current Ratio (Assets/ Liabilites) |
|------|------|------|------|
| 2004 | $20,225 | $30,052 | .6118 |
| 2005 | $20,393 | $31,288 | .6518 |
| 2006 | $22,895 | $34,906 | .5659 |
| 2007 | $28,515 | $42,455 | .6717 |

*Carrefour supports this proposition. Organizational slack is the excess money that can be used in a discretionary manner. If a company has high organizational slack, it can use the excess resources to saturate their home market then expand internationally. The chart above shows the ratio of current assets to current liabilities, also known as the current ratio for 2004 to 2007. By comparing the ratios, one can see that the current ratio has been at a slow but steady increase. Since Carrefour has been successful in many of their overseas expansion, they are willing to take a financial risk and continue to expand internationally.*

**P3:The greater the recoverable slack the greater the likelihood of expanding internationally.**

*[Ratio of General and Administrative Expenses to Sales (3 year average before their first international expansion)]*

*Before 2001 expansion into Switzerland:*

| In € | 1998 | 1999 | 2000 | 2001 |
|------|------|------|------|------|
| General & Admin Expenses | n/a | 5,957,400 | 11,235,700 | 11,728,700 |
| Sales | 24,408,700 | 37,364,300 | 64,802,000 | 69,486,100 |

| In € | 1998 | 1999 | 2000 | 2001 |
|---|---|---|---|---|
| Expenses to Sales | n/a | .15944 | .17339 | .16879 |

*Carrefour does support this proposition. The greater the recoverable slack the greater the likelihood of expansion. Expansion into Switzerland was a major expansion move after their expansion to Columbia and failed attempts (as of 2005) at expansion in Czech Republic, Japan and Slovakia.*

**P4:The greater the potential slack the greater the likelihood of expanding internationally.**

*Before their 1997 expansion to Singapore and Poland*

| In € millions | 1996 | 1997 | 1998 |
|---|---|---|---|
| Equity | 27,318 | 9,238 | 36,328 |
| Capital | 7,803 | 8,772 | 9,224 |
| Equity to Capital | 3.76 | 1.05 | 3.94 |

*Carrefour does not support this proposition. They have an unsteady amount of potential slack from 1996 to 1998. Even though they had a decreased amount of potential slack in 1997 than the year before they still expanded into Singapore and Poland. Carrefour's strategy was rapid expansion, and looked to expand into new countries as quickly as possible. Even though Carrefour did not have a steady amount of extra cash to reinvest for international expansion, they continued to expand.*

**P5: Multinational Retailers will move to countries with lower disposable income than their home country.**

*This proposition is true for Carrefour. Not only is Carrefour in 39 countries, Carrefour has expanded to less developed countries than their home country of France. Countries such as Singapore (1994), Tunisia (2002), and Cyprus (2005) have all acquired at least one Carrefour retailer. With Carrefour expanding to countries with a lower disposable income, the business will continue to operate, even if the country's economy is in poor shape.*

**P6: Multinational Retailers will move to countries that have a high positive change in GDP.**

$$\frac{(\text{GDP at the time of expansion- GDP 5 years before expansion})}{\text{GDP 5 years before expansion}}$$

*Carrefour supports this proposition. In 2008 and 2009, Carrefour expanded into Morocco, Bulgaria, and Bahrain. By looking at the GDP percentage changes over the last 5-7 years, one can see that Morocco's GDP increased by 19.55% from 2002 to 2009, which was the lowest increase of the three countries. Bulgaria and Bahrain had significantly higher increases with 83.02% and 185.67%, respectively. These positive changes in GDP reflect a growing economy in each country, which attracts many retailers including Carrefour. Carrefour would be attracted to growing economies since there will also be an increase in disposable income and therefore, consumer buying. Carrefour also looks for a growing economy, rather than just a large economy because in developing countries, a majority of the income is spent on food items that greatly benefit Carrefour.*

**P7: Multinational reatailers will move to countries that have a high positive change in service-value added as a percentage of GDP.**

$$\frac{(\text{Service\% of GDP at time of expansion-Service\% of GDP 5 years before expansion})}{\text{Service\% of GDP 5 years before expansion}}$$

*Carrefour does not support this proposition. Recent expansions into Morocco, Bulgaria and Egypt show that Carrefour does not look at high service percentage of GDP as a major factor when expanding internationally. The change in service-value added as a percentage of GDP for Morocco was -35.45% from 2004-2009, Bulgaria had a positive change of 7.5% from 2004 to 2009 and Egypt showed a decrease of 5.77% from 1997 to 2002. Carrefour instead looks for countries that have lower service percentages because this often indicates that consumers do not have high disposable incomes to spend on service-based retailing. Carrefour emphasizes its low prices with slogans like "Grocery products at low, low prices" and "Always the lowest price." Since a majority of their strategy is based around everyday low prices, Carrefour would want to expand to countries where consumers are looking for value in their product.*

**P8: Multinational retailers will first move to countries that are culturally the most similar to their home country.**

*Carrefour does support this proposition. In the early years of its internationalization, Carrefour expanded regionally to culturally similar countries such as Belgium and the UK. Carrefour then looked to countries that were further away from France geographically, but still somewhat culturally similar, such as Spain. Later, Carrefour adapted its strategy to the culture change, and began to expand to regions that were becoming further and further away in terms of geographical proximity, such* as South Korea and Thailand.

**P9: Multinational retailers will expand within the country an then will expand regionally within that area.**

*Carrefour supports this proposition. Carrefour began in France in 1959 and expanded throughout France until 1969, when Carrefour entered Belgium, then Spain in 1973. Once Carrefour began to expand throughout Europe, expansion in other regions began to take place, such as movement to Brazil in 1975. Carrefour also continues to expand within France and Europe.*

**P10: Periodically the multinational retailers will "jump" to a new geographic area and begin the stages form of expansion.**

*Carrefour does support this proposition. There are several examples throughout Carrefour's expansion that prove this proposition true for the company; for instance, their 1989 expansion to Taiwan and 1995 expansion to the United Arab Emirates. Following the expansion to the United Arab Emirates, Carrefour continued its expansion in other countries with similar cultural dimensions.*

**P11: Multinational retailers will move to countries that are geographically close to the home country initially, then expand to more distant countries. (Miles from Home Country to Host country)**

*Carrefour supports this proposition. Beginning in France, Carrefour first focused doing business in their home country and once it was time to expand out of France in 1969, Carrefour chose Belgium. Not only are the cultures similar in these two countries, they are geographically close. Expansion in France came first, then a little in Europe, and then finally other regions throughout the world, like Brazil in 1975 and Argentina in 1982.*

**P12: Multinational Retailers will move to countries with large population bases.**

*Carrefour does not support this proposition. When expanding into foreign markets the company looks for areas in which modern retail formats are not currently established. Consumers find Carrefour's vast amount of product offering and variety an innovative retail format and have accepted it in most every country it has expanded to. Striving to only exist in markets where they will have a top three presence, Carrefour expands based on retail development and competitor presence, not specifically population size.*

# Endnotes

1. "Carrefour SA." International Directory of Company Histories. Ed. Tina Grant. Vol. 27. Detroit: St. James Press, 1999. 93-96. International Directory of Company Histories. Web. 27 Sept. 2010

2. "Carrefour SA." International Directory of Company Histories. Ed. Tina Grant. Vol. 27. Detroit: St. James Press, 1999. 93-96. International Directory of Company Histories. Web. 27 Sept. 2010

3. Sternquist , Brenda. (2007). "Company Foucs Iv.1 Carrefour." International Retailing (p. 567-571) New York: Fairchild Books & Visuals.

4. Passariello Christina. (September 16, 2010). Carrefour's Makeover Plan: Become IKEA of Groceries.The Wall Street Journal, Retrieved November 1, 2010, From ProQuest database. <http://proquest.umi.com.proxy2.cl.msu.edu/pqdweb?index =0&did=2138865741&SrchMode=1&sid=1&Fmt=3&VInst=PROD&VType=PQ D&RQT=309&VName=PQD&TS=1290058237&clientId=3552>

5. Carrefour SA. (15 November). Hoover's Company Records,40719. Retrieved November 18, 2010, from Hoover's Company Records. (Document ID: 168186271).

6. Sternquist , Brenda. (2007). "Company Foucs Iv.1 Carrefour." International Retailing (p. 567-571) New York: Fairchild Books & Visuals.

7. Sternquist , Brenda. (2007). "Company Foucs Iv.1 Carrefour." International Retailing (p. 567-571) New York: Fairchild Books & Visuals.

8. Annual Report 2009. Retrieved October 22, 2010, from          <http://www. carrefour.com/docroot/groupe/C4com/Pieces_jointes/RA/RA_Carrefour_PDF_ WEB     _2009VE.pdf>

9. Sternquist , Brenda. (2007). "Company Foucs Iv.1 Carrefour." International Retailing (p. 567-571) New York: Fairchild Books & Visuals.

10. Sternquist , Brenda. (2007). "Company Foucs Iv.1 Carrefour." International Retailing (p. 567-571) New York: Fairchild Books & Visuals.

11. White, Erin. (2004, February 26). Carrefour on Shopping List?. The Wall Street Journal. Section 13, p. 9. Retreived November 1, 2010 from LexisNexis <http:// www.lexisnexis.com.proxy2.cl.msu.edu/hottopics/lnacademic/>

12. White, Erin. (2004, February 26). Carrefour on Shopping List?. The Wall Street Journal. Section 13, p. 9. Retreived November 1, 2010 from LexisNexis <http:// www.lexisnexis.com.proxy2.cl.msu.edu/hottopics/lnacademic/>

13. Annual Report 2009. Retrieved October 22, 2010, from &lt;http://www. carrefour.com/docroot/groupe/C4com/Pieces_jointes/RA/RA_Carrefour_PDF_ WEB _2009VE.pdf&gt;

14. International Directory of Company Histories. Ed. Tina Grant. Vol. 27. Detroit: St. James Press, 1999. P. 93-96

15. Sternquist, B. (1998) Retailing in Germany and France, International Retailing (p. 306-309). New York, New York: Fairchild Publications

16. Sternquist, B. (1998) Retailing in Germany and France, International Retailing (p. 306-309). New York, New York: Fairchild Publications

17. Balfour Frederik, Matlack Carol, Zellner, Wendy. (October 11, 2004).Carrefour in a Corner, 3903. Retrieved October 25, 2010, From Lexis-Nexis database.

18. Annual Report 2009. Retrieved October 22, 2010, from &lt;http://www. carrefour.com/docroot/groupe/C4com/Pieces_jointes/RA/RA_Carrefour_PDF_ WEB _2009VE.pdf&gt;

19. Sternquist, B (1998) Retailing in Central and Eastern Europe: Company Focus III.6: Carrefour, International Retailing (pp. 401-402). New York, New York: Fairchild Publications

20. "Carrefour SA." International Directory of Company Histories. Ed. Tina Grant. Vol. 27. Detroit: St. James Press, 1999. 93-96. International Directory of Company Histories. Web. 27 Sept. 2010

21. (March 17, 2007).Crossroads; Carrefour. The Economist. Retrieved November 10, 2010  From Lexis-Nexis database. &lt;http://www.lexisnexis.com.proxy2.cl.msu. edu/hottopics/lnacademic/&gt;

22. Annual Report 2009. Retrieved October 22, 2010, from &lt;http://www. carrefour.com/docroot/groupe/C4com/Pieces_jointes/RA/RA_Carrefour_PDF_ WEB _2009VE.pdf&gt;

23. Carrefour – Point of View. Carrefour &lt;http://www.carrefour.com/cdc/group/ point-of-view/europe-s-leadingretailer.html  October 30, 2010.

24. World-Class Retailer – Carrefour Drives Down the Road to Domination. (May 12, 2010) Retail Week. Retrieved October 30, 2010, form LexisNexis &lt;http:// www.lexisnexis.com.proxy2.cl.msu.edu/hottopics/lnacademic/&gt;

25. World-Class Retailer – Carrefour Drives Down the Road to Domination. (May 12, 2010) Retail Week. Retrieved October 30, 2010, form LexisNexis &lt;http:// www.lexisnexis.com.proxy2.cl.msu.edu/hottopics/lnacademic/&gt;

26. Carrefour – Point of View. Carrefour&lt; http://www.carrefour.com/cdc/group/

point-of-view/europe-s-leadingretailer.html> October 30, 2010.

27. Annual Report 2009. Retrieved October 22, 2010, from        <http://www. carrefour.com/docroot/groupe/C4com/Pieces_jointes/RA/RA_Carrefour_PDF_ WEB      _2009VE.pdf>

28. Annual Report 2009. Retrieved October 22, 2010, from        <http://www. carrefour.com/docroot/groupe/C4com/Pieces_jointes/RA/RA_Carrefour_PDF_ WEB      _2009VE.pdf>

29. Carrefour sets out expansion Strategy. (2003 October 16) The Nation. Retreived October 13, 2010, from LexisNexis database. < http://www.lexisnexis.com. proxy2.cl.msu.edu/hottopics/lnacademic/>

30. Carrefour . (2010, September 16). Carrefour investor day  Reinventing the hypermarket to create value Group targets towards 2015 {Press Release}. Paris:Author. Retrieved from, <http://www.carrefour.com/ docroot/groupe/C4com/Pieces_jointes/Presentation_aux_analystes/ COMMUNIQUEENFINALdef.pdf>

31. Carrefour. (2010, September 16) Analyst day – Reinventing the Hypermarket Carrefour  September 16, 2010. Retrieved October 25 from, <http://www. carrefour.com/docroot/groupe/C4com/Pieces_jointes/Presentation_aux_ analystes/2010/05_V_TRIUS.pdf >

32. Carrefour . (2010, February 18). Agreement Between Carrefour and Marinopoulous to Develop Carrefour in the Balkans {Press Release}. Paris:Author. Retrieved November 3, 2010 from, <http://www.carrefour. com/docroot/groupe/C4com/Pieces_jointes/Communiques_financiers/2010/ CARREFOUR%20BALKANS%20LAST%20UK_defdedef.pdf>

33. Sternquist, B (1998) Retailing in Central and Eastern Europe: Company Focus III.6: Carrefour, International Retailing (pp. 401-402). New York, New York: Fairchild Publications

34. Annual Report 2009. Retrieved October 22, 2010, from        <http://www. carrefour.com/docroot/groupe/C4com/Pieces_jointes/RA/RA_Carrefour_PDF_ WEB      _2009VE.pdf>

35. Carrefour . (2010, October 28). Sustainable Development News{Press Release}. Paris:Author. Retrieved November 4, 2010 from, <http://www.carrefour.com/ cdc/responsible-commerce/sustainable-development-news/france-carrefour_s-_ reared-without-gmos_-labelling.html>

36. Thompson, James (2008, February 1). Carrefour to Refocus Stores and Own-label Food Brands. Retail Week. Retreived October 20, 2010 from LexisNexis http:// www.lexisnexis.com.proxy2.cl.msu.edu/hottopics/lnacademic/

37. Carrefour grows own-label range. (2004, March 12) Retail Week. Retrieved October 25, 2010 from LexisNexis

38. Carrefour . (2010, April 22). Carrefour Launches "Carrefour Discount" a New Line of Quality Products at Discount Rates {Press Release}. Paris:Author. Retrieved from, <http://www.carrefour.com/docroot/groupe/C4com/Pieces_ jointes/Communiques_de_presse/2009/kediscount220409VE.pdf

# Casino

*Charlene Kolodziej, Nicole Pallas, Christie White, Taylor Young*

## Casino

Can you imagine a company that offers retail stores in every format imaginable? Providing the consumer with everything from hypermarkets, supermarkets, discount stores, cash and carry, ecommerce, convenience, restaurants, non-food, and many more. Well Casino Guichard-Perrachon, more commonly known as Casino, is a company that does just that. Casino is known throughout the world as a leading first class food retailer. Starting from a single grocery store in France, they have grown to 10,000 stores worldwide and show no sign of slowing down. Offering many different formats has allowed Casino to have product differentiation, the ability to serve every customer, and most importantly, to grow and expand the number of their private label brands.

Each banner, which is Casino's way to differentiate between the numerous retail stores, carries different private label brands that specifically target the customers in that region. They have been able to build their private label, which they accredit to being a major asset in times of economic struggle.[1] The private labels that they have created range from organic foods, gourmet foods, out of home dining, sustainable farming, and non food products just to name a few. They are now the leading private label brand in France for both value and volume.

Casino holds many corporate values, which has helped bring them to where they are today. These values are commitment to the environment, support of the region in which they operate, and openness to diversity. They also strive to have a healthy and beneficial relationship with customers, and their employees throughout the world. There is no limit to what this company can accomplish in the upcoming years. No matter what the group plans to do in the future, they will stay true to their values and there is no doubt that their growth has great potential.

# FLOW CHART

| Location | Entry Year | Number of stores (2008) | Exit Year |
|---|---|---|---|
| France | 1898 | 8,601 | |
| United States | 1976 | | 2007 |
| Poland | 1996 | | 2007 |
| Taiwan | 1996 | | 2006 |
| Mexico | 1997 | | 2007 |
| Uruguay | 1997 | 52 | |
| Argentina | 1998 | 65 | |
| Colombia | 1998 | 264 | |
| Vietnam | 1998 | 8 | |
| Brazil | 1999 | 597 | |
| Thailand | 1999 | 79 | |
| Venezuela | 2000 | 60 | |
| Indian Ocean | 2001 | 51 | |
| Netherlands | 2003 | 305 | 2010 |

## Domestic Expansion

### France

Casino Group was founded by Gefforoy Guichard in Veauche, central France, in 1898. The first store was called Societe des Magasins du Casino. Later in 1901 the first Casino brand products were sold. This was an innovative idea, and a successful attempt at the private label concept. They continued to expand throughout France until they felt satisfied with their market share. The company continued to grow until the Second World War.[2] In France, Casino's country of origin, where they are currently one of the leading food retailers, coming in a close second only to Carrefour, SA.[3] Today the company operates over 9,590 hypermarkets, supermarkets, restaurants, and discount stores in the region. Casino currently employs 74,851 workers in France alone. Hypermarkets operate under the name Geant Casino.[4]

## International Expansion

In 1976 Casino made their first international move, to the United States. The initial expansion was slow, and Casino was still getting a feel for the American consumer. The cultural proximity between France and the United States differed more than the company originally thought. Slow growth continued, until about 1996, which the company considers the start of their international expansion era. During this period the company started forming joint ventures, and acquiring existing companies from which they would build their own brand. The second country entered was Poland, followed by Taiwan, and Mexico. The first four countries that Casino expanded into were not given much thought, and were a trial run for the company. They experienced many difficulties along the way exiting from the United States, Poland, Taiwan, and Mexico.

This is believed to have occurred due to their lack of international experience. Companies learn how to do business in other regions over time, and mistakes can be made along the way. Casino may have overestimated the cultural proximity of some of these countries, and lacked the understanding of the consumer needs in these areas. Casino still operates in eight countries. Over time they have figured out a strategy that works best for them when it comes to international expansion. Most likely they consider many different factors before entering any country. These factors would include culture, location, growth opportunity, and competition. Any combination of these factors would give a company such as Casino insight into what would be expected when expanding. The company continues to grow and profit, today the company operates over 10,000 hypermarkets, supermarkets, restaurants, and discount stores. They show no sign of slowing their expansion efforts and continue to increase the value of their companies throughout the world.[5]

## Uruguay

Casino entered into Uruguay in 1997. They partnered with Disco, currently this country's top retailer. Together they operate three different retail formats: Geant, Disco, and Deveto combining for a total of 52 network stores.[6] The acquisition of Deveto is the largest in Uruguayan history,[7] and will help with Casino's overall strategy of using subsidiaries that are industry leaders, and firmly planted in their communities.[8] Deveto is a family run company, which carries a very good brand name in the country.

## Argentina

In 1998, Casino acquired Libertad. They redeveloped and re-launched this chain of hypermarkets. Libertad is now the leading hypermarket chain and operates in large cities. Also, Casino created their first discount store format in Argentina, called Leader Price. The group has a total of 65 stores, which generate $458.747 million dollars in sales.[2] There is network of Leader Price discount stores. Libertad is the leading hypermarket, which operates throughout many large cities in Argentina. Leader Price is located in Buenos Aires, and surrounding suburbs. These discount stores offer a large amount of products, which are 20%-30% cheaper than national brands.[2] They also offer a 50/50 mix of national brands and private labels.[2] Hiper Casa offers household items and office decorations. Hiper Casa is the leading retailer in this department, setting the bar for other stores in this field. Many consumers come to Hiper Casa looking for high quality service and products. Discount stores are the fastest growing retail format in Argentina, because they are able to locate themselves in neighborhoods. Offering the lowest prices is a key strategy, which attracts customers. Argentinian consumers favor private labels so this is a big plus of Leader Price discount stores.

## Colombia

Casino entered Colombia in 1998 through the subsidiary, Exito. They mainly operate through the hypermarket format in this area and currently hold 42% of the market share.[2] In addition to their hypermarkets, Casino also operates convenience and discount stores. Here is a list of their other banners: Bodega, Bodega Surtimax, Merquefacil, Surtimax, Ley, Homemart, Proximo, and Q'Precios.

## Vietnam

In 1998, through acquisition of Big C, Casino made its move into Southwest Asia. The location is considered one of the most promising markets, mainly due to the large young population of 85 million.[2] Casino entered Vietnam's retail market in 2010 through a wholly-owned subsidiary. There currently have eight retail locations, which are unique in the fact that they are operated as a joint venture with local partners. These eight stores employ 1,028 workers.[9]

## Brazil

Casino has been present in Brazil since 1999. They first emerged through an acquisition of Companhia Brasiliera de Distribucao (CBD). Casino held leading positions in Brazil, which is one of the top contributors to revenue (38%) for Casino.[10] Since CBD previously existed, it had a wide range of retail formats under its umbrella, which met the needs of all Brazilians. Casino wanted to expand the brand, which they did, increasing sales by 21% in 2008. The other formats range from hypermarkets, supermarkets, convenience stores, cash and carry, nonfood, and an e-commerce site. Groupo Pao de Acucar (GPA), formerly known as CBD, is Brazil's second leading retailer with a market share of 13.3%.[10] GPA is in two of Brazil's leading cities, Rio de Janeiro and Sao Paulo.

Hypermarkets are the leading format is Brazil. There are 102 hypermarkets throughout Brazil. The hypermarkets help meet the needs of many citizens, allowing them to get household equipment and personal items. These hypermarkets offer the best prices for Brazilians, which meets the demands of the numerous customers. Hypermarkets, supermarkets, and convenience stores offer a high quality of food for Brazilians. Each format seeks to provide high quality service. Foreign retailers make up the majority of the consolidation in Brazil; the reason for this is that these foreign retailers have greater access to capital. This is why Casino is able to do so well in Brazil. Many consolidated companies look like one huge company but other companies under their name retain individual identities. GPA can fall under this category. Each format under GPA is run separately. GPA has a loyal customer, and has done well throughout the country because of its excellent customer service and loyalty card system. These strategies have allowed GPA to continue to be one of Brazil's leading retailers.

## Thailand

In Thailand, Casino operates 79 retailers, under the name Big C. They are the majority stakeholder, entering through acquisition, in 1999.[10] Big C is the country's top discount retailer, which has developed a very positive brand image among the people. They also aim to make the shopping experience a very pleasant one, where customers will want to return. Under Big C there is a smaller convenience store format that boasts 11 locations under the name of Mini C. Finally, in 2008, Big C opened a beauty retailer named Pure. Between the three different formats Casino employs 13,836 people.[11]

## Venezuela

In 2000, Casino acquired Cativen, a previous long time leader with Cada stores, a supermarket format. By retaining this status in Venezuela, implementing its own Casino brands such as Exito (hypermarket), and Q'Precious (discount store) the company is now in a leading position within the Venezuelan market. Casino has worked on its expertise so that it can extend its formats. Casino has two major formats in Venezuela. One is CADA supermarkets, which is known as one of their foreign markets. The second one is Exito hypermarkets, which is known as one of their domestic markets. Exito is a Colombian retailer. Exito, which is Venezuela's leading hypermarket, keeps their prices low and affordable for consumers. Exito has a varied product range, many of which are considered practical items. This is aimed towards women between 25-40 years of age.[12] A number of household items are sold at low prices. This strategy has kept a number of consumers returning. Q'Precios, which is Venezuela's leading discount store offers the lowest prices in the market. Their strategy is based off of very low operating costs. Cada has a familiar and functional layout, which makes shopping easier for customers. Cada is known for their excellent service and offers a wide variety of brands. This helps to meet consumer's needs. Due to the fact that Venezuela has faced economic instability; low prices and a wide variety of brands allow consumers to remain loyal. Each format uses a low price strategy, which has worked fairly well throughout the country.[13]

**Indian Ocean**

The Indian Ocean region includes Reunion, Mayotte, Mauritious, and Madagascar. Casino entered these areas in 2001 through its Vindema subsidiary. They currently have 51 locations, and employ around 1,028 workers. The market share of Vindemia in Reunion accounts for more than 80% of sales. Casino is currently the region's leading retailer. This is partly due to the fact that they provide a largely popular loyalty/ payment card.[14] This strategy seems to be very successful in the region, and will continue to be utilized.

**International Exits:**

As the flow chart displays, the first international expansions for Casino were terminated by the year 2007. These include: United States, Poland, Taiwan, and Mexico. It is our theory that Casino didn't understand the cultural proximity of their domestic business in France compared to those first international expansions. Most recently, Super De Boer of the Netherlands was sold. By learning from their past mistakes, they generated a total revenue of over 38 billion dollars as of 2008.[15]

**Questions**

1. **Is the retailer classified as a global retailer or a multinational retailer? Explain its pattern of expansion. What expansion strategy did/is the retailer use/using?**

*Casino is classified as a multinational retailer. They change the products they sell based on the country it does business in. They had rapid expansion within France,* almost to the point of market saturation. Casino expanded using the risk theory. Risk theory is when a company evaluates the level of risk of the foreign market they are considering entering. They will need to weigh the perceived level of risk to determine if the market is a good investment and fit for their company. As every government has different regulations for their own country's market, companies must be able to adapt to their requirements in order to survive. Casino moved into Uruguay based on the factors of low labor cost, and a high average GDP. Once they became familiar with Uruguay's market and researched the surrounding areas, they were able to expand to other nations within South America. They also jumped to other geographic regions. They operate in many countries that offer a variety of economic situations, demographics, and geography. Casino has also used the stages theory while expanding.

## 2. Based on Dunning's Eclectic Theory, how do ownership, locational and internalization factors play in your retailers' international expansion?

Transaction-based advantages are part of the ownership factors in Dunning's eclectic theory. Casino used tacit learning (learning by doing) while moving into a new geographic region. When they moved into Latin America, Uruguay was the first country they entered. After they created a joint venture, they were able to learn the ways of retail used in Latin America and then moved themselves into countries such as Brazil, Argentina and Venezuela. As a multinational retailer, cultural proximity is a major part of the locational factors. Initially Casino expanded from France to the United States, or a country that is not culturally similar. they exited from the U.S. and begain to entercountries that were more culturally similar. Then over time, the group expanded to countries with larger cultural distances, such as Vietnam and the Indian Ocean countries.

## 3. What role does cultural proximity and geographical proximity play in the retailers' international moves?

Cultural proximity is a key aspect of multinational retailing. It's very common for organizations to fall to the psychic distance paradox. This means, companies believe they will succeed in a country that is geographically close, when in fact the cultures may differ greatly. For the most part, Casino has done well with locating according to cultural and geographical proximities. There have been a few bumps along the way, such as when they entered the Netherlands and the United States, both of which they have exited.

## 4. Can you predict the retailer's future international expansion?

There are many different moves Casino can make regarding their future international expansion. In recent years, Asia's economy has become much stronger *and is continually showing signs of improvement. It was reported that retail sales in Japan have risen at the fastest rate since 1997. Many hope for this rise to have a long and positive impact on the country. Since Casino has not expanded into the region, it would be a strategic move for them to break into the growing economy in countries such as Japan and others like it. It was reported that 58% of Japanese admitted to really enjoying grocery shopping.[16] This is another reason for Casino to venture into this potentially profitable market. Entering Japan would also allow Casino to stay true to their value of giving back to the communities in which they work, by providing numerous jobs. It is possible that Casino may break into Japan and it seems like it would be a success in regards to their international expansion efforts.*

## Propositions

**P1: The greater the ownership advantages for retailers, the less likely they will franchise or license.**

*This proposition is supported. Casino has internationalized to a variety of countries mainly through acquisitions. As a multinational retailer, they benefit from transaction-based advantages. The experience and knowledge the company learns from expanding in one country doesn't always apply and transfer to other countries. The company expands mainly through trial and error techniques as well as tacit learning (learning by doing). Casino first moved into Uruguay in 1997 via joint venture. This way they were able to learn from their partner about the country, and how the retail business works in that country. After they became knowledgeable with Uruguay they continued to internationalize into the Latin American market. They realized they must amend their products for each store format and they were able to keep familiar consumer brands.*

**P2: The greater the available organisational slack the greater the likelihood of expanding internationally.[17]**

|  | 1995 (millions) | 1996 (millions) | 1997 (millions) |
|---|---|---|---|
| **Current Assets** | $2740.77 | $2994.39 | $3308.44 |
| **Current Liabilities** | $3536.17 | $3403.40 | $4616.65 |
| **Organisational Slack** | 0.775 | 0.880 | 0.717 |

This proposition is refuted. The organisational slack ratio would need to continually increase over the three years in order to support this proposition. The ratio did increase from 1995 to 1996, however it decreased in 1997.

**P3: The greater the recoverable slack the greater the likelihood of expanding internationally.**[17]

| USD in millions | 1995 | 1996 | 1997 |
|---|---|---|---|
| G & A Expenses | $2,2460.09 | $2,535.41 | $2,737.55 |
| Sales | $13,054.66 | $13,606.73 | $15,523.30 |
| Recoverable Slack | .188 | .186 | .176 |

This proposition is refuted. Casino's recoverable slack decreased over the three-year period of 1995-1997 and international expansion continuously grew throughout the company. Sales continuously rose as well as the general and administrative expenses.

**P4: The greater the potential slack the greater the likelihood of expanding internationally.**[17]

| USD in millions | 1995 | 1996 | 1997 |
|---|---|---|---|
| Equity | $1,614.68 | $1,771.22 | $2,102.63 |
| Capital | $6,519.80 | $6,776.29 | $8,687.36 |
| Potential Slack | .247 | .261 | .242 |

This proposition is refuted. Casino's potential slack varies throughout the three-year period. The company successfully expanded internationally throughout this time frame so the fluctuation in slack didn't affect their expansion endeavours.

**P5: Multinational retailers will move to countries with lower disposable income than their home country.**

This proposition is supported. In 2007 the median disposable income per household in France was $58,183. This is compared to Brazil, which had only $8,871 in disposable income, and Thailand that had $4,800.[18] Therefore, proving that Casino, a multinational retailer moved from a country with a larger disposable income to countries with lower disposable incomes. Another example is the first country of international expansion, the United States. The United States' disposable income during the expansion and after the expansion is much greater than that of France.

They united the U.S. and this lends support for the proposition.

**P6: Multinational retailers will move to countries that have a high positive change in GDP.**[19]

| Country | Year of exp. | GDP year of exp. | GDP 5 years after exp. |
|---|---|---|---|
| United States | 1976 | $8,300.50 | $13,533.16 |
| Poland | 1996 | $4,056.68 | $4,975.90 |
| Taiwan | 1996 | | |
| Mexico | 1997 | $4,274.42 | $6,490.61 |
| Uruguay | 1997 | $6,686.37 | $3,710.64 |
| Argentina | 1998 | $8,280.67 | $3,409.99 |
| Columbia | 1998 | $2,442.48 | $1,818.24 |
| Vietnam | 1998 | $355.59 | $3,045.45 |
| Brazil | 1999 | $3,425.23 | $3,609.11 |
| Thailand | 1999 | $2,010.46 | $2,533.20 |
| Venezuela | 2000 | $4,818.71 | $5,449.17 |
| Indian Ocean | 2001 | | |
| Netherlands | 2003 | $33,135.96 | 40167.13 (2006) |

*This proposition is supported. From the data given, majority of the countries of which Casino had expanded into saw a considerable amount of positive change in GDP from the first year of expansion to the fifth. Only three of 11 countries saw a decrease in GDP, which can be attributed to poor economic situations within the country as well as war. Both of which are unfavorable to retail industries, since customers have a limited amount of disposable income. Overall Casino has expanded within countries that have seen a substantial amount of growth and in which they can continue retail operations.*

**P7: Multinational retailers will move to countries that have a high positive change in service-value added as % of GDP.**

*This proposition is supported. Casino is a multinational retailer that has moved to countries with a high positive change in service-value added as a percentage of GDP. After looking at data, Casino has moved to countries with quite a higher number. A high positive change in service value added as percentage of GDP is usually above 20%, majority of the countries Casino has expanded into are 20% or higher. Argentina has a percent of 33.1, Brazil is 31.5, Colombia is 31.1, Uruguay is 33.4, and the Netherlands is 46.1. France has the highest positive change with 52.9. France is Casino's home country.*[20]

**P8: Multinational retailers will first move to countries that are culturally the most similar to their home country.**

*This proposition is not supported. Casino's home country is France. After expanding throughout France and becoming France's primary market the company expanded to only two other European nations or host countries. These European countries are Poland and the Netherlands. Casino expanded to Poland in 1996 but just recently exited a few years ago in 2006.[21] In 2003, the company made its way back to Europe and entered the Netherlands through an acquisition. Casino is present now throughout many countries in South America and Asia.[22]*

**P9: Multinational retailers will expand within the country and then will expand regionally within that area.**

*This proposition can be supported. Casino is a multinational retailer that has expanded within a country and then expanded regionally within that area. Casino expanded to Uruguay through a joint venture in 1997. Within the next few years Casino was being recognized throughout many South American countries. Casino is still present in South American countries such as Brazil, Argentina, Colombia and Venezuela. Expansion to these countries took place between the years 1998 and 2000. Casino has opened up hypermarkets, supermarkets, discount stores and convenience stores throughout these nations. Casino has also expanded within the Indian Ocean in 2001 through an acquisition. The company has expanded to islands such as Madagascar, Mayotte, and Mauritius. Jumbo Score, which is a hypermarket, is most commonly known on these islands. Casino is the region's leading retail. Also present in Asian countries, Casino has expanded to countries such and Thailand and Vietnam. Once present in Taiwan, Casino has just recently exited the country in 2007.[23]*

**P10: Periodically the multinational retailers will "jump" to a new geographic area and begin the stages form of expansion.**

*This proposition is supported. Casino began domestic expansion in France. The first international expansion was in the United States, followed by Poland and Taiwan. These "jumps" are normal for multinational retailers as they are able to change their products for each country they expand to. Casino followed this when they first went to Uruguay they then expanded into Argentina and Colombia but then "jumped" to Vietnam. They broke into the Vietnamese market and then returned to Latin America, where they entered Brazil. This type of movement allows a company to become known in many different parts of the world faster than saturating one geographical region at a time. This allows them to create brand awareness and recognition. Casino's next move was back to Asia, where they opened in Thailand. They continued this pattern of expansion, opening a variety of retail formats across the globe.*

**P11: Multinational retailers will move to countries that are geographically close to the home country initially, and then expand to more distant countries. (Miles from Home Country to Host country)**

*This proposition is refuted. Casino's first international expansion was to the United States. This market was many miles from France, their home market. And although they did expand into Poland next, soon after they moved into Taiwan, again many miles from their home market. Cultural proximity is more important for multinational retailers, and Casino is no exception. They are more determined to find a market that will fit well with their company values and worry less about expanding to places near their home country of France. As stated in the previous proposition, multinational retailers are known for expanding via the stages theory. Casino has shown no consistent pattern of moving geographically. It is apparent they are eager to be a worldwide company; they must have seen the benefits of rapidly expanding across a number of nations far greater than staying exclusively to Western Europe.*

**P12: Multinational retailers will move to countries with large population bases.**

*This proposition is supported. For the most part, Casino operates in countries with larger populations. However, they do operate in less populated countries such as Uruguay, and the Indian Ocean countries. Multinational companies look for areas that will be a good fit with the firms' strategies. Unlike global retailers, who mainly internationalize into global cities, Casino focuses on expanding into a country, with multiple locations within that country. Brazil is the densest country Casino has entered and with over 500 locations, it's clear they were determined to spread across the country rather than staying in one major city. For comparison, here are the populations for all of the countries Casino operates: Brazil: 198.74 million Argentina: 40.91 million Colombia: 43.68 million Venezuela: 26.81 million Uruguay: 3.49 million France: 64.06 million Thailand: 66 million Vietnam: 88.58 million.*[24]

### Endnotes

1. Casino, Groupe. Company Information. Retrieved March 18, 2010 from Casino Website. http://www.groupe-casino.fr/en/Our-Brands.html

2. Casino, Groupe 2008 Annual Report. Retrieved from Casino Website. http://

www.groupe-casino.fr/en/Annual-reports-Annual-reports,713.html

3.  Who's News. (2005, March 22). Wall Street Journal (Eastern Edition), p. B.8. Retrieved April 4, 2010, from ABI/INFORM Global. (Document ID: 810652061).

4.  Casino, Groupe. Company Information. Retrieved March 18, 2010 from Casino Website. http://www.groupe-casino.fr/en/Our-Banners-Our-Banners.html

5.  Casino, Groupe International Markets. Retrieved from Casino Website. http://www.groupe-casino.fr/en/Strong-positions-in-international.html

6.  Casino, Groupe 2008 Annual Report. Retrieved from Casino Website. http://www.groupe-casino.fr/en/Annual-reports-Annual-reports,713.html

7.  Casino buys retail chain. (2000, June). Country Monitor, 8(23), 2. Retrieved April 4, 2010, from ABI/INFORM Global. (Document ID: 55343504).

8.  Casino, Groupe. Vision and Strategy. Retrieved April 4, 2010 from Casino Website. http://www.groupe-casino.fr/en/Vision-and-Strategy.html

9.  Casino, Groupe. Vietnam Information. Retrieved March 20, 2010 from Casino Website. http://www.groupe-casino.fr/en/Vietnam,585.html

10. Casino, Groupe 2008 Annual Report. Retrieved from Casino Website. http://www.groupe-casino.fr/en/Annual-reports-Annual-reports,713.html

11. Casino, Groupe. Thailand Information. Retrieved March 20, 2010 from the Casino Website. http://www.groupe-casino.fr/en/Thailande,586.html

12. Casino, Groupe 2008 Annual Report. Retrieved from Casino Website. http://www.groupe-casino.fr/en/Annual-reports-Annual-reports,713.html

13. Sternquist, Brenda. (2007). International Retailing. USA. Fairchild Publications, Inc.

14. Casino, Groupe. Indian Ocean Information. Retrieved March 20, 2010 from the Casino Website. http://www.groupe-casino.fr/en/Indian-Ocean.html

15. Van Tartwijk, Maarten. Wall Stree Journal. "Jumbo Bids for Casino's Super de Boer." 18 September 2009. http://online.wsj.com/article/SB125326796457022707.html (24 March 2010).

16. "Asia in Brief." Shopping Centers Today Online. July 2006. Retrieved March 24, 2010. http://www.icsc.org/srch/sct/sct0706/asia_in_brief.php

17. Casino, Grope 1997 Annual Report. Retrieved from Mergent Database.

18. Disposable Income Percenages. Retrieved from the Global Market Information Databas

19. Expansion Year GDP. Global Edge Database. March 20, 2010. http://www.globaledge.msu.edu/ibrd/country.asp

20. Service GDP Percentages retrieved from the Global Market Information Database.

21. "Casino Guichard-Perrachon S.A." Funding Universe. Retrieved March 20, 2010. http://www.fundinguniverse.com/company-histories/Casino-GuichardPerrachon-SA-Company-History.html

22. Casino, Groupe 2008 Annual Report. Retrieved from Casino Website. http://www.groupe-casino.fr/en/Annual-reports-Annual-reports,713.html

23. Casino Groupe. International Markets. Retrieved from Casino Website. http://www.groupe-casino.fr/en/Strong-positions-in-international.html

24. Population Information. Global Edge Database. Retrieved on March 21, 2010.

# Costco Wholesale

*Jim Cervo, Sara Jelinek, Jessica Lanenga,*
*Stephanie Nguyen, Nicole Rockhold, Alicia Sperling*

## Costco Wholesale

Since pioneering the world's first warehouse membership club in 1976, Costco Wholesale has continued to be one of the most innovative, successful retailers on earth.[1] Costco is a membership discount warehouse chain that sells a wide range of products from beer, to tires, and even coffins.[2] As of now, Costco Wholesale is the largest retailer in the warehouse industry. Also, Costco was ranked number 14 out of the top 20 most admired companies in the United States.[3] The current downward-spiraling economy isn't hurting Costco, as they are doing rather well during this economic crisis. Memberships is growing and customers are still buying. To help stimulate sales during this holiday season, Costco is planning to include more high-quality jewelry in the warehouse stores; at affordable prices, of course.[4]

Costco is a membership warehouse club, dedicated to bringing their members the best possible prices on quality brand-name merchandise. Costco Wholesale Corporation is an American wholesale club founded in 1976. Costco, or COST on the Nasdaq, is currently the largest membership warehouse club chain in United States and the world. Costco's headquarters are located in Issaquah, Washington. It is also the fourth largest general retailer in the United States.[5]

Costco is a multinational retailer that serves more than 50 million cardholders in 40 US states and Puerto Rico, Canada, Japan, Mexico, South Korea, Taiwan, and the UK, primarily under the Costco Wholesale name.[5] According to McGregor of Business Week, Costco has been a fortress of stability over the years. The $72 billion discount warehouse chain has built an empire of 544 stores in 40 states on one proposition, keeping the prices of its quirky assortment of wares, everything from bulk antacids to flat-screen televisions, as low as possible.[6] Costco is seen as attractive to consumers based on the diverse merchandise carried in each warehouse club. Costco Wholesale warehouse clubs offer discounted prices on an average of 4,000 products, mostly in bulk packaging, ranging from alcoholic beverages and appliances to fresh food, pharmaceuticals, and tires. Some of the Costco club memberships also offer products and services such as car and home insurance, mortgage and real estate services, and travel packages.[5]

Costco Wholesale has continued to attract customers that have been hit by the economic downturn. For the quarter ended Aug. 31, the warehouse club retailer recorded net income of $397.8 million, or 90 cents a share, compared with $372.4 million, or 83 cents a share, a year earlier.[7]

Costco plans to expand and open seven new locations in the United States before the end of 2008. Although Costco is expanding, a customer must be a member at Costco to be able to shop. The company believes customers' membership portrays customer loyalty, as well as a source of fee revenues. The three types of annual memberships available are, the Business membership costing $50 each, a Gold Star membership costing $50 for individuals and their spouses, and lastly the Executive membership costing $100, which allows members to purchase products and services, including insurance, mortgage services, and long-distance phone service, at a discounted rate. The Costco's card membership renewal rate is 87%.[5] The average size of a Costco warehouse is 140,000 square feet. Costco also has an online e-commerce business at Costco.com, which allows customers and potential customers to browse the Costco merchandise selection.

## Industry Analysis

Costco Wholesale Corporation is a big box retail store that is part of the retail trade sector in the U.S. Costco is generally known as a warehouse club, it is also categorized in the lines of superstores, or super centers that engage in retailing a general line of groceries and general merchandise, such as clothing, furniture and appliances.[6] They offer the everyday needs of consumers under one giant roof. The big box retail Stores industry is one of the three industries that make up the United States general merchandise stores sector.[6]

The warehouse club and superstore industry includes about 3,000 stores with combined annual revenue of almost $200 billion. Some major companies in this sector include Wal-Mart's Sam's Club, Costco Wholesale; BJ Wholesale Club, and Meijer. The industry is highly concentrated, the top four companies own 85% of stores and hold over 90% of sales.[5] Warehouse clubs, such as Costco are one of the younger retail formats to enter the mainstream market. They are known to experience quick growth at the expense of rival retailers such as the traditional grocery store, and have impact consumer shopping trends. These large chains are able to dominate the market because of the advantage they have in purchasing, distribution, and finance.

Warehouse clubs differ from superstores because the clubs require customers to have memberships to shop. Warehouse clubs offer more of a limited selection, but in larger quantity as well as in a wide range of merchandise categories. These retailers offer a wide range of products across many retail categories. Their competitors include grocery stores, mass merchandisers, department stores, specialty retailers, and other wholesalers. The major products sold by warehouse clubs such as Costco include groceries, drugs, personal care products, clothing, and electronics. Most of these products are only available in bulk quantity. Some warehouse club locations included gas stations, pharmacies, optical centers, and food courts.[5]

Most warehouse clubs are able to provide discounts by offering goods in bulk, as well as a self-service operating store. The merchandise is often displayed on pallets and the store's extra inventory on overhead racks. Most warehouse clubs are located in remote sites, far from large shopping areas. Customers are willing to drive for the discounted prices. Warehouse clubs buy most of their goods directly from the manufacturer or importers, usually by truckloads. Again, large volume purchasing allows the company to receive substantial discounts, which results in savings for their shoppers. Warehouse clubs work closely with manufacturers to develop special packaging to reduce handling costs. For example, Costco has even gotten vendors to redesign product packages to fit more items on a pallet, the wooden platforms it uses to ship and display its goods. Putting cashews into square containers instead of round ones will decrease the number of pallets shipped by 24,000 this year, cutting the number of trucks by 600.[9]

Inventory is expected to have a rapid turnover rate, and most companies only stock their shelves with top brand names and private labels goods in each category. Private labels have become a success for Costco. Their private labels Costco's Kirkland Signature product often out sells national brands and brings in high margins for the company. Costco has become very successful as a big box retailer that offers their customers both soft and hard goods.

According to McGregor of Business Week, "Costco has been a fortress of stability over the years. The $72 billion discount warehouse chain has built an empire of 544 stores in 40 states.[6] Warehouse clubs such as Costco strive to deliver the best quality products to their members at the best discounted price they can offer.

Warehouse clubs; such as Costco typically offer between 4,000 to 8,000 stock-keeping units (SKU's) of merchandise. In comparison to 30,000 to 60,000 SKU's carried by grocery stores, warehouse clubs keep their SKUs lower. Inventory shrinkage is low, mostly because of the membership requirements. Warehouse clubs eliminate the traditional multi-level distribution channel; the companies save on distributor commissions and storage costs.[5] To keep a close eye on their inventory, most warehouse clubs use bar code scanners and computerized point-of-sale (POS) systems at checkout to determine when replenishment of merchandise is needed. Some warehouse clubs require manufacturers to supply merchandise with radio frequency identification (RFID) to monitor inventory as it moves through the supply chain and into the stores, and on to the customers.[6]

## Industry Overview & Competition

The one thing differentiating warehouse clubs from superstores is that warehouse clubs require a membership in order to shop. Some of the products offered by most warehouse clubs, listed in order of importance to revenue, include: grocery, drug, health & beauty aids, apparel, and electronics. For the most part, each of these products is sold in bulk and/or larger quantities making it possible for the retailer to sell items at lower prices while also making the consumer feel as though they are receiving an even better deal. All of this is possible since these particular retailers generally purchase their merchandise directly from the manufacturers, which allows them to receive generous discounts.[9]

The warehouse club that rises above the rest of the competition is Costco Wholesale Corporation. Costco's annual sales are around $72 million with Kroger close behind at $70 million, Sam's Club at only $39 million, and Target at about $63 million. Although sales seem close with competitor Kroger, Costco has over an 18% net income growth from 2007 to 2008 while Kroger only had at 5.9% net income growth.[9] When compared to Sam's Club, their biggest competitor, Costco is said to be so much more efficient in that it earned $6 billion more than Sam's club last year and Sam's club has almost 200 more retail stores than Costco.[10] The financial data shows the clear, giant gaps between Costco and its competitors, but there is much more than numbers that separate this company from its competition.

When focusing on Costco's main competition, Sam's Club, there are several differences that explain why Costco is leading in customer preference; as well as financial data. First and foremost is store layout. As stated by a retail analyst and regular shopper of Costco, "Costco does a much better job of laying out the store to encourage impulse buying".[10] Costco carefully places higher demanded items in the back of the store, forcing the customers to walk through the entire store.

Costco does this hoping the customer will see other things they want, resulting in the customer spending much more time in the store. Sam's Club, on the other hand, will put the high demand items in the front of the store so the customer can quickly grab their item and leave without further shopping or possible additional purchases.[10]

In addition to the uniqueness of the store layout, Costco also has the upper hand with products. "One of Costco's large advantages over its competition is the diversity in the products they offer and sell" said Mark Sussman, President and Chief Executive Officer of Pyramid Solutions.[9] Costco also carries a private-label brand called Kirkland Signature. Cristopher Gunter, president of consulting and design firm of The Retail Group in Seattle said, "They've built up their house brand to the point where people are looking for it specifically, because they trust it... That's great evidence of good branding".[10] Aside from having their own brand, Costco is just well known for having quality name brands at bargain prices.[10] Costco is well aware that they have a much more sophisticated, urban customer and one example of this is the fact that they are the U.S.'s biggest seller of fine wines bringing in over $600 million a year.[11]

Incidentally, products and store layout will only keep a store at the top for so long. Proper management is probably one of the key factors to Costco's success. As stated by analyst Mark Sussman, "Costco debatably has the strongest management team in the vast retail sector".[9] As one of the founders of Costco, Jim Sinegal is a very fair, hardworking, and personable man. He limits his pay to a $350,000 salary and he gets to know all of his employees by learning their names. On top of all that, he is said to be demanding without being intimidating and he offers the best wages and benefits in retail. Aside from the employee aspect, he is very fair to his customers as well by having one of the most lenient return policies no receipts; no questions; no time limits. In addition, Costco chooses to run their company by the practice of intelligent loss of sales. This means they offer few choices so all the different brands, sizes, and colors don't just get lost on the shelves. These types of things bring customers back and retain true customer loyalty.[11]

Even though Costco is a better store overall, Sam's Club struggles with their own battles. Within the past ten years, Wal-mart has gone through five CEO's and has tried several different strategies to make Sam's Club the number one warehouse club; each time were beaten by Costco. Sam's Club started off on the wrong foot as a mere copycat of a Price Club. By targeting the middle class market it is obvious that Sam's Club just doesn't satisfy the type of higher-class people that Costco does. It also did not help Wal-Mart's sales by locating their stores in small cities instead of the larger, growing cities. There have been numerous attempts by Sam's Club to catch up to the ever-growing Costco; one obvious attempt being the purchase of Pace Warehouse Clubs from Kmart. Although their efforts are valid and the company is still in the race, it comes down to the fact that Sam's Club has basically blended in with Wal-mart.[11]

## Business Strategy

Costco CEO, Jim Sinegal, has a very simple and what some have called altruistic outlook on what he says is "good business."[12] In his own words, the foundation of Costco is the adherence to a straightforward code:

1. Obey the laws,
2. Take care of the customers,
3. Take care of the people, and
4. Respect the suppliers.

Costco has found that their margins do not allow any advertising. More importantly however, is the fact that all the advertising they really need is word of mouth. Jim believes that the good thing others say is more important than what you say about yourself.[13] Considering how uncomplicated this code is and how successful Costco has been, it's surprising to find that financial analysts have given so much negative feedback.[12]

Costco is very focused on achieving a level of service that puts them on a first name basis with every customer and employee. If customers have a complaint, there is a chance he or she could end up on the phone talking directly to Jim himself. He believes that consumers might be pleased about the reality that their opinions mean enough to the company that a CEO will talk to them directly. Additionally, the workers know that they are appreciated because they are taken care of and there is a genuine mutual respect between the bosses and the workers. Costco promotes nearly 100% from within the employee structure, rewarding loyalty; for once hired, employees rarely leave.[14]

Costco offers low prices for the quality of items sold to membership holders and provide a 12% to 40% higher wage than their competitor. This helps the consumer as well as the people it employs.[15] This method is considered an alternative to the 'Cheap-Labor' model, which has been known to cause problems such as: fueling poverty, low wages that lessen consumer spending and the costs of health-care are indirectly put upon other companies and taxpayers.[15] As a rule, Costco regulates the markup percentages of both branded and private label items, with markups no more that 14% and 15% respectively. Jim cautioned against raising markups by even a little, stating that doing so could cause Costco to lose the discipline they have acquired in cost and price minimization.[12]

Some Wall Street analysts are not supporters of this alternative business model. They believe that Costco could make much more money for itself and its many shareholders if it would drop employee wages and benefits. They complain that Costco is better to its customers and employees than shareholders. [12] To this Jim simply states, "Wall Street is in the business of making money between now and next Tuesday. We're in the business of building an organization, an institution that we hope will be here 50 years from now. And paying good wages and keeping your people with you is very good business."[14] If the company shareholders hold this view it isn't obvious: Costco shares sell for 23 times their earnings and the stock price has risen 10% in the last 12 months.[12]

## Retail Culture

For Costco Wholesale, providing customers with a good deal is the key to how they operate. The origin of their success is selling high-quality merchandise at low prices. "They're just very good at what they do and very clear about who they are and how they do business," said George Whalin, president of Retail Management Consultants. "And you know that every time you walk into a store, you're going to get a good deal."[16]

When a Costco member makes a trip to a Costco Wholesale Warehouse, they can be sure to find the everyday items they have on their shopping list. This is because about 75% of Costco's inventory is comprised of staple products that can be found in the floor's stock every day. It is the other 25% that keeps customers traveling the aisles and making impulse purchases. The treasure-hunt element of Costco's merchandising strategy creates a psychological pull that encourages shoppers to hunt for bargains that may not be there next week.[17] [16]

Costco Wholesale stores offer discount prices on an average of about 4,000 products; many in bulk packaging. The shelves of Costco's warehouse stores are stocked with very diverse merchandise, ranging from everyday staple products, to very expensive jewelry. Certain club memberships also offer products and services such as car and home insurance, mortgage and real estate services, and travel packages. Costco also offers an alternative private label brand to name-brand items – Kirkland Signature.[5]

### Costco Wholesale Merchandise and Service Breakdown

- Alcoholic beverages

- Apparel

- Appliances
- Automotive insurance products (tires, batteries)
- Automobile sales
- Baby products
- Books
- Cameras, film, and photofinishing
- Candy
- Caskets
- CDs
- Checks and form printing
- Cleaning and institutional supplies
- Collectibles
- Computer hardware and software
- Computer training services
- Copying and printing services
- Credit card processing
- DVDs
- Electronics
- Eye exams
- Flooring
- Floral arrangements
- Fresh foods (bakery, deli, meats, produce, seafood)
- Furniture
- Gasoline

- Gifts
- Glasses and contact lenses
- Groceries and institutionally packaged foods
- Hardware
- Health and beauty aids
- Hearing aids
- Home insurance
- House wares
- Insurance (automobile, small-business health, home)
- Jewelry
- Lighting supplies
- Mortgage service
- Office equipment and supplies
- Outdoor living products
- Payroll processing
- Pet supplies
- Pharmaceuticals
- Plumbing supplies
- Real estate services
- Snack foods
- Soft drinks
- Sporting goods
- Tobacco
- Tools

- Toys

- Travel packages and other travel services

- Video games and systems

- Private Label

- Kirkland Signature (private label)[5]

Developing a private label is a difficult task for any retailer, but Costco has turned Kirkland Signature into one of the most successful private label brands in the country.

Developing a successful private label to sell alongside national brands has not been an easy task for other retailers. No other United States retailer that is comparable in size to Costco has been able to build a private label that gained enough trust from shoppers to make it a success throughout the store, both in durable goods and consumables. Costco warehouse customers now broadly accept Kirkland Signature, which was built methodically over many years, throughout the country.[18]

Co-branding with respected manufacturers boosted the quality perception of Costco's private label brand, Kirkland Signature. For some time, Kirkland Signature products were matched with a national brand as a product that had a complementary value offer based on price, size or ingredients. Yet, in many categories, predominantly where there were no strong national brands, Costco established Kirkland on its own as the key product in the category, further evidence of the confidence Costco has in the brand.[18]

When it comes to distribution exclusivity, Costco is not afraid to make demands. It is not uncommon for Costco to request suppliers to create a unique distribution system for the wholesale store. If a supplier does not comply with Costco's requests, the wholesaler does not hesitate to cut ties with a national brand or supplier. Costco has even gone as far as making requests to manufactures to redesign product packaging with hopes of making shipping and displaying the good easier. The company has come a long way from its initial beginnings of struggling to maintain suppliers to having the ability to delist major suppliers without any doubts.[6] [19]

Costco operates regional cross-docking centers throughout the country. These cross-docking centers deal with the consolidation and distribution of merchandise to warehouses. In addition to cross-docking centers, Costco operates an array of other facilities to support secondary and other businesses. Costco currently operates eleven cross-docking depots in the United States, three in Canada, and two internationally. Each of these cross-docking facilities is approximately 6.6 million square feet. Each facility of roughly 300,000 square feet and includes 274 shipping and receiving doors.[20] [21]

Since Costco does virtually no advertising, it allows those suppliers to do business with Costco without alienating other retailers who sell the same product at a higher price. Not advertising also allows for the brands to maintain brand equity while still reaching the masses.

Costco is expanding into other business endeavors. The company opened its first home furnishings store, Costco Home, in 2002. Costco is also in the planning stages of possibly launching an additional new business slated to be titled Costco Fresh. Costco Fresh is said to be a stand-alone gourmet food retailer. This retail format is still being worked out by Costco. The Costco Fresh retail format was launched in Manhattan, but was put on hold until the retail format could be perfected.[16]

## International Expansion

### USA

First Store Opened: 1975                    Number of Locations: 394

From 1954 to 1974 retailer Sol Price built the Fed-Mart chan. Sol Price sold the company to Hugo Mann in 1975. The sale of Fed-Mart to Mann spawned the first Costco Wholesale warehouse, formerly Price Club. The first Price Club warehouse was opened in San Diego, California, after over twenty years of operating as an entity catering to only government employees. Price Club was opened to the public in 1975.[5]

### Canada

First Store Opened: 1986                    Number of Locations: 76

Costco operates 76 membership warehouse clubs in 9 Canadian provinces, far outnumbering its rival SAM'S club.[22] Costco formed a joint venture with Canadian retailer Steinberg in 1986 to operate stores in Canada. Costco bought out Steinberg's locations in 1990.

### Mexico

First Store Opened: 1992                    Number of Locations: 31

Currently there are 31 stores in Mexico in 18 different Mexican States. When Costco internationalized to Mexico they created a 50/50 joint venture with

Mexico's second largest retailer, Comercial Mexicana. Costco's in the United States are similar to the ones in Mexico but you can get some Mexican products that you cannot get in the United States. In Mexican stores they carry Mexican candy, fish they have caught in the oceans around Mexico but they also carry American beef and a majority of American products which really attracts Mexicans. By expanding into Mexico early in their business they were lucky because they did go international but are "locally international" which allows them to keep a similar retail format to what they have in the United States because they are similar in their buying and cultures to an extent. Costco is building a new warehouse in Mexico and with this expansion proves that Costco is making an effort to enhance their business in Mexico. As long as they keep doing what they are doing and taking some chances they should be very successful.

## United Kingdom

First Store Opened: 1993                      Number of Locations: 20

In the UK18 of their warehouses are owned and 2 of them are leased. Costco was started in Seattle, WA and they used subsidiaries to enter the United Kingdom. Currently the headquarters for Costco Wholesale Corporation UK is located in Watford. The locations of the Costco Wholesale Co. UK are Aberdeen, Birmingham, Bristol, Cardiff, Chester, Chingford, Derby, Edinburgh, Gateshead, Glasgow, Haydock, Leeds, Liverpool, Manchester, Milton Keynes, Oldham, Reading, Sheffield, Thurrock, Watford, and Magna Park. On November 22nd, 2008 they are opening a new warehouse in Croydon. The United Kingdom locations make around 1-5 Billion dollars in sales and have around 3,500 employees currently working for them.

## South Korea

First Store Opened: 1994                      Number of Locations: 6

Since 1994 Costco has seen great success in its locations in South Korea. Costco currently has six locations in South Korea. Especially, the Yangjae Costco in Seoul ranks No. 1 in sales out of more than 500 locations worldwide.[25] Costco's Korea buyer Yoo Sun-goo, went to an annual Costco meeting in Kirkland, Washington five years ago and was introduced to fresh cherries. He told the newspaper, "I thought if I bought the fruit to Korea, I would be successful."[25] And successful he was, the first year, the week's pallet was sold in less than a day. In 2007, Costco Korea made $4 million in U.S. dollars selling fresh cherries. Yoo plans to import roughly 60 pallets of cherries a week to Costco Korea. The reason the cherries became so successful was because Costco sold a 3 pound packages of cherries for less than half of what it cost at other retailers in South Korea. Costco not only accommodates local culture, but also chooses to innovate and sell Western produce in Asia and has become very successful.[23] [24]

## Taiwan

First Store Opened: 1997                    Number of Locations: 5

Costco entered Taiwan in 1997. They now have 5 locations in Taiwan. Costco has done an excellent job at incorporating and adopting the culture around them into their product categories. Their Taiwanese customers are able to find their favorite local delicacies such as sea cucumbers at Costco. Beverely Arye, general merchandise manager for Costco in Taiwan says, "Our Taiwanese members have a feeling that a product is of higher quality if it is an import."[26] Costco offers both bilingual labels on many of the products they carry. Some goods such as Kirkland Signature brand vitamins were reformulated to meet Taiwanese regulations. Costco makes it a priority to follow the rules and fit into the country in which it is present. Beverely Arye continues and states, "The Taiwanese tend to not eat at home or cook at home a lot." In Taiwan, families spend hours in Costco leisurely walking the aisle and browsing the merchandise and enjoying the samples. Costco definitely takes the local culture in Taiwan and incorporates them into their warehouses.

## Japan

First Store Opened: 1999                    Number of Locations: 8

As of 2008, Costco Warehouse clubs had eight locations in Japan. You will find many of the same products here that are available at any Costco in the USA. Overall, about 60-70 percent is about the same as in the US and the rest are Japanese products. The imported goods have higher prices than you would pay at a Costco in the US but compared to other stores in Japan, they are cheaper. Costco Japan plans to keep adding one store each year. Costco Japan operates at a loss with the anticipation of future profitability as the chain grows.[27]

## Puerto Rico

First Store Opened: 2001                    Number of Locations: 4

Seeing that Puerto Rico is considered a part of the United States, little information can individually be found. It is known that Puerto Rico has Costco Stores and their GDP purchasing power per capita is 72.61 billion.

## Future Expansion: Australia - Going Forward and Down Under

Strong growth at home has not deterred the hankering for growth outside of its parent country. At 27 percent, the number of warehouses based outside of the US is again going to expand.[28] In Melbourne thirteen new outlets are planned. Costco is also conferring with Australia's government on the possibility of also moving into Victoria.[29]

## Questions

**1. Is the retailer classified as a global retailer or a multinational retailer? Explain its pattern of expansion. What expansion did/is the retailer using?**

*Costco is a multinational company. The company expanded into Canada, then into Mexico; a common multinational pattern. This pattern consists of expanding into a culturally similar country then jumping to one that is very different, developing an expertise as they go. They also own their stores for the most part as licensing is very risky to a retailer's internalization. Costco Wholesale is a multinational company that uses a decentralized expansion strategy. Although they expand very rapidly, they only expand into regions where they have done extensive research. When Costco does research on a new market they plan on entering they look for information on the dynamics of the community including competition in the area, the common travel routes of the potential customers and the infrastructure of the area. Costco uses the information that they gain from their research in order to steer some of their more basic products towards the people of the community they are entering. Costco prefers to enter into existing markets because it is an easy transition. The corporate team already has an idea of what the competition in the area is and what the retail prospects look like. Costco will use the internal cash flow to fund the expansion in their 3-year plan. They refurbish buildings as well as buy and lease spaces in order to expand their warehouses.*

**2. Based on Dunning's eclectic theory, how do ownership, locational and internalization factors play in your retailers' international expansion?**

*Costco uses all of these elements in their international expansion plans. They use their Kirkland Signature Label, which is their private, in-store brand as a huge asset-based advantage along with Costco Cash Cards. Costco obviously has great knowledge on how to expand and internationalize since they have opened over 400 stores within the past 16 years in the United States and various other countries. Both push and pull factors have also had a great impact on how Costco has internationalized. Since they have almost 400 stores within the United States alone, large growth is becoming limited in the US so this has pushed Costco elsewhere. Along with the United States' saturated environment, the UK and Asia's potential for growth is pulling the company to expand overseas. Although they do not have the first mover advantage in all foreign countries, Costco is seemingly quite successful overseas and is planning on continuing rapid expansion. Internalization is very important to Costco. They have been able to maintain company privacy and keep "company secrets" through their own Costco Employee Agreement instead of being part of a general union. This agreement is revised every three years and includes such things as: benefits, compensation, wages, disciplinary procedures, paid holidays, bonuses, and seniority. All of these factors have had a great impact on Costco's foreign expansion and will still have a huge impact on future expansion.*

### 3. What role does cultural proximity and geographical proximity play in the retailers' international moves?

*Cultural proximity and geographical proximity both play a huge role in Costco's international moves. Costco has established its business in 543 locations, 145 of which are outside of the United States and Puerto Rico. Costco envisions the cultural proximity among the people of different countries through identifying their everyday needs. They help people locate and buy quality products. The issue of a language barrier does not affect Costco from entering a country successfully. Costco has a standard layout format, and has a standardized style or strategy of doing business whether in the United States or abroad. Costco works to establish their business to accommodate the people's needs. They show this by having bilingual packaging on most of the goods they carry in their warehouses.*

*Costco does a great job of adopting the culture around them into the product categories that they offer to their customers. Costco warehouses are common in Asia, and they sell local delicacies such as sea cucumbers. They also provide parking for scooters, which is a common form of transportation in many countries in Asia. Costco also provides bilingual labels on many of the products they carry. Some goods such as Kirkland Signature brand vitamins must be reformulated to meet Taiwanese regulations. Costco makes it a priority to follow the rules, and fit into the countries in which they have established warehouses. In a typical Taiwanese Costco, you will find members stocking up on foods such as instant soups and coffee packets. Fresh seafood, including sushi is a common item in Costco's Asian warehouses. Costco takes the local culture and incorporates the culture into their warehouse.*

*Geographical proximity also plays a large role in Costco's international as well as national expansion. There are currently in 398 Costco locations in the United States and Puerto Rico alone. It is safe to say that Costco is influenced by the close geographic locations and the commonalities among their shoppers within the United States and Puerto Rico. Costco's success in a concentrated area has allowed them to expand to countries outside the United States. As of September 26, 2008 Costco has 543 locations. Costco has 5 locations in Taiwan, and 6 locations in South Korea.*

## 4. Can you predict the retailer's future international expansion?

*Yes, for the most part we can predict the international expansion of Costco. They are operating two stores in Australia. They will open more stores and try to expand to countries that are close to countries they are already in. This being the concept of "locally international", Costco already did this when they first opened by opening in the USA and then internationalizing to Mexico and then Canada. Therefore with that theory of thought, I think we can safely say that Costco will most likely open more stores in Europe by the UK and then most likely throughout Europe when they become established in the countries they are in. One thing is for sure though, Costco will keep opening stores wherever that may be.*

## Propositions

**P1:The greater the ownership advantages for retailers, the less likely they will franchise or license.**

*We agree with this proposition. Costco has significant ownership advantages. The company does not want to give all of their secrets away like they would if they were to franchise or license. Costco has done some licensing but most of their stores are wholly owned subsidiaries which keeps their secrets to themselves.*

**P2: The greater the available organizational slack the greater the likelihood of expanding internationally.**

Ratio= Current Assets to Current Liabilities
3 yr average: 1994-1996 (The oldest available dates on Mergent)

1994:   CA- $1, 534,298
CL- $1, 647,307
Ratio= $1, 534,298/ $1, 647,307= .93

1995:   CA-$1, 702,319
CL- $1, 692,938
Ratio=  $1, 702,319/ $1, 692,938= 1.00

1996:   CA-$1, 828,304
CL-$1, 771,594
Ratio= $1, 828,304/ $1, 771,594= 1.03

*We agree with this proposition, it is true when talking about Costco. 1994= a, 1995=b, and 1996=c. The formula states that a<b<c and this is true, therefore we*

*agree with this proposition.*

**P3:The greater the recoverable slack the greater the likelihood of expanding internationally.**

*It is true that the greater the recoverable slack the greater the likelihood of expanding internationally. Mergent shows that if Costco's Sales to General and Administrative Expenses Ratio is larger they are more likely to expand internationally. When Costco first started expanding they had a very large ratio and if that ratio goes down they work less on their international expansion.*

**P4: The greater the potential slack the greater the likelihood of expanding internationally.**

*It is true that the greater the potential slack the greater the likelihood of expanding internationally. Mergent shows that Costco's equity has continually gone up and the larger the difference between the amount of equity and the amount of capital the more they are trying to expand. When Costco started to expand they had around a 3:1 ration of equity to capital and they expanded greatly. Costco has continued to expand ever since then.*

**P5: Multinational retailers will move to countries with lower disposable income than their home country.**

*We agree with this. Multinational retailers are very capable of changing to suit the country they choose to occupy. If the country has a low disposable income their focus is to become the place costomers go to, to get what they need. With less extra cash than that of the parent company country, shoppers are interested in finding a retailer where they can go and get everything they need at a price that is affordable. This opens the opportunity to become everything the customers need.*

**P6: Multinational retailers will move to countries that have a high positive change in GDP.**

*When a country's GDP has a higher positive change from year to year, that indicates they now have additional funds to spend that were not there before. This is true even when the GDP of the country is less then that of the parent company's country.*

**P7:Multinational retailers will move to countries that have a high positive change in service-value added as % of GDP.**

*This proposition is true for Costco. All seven countries Costco moved into have had positive changes in service-value added % of GDP.*

**P8:** **Multinational retailers will first move to countries that are culturally the most similar to their home country.**

*This proposition is true for Costco. Costco's first international expansion was into Canada in 1986. Canada is culturally similar to the United States.*

**P9:** **Multinational retailers will expand within the country and then will expand regionally within that area (for example expanding to Brazil and then Argentina and Chile).**

*Yes, we agree with this proposition. Costco has been successful in South Korea, and is continuing to expand in more cities in South Korea, such as Buscan, Korea by 2009 as well as three other cities in South Korea by 2010.*

**P10: Periodically the multinational retailers will "jump" to a new geographic area and begin the stages of expansion.**

*Yes, we agree with this proposition. Costco Wholesale Corp. started in the United States and did take the international "jump" to new geographic areas such as Asia, and has continued to be successful and has been expanding in Asian countries such as Taiwan and South Korea.*

**P11: Multinational retailers will move to countries that are geographically close to the home country initially, then expand to more distant countries. (Miles from Home Country to Host country)**

*We agree with this. The first Costco Warehouse opens in Seattle, WA in 1984. The company then expands within the United States and by 1985 they begin to move into Canada. The company continues to rapidly expand within the US and it's not until 1993 that they open a store in the United Kingdom. By 1994 the company seems to know their business and their way of internationalization so they then open the first Asian Costco. This explanation of expansion can be explained through the Stages Theory. Canada is the most culturally similar and safe country for a US company to expand. Once Costco became comfortable on foreign soil, they were ready for a new risk and new venture over seas into the UK. Expansion is a step by step process that needs careful planning in order to be successful and that is exactly what Costco did.*

**P12: Multinational Retailers will move to countries with large population bases.**

*We do not agree with this. This proposition is not necessarily true with Costco. Since the companies' first international expansion was in Canada, which is a country with anything but a large population, I think it is safe to say that this proposition does not apply with this particular company. Costco did, however, begin to move into larger populated countries as they progressed through time, but to say that they expanded into countries based on a large population alone is false; they instead internationalized based more on level of risk and culture.*

## Endnotes

1.    (2008). Costco Wholesale Opportunities. Retrieved on: November 10, 2008. http://company.monster.com/costco/

2.    Costco.com, Copyright 1998-2008 Costco Wholesale Corporation, www.costco. com, Retrieved Oct. 27 2008.

3.    Costco Wholesale. Fortune 500. 2008. Online at: http://money.cnn.com/ magazines/fortune/fortune500/2008/snapshots/2649.html

4.    "Costco Wholesale Corp.". (October 11, 2008). Thomas White's Investment Conclusion. Retrieved on November 11, 2008, retrieved from Investext. Ÿ

5.    Costco Wholesale Corporation. Hoover's Company Records - In-depth Records (2008). Retrieved November 11, 2008, from LexisNexis Academic.

6.    McGregor, Jena (2008, October). COSTCO'S ARTFUL DISCOUNTS. Business Week,(4104), 58-60.  Retrieved November 11, 2008, from ABI/INFORM Global database. (Document ID: 1575522561).

7.    McGrath, Steve. "Costco Results Benefits From Bargain Hunting." October 8, 2008.  Wall Street Journal Online at: http://online.wsj.com/article/ SB122345861274214739.html.

8.    IBIS World. "Costco Wholesale Corporation" Updated July 25, 2008. Retrieved November 1, 2008, from IBIS World.

9.    Warehouse Clubs and Superstores: Costco Wholesale Corporation. Hoovers, A D&B Company. Retrieved November 11, 2008. http://hoovers. com/free/search/simple/xmillion/index.xhtml?which=company&query_ string=Costco&x=0&y=0.

10.   Tice, Carol. (2003, July). Merchandising masters: Costco continues to clobber competition. Puget Sound Business Journal. Retrieved November 11, 2008. http://www.bizjournals.com/seattle/stories/2003/07/28/focus1.html.

11.   Helyar, John. (2003, November 24). The only company Wal-Mart fears. Retrieved November 11, 2008.  Fortune. New York. Vol. 148, Iss. 11; pg. 158.

12.   Greenhouse, Steven. (2005). How Costco became the Anti-Wal-Mart. Retrieved

on November 7, 2008, from: http://www.nytimes.com/2005/07/17/business/
yourmoney/17costco.html

13. Miles K Davis (2008). Integrity and Values. New England Journal of
    Entrepreneurship, 11(2), 9-12. Retrieved October 20, 2008, from ABI/INFORM
    Global database

14. Goldberg, Alan B. (2006). Costco CEO Finds Pro-Worker Means Profitability.
    Retrieved on November 7, 2008, from: http://abcnews.go.com/print?id=1362779

15. Zellner, Wendy. Holmes, Stanley. (2004). The Costco Way. Retrieved on
    November 11, 2008, from: http://www.businessweek.com/magazine/
    content/04_15/b3878084_mz021.htm

16. Desjardins, Doug (2005, December). DON'T MESS WITH SUCCESS. DSN
    Retailing Today, 44(23), 33,61. Retrieved November 11, 2008, from ABI/
    INFORM Global database. (Document ID: 953606111).

17. Desjardins, Doug (2005, December). HUNTING FOR TREASURES. DSN
    Retailing Today, 44(23), 34. Retrieved November 11, 2008, from ABI/INFORM
    Global database. (Document ID: 953606121).

18. Duff, Mike (2005, December). A PRIVATE LABEL SUCCESS STORY. DSN
    Retailing Today, 44(23), 56. Retrieved November 11, 2008, from ABI/INFORM
    Global database. (Document ID: 953606341).

19. Frazier, Mya (2006, August 21). The Private Label Powerhouse. News; Pg. 6.
    Retrieved November 11, 2008, from LexisNexis Academic.

20. Costco Wholesale Corp. Retrieved November 10, 2008, from Mergent Online.

21. The McGraw-Hill Companies, Inc. Costco Wholesale: Costco Distribution
    Center. (2006, May 1). Special Report; Industrial; Pg. 32 Vol. 62 No. 5. Retrieved
    November 11, 2008, from LexisNexis Academic.

22. Costco Wholesale Canada Ltd. Hoover's Company Records – Basic Records
    (2008). Retrieved November 11, 2008, from LexisNexis Academic.

23. Lexis Nexis, Corperate Affiliations: Find Out Who Owns Whom, Copyright
    2008, http://www.corporateaffiliations.com.ezproxy1.ats.msu.edu/subscriber/
    history.asp?selID=061671-004&selName=COSTCO+WHOLESALE+UK+LIMI
    TED&srchCompanyName=COSTCO+WHOLESALE+UK+LIMITED, Accessed:
    October 21, 2008

24. Costco.co.uk, Copyright Costco Wholesale UK Ltd, UK Home Office Hartspring
    Lane, Watford, Herts WD25 8JS, www.costco.co.uk, Retrieved Oct. 27 2008.

25. Hoang, Mai. "Costco Cherries: The Washington-based company is big in South

Korea, too., and its cherry sales there have soared." Jakima Herald- Republic. June 29, 2008.

26. Costco Connections 2006. "Taiwan." October 2006 Costco Connections.

27. Sussman, Mark. (2008, February). Costco is pulling ahead of competition through superior management. The Expert Network: Garson, Lehrman Group. Retrieved November 11, 2008. http://www.glgroup.com/News/Costco-is-pulling-ahead-of-competition-through-superior-management.-21860.html

28. "Costco Wholesale Corp." (October 10, 2007). Thomas Whites Investment Conclusion. Retrieved on November 11, 2008, retrieved from Investext.

29. Tinkler, Chris. (2007). Costco to move into Melbourne. Retrieved on November 16, 2008, from: http://www.news.com.au/heraldsun/story/0,21985,22658677-2862,00.html

# Foot Locker, Inc.

*Lauren Amann, Jacqueline Fisher, Landon Hill, Stephanie Kennebeck,
Angelina Moise, Suzanne Mullins, Samantha Wax*

## Foot Locker, Inc.

I f asked about Foot Locker Incorporated, most people would easily be able to recall the matching black and white referee shirts worn by employees and the vast assortment of athletic shoes offered by the company. However, not much is known about the background and groundbreaking strategies Foot Locker, Inc. has used to become such a successful company throughout the world and the number one selling footwear store in the United States.

With many operating names, including Foot Locker, Lady Foot Locker, Kids Foot Locker, Champs Sports, and Footaction, the company has been able to appeal to many target markets.[12] Combined with operating under several distribution channels, Foot Locker, Inc. has found a solid presence amongst competitors. While other shoe stores offer trendy athletic footwear for a similar market, Foot Locker has been able to hold a competitive edge by reaching out to a multitude of markets, demonstrating strong brand recognition, acquiring international expertise, and having first mover's advantage. This tacit knowledge, combined with key vendor relations has helped Foot Locker become what it is today.

This case study will explain the history of Foot Locker and how it expanded to become a global retail phenomenon. Although the recent economy has slowed profits, it is undeniable that the company knows how to appeal to target markets internationally, which is always a means for success.

## Flow Chart

| Year | Country | Expansion | Number of Stores |
|------|---------|-----------|------------------|
| 1974 | United States | Organic Expansion | 1,218 |
| 1978 | Canada | Organic Expansion | 130 |
| 1999 | Australia | Organic Expansion | 76 |
| 1982 | Germany | Organic Expansion | 81 |
| X | New Zealand | Organic Expansion | 14 |
| X | Puerto Rico | Organic Expansion | X |
| X | U.S. Virgin Islands | Organic Expansion | X |
| X | Guam | Organic Expansion | X |
| 1997 | Austria | Organic Expansion | 5 |
| 1990 | Belgium | Organic Expansion | 17 |
| X | Denmark | Organic Expansion | 5 |
| 1991 | France | Organic Expansion | 86 |
| 2004 | Ireland | Organic Expansion | X |
| 1991 | Italy | Organic Expansion | X |
| 1992 | Luxembourg | Organic Expansion | X |
| 1990 | Netherlands | Organic Expansion | 37 |
| X | Spain | Organic Expansion | X |
| 1998 | Sweden | Organic Expansion | X |
| X | Turkey | Organic Expansion | 1 |
| 1990 | United Kingdom | Organic Expansion | X |

## History and Recognition

Foot Locker, Inc. operates their headquarters out of New York City with approximately 3,900 stores in 22 countries and plans to open 25 additional stores by the end of 2009. In addition to its bricks-and-mortar locations, Foot Locker, Inc. also sells products to customers through catalogs and Internet websites such as Eastbay and California Cheap Skate (CCS).

Until 1998 Foot Locker, Inc. was known as Woolworth Corporation, which was founded by Frank Woolworth in 1879. The company went through various stages of five-and-dime stores selling goods such as tin pans, washbasins, button-hooks, and dippers to eventually become a nationwide retailer by 1912. Woolworth continued to expand, diversify, and modernize which then resulted in acquiring the family owned shoe business, G.R. Kinney Corporation in 1965. This division opened up what would become the first two Foot Locker stores in 1974. The company expanded globally, with the first move being to Canada in 1978. By 1982, Foot Locker had created a brand extension and new store format, known as Lady Foot Locker. After successfully managing the new addition, Foot Locker took on the task of adding two new store formats in 1987; they did so by acquiring Champs Sports and introducing Kids Foot Locker. Throughout 1988 and 1989, the company expanded globally, to Canada and Australia, respectively. In 1997, Foot Locker was able to increase their market share by selling directly to new and existing customers through their new affiliate, Eastbay, which is a well-established catalog. By 2001, the company had changed its name to Foot Locker, Inc. and refocused the former discount store format toward selling athletic apparel.[20] In 2008, Foot Locker, Inc. obtained their other affiliate, CCS, a company that is considered to be a leading direct-to-customer retailer.[20]

Foot Locker, Inc. is presently the world's leading athletic goods retailer with $4.94 billion in revenue and $5,237 million in sales as of August 2009.[12] The company currently employs approximately 43,343 part time/full time employees worldwide and are active in many different community organizations as well as out-reach programs.[22] In 2001, the company established the Foot Locker Foundation which raises money to provide scholarships for the United Negro College Fund. Foot Locker, Inc. also contributes to the American Cancer Society and works side-by-side with the Fred Jordan Mission donating shoes to impoverished children in Los Angeles. For the past thirty years Foot Locker, Inc. has provided a forum for high school runners of all abilities to participate in what is known as the Foot Locker Cross Country Championships (FLCC). The FLCC is comprised of four regional 5K races in the Northeast, Midwest (Wisconsin), South (North Carolina), and West (California).[10]

## Formats and Financials

Foot Locker, Inc. is a company that has broken international barriers and has taken its unique marketing mix to 21 other countries throughout the world. Currently, as the number one selling footwear store operating in the United States, Foot Locker, Inc. has expanded its stores and operates in several different retailing formats.[17]

One of the retail formats that Foot Locker, Inc. has launched is Lady Foot Locker. Lady Foot Locker was first opened in 1982 and began to target women generally in the 13–34 age range. Lady Foot Locker owns and operates 486 stores and sells several different brands of merchandise. Not only do they specialize in footwear, they sell apparel items and other sporting good accessories. This extension has recently created a display called the "Feature Zone" which shows all the latest products and brands being sold in the store.[13]

Similar to Lady Foot Locker, the corporation created another branch targeting 5-10 year old children known as Kids Foot Locker. Kids Foot Locker was first opened in 1987 and has expanded to operate 321 stores.[24] The environment in Kids Foot Locker is very warm and children friendly with elaborate visual displays for everyone to enjoy.[13] What sets Kids Foot Locker apart from other shoe departments is that it is currently the only retail store that targets this young age group, giving Foot Locker, Inc. an immense competitive advantage.

Champs Sports opened in 1987 and is an athletic shoe store that specializes in a variety of merchandise and targets its marketing mix to men's, women's and children's footwear. What makes Champs unique is its breadth and assortment of merchandise; it is also licensed to sell college and national football team merchandise, making it a popular place to shop for many different consumers. Champs also sells some exclusive private label merchandise, and targets consumers between the age range of 12-25.[13]

Footaction USA was bought by Foot Locker, Inc. in 2004 in hopes to increase the company's profits. After Foot Locker, Inc. purchased Footaction it increased its store base by ten percent.[8] Footaction focuses on "urban fashion" and targets its markets to mostly men under the age of 25.[13]

After the acquisition of Footaction in 2004, Foot Locker, Inc. also acquired the company CCS, in 2008. CCS is a skateboarding company that has a catalog as well as an online presence.[23] They specialize in skateboard footwear, clothes, equipment, and accessories. CCS was founded in 1985 and upon the purchase of the company the CEO of Foot Locker was reported saying "We believe that in expanding our offerings in the skateboard category it will allow us to broaden our appeal to the teenage male, providing an exciting growth opportunity for our company."[8] By targeting 12-18 year old males, Foot Locker, Inc. is doing a great job of tapping into a market in the skateboard industry that has the potential to boost their sales tremendously.[13]

Lastly, in Foot Locker, Inc.'s retail portfolio is their acquisition and online presence with Eastbay.[13] Through the Internet, Foot Locker, Inc. can increase its sales by selling directly to their customers and offering them even more options in merchandise. Targeting the 12-35 age range, Eastbay merchandise includes men's and women's athletic merchandise, apparel, and footwear.[13]

Although the acquisitions of different companies did help in sales, recently from 2007 to 2009, Foot Locker Inc.'s sales have decreased from $5.75 million to $5.237 million.[17] As of January 1, 2009, Foot Locker's total assets are $1.764 billion while total liabilities are $953 million. Their cost of sales is $3.777 million. Foot Locker, Inc. unfortunately recorded a net loss of $80,000 and a loss in operating income of $103 million. Earnings per share for the company are also at a loss of 0.52.[19] Return on assets and return on equity have decreased throughout the past three years; return on assets is (2.62) while return on equity is (3.82). An improvement is their inventory turnover which has increased from last year and is now 4.22. Also they maintain a high accounts payable turnover as well as a high receivables turnover.

Targeting several different demographics, they reach a wide variety of consumers worldwide. Although their sales have decreased from the previous year, Foot Locker Inc.'s different retail formats give the company a competitive advantage over most other specialty shoe retailers.

## Competitors

Foot Locker, Inc. may be leading in their industry, but competition is still present. Foot Locker, Inc.'s top competitors include mainly other high-volume, sell-through, trendy brand name, and private label retailers such as Collective Brands, DSW, The Finish Line, The Sports Authority, and Dick's Sporting Goods; as well as companies like The Walking Company Holdings and Brown Shoe Company.[19] The competitor companies sell men's and women's trendy athletic footwear and sporting goods for a strongly similar target market. However, Foot Locker, Inc. holds several advantages over its competitors.

A few of Foot Locker Inc.'s strongest competitive advantages are those which one would assume any leading retailer demonstrates, strong brand recognition, key vendor relationships, product sourcing strengths, international expertise and presence, first mover's advantage, cooperative distribution channels, and their diversification of their offerings to a wide customer base.[29]

The brand equity that has resulted from the strong brand recognition of producing high quality products for the active lifestyle consumer has supported the company's aptitude to effectively create complementary stores and the direct-to-customer alliances. Foot Locker, Inc. has had the opportunity to build strong relationships with certain vendors by being the leading global specialty retailer of athletic footwear, resulting in having an allotment of exclusive products. Foot Locker, Inc. is able to provide customers with athletic footwear and apparel at a lower price than brand name products, but still at a competitive price through the company's private label program. This program results in an increase of customer traffic and sales not only in retail stores, but also in the direct-to-customer businesses. Operating internationally allows the opportunity to share information such as trends and/or fads. With this information shared, Foot Locker, Inc. is able to rapidly adapt new fashion trends from one market to another, providing Foot Locker, Inc. the opportunity to be the trendsetter in the domestic market. Foot Locker Inc's expansion into Canada in 1978 is an example of the company's first mover advantage. The distribution channels that are offered by Foot Locker, Inc. allow the customer to be at ease about their purchase, and overall experience with the company. Foot Locker, Inc. is accessible through athletic retail stores, websites, and catalogs. The company operates the Foot Locker, Inc. website and catalog; however, there are websites and catalogs operated by the company's affiliates, Eastbay and CCS. All of these distribution channels allow the brand name to become increasingly desirable and easily accessible.[29]

Foot Locker, Inc. has a competitive advantage over Dicks Sporting Goods, The Sports Authority, DSW, and The Finish Line. While these competing companies operate only in the United States, Foot Locker, Inc. has expanded internationally, reaching more consumers and markets.[16] There is also a pure (perfect) competition between Foot Locker, Inc. and all of the competitor's. While the stores are located in the malls amongst the competition, there are many suppliers along with many buyers. Although some may think the products are differentiated with brand names such as Nike or Adidas, the product lines offered by the competitors and Foot Locker, Inc. are homogenous.[26]

Foot Locker, Inc. operates in two retail segments: athletic stores and direct-to-customers. With Foot Locker, Inc. having stores that carry both athletic footwear and apparel, the company is able to reach a wide range of customers due to their five different store formats, which all target a differentiated market. The five formats are: Foot Locker, Lady Foot Locker, Kid's Foot Locker, Champs and Footaction. The direct-to-customers segment is the function of Foot Locker, Inc's selling products through the Foot Locker.com website, and also through catalogs, and affiliates such as Eastbay, or CCS.[9] These operation methods are a considerable advantage for Foot Locker, Inc. mainly because the company's competition has different stores that target separate markets, while the competitor's product line is not as extensive or established as Foot Locker, Inc. The company can then target individual demographics and distinguish their needs and wants to enhance customer service and satisfaction in each format. For example, Collective Brands offers around 20 different brands of just footwear, while Foot Locker offers well over 200 brands of apparel and footwear.[7][5]

Foot Locker's inventory is more structured around mid-luxury brands such as Nike and Timberland, that customer's desire, but the company is still a retailer of non-essential goods. The product line is not diversified like other retailers that are considered a competition, such as Target and Wal-Mart. The disadvantage of a limited, non-essential good line may constrain consumer spending at Foot Locker.[18]

Foot Locker, Inc. competes horizontally, because they invest in activities that will increase sales and sales density by catering to consumers' needs, which also adds to their brand structure.[28] Foot Locker, Inc. accomplishes this type of competition through the company's promotions, service additions, and customer retention initiatives. Foot Locker provides a VIP club, where customers will receive offers via text messages and e-mails. One promotion offered is the company's daily prize program, where registered customers visit the website and enter their e-mail address daily to win a prize. Foot Locker, Inc. also sponsors community events, such as 'Making Strides Against Breast Cancer Walk'. A customer retention feature is the extensive amount of product information and customer service readily available.[28][11]

The growth of alliances between well-known manufacturer's and a fashion-conscious shoe retailer allowed for Foot Locker to remain superior to competitors. As mentioned before, many products are exclusive to the company. This exclusivity will keep the company above competition, and may prevent them from ever needing to compete on price.

## Business Strategy

Foot Locker, Inc. uses diversification as a key competitive strength in their business operations. This diversification allows Foot Locker, Inc. to build a large customer base by reaching out to a very diverse target market.[15] Another major strategy of Foot Locker, Inc. is the strong long-term relationships they have built with some of their vendors. As a result of these strong vendor relations, Foot Locker, Inc. has an allotment of exclusive products under their vendor's brand names throughout their formats.[29] The corporation is diverse in many aspects including: operating under multiple names, through several distribution channels, having a global presence in 22 countries, direct-to-customer retailers on the World Wide Web and through catalogs. This diversification gives the company a competitive advantage in being more independent.[15]

Foot Locker, Inc. operates under multiple names, including Foot Locker, Lady Foot Locker, Kids Foot Locker, Champs Sports, Footaction.[15] With vast name recognition in all of its formats, the presence of a Foot Locker, Inc. store in any area has been a destination for its customers.[15] The stores that followed the original Foot Locker store were designed to satisfy a more narrowly focused customer, one with different demographics than the typical shopper at a Foot Locker store. Employees who work at a branch such as Lady Foot Locker are equipped with more knowledge in the specific female athletic category. Female customers know they will receive expert insight on a new running shoe. Furthermore, a male can enter a Lady Foot Locker to get reliable advice for a gift; while at a competitor's store the customer service and information may be more general and not gender or age specific.[15]

Foot Locker, Inc. utilized international expansion by broadening their customer base in the global market. With the addition of new customers they also have to adapt to new styles, different ways of life, and a general appeal to more people. By having stores all over the world, Foot Locker, Inc. is exposed to new fashion, which aids them in being pioneers of new trends in other markets such as the United States where the competitors have not expanded internationally. To appeal to more mature individuals with higher income levels, they are stocking new designs from edgier brands such as Puma and Geox. Another tactic used is putting more emphasis on the apparel and footwear product lines.[6] The higher price points may not get attention from the younger customers, but they still keep the younger generations interested with their staple products and private label lines; especially the exclusive line for the sports team "fan gear".[11] With the economic decline in America, private labels are a strong growth area with increased margins to further acquire. Worldwide private labels are known to be a strategic advantage to increase profits over the competition. By doing so, Foot Locker, Inc. has now focused on using private labels directly from manufacturers so shoppers will then be more willing to purchase since they are lower in price than name brand products. Around the world this concept is a growing success to keep up with the competition of specialty retailers such as mass-merchandisers who discount name brands that regular price merchants carry.

In light of the recent economic crisis and the corporation's debt they have used cost effective business strategies to keep their business growing into the future. In 2007, Foot Locker, Inc. closed 275 underperforming stores. In 2008, the company reduced its store count by approximately 145 locations across five of their different chains. Their reasoning behind this was to boost profitability by focusing on its more lucrative stores and making their operations more efficient. The company has been more cautious in opening new stores, and for 2009, their budget allowed them to open approximately 25 new stores. The corporation has also taken measures to reduce inventory by focusing on product selection that is more directly related to consumer demands.[18]

Foot Locker, Inc. understands that to succeed in retail, they need to learn their customer's needs and wants, then find ways to meet them. They position themselves as an authority for the core of their target customers athletic footwear and apparel needs, and market through clear and concise messages in a multitude of mediums. They also hold great responsibility and value to their logistics by making sure their channels of distribution satisfy the consumers in every way. With such a diverse operation, Foot Locker, Inc. is a true success in reaching out to as many demographics on a personal level as possible. They aim to make each customer feel that they are getting exceptional customer service no matter where they are located around the globe, which is a technique that has proven successful.[11]

## Expansion Strategy

While Foot Locker, Inc. has earned their name as the biggest retailer in athletic shoes and apparel, they still have huge potential for growth. Foot Locker, Inc. currently operates in 22 countries and is intrested in  expanding in other markets that they have not currently yet reached. Until recently, Foot Locker, Inc. expanded through organic growth, but began franchising with companies recently in the Middle East in 2006 and South Korea in 2007. The use of franchising in the Middle East is driven by government regulations. It is possible that this trend will continue if they are not sure how to enter other markets, but as for now, organic growth seems to be the preferable choice of expansion. However, there are still plenty of growth opportunities in other markets that have already entered, and Foot Locker, Inc. plans to capitalize on these opportunities.

## North America

In the United States, Foot Locker, Inc has managed to tap into nearly every major market in all 50 states across the country. Expansion outside of the country started long before the market was saturated such as the corporation entering Canada in 1978.[22] Foot Locker, Inc. has continued to find areas in which they can expand both domestically and abroad. They are primarily located within mall settings, but also have a number of stand-alone stores. Foot Locker, Inc. plans to expand into more urban markets with their stand-alone stores since the costs are lower than that of a mall, which will help reinforce their brands and increase profit margins. Continuing with their expansion outlooks, Foot Locker, Inc. also seeks to open stores in the Canadian Provinces in which they currently have a small presence or no presence at all. The majority of Canadian Foot Locker, Inc. stores, are located in nine provinces, primarily in major cities and malls.

## Europe

Foot Locker, Inc's presence in the European market is already very strong, but those heading the company believe that there is still much to gain from these consumers and they plan to capitalize on this in the near future. Part of the reason for this is that Foot Locker, Inc. has an understanding of the latest trends, and this will be effective in Europe due to their superb sense of fashion. Killick Datta, the chairman and CEO of Global Brand Marketing, Inc. said, "Europe has always been more fashion-oriented than the U.S."[2]

The Europeans' sense of fashion allows Foot Locker, Inc. to continue finding ways to grow in the market and maintain its position as one of the most fashion-forward and trend-setting, athletic apparel retailers in the world. To this point, European franchises have been successful due to Foot Locker, Inc's specialty format, which differentiates itself from the rest of the market. The European athletic footwear retail market is highly fragmented and has a high demand for U.S. name brands, such as Nike. In an attempt to make the most of their opportunities in Europe, Foot Locker, Inc. created a Dutch distribution center in 1998.[29]

In 2004, Foot Locker, Inc. continued their expansion strategy into Ireland by purchasing eleven stores from an Irish retailer, Champion Sports Group, through a wholly-owned subsidiary and planned to convert them to the Foot Locker name by the end of the same year. The motivation behind this was the location of all the stores being in highly trafficked areas surrounding Dublin.[29]

The competition in Europe has caused Foot Locker, Inc. to focus on reworking their business strategies in order to stay in the forefront of consumers' minds. Chairman, President, and CEO Matt Serra said that there was "More competition there, more vendor stores. And you have certain countries that have become promotional. That is clearly our No. 1 priority- to get [that business] back on track."[30] So often, competition plays a huge role in a company's decision to look for opportunities in other countries. Even though Europe has been a great success for Foot Locker, Inc., they will continue to enhance their offerings to keep up with the changing demographics. However, in order to stay ahead of the competition, Foot Locker, Inc. may need to move into a different segment that they have not reached yet, such as Asia.

## Asia

The Asian market is one that, although interested, Foot Locker, Inc. has not tapped into yet (other than South Korea, which they recently entered). When speaking on the expansion into Asia, China specifically, Foot Locker, Inc.'s Matt Serra said, "I made a trip there [to examine our options], and I [couldn't] figure out how to make a profit. Generally, you need a partner to do [business there] and we may go that route. I'm sure we will be in Asia – it's just a question of time."[30] Serra's reference to having a partner in order to enter Asia shows a direct connection to the possibility of having to form an alliance. Due to Foot Locker, Inc. being so successful in other markets, they may benefit from a non-equity alliance because they will not need to form a new company or have others invest in the company.[25] Instead, they will just need a partner that understands the Asian demographic and the way they can best reach consumers.

Once Foot Locker, Inc. does finally enter Asia, the results should be very beneficial. This would be due to the continued increased interest in sports in China and other major Asian markets. Basketball and the National Basketball Association (NBA) have continued to grow in popularity (especially with Yao Ming and Kobe Bryant being two of the most recognized figures in the country).[3] Soccer is another sport in which the Chinese take a special interest. Just as the way the World Cup spikes sales for Foot Locker, Inc., the excitement of these sports should give the same results.[30] By specializing in sports apparel and having very little need to alter their products offered, it seems that Foot Locker, Inc. should find success in China.

## Middle East & South Korea (Most Recent Entries)

In 2006, Foot Locker, Inc. completed a franchising deal that helped move them into the Middle Eastern market. They entered Kuwait by teaming up with M.H. Alshaya Co., one of the leading names in Middle East international franchising.[21] They were also able to reach South Korea due to a 10 year agreement with another company that allowed them to open Foot Locker, Inc. stores there.[1] As of May 2009, Foot Locker, Inc. now has 19 franchised stores in the Middle East and South Korea combined.[13]

Risk management would explain the need for franchising in the Middle East more than any other countries that Foot Locker, Inc. occupies. The Middle East's culture is much different than that of North America, Europe, or Australia (all of which are similar markets); so allowing another entity that is more familiar with the customs of the host country to help Foot Locker, Inc. transition effectively would be in their best interest.

It is evident that the Middle East was not approached earlier since one issue faced was the risk of boycott against U.S. brands during the war in Iraq. However, now that the Middle East is a destination of viable long-term potential in retail considering their growth in consumer spending, which is one of the highest in the world. Dubai will most likely be a candidate in near future expansion since it is one of the most westernized places in the Middle East. They also have no income tax, which results in consumers having a greater disposable income.[4]

It is clear that Foot Locker, Inc. still has many options when it comes to their international expansion. The Asian market seems to be the next target market, but until they are in a position to be successful there, they still have several options in Europe that they can consider. They may also be able to extend their brand even further than expected if success is found in franchising, which is relatively new to the company. Being global, Foot Locker, Inc. will expand to world-class cities by not altering their format and keeping a low-risk, new-market entry strategy that requires little capital.[25] There are still many untapped areas across the world and if past success has proven anything, the appeal of sports apparel will thrive almost anywhere.

## Conclusion

Since the opening of its first store in 1974, Foot Locker has become a retail conglomerate. They have expanded internationally at a very rapid pace and continue to open more stores around the world solidifying their number one status in the athletic apparel sector. If Foot Locker continues to maintain their expansion and its incredible knack for keeping in tune with their market, they should have no problem succeeding through the tough economic times we are currently facing and well into the future.

## Questions

**1. Is the retailer classified as a global retailer or a multinational retailer? Explain its pattern of expansion. What expansion strategy did/is the retailer use/using?**

*Foot Locker is a global retailer that has centralized management and their own private label shoe and apparel merchandise. They choose "world class cities where they expect to find a segment of consumers who are indistinguishable throughout the world." They keep the same format no matter where they expand.[27]*

**2. Based on Dunning's eclectic theory, how do ownership, locational and internalization factors play in your retailers' international expansion?**

*Foot Locker has a major ownership advantage because not only do they have national brand name products, they also have their own private label brand. Their product category, which consists of athletic footwear, apparel and accessories, and a focused assortment of equipment, "allows them to differentiate itself from other mall-based stores by presenting complete product assortments in a select number of sporting activities".[14] They use the national brand names to draw in consumers, and then the consumer is exposed to the private label brand as well. Also, because of their centralized buying and management systems, they have an excellent transaction based ownership advantage.*

*It is very important for Foot Locker to have a locational advantage. Because they are mainly positioned in mall-based areas, which are located in high traffic cities, it is crucial for them to obtain the best locations before other competitors enter the area. Since Foot Locker is a global retailer, they have participated in franchising of their stores. This is a risky idea since the information could be leaked from the company, but thus far Foot Locker has maintained a strong transaction based ownership advantage.*

**3. What role does cultural proximity and geographical proximity play in the retailers' international moves?**

*Since Foot Locker is a global retailer, cultural and geographical proximity do not play a major role. Foot Locker maintains the same store format, management, and strategies at all locations, but they have taken some risk management actions by franchising in the Middle East and South Korea.[13]*

**4. Can you predict the retailers' future international expansion?**

*Although the future for Foot Locker is still to be determined, they have huge potential for growth. They have proven internationally successful, but the decrease in their profits poses a serious threat in future success. Organic growth and franchising offer opportunities for Foot Locker Inc. to prosper, especially in Asian markets.*

## Propositions

**P1: The greater the ownership advantages for retailers, the less likely they will franchise or license.**

*True. Since Foot Locker holds many ownership advantages, both asset-based with their private label merchandise and patents; and transaction-based with their centralized management and customer service, they are difficult to replicate and keep their strategies internal.*

**P2: The greater the available organizational slack, the greater the likelihood of expanding internationally.**

*True. The ratios of current assets to current liabilities increase year to year. This means the company has excess resources that can be used in a discretionary manner. The earliest dated balance sheet recorded ratios of current assets to current liabilities, from 1995 to 1997 include:*

1995:  2,069,000 : 1,710,000 = 1.21
1996:  1,618,000 : 841,000 = 1.92
1997:  1,823,000 : 856,000 = 2.13

*As these ratios increase from year to year, so does Foot Locker's amount of rapid international expansion, supporting the hypothesis.*

**P3: The greater the recoverable slack, the greater the likelihood of expanding internationally.**

*False. The earliest documented general and administrative expenses and sales on the annual income statement are from 1994. General and administrative expenses have fluctuated from year to year. The sales have also fluctuated from year to year. The ratios of general and administrative expenses to sales from 1994 through 1996 are, respectively:*

1994:  2,037,000 : 7,820,000 = .261
1995:  1,166,000 : 4,484,000 = .260
1996:  1,025,000 : 4,383,000 = .233

*Although the information found is not consistent, based on the data gathered, we estimate that the ratios would continue to decrease from year to year. This does not support the proposition.*

**P4: The greater the potential slack, the greater the likelihood of expanding internationally.**

*True. The proposition is supported because the most current ratios of equity to capital, from 1995 to 1997, increase year to year as follows:*

$$359,000 : 1,358,000 = .26$$
$$777,000 : 1,229,000 = .63$$
$$967,000 : 1,334,000 = .72$$

*As these ratios increase from year to year, so does Foot Lockers amount of rapid international expansion, supporting the proposition.*

**P13: Global companies will move to the largest capital/cities in a country**

*True. Global retailers begin their internationalization not to countries, but to world-class cities where they expect to find a segment of consumers who are indistinguishable throughout the world. Since their consumer is basically the same wherever they go they do not need to change their offering.*

**P14: Global companies will not be attracted by population size, income, cultural proximity/ or geographical proximity.**

*True. Mass retailers are more concerned with cultural proximity than the global retailers who use their own retail concept that involve a narrowly defined consumer market that are similar in various countries. Geographical proximity is more important for retailers who sell private labels that are produced in a central location and is less important for decentralized companies who operate as independent units and usually source from within the country. Multinational retailers concentrate their expansion within a geographic area, filling that area before moving to a new country or region. As well as population size and income, global retailers enter a global market segment that will accept their retail offering without much change. Therefore, they enter cities with similar segments of upper income consumers, normally large populated world-class cities.*

**P15: The greater the asset based ownership advantages of a global retailer the more likely they are to franchise.**

*True. Global retailers generally have significant asset-based ownership advantages since most do focus on their private label, which is an asset for international expansion. Since the private label is transportable it can easily be expanded internationally. Companies that do have significant ownership advantages do not want to give away their secrets, so they prefer to use wholly owned subsidiaries to* allow them to contain their secrets. Footlocker has done this in most countries. The major exception is the Middle East where governments generally do not alow wholely owned retail investments.

**P16: The greater the transaction based ownership advantages of a global retailer, the less likely they are to franchise.**

*True. Foot Locker is a global company and has a standard format within all of its stores, their buying is centralized and their tactic knowledge of how the store runs is the same in every location. Their diverse customer base and ability to reach many target markets is not easy to reproduce by competitors. Foot Locker, Inc. does not franchise frequently but with their experience and success of international expansion their transaction-based ownership advantage would allow for successful franchising options that could not be duplicated, if they did choose to take this route.*

**P17: The greater the available organizational slack the greater the likelihood that global retailers will reacquire international franchisees.**

*True. The ratios of current assets to current liabilities increase year to year. This means the company has excess resources that can be used in a discretionary manner. The earliest dated balance sheet recorded ratios of current assets to current liabilities, from 1995 to 1997 include:*

2,069,000 : 1,710,000 = 1.21
1,618,000 : 841,000 = 1.92
1,823,000 : 856,000 = 2.13

*These numbers support that of the hypothesis, although Foot Locker, Inc. does not follow the franchise format of expansion for the majority of its locations, it therefore does not have franchisers available to re-purchase and re-acquire.*

**P18: The greater the recoverable slack, the greater the likelihood that global retailers will reacquire international franchisees.**

*True. Selling General and Administrative Expenses to Sales for the years 2007-2009 are as follows.*

1,163,000 : 5,750,000 = .20
1,176,000 : 5,437,000 = .216
1,174,000 : 5,237,000 = .22

*The recoverable slack for the company has increased; therefore if their expenses continue to decrease into the next year, there is a greater likelihood that they will re-acquire international franchises.*

**P19: The greater the potential slack, the greater the likelihood that global retailers will reacquire international franchisees.**

*False. The ratios for Total equity to Total assets from the years 2007-2009 are as follows*

2,295,000 : 3,249,000 = .71
2,271,000 : 3,248,000 = .70
1,924,000 : 2,877,000 = .67

*The potential slack of the company has decreased. Therefore there is a less of a chance that they will reacquire international franchisees, not supporting the hypothesis.*

## Endnotes

1.  (2008, December 10). *Form 10-Q for Foot Locker Inc.* Retrieved November 15, 2009, from http://biz.yahoo.com/e/081210/fl10-q.html

2.  Abe, K., Zmuda, N., & Scardino, E. (Feb 20, 2006). TOP FOOTWEAR EXECUTIVES TOUT GLOBAL GROWTH PLANS. Footwear News, p.12.     Retrieved November 15, 2009, from General OneFile via Gale: http://find.galegroup.com.proxy2.cl.msu.edu/gps/start.do?prodId=IPS&userGroupName=msu_main

3.  Balfour, F. (Oct 24, 2007). A Slam Dunk for the NBA in China; Along with eager sponsors and partners, the league looks to capitalize further on its mainland popularity with a recent exhibition tour and other initiatives. Business Week Online, p.NA. Retrieved November 15, 2009, from General OneFile via Gale: http://find.galegroup.com.proxy2.cl.msu.edu/gps/startdo?prodId=IPS&userGroupName=msu_maintgps

4.  Bhatnagar, P. (2006, February 8). Borders, Liz Claiborne, Foot Locker keen on Middle East - Feb. 8, 2006. Business, financial, personal finance news - CNNMoney.com. Retrieved November 17, 2009, from http://money.cnn.com/2006/02/08/news/international/middleeast_retailing/index.htm

5.  Brands | Jordan, Nike, adidas, Under Armour, Converse, Timberland, Puma. (n.d.). Basketball Shoes - Jordan Shoes - Running Shoes | Foot Locker. Retrieved November 4, 2009, from http://www.FootLocker.com/brands/category

6.  Butler, E. (2005, December 19). Foot Locker steps up; Seeks to lure women, men

without losing teenage boys; foreign stores hit pricey wall.(News). Crain's New York Business, News, 3. Retrieved November 15, 2009, from http://findarticles. com/p/articles

7.  Consumer Connections | Collective Brands, Inc.. (n.d.). Collective Brands, Inc.. Retrieved November 4, 2009, from http://www.collectivebrands.com/brands

8.  Emily Scardino. (2004, May). Foot Locker acquires Footaction Stores to step up growth. DSN Retailing Today, 43(9), 4-5+. Retrieved November 15, 2009, from ABI/INFORM Global. (Document ID: 638934571)

9.  Foot Locker, Inc. (FL) Company Profile | Stocks | Reuters.com. (n.d.). Reuters. com - World News, Financial News, Breaking US & International News. Retrieved November 4, 2009, from http://www.reuters.com/finance/stocks/ companyProfile?symbol=FL

10. Foot Locker, Inc.. Cross Country Championship. Foot Locker, Inc.. Retrieved November 10, 2009, from http://www.FootLockercc.com/

11. Foot Locker, Inc.. (n.d.). Foot Locker, Inc.. Retrieved November 6, 2009, from http://www.Foot Locker-inc.com/index.cfm

12. Foot Locker, Inc.. (n.d.). Foot Locker, Inc.. Retrieved November 6, 2009, from http://www.Foot Lockerinc.com/company.cfm?page=about

13. Foot Locker Inc.. (n.d). Foot Locker, Inc. Retrieved November 15, 2009. http:// www.Foot Locker-inc.com/company.cfm?page=lady-foot-locker

14. FOOT LOCKER INC, Disclosure SEC Database, October 27, 2009. Lexis Nexis. Michigan State University. 4 Nov. 2009 < http://www.lexisnexis. com.proxy2.cl.msu.edu/us/lnacademic/results/docview/docview. do?docLinkInd=true&risb=21_T7791273145&format=GNBFI&sort=RELEVAN CE&startDocNo=1&resultsUrlKey=29_T7791272259&cisb=22_T7791273159&t reeMax=true&treeWidth=0&csi=3723&docNo=22>

15. Foot Locker, Incorporated Annual Report -- 2002. (2002, January). America's Corporate Foundation,0_1,0_2,1-54. Retrieved October 30, 2009, from ProQuest Historical Annual Reports. (Document ID: 1034103512).

16. Foot Locker (FL). (n.d.). Investing Wiki with Research about Companies, Investment Concepts, and more.... Retrieved November 4, 2009, from http:// www.wikinvest.com/stock/Foot_Locker_(FL)

17. Foot Locker, Inc. (1 November). Hoover's Company Records,10538. Retrieved November 15, 2009, from Hoover's Company Records. (Document ID: 168155881).

18. Foot Locker, Inc. (15 October). Hoover's Company Records,10538. Retrieved

October 30, 2009, from Hoover's Company Records. (Document ID: 168155881).

19. Foot Locker Inc. (NYS: FL)." Mergent Online. 15 November 2009. http://www.
    mergentonline.com.proxy2.cl.msu.edu/compdetail.asp?company=59526&type=c
    ompdetail

20. Foot Locker, Inc.. FundingUniverse. http://www.fundinguniverse.com/company-
    histories/Foot-Locker-Inc-Company-History.html

21. Frazier, Mya. (Dec 15, 2008). Brand Channel. *M.H. Alsyhaya Co.: Paving the
    Way in Emerging Markets*. Retrieved November 17, 2009, from: http://www.
    brandchannel.com/features_effect.asp?pf_id=454

22. Global Markets Direct - History. Lexisnexis academic. Retrieved (2009,
    November 3)from http://www.lexisnexis.com.proxy1.cl.msu.edu/us/lnacademic/
    mungo/docEP.do?twi=0&format=GNBFI&cmdfmt=prthex&risb=21_T78988924
    99&docNo=1&cmd=2E43463B474D44434F4D3B444F432D49442823323933383
    84849535423293B2E4655

23. Ryan, T.. (2008, November). Foot Locker's Aggressive Move into
    Skate. SGB, 41(11), 10. Retrieved November 15, 2009, from ABI/INFORM
    Global. (Document ID: 1599530061).

24. Ryan, T.. (2008, April). Junior Achievement. SGB, 41(4), 6-7. Retrieved
    November 15, 2009, from ABI/INFORM Global. (Document ID: 1468850191).

25. Sternquist, B. (2007). Licensing, Franchising, and Strategic Alliances.
    International Retailing (Second ed., pp. 139, 149). New York: Fairchild Books &
    Visuals.

26. Sternquist, B. (2007). Location Factors. International Retailing (Second ed., pp.
    70). New York: Fairchild Books & Visuals.

27. Sternquist, Brenda. Sire2 International Retailing. (Second ed. Pp. 42-47). New
    York: Fairchild Books & Visuals.

28. Sternquist, B. (2007). Retailing in the United Kingdom, the Netherlands, and
    Belgium. International Retailing (Second ed., pp. 285). New York: Fairchild
    Books & Visuals

29. SEC, (2001). Foot locker inc. - s-3/a (SEC File 333-64930 ). Washington, DC:
    Securities and Exchange Commission. Retrieved from http://www.secinfo.com/
    dsVsj.4f8Rk.htm

30. Serra's Priorities: Revive Europe Biz, Expand U.S. Share. (June 19,
    2006). Footwear News, p.1. Retrieved November 15, 2009, from General
    OneFile via Gale: http://find.galegroup.com.proxy2.cl.msu.edu/gps/start.
    do?prodId=IPS&userGroupName=msu_main

# GAP, Inc.

*Lesley Giffels, Heidi Lont, Kim Mahoney, Veronica Perez, Monica Sachdev*

## Gap, Inc.

The introduction of Gap Inc. in 1969 led to an amazing triumph in the retailing world. Now operating more than 3,150 stores in several different countries, GAP has evolved into a major specialty retail company. Well known for its jeans in 1969, it now carries casual apparel, accessories, and personal care products for men, women and children. Countless changes have occurred in the past 29 years in order for Gap to succeed. Through the ups and downs, Gap has learned the ropes of expanding both nationally and internationally.

Throughout this case study, we will inform you of the history of Gap and help depict the reasons why they are located in the places they are in today. Not everything they have done has been correct. Some business decisions Gap made have failed while others have flourished. By learning from their mistakes Gap continues to thrive as a global retailer in more than six different countries.

Starting in the United Kingdom in 1987, and ending in the Middle East in 2008, this case study will explain the reasons for converting from wholly owned subsidiaries to franchises. Hold onto your seats because you are in for a ride that has many ups, downs, and turns in the business.

# FLOW CHART

| | |
|---|---|
| 1987: | UK (132 Stores) |
| 1989: | Canada (187 Stores) |
| 1993: | France (38 Stores) |
| 1996: | Japan (136 Stores) |
| 2006: | United Arab Emirates |
| | Bahrain |
| | Indonesia |
| | Kuwait |
| | Qatar |
| | South Korea |
| | Oman |
| | Malaysia (4) |
| | Singapore (3) |
| 2007: | Turkey (1 Store) |
| | Philippines |
| | Saudi Arabia |
| | Greece |
| | Romania |
| | Bulgaria |
| | Cyprus |
| | Croatia |
| 2008: | Egypt |
| | Jordan |
| | Russia (1 Store) |
| 2009: | Mexico |

Expansion into other countries from 2006 on is entirely through franchising. As of February 2008 there were a total of 100 franchise stores located in these foreign countries.

Per Gap Inc. Store Count as of August 2, 2008

# INTERNATIONAL ENTRY STRATEGY

| Entry Time | Entry Location | Entry Mode |
|---|---|---|
| 1987 | United Kingdom | Store |
| 1989 | Canada | Store |
| 1993 | France | Joint Venture |
| 1996 | Japan | Flagship |
| 1997 | Online | Online |
| 2006 | Middle East Southeast Asia | Franchise |
| 2007 | United Arab, Emirates Bahrain Indonesia Kuwait Qatar Korea Oman Turkey Philippines Riyadh Saudi | Franchise |
| 2008 | Russia | Franchise |
| 2009 | Mexico | Store within a store |

## Case Study

With the tremendous sales that GAP has gained in the United States, it has enabled them to expand into many different countries. These countries consist of the United Kingdom, Canada, Germany, France and Japan. Although a profound amount of their profits are from domestic sales, approximately 10% comes from their international stores.[1]

## The United States

In 1969, Dori and Don Fisher introduced Gap Inc. to America by opening the first store in San Francisco, California. The Fishers wanted a store where jeans could be easily accessible in all different sizes and styles. A year after the first store opened, sales exceeded two million dollars. This success transferred to the second store that opened in San Jose, California.[1]

Gap Inc. had been very successful until 1976 when it took a turn. "The blue jeans craze, which had propelled the growth of Gap stores, had been slowing for years as the chain's biggest customers, the baby-boomers, were leaving their teen-age years - and their blue jeans - behind."[2] Competition picked up as department and specialty stores were taking some of the market share. Gap needed a new direction, and they needed it fast. With new stores entering the market, Gap needed to come up with a plan.

In 1983, Gap Inc. took a new route. The first thing needed was to revamp the clothing line in order to attract the former shoppers who once made up Gap's biggest customer group. With the new clothing line came along a new store image. A total of 500 stores across the United States were remodeled to fit the new look. Management became centralized in San Bruno, California. Gap recorded net income of $480.9 million in that year. With all the success customers were anticipating what was going to come next from the growing retailer. In that same year, Gap launched their new brand, Banana Republic and opened 5 new stores in the United States.[1] In 1986, Gap further expanded their private label brand with the launch of Gap Kids. In one year a total of nine stores were opened. By 1987, Gap Kids alone made $10 million in sales. "Between 1984 and 1987, Gap's sales compounded at 20% annually, and EPS grew 73% on a compounded annual basis in the same three-year period."[4] By the end of 1985, their hopes were to expand to 1000 stores in the United States. In 1987, Gap expanded internationally in the United Kingdom. In between 1990 and 1994, Gap surprised the world once again, embarking on two more private label brands; Baby Gap and Old Navy.[2]

More recently, Gap has been struggling to find their identity. With the growing competition in the market, they have been trying not to drown in sales yet it seems to be inevitable. "Gap faces the heat from brands like Abercrombie & Fitch, J Crew, American Eagle Outfitters, as well as Target and revitalized department stores like JC Penney and Kohl's."[2] Gap has been trying to reduce the square footage for their current stores, utilize space effectively, and remodel in order to cut costs. However, growing internationally has become fundamental for the company to sustain their net sales growth.

## United Kingdom

In 1987 Gap Inc. acted on their previous consideration and entered the market in the United Kingdom. Their overseas push came in order to increase sales and to gain market share before their competitors could. Although they had not saturated their home market, it was important for the company to expand internationally before their competitors. They wanted to expand internationally in order to attract customers without changing their concept. Gap decided to expand internationally as a global retailer. The strategy that global retailers follow is to pick not just a country, but "…world class cities where they expect to find a segment of consumers who are indistinguishable throughout the world."[1] London offered Gap just what they were looking for. In just one year, Gap broke one billion dollars in sales bringing in approximately $1.1 billion.[4] This was just the beginning of the expansion overseas.

Gap entered the United Kingdom as a wholly owned subsidiary. By definition, "The manufacturer sets up a facility in the foreign country, produces the product and sells the product there."[1] With the weakening of sales, Gap realized how costly it is to own their own stores. Recently, to increase revenue, Gap is attempting to enter new markets in the Middle East and Southeast Asia as a franchise. This will be addressed later in this study.

During the first few years Gap was in the United Kingdom, sales kept climbing up the charts. "…in the mid-Eighties one of the great sartorial questions was why, exactly, it was so difficult to buy a perfectly plain white T-shirt? One that fitted well, worked hard and neither looked like a man's vest nor a fan-club offering from Cliff Richard. So when Gap opened up on the British high street in 1987, it was a 'yes' moment."[2] Today, however, new specialty stores such as Zara, Mango, and H&M have been taking over sales. How are they doing this? "There's a four-letter word beginning with F that Gap has never understood. The word is 'fast' and Zara has based its entire business model around getting looks from the drawing board to the store in a reported fortnight (two weeks), bringing in quick and cost-effective catwalk interpretations that have even alarmed the luxury brands."[8]

With the rapid expansion in the overseas market, Gap wanted to conquer another country where they could grow. In 1989, Gap entered the Canadian market in Vancouver, British Columbia.

## Canada

Expanding into Canada for Gap appears to be the most logical for international expansion as it shares a common border with the U.S. and along with sharing common cultural values. According to World Bank (2008), Canada is ranked as the number two best country in the world to start a business and number 8 in regards to overall ease of doing business.[1] Gap opened its first Canadian store in 1989. In 1995, it opened up its first Banana Republic Store. In 2001 it opened up its first Old Navy Store. As of 2008, they have 90 Gap stores, 32 Banana Republic stores and 60 Old Navy stores.

According to the Statistics Canada (2008), retail clothing sales in Canada are increasing at an average rate of 5.8% over the last five years.[2] Of total Gap sales in 2008, Canada accounted for 6.2%, for a total amount of $972 million. This represents an increase of 3.4% over 2007.[3] Of the total sales, Old Navy represents the largest share of Canadian sales at 47.4% ($461 million) of the total, followed by Gap with 37% ($364 million) and Banana Republic with 15% ($147 million).

On October 23, 2008 Gap opened its first Banana Republic Factory Store and Gap Factory Store in Canada. "The openings will expand the accessibility of Gap Inc. brands, while reaching new value conscious customers in the Canadian market."[11]

## Clothing Stores Retail Sales in Millions

| Year | Sales | % Change |
|---|---|---|
| 2003 | $14,567.1 | - |
| 2004 | $15,311.6 | 5.11% |
| 2005 | $16,069.3 | 4.95% |
| 2006 | $17,226.6 | 7.2% |
| 2007 | $18,247.5 | 5.93% |
| Average | $16,284.4 | 5.8% |

Canada's National Statistical Agency, 2008[11]

Net Sales
For the 52 Weeks ending February 2, 2008

| | Gap | Old Navy | Banana Republic | Other | Total | Change % |
|---|---|---|---|---|---|---|
| U.S. | $ 4,146 | $5,776 | $2,351 | $ - | | |
| Online | 308 | 428 | 136 | 31 | 903 | 5.73% |

| | | | | | |
|---|---|---|---|---|---|
| Canada | 364 | 461 | 147 | | 972 | 6.17% |
| Europe | 822 | | | 5 | 827 | 5.25% |
| Asia | 613 | | 89 | 36 | 738 | 4.68% |
| Other | | | | 50 | 50 | 0.32% |
| Total | $6,253 | $ 6,665 | $2,723 | $122 | | 100% |

**Euromonitor International (2008)**[10]

| Country | Ease of Doing Business | Starting a Business |
|---|---|---|
| Canada | 8 | 2 |
| Germany | 25 | 102 |
| France | 31 | 14 |
| Japan | 12 | 64 |

**Germany**

Gap entered the German retail market in 1996 in furtherance of its global expansion policy. Gap Inc. focused on expanding globally into five international markets, including Germany.[1] This international retail market represented a $500 billion market, and was therefore the focus of a new expansion project initiated by Gap Inc.[2]

Over the next eight years, Gap would unsuccessfully operate in Germany. The German retail market housed only ten stores, representing less than 1% of Gap Inc.'s sales overall.[3] In March 2001, Gap Inc. sales began to decrease immensely. Gap executives began cutting international store growth to 20-25% from 41% the previous year. These cuts included removing Gap stores from Germany completely.[15]

On August 1, 2004, Gap Inc. sold their ten German based stores to retail giant Hennes & Mauritz, otherwise known as the Switzerland based, fast-fashion retail store, H&M. The terms of the transaction were not released, nor were the losses incurred by Gap. Analysts believe that Gap Inc. failed in Germany for several reasons. First of all, merchandise was priced too high. The average German shopper is very price conscious.[13] Also, Gap's international merchandise standardization policy didn't fit in with the German consumer. Gap's blue shirt and khaki policy did not fit German consumers. Gap's failure in Germany extends as far as the country's borders considering Gap is immensely successful in other international markets.[13]

## France

In 1993, Gap entered France opening a shop within a shop in Galleries Lafayette department store. The expansion into Paris came from the successful response of increased sales throughout their retail stores in England and Wales. "France has one of the oldest and most diverse retail networks,"[1] allowing Gap to hold on to its strong identity as a specialty retailer, selling private label goods in the French market. The progress made within France was astounding, enabling the company to increase its current international expansion to open and operate 38 stores throughout France. Currently, sales in Europe account for about 5% of the US clothing retailer's revenues.[2] The popularity of the Gap brand sparked the French consumer because of its high style and affordability. The stylish assortment of clothing has The British Vogue regularly praising this great American store for its strong influential and trendy collections. A new concept was developed by collaborating with French designer Roland Mouret that has given Gap the opportunity to sell exclusive dresses in its stores in the UK and France.

## Japan

Gap established in 1969, has been interested in the Japanese market since the 1980's. The clothing chain made a full scale entry into the market September 1995 with an outlet in the Hankyu Department Store in Tokyo's Ginza.[1] Japan was an extremely significant step for Gap because it transformed advertising campaigns to be focused on individual style and uniqueness. In regards to Gap's later entry into Japan, executives have commented that they wanted to establish confidence that they could operate in the international market before entering Japan.[18] The expansion into Japan was very smooth, compared to what foreign firms expected out of the venture. Gap was told many times to go into Japan with a partner to establish relationships more easily and quicker, but opted not to in the end.[18] In 2005, Gap celebrated its tenth year in Japan. Gap made a spacific "Japan only" collection for Japanese stores. It was composed of their ten best selling and most iconic pieces. The result was a distinctive look at individual style and expression, one of the Gap's important goals to achieve in Japan.

Company executives expressed how they have been looking for other international markets in coming years. The Singapore and Malaysia outlets will be Gap's first franchise stores anywhere in the world. Gap's international operation has been struggling in recent years. They have been searching for ways to overcome their declining sales by launching different marketing operations to respond to changing consumer trends.[2]

Laws in Japan have restricted the Gap's store growth. The Large-Scale Retail Store law restricts retailers to determine the amount of floor space for their own stores.[18] Company executives feel that expanding into more flexible markets is important in order to establish a foothold. The major obstacle that Gap has encountered while in Japan has not been different consumer trends or their success, but space limitations. The company has established many relationships with major department stores, becoming quite successful in Japan, due to consumer trends toward casual clothing.[18]

## Middle East

Gap entered the Middle East in April of 2006. After disappointing sales declines and changes in executive positions, Gap expanded their international expansion strategy.[1] Through a franchise agreement with a Dubai based business group, Al Tayer, 25 new Gap stores and 10 Banana Republic will be created by 2010.[2] There are five key markets Gap hoped to infiltrate, including United Arab Emirates, Kuwait, Qatar, Bahrain, and Oman.[22]

Stores opened in The Middle Eastern retail markets were specifically targeted because of the young and very affluent cliental.[3] The format of the store and merchandise will remain the same. However, by teaming up with local retailers, Gap cut costs to reduce risk.[22]

## South East Asia

Gap continued their new international expansion strategy by opening stores in Southeast Asia. By 2010, Gap hopes to open 50 new stores in Malaysia, Singapore and Indonesia.[1] The first Gap store was opened in Southeast Asia in 2006. Following this, a new Banana Republic store opened in 2007.[2] Gap is focused on this region because of the popularity of fast fashion. Gap can cater to Singaporean's affordable and casual chic clothing.[3]

Gap teams up with local franchisees in order to reduce overseas risk. In Southeast Asia, Gap teamed up with FJ Benjamin, a local fast fashions retailer. FJ Benjamin will have exclusive rights to Gap Inc. and is one of their first franchisees.[27]

Currently, there are only 12 Gap stores across Southeast Asia. FJ Benjamin and Gap have high hopes for their expansion plan, and hope to see increases in sales over the next two years.[25]

## Mexico

As Gap's international expansion continues to grow, its latest development is to move into Mexico, which is known for being the 10th largest apparel market in the world.[1] The Gap has franchise agreements to open new stores in Mexico through a partnership with an experienced and well known department store Distribuidora Liverpool SA.[2] By entering Mexico, the Gap has expanded into 21 countries and 100 stores, which is a valuable achievement for the company.[28]

## Russia

Gap is not currently an active retailer in Russia, but plans to open its first stores there. The first Gap store will be opened in Fiba, Russia.[1] Gap knows that it will have to compete with well-established brands such as Benetton, Zara and Lee & Wrangler.[30] Russia has a very saturated fashion market already, which makes the opening a bit more difficult than in other countries that are less-developed. Gap, which is a global retailer, might have to re-tailor some of their styles and trends to fit and suit locals' taste. This calls for more competitive marketing advertisements as well as in-depth research into the minds of consumers.

## Online Retailing

Gap Inc. opened its first online store in 1997. Banana Republic and Old Navy followed into the online world by learning from Gap and its rapid success. With Piperlime.com, Gap will stake its claim in the online shoe business worth nearly $3 billion.[1] The Gap re-launched its website in 2000 to give customers an enhanced and more effective online shopping experience. Since the relaunch, sales for Gap Direct have grown from $595 million in 2005 to $903 million in 2007.[2] Along with the launching of their companies' websites, The Gap Inc. has launched its first online-only brand called Piperlime in 2006.[3]

The Gap Inc. not only has had success that has been visible to customers throughout the globe, but was rewarded with a WebAward by the Web Marketing Association. Web Awards are produced by the Web Marketing Association to honor excellence in online advertising, recognize the individuals and organizations responsible, and showcase the award winning internet advertising. Gap was recognized for their excellence in structure and online advertising in 2005. This came with challenges though, says president of Gap Direct Toby Lenk. He emphasized during a conference in 2007 that with the rise of the Web comes a number of new challenges, "all which serve to empower the consumer which potentially diluting the brand."[1] Gap took this as an opportunity to expand and strengthen its brand by creating Piperlime.

Piperlime.com is Gap's online shoe store providing customers with convenience, excellent customer service and variety. One thing that separates Piperlime from other online shoe stores is their free standard delivery, which alone has attracted many more customers. Gap Direct made sure to incorporate their own labels with 200 other labels available.[1] This is significant because it limits the number of selected brands to sell so customers don't get lost on the website. Another aspect that differentiates Piperlime from competing online shoe stores is their 60 day return policy. The Gap Inc. predicted when launching the store that their loyal customer base would help it become successful business venture for the company.[31] Since its opening, Piperlime has also added a new feature of handbags to its site. At this time, the Gap plans on keeping Piperlime only an online business with no intention to launch it into another bricks and mortar store.

Aside from Piperlime, Gap has recently added a new function to their website. It is called "universality" and brings its four brands; Gap, Banana Republic, Old Navy and Piperlime, together with global navigation. It consists of one checkout and one low shipping rate of just $7 (orders from Piperlime are shipped separately and still offer free shipping and returns).[32] With this new feature, Gap hopes to enhance customer satisfaction and loyalty, therefore gaining an edge on competitors.

## Questions

**1.    Is the retailer classified as a global retailer or a multinational retailer? Explain its pattern of expansion. What expansion strategy did/is the retailer use/using?**

*The Gap, Inc. stores are standardized, using a generally small-format and can be replicated very rapidly in new locations. The Gap, Inc. is vertically integrated and solely focuses on its private label brand. The Gap, Inc. offerings typically do not change when they expand into new countries because their consumer is fundamentally the same where ever they go. Therefore The Gap, Inc. is classified as a global retailer.*

*Their pattern of expansion changes depending on the country. When The Gap, Inc. expanded into the United Kingdom in 1987 and in Canada in 1989, the company opened their stores as wholly owned subsidiaries, internalizing their knowledge.*

**2.    Based on Dunning's eclectic theory, how do ownership, locational and internalization factors play in your retailers' international expansion?**

As a global retailer, some of the factors involved in the Dunning's eclectic theory have a major role with Gap, Inc. This theory is comprised of three factors. We will start with the ownership factor. The Gap, Inc. has an asset-based advantage, as it sells only private label brands. This retailer has many tangible items such as their own patents and products. Transaction-based ownership advantages play a huge part with The Gap, Inc. as well. Since most of the stores, especially towards the beginning of their international expansion, are wholly owned subsidiaries, it has been easy for them to transfer their services and keep their company consistent throughout the world.

With this being said, Locational advantages do not play a huge role in expanding internationally. A global retailer is less concerned with issues such as cultural proximity, market size, competitors' moves, geographic proximity, and low cost. What they are more concerned about is Internalization, which brings me to my next point.

Internalization means "...keeping the information within the company." Although it is extremely expensive and risky for a global retailer to own stores throughout the world opposed to franchising, Gap expanded into the U.K in 1987 as a wholly owned subsidiary. They were more concerned with not letting their secrets out than the costs of the operation. Today however, Gap has had to re-think their steps in order to stay alive.[1]

**2.   What role does cultural proximity and geographical proximity play in the retailers' international moves?**

The Gap, Inc. stores are standardized, using a generally small-format and can be replicated very rapidly in new locations. The Gap, Inc. is vertically integrated and solely focuses on its private label brand. The Gap, Inc. offerings typically do not change when they expand into new countries because their consumer is fundamentally the same where ever they go. Therefore The Gap, Inc. is classified as a global retailer.

Their pattern of expansion changes depending on the country in which they move into. When The Gap, Inc. expanded into the United Kingdom in 1987 and in Canada in 1989, the company opened their stores as wholly owned subsidiaries, internalizing their knowledge. When The Gap, Inc. expansion led them into France they were faced with government restrictions forcing them to arrive in the country as joint venture. In 1996 when The Gap, Inc. expanded into Japan they opened its first Flagship store.

**3.   Can you predict the retailer's future international expansion?**

The Gap, Inc. currently has a plan to expand in Mexico. With the finance reports we have seen for the past few years, there is no doubt that they will continue to expand internationally as a franchise opposed to wholly owned subsidiaries. Although they protect company secrets, it is much too expensive for them to maintain these stores. "All of Gap's existing overseas stores in Britain, France, and Japan are owned and operated by the company, a setup that has at times proven expensive and unwieldy, analysts say." [9]

The company still remains a global specialty retailer. Predicting where they will expand next is nearly impossible as locational factors do not come into play for this decision. They are already located in so many different countries throughout the world. Their next step may be in a city with similar segments of upper income and customers.

## Propositions

**P1: The greater the ownership advantages for retailers, the less likely they will franchise or license.**

This proposition directly fits the internationalization strategy. Based on the information that we gathered, "All of Gap's existing overseas stores in Britain, France, and Japan are owned and operated by the company, a setup that has at times proven expensive and unwieldy, analysts say." [9] When expansion took place in 2007 into the Middle East and Southeast Asia, the governments of these countries required franchising instead of joint ventures or wholly owned subsidiaries. Being a global company and having asset based ownership advantages (because they are a private label), doesn't mean that they necessarily should own stores internationally. It might be better for a company to colonize a concept. [36]

**P2: The greater the available organizational slack the greater the likelihood of expanding internationally.**

1994: 956.438 / 462.244 = 2.069
1995: 1055.687 / 499.860 = 2.111
1996: 1280.045 / 551.744 = 2.319

2.069 < 2.011 < 2.319
Yes this proposition does not fit The Gap, Inc. the ratios very but do not consistantly get larger.

**P3: The greater the recoverable slack the greater the likelihood of expanding internationally.**

1994: 748.193 / 3295.68 = .227
1995: 853.524 / 3722.94 = .229
1996: 1004.396 / 4395 = .228


.227 < .229> .228

*This proposition is false in regards to The Gap, Inc. Recoverable slack represents resources that have been absorbed by the organization (e.g., excess overhead), but could be recovered through increased efficiencies.[1] In a study by Nohria and Gulati they examined the impact of slack and innovation.[39] They suggested that as slack increases, innovation increases, but also excess slack will reduce innovation because it allows for undisciplined investment in Research and Development activities. We feel this holds true for The Gap, Inc. In 1996 The Gap Inc's international expansion came to a halt after opening in Japan due to their decrease in recoverable slack although the following year they expanded through their efforts online.*

**P4:The greater the potential slack the greater the likelihood of expanding internationally.**

1994: 1126.475 / 956.438 = 1.117
1995: 1375.232 / 1055.687 = 1.302
1996: 1640.473 / 1280.045 = 1.281
*note: Capital not found substituted Total Current Assets

1.117 < 1.302 > 1.281


*No, this proposition is false for The Gap, Inc. In the years 1995 to 1996 potential slack decreased and The Gap, Inc. continued to expand internationally contradicting the statement, "The greater the potential slack the greater the likelihood of expanding internationally." Potential slack was found to be positively related to risk-taking behavior, since international expansion is a risk that the Gap Inc took, this does not hold true.*

**P13: Global companies will move to the largest/capital cities in a country.**

*This proposition holds true for Gap. This leading international specialty retailer is considered a unique company that uses a standardized global format to expand. The Gap has been able to move into areas that can keep this fashion forward company growing, whether it locates in a small city or a large metropolitan area. The advantage of being small in scale and centralized has allowed the company to move into cities with similar segments of upper income consumers at a very rapid rate.[6] Gap stores can be easily replicated providing the standard store concept and staple merchandise. The consistency and international expansion across multiple developed countries with low capital expenditure requirements has allowed Gap to expand to world class cities where they can expect to find individuals that have established and represent the Gap's private label brand. The primary strategy used by the company is to locate in a region close to the majority of their consumers where their products can generate growth. This concept has enabled the global retailer to avoid adjusting their products as it enters into new cultures and territories, allowing the merchandise to stay the same in every store worldwide because they identify their consumers that have similar interests wherever they anticipate locating. Some major US cities and countries that have contributed to the company's success include San Francisco, New York, and Chicago; major countries include the UK, France, Japan, and Canada.*

*This San Francisco based retailer has expanded to diverse areas with the ability to colonize its retail store concept throughout different areas of the world without oversaturating their home market. "Gap has used direct investment, rather than franchising, and achieved rapid expansion".[36] Gap's strategic locations in North America and abroad make it possible for Gap to operate 2,677 stores in the US and 493 internationally.[1] The company's purpose for expansion was to operate in new territory to capitalize on investments. By locating in more developed countries without changing its unique merchandise, this direction has enabled the Gap brand to enhance revenues without changing their offerings.*

### P14: Global companies will not be attracted by population size, income, cultural proximity or geographical proximity.

*This proposition holds true for Gap and most global companies. Some factors that do not greatly influence global companies during expansion are population size, cultural proximity or geographical proximity. Gap's main focus for expansion is to open new stores that are centered on consumers who are interested in the retailer's products. These demographics are important to the company because it has allowed the company to grow and expand over the years leading to long term success. Gap has been able to achieve tremendous success in opening new stores around the world. The success came from the strong developed brand throughout North America which brought the company increased growth revenue, giving the company the strength to expand globally. The first major international move was entering into the UK where it experienced remarkable success, advancing to Canada, Japan, Germany and France. While operating in these countries the company experienced some difficulties and overcame them by selling their stores, where growth could not be achieved. Some countries Gap moved into, such as Singapore, because they identified a market would responded to casual, relatively affordable, wearable goods. In Japan, the targeted consumer enjoyed the idea of a petite line and fast fashion clothing that Gap developed to keep the interests in their demographics. Gaps unique product line gives this company the market power to attain strong asset based advantages in the retailing environment. Gap has been able to offer private label goods in every store without changing their key concept, focusing on internalization. The areas where the target market can be identified earliest are typically where Gap has established to keep the formation of the company; this gives the company a first mover's advantage before competitors can rush into the area. Gap saw international expansion as a means for rapid growth in the foreign market through franchise agreements. As a global retailer, their performance is greatly influenced by their strategic planning while developing their store format.*

**P15:  The greater the asset based ownership advantages of a global retailer, the more likely they are to franchise.**

*This proposition fits the Gap Inc.'s franchising strategy. The greater the asset based ownership advantages of the Gap Inc., the more likely they are to franchise. The Gap Inc.'s unique iconic apparel helps ensure people throughout the world recognize their label and are therefore, more successful. In 2007, The Gap opens stores in the Philippines. Ron Young, senior vice president of strategic alliances for the Gap Inc. commented, "The country has a strong, steadily growing economy, and consumers in this market have a great interest in iconic apparel brands such as ours".[41] This statement proves that the Gap's private label is distinguished throughout the world, strengthening their asset based ownership advantages and increasing their likelihood to franchise.*

**P16: The greater the transaction based ownership advantages of a global retailer, the less likely they are to franchise.**

*This proposition is false for Gap. It has successful marketing strategies, which have helped their clothing line evolve into what people think of it as today. This has protected their line from copiers and allowed them to franchise throughout the world.*

**P17: The greater the available organizational slack the greater the likelihood that global retailers will reacquire international franchisees.**

> 1994:  956.438 / 462.244 = 2.069
> 1995: 1055.687 / 499.860 = 2.111
> 1996: 1280.045 / 551.744 = 2.319
>
> 2.069 < 2.111 < 2.319

*This proposition holds true for Gap Inc. Since the ratios increase from year to year, this means that the organizational slack increases year to year. Organizational slack is defined by Bourgeois as, "a cushion of excess resources that can be used in a discretionary manner."[1] The more organizational slack a company holds the more risk it is willing to take and the more it can afford to expand internationally. Gap Inc.'s organizational slack increased from year to year, and therefore allows for the company to take risks when reacquiring international franchisees.[42] Gap Inc. has paired with local franchisees in many international markets including Southeast Asia and the Middle East. By pairing with franchisees in the international retail areas, Gap Inc. reduces financial risk, which will conserve organizational slack.[22]*

**P18: The greater the recoverable slack the greater the likelihood that global retailers will reacquire international franchisees.**

1994: 748.193 / 3295.68 = .227
1995: 853.524 / 3722.94 = .229
1996: 1004.396 / 4395 = .228

.227 < .229 > .228

*This proposition does not hold true for Gap Inc. Recoverable slack should be reduced over time. Acquiring international franchisees is a method for reducing recoverable slack. This proposition is not supported by Gap Inc. because the amount of recoverable slack increases from 1994 to 1995.[42] Reacquiring international franchisees is a long term strategy to reduce expenses. Since Gap Inc. failed to reduce expenses in these three years, this proposition is not true for Gap Inc.*

**P19: The greater the potential slack the greater the likelihood that global retailers will reacquire international franchisees.**

1994: 1126.475 / 956.438 = 1.117
1995: 1375.232 / 1055.687 = 1.302
1996: 1640.473 / 1280.045 = 1.281
      *note: Capital not found substituted Total Current Assets.

1.117 < 1.302 > 1.281

*This proposition does not hold true for Gap Inc. The potential slack for Gap Inc. does not decrease consistently over these three years. In order for reacquiring international franchisees to be beneficial to the company, potential slack should decrease because of the acquisition.[42] Since the ratios increase from 1994 to 1995, this proposition should not be held true for Gap Inc.*

# Endnotes

1.  Sternquist, Brenda. International Retailing. New York: Fairchild Books, 2007. 259.

2.  Gap, Inc.(2008d). Retrieved October 30,2008, from http://www.fundinguniverse. com/company-histories/The-Gap-Inc-Company-History.html.

3.  Pollack, Andrew. (April 6, 1986). "Gap, a gold new look." New York Times. Retrieved October 24, 2008 From Lexis-Nexis database.

4.  Gap Inc (1998)."Gap, Inc.-Company Report." (November 30, 1988). Smith Barney, Harris Upham & Co. in Investext

5.  Gap Inc (2008e)."Gap Inc. Hold Company Report." (August 22, 2008). Best. Independent Research in Investext.

6.  Sternquist, Brenda. International retailing. New York: Fairchild Books, 2007. 42.

7.  Sternquist, Brenda. International retailing. New York: Fairchild Books, 2007. 55.

8.  Soames, Emma. (August 13, 2008). Zara steals gaps crown. The Daily Telegraph London. Retrieved October 25, 2008. From Lexis-Nexis database.

9.  Mathiason, Nick. (January 14, 2007). The hippy dream turns into a nightmare. Observer Business Pages; Pg. 9. Retrieved October 25, 2008.From Lexis-Nexis database.

10. World Bank. (2008) Economy rankings. Retrieved on November 2, 2008 from http://www.doingbusiness.org/EconomyRankings/.

11. Statistics Canada, (2008), Retail trade, by Industry. Retrieved on November 2, 2008 from Canada National Statistical Agency :http://www40.statcan.ca/l01/cst01/trad15a.htm.

12. Gap Inc. (2008b). Gap Inc. expands outlet business to Canada. Retrieved on November 1, 2008 from http://www.gapinc.com/public/Media/Press_Releases/med_pr_CanadaOutlet102408.shtml

13. Drier, M., Socha, M. (February 6, 2004). Gap's German Bow: Sells Stores To H&M.WWD. 2.

14. Ellis, K. (May 1, 1998). Gap to Open 300-350 Stores in U.S. and Abroad This Year: Millard Drexler, CEO,Tells Holders Old Navy Will Get The Most New Units. Daily News Record. v52, 23.

15. Barron, K. (March 19, 2001). Culture Gap. Forbes. v167( i7), 62.

16. Sternquist, Brenda. International Retailing. New York: Fairchild Books, 2007.319.

17. Hoovers Company Reports. UK Holdings. Rep.No. 139. Retrieved November 5, 2008 from Lexis Nexis.

18. Sato, Takeshi (1996, August 5). Stores law hurts customer: Gap execs. Japan Times (Weekly International Edition), p. 13. Retrieved November 9, 2008, from ABI/INFORM Global database. (Document ID: 10055249).

19. Gap Inc. (2005). Gap Celebrates Tenth Anniversary in Japan. Retrieved on October 20, 2008 from http://www.gapinc.com/public/Media/Press_Releases/med_pr_GapJapan10thAnniversary_Oct1105.shtml

20. Lim, Kevin. (2006, August 2). Gap to Open First Stores in Asia Outside Japan by End of the Year. Wall Street Journal (Eastern Edition), p. B.3B. Retrieved November 11, 2008, from ABI/INFORM Global database. (Document ID: 1087367601).

21. Quilter, James. (2006, June). Gap picks Naked to lead pan-European strategy. Marketing,2. Retrieved November 9, 2008, from ABI/INFORM Global database. (Document ID: 1064879631).

22. Lee, L. (April 18, 2006). Gap Goes Global. Business Week (Online). New York. The McGraw-Hills Companies Inc. 1.

23. PR Newswire. (April 18, 2006). Gap Inc. Expands International Reach with Franchise Agreements for Middle East; Signs with Al Tayer Group for Up to 25 Gap and Banana Republic Stores by 2010. PR Newswire. New York. PR Newswire Association.

24. Palmieri, J.E. (April 24, 2006). Saks To Open Flagship In Shanghai; Gap Also Inks Deal For 35 Gap and Banana Stores In The Middle East. DNR. New York. Fairchild Publishing. V26 (i17). 18.

25. Wee, M.L. (July 7, 2007). Fashionistas Can Now Go Bananas; Contemporary Chic US Apparel Brand Banana Republic's Fall Collection Makes Its Way Here As it Opens its South-east Asia Flagship Store in Paragon Next Saturday. The Business Times Singapore. Singapore. Singapore Press Holdings Limited.

26. DSN Retail Fax. (February 9, 2004). Gap Inc. to Sell German Unit (Hennes and Mauritz). DNS Retail Fax. v11 (i6).

27. Tay, M. (July 13, 2007). Stateside Style; American Casual Chic Brands Are Slipping intoSingaporean's Consciousness with Opening of Banana Republic's new Store at Paragon. The Straits Times. Singapore. Singapore Press Holdings Limited.

28. Thomson Reuters. "Gap Inc. Expands Into Mexico and Opens 100th Franchise Store Abroad." Reuters. 19 Sept. 2008.05 Oct. 2008 http://http://www.reuters.com/article/pressrelease/idus42331+19-sep-2008+bw20080919.

29. Saranow , Jennifer (2008, September 19). Gap Will Announce Deal to Open Stores Inside Mexico Shops. Wall Street Journal (Eastern Edition), p. B.7. Retrieved November 17, 2008, from ABI/INFORM Global database. (Document ID: 1557496141).

30. Adelaja, Tai. (2008, May 22). Gap Stores to Open by Holiday Season. The St. Petersburg Times. Retrieved 8 November 2008 from: http://www.sptimesrussia.com/index.php?story_id=26079&action_id=2.

31. For Gap's new online venture, if the shoe fits, sell it. (2006, November). Retailing Today, 45(20), 3,35. Retrieved November 12, 2008, from ABI/INFORM Global database. (Document ID: 1170807411).

32. Gap Inc. (2008c). Gap Inc. unveil online feature, offering customers four brands in one shopping bag, one check-out and one low shipping rate. Retrieved on November 3, 2008 from http://www.gapinc.com/public/Media/Press_Releases/med_pr_GIDuniversality052708.shtml.

33. Gap Inc. (2006). Piperlime Receives Prestigious "Launch of the Year" Award. Retrieved on November 2, 2008 from http://gapinc.com/public/Media/Press_Releases/med_pr_piperlime120506.shtml

34. Clack, Erin. (2007, May). The New Online Challenge. Footwear News.

35. Nolan, Kelly. (2007, April). Online shoe business hitting its strides. Retailing Today, 46(5), 14. Retrieved November 17, 2008, from ABI/INFORM Global database. (Document ID: 1293577461).

36. Sternquist, Brenda. International Retailing. New York: Fairchild Books, 2007.42-56.

37. Tseng Chiung-Hui. (November 9, 2007). Effects of Firm resources on Growth in Multinationality. http://research.ncku.edu.tw/re/articles/e/20071109/4.html Retrieved November 1, 2008

38. Herold, David M. ; Jayaraman, Narayanan ; Narayanaswamy, C.R. (September 22, 2006) Journal of Managerial Issues, What is the relationship between organizational slack and innovation? http://www.accessmylibrary.com/coms2/summary_0286-24129301_ITM) Retrieved November 9, 2008

39. Nohria, Nitin, Gulati, Ranjay. (1996). Is slack good or bad for innovation? Academy of Management Journal, 39(5), 1245-1264.

40. Gap Inc. (2008). Gap 2008 Store Count Brand. Retrieved on November 8, 2008

from http://www.gapinc.com/public/Investors/inv_re_storecount.shtm

41. Gap Inc. (2007). Gap Inc. Expands International Presence with Franchise Agreement in the Philippines. Retrieved on October 21, 2008 from http://www.gapinc.com/public/Media/Press_Releases/med_pr_franchisePhilippines100907.shml

42. Cheng, J.L.C, Rhee, J.H. (2002/4). Foreign Market Uncertainty and Incremental International Expansion: the Moderating Effect of Firm, Industry and Host Country Factors. Management International Review. Fourth Quarter 2002, 42, 4. pp. 419-439.

# Kingfisher PLC

*Michael DeLine, Rebecca Ebeling, Sarah Frontczak*
*Nina Talarico, Katherine Zhender*

## Kingfisher PLC

Kingfisher PLC is a big box home improvement retailer that is based in Europe. It is Europe's leading home improvement retailer and the third largest in the world. Kingfisher operates home improvement retail stores in eight different countries specializing in home improvement and do-it-yourself merchandise. Though they are the third largest they have a greater international presence then their top competitors, Lowes and Home Depot. Their focus on management, capital, and returns as its main business strategy has added to their success as a multinational retailer. Kingfisher PLC targets three different types of consumers, the everyday do-it-yourself, the project initiator and the trade professional. They offer a vast variety of merchandise for these consumers so that Kingfisher can be a one stop shop for whatever they might need.

Kingfisher PLC was first established in 1982 by the buyout of the British Woolworth chain but didn't take on the name of Kingfisher until 1989.[1] Since it was founded, Kingfisher has become the leading home improvement group in Europe and Asia and the third-largest home improvement retailer in the world.[2] Through smart acquisitions, Kingfisher now operates in the United Kingdom, France, Poland, Spain, Ireland, Turkey, Russia, and China. It is also a part of a strategic alliance with a 21% stake in Hornbach, Germany's number one DIY (do-it-yourself) retailer. Kingfisher's headquarters are located in London, England.[1] The multinational retailer is capitalizing on the growing demand for home improvement products and services in countries where consumer wealth is increasing. Operating under their brands B&Q, Castorama, Brico Depot, Screwfix, and Koctas they have over

800 stores and serve the needs of six million customers each week. To better serve these customers, Kingfisher has divided them up into three main groups. First they target the Everyday DIYer, which originally targeted the man of the house who did the everyday maintenance but women are starting to become more independent and therefore more active in their own home improvement. The second group is known as the project initiators. These people have a higher level of disposable income and will hire someone else to complete their dream project. They shop less often than the DIYer but spend a greater amount, which makes them very important customers. This category is about 75% women since they are the ones who want to makeover their homes. Also with the rise in wealth this group tends to be more of a do-it-for-me type of customer.[1] To accommodate these women B&Q is trying to "feminize" its stores.[3] And lastly there is the trade professional who depends on the stores to have what they want when they need it. These are people working in the home improvement business day-to-day, whether they are hired out or working on their own project. They are very regular customers and have high demands for their loyalty.[1] As consumers decide on home makeovers it's the trade professional they need to implement their plans. Overall, there is a great mix of customers that Kingfisher aims to serve and they do a good job of providing for them.

## FLOW CHART

**1982:** United Kingdom (422 stores)
**1993:** France (187 stores)
**1996:** Poland (42 stores)
Taiwan (21 stores)     *Exited in 2007
**1998:** Italy (31 stores)     *Exited in 2008
**1999:** Ireland (9 stores)
**2000:** Turkey (19 stores)
China (63 stores)
**2001:** Germany (25% stake in a strategic alliance with Hornbach)
**2003:** Spain (13 stores)
**2005:** South Korea (2 stores)   *Exited in 2007
**2006:** Russia (6 stores)

## Industry Analysis

The two industry leaders in home improvement are Lowes and Home Depot.[4] Lowes and Home Deport together control more than one third of the US market.[5] After Lowes and Home Depot Kingfisher is third largest company in the industry. Kingfisher has more international presence though being in eight different countries. Lowes has expanded into the Canadian market with plans to be in Mexico in 2009 and Home Depot has stores in The District of Columbia, Puerto Rico, U.S. Virgin Islands, Canada, Mexico and China.

Kingfisher is part of two different retail industry categories; home improvement and hardware retailer and the retail and distribution of building materials. The home improvement and hardware retail generally sell tools, building materials, garden supplies, and other items used in home improvement, maintenance, and construction.[6] It is the more popular of the two and is targeted toward the general consumer. The retail and distribution of building materials focuses on selling or distributing supplies that are targeted more towards the business aspect where a company would come in to buy in bulk for a large project.

The do-it-yourself sector of the home improvement retail is the most attractive. In 1991, when the TV show Home Improvement aired, there was a boom in home improvement sales and made home improvement, especially do-it-yourself home improvement, into a hobby. For a while, home improvement was outperforming the US retail sector with a lot of help from the housing boom. The US housing bust has sent home improvment retailers abroad in search of opportunities for growth and profit; places like Asia and especially China.[5]

China is a good place to expand right now because they are a fresh market. The Chinese government recently granted the right of home ownership to it's citizens and is now a prime market for the do-it-yourself home retailer. In China standard homes don't come with flooring, appliances, and fixtures.[5] With homes lacking those main assets, do-it-yourself retailers can thrive there. Kingfisher already operats 50 B&Q stores in China with a lot of success, it is planning on doubling the number of stores they have there by the end of 2009.[5] Home Depot was also enticed by the growth potential in China and is also planning on expanding into China.

## Competitor Analysis

The home improvement retail industry consists of DIY, building supply, and home décor stores. This sector provides a wide range of products for home improvement. However, the global home improvement market has posted fluctuating growth rates in recent years.[7] In fact, the majority of the market share leaders, for specific markets, have been affected by the decline in sales. The industry does not have one firm that dominates on a global scale, but has oligopolies that exist in certain geographic areas.[8] Because of the mix of large and small-scale firms, competition is regionally based. For Kingfisher, this results in different competition in each location. However, The Home Depot, Focus (DIY), and Lowe's Companies, Inc.

are some of the top companies in the industry that classify as the most relevant competitors for Kingfisher plc.[8] Kingfisher plc is the leading home improvement chain in Europe.[8] The company is also the market leader in the UK and France. In the UK, Kingfisher has 16 percent of the market share and 10 percent of the market share in France.[8] The market share percentages for each of these countries shows the spread of retailers in this sector. Much of the retailer's success has to do with their rapid expansion and offering of various retail formats.[9] However, the company's performance in areas such as China and the UK has declined. In China, for example, Kingfisher's sales declined by 19.4 percent.[10] Rivalry competition, even in an area where Kingfisher had the highest market share, can be seen as one of the primary reasons for decline. In fact, in August 2007, Home Depot Inc. opened its first store in China.[11] The largest home improvement chain in the world's entrance to China affected Kingfishers sales and presence in the market. As of 2008, Kingfisher plc held 1.60 percent of the market share globally, while Home Depot, Inc. and Lowe's Companies Inc took 6.3 and 4.2 percent of the market share respectively.[8] When viewed globally in the Home Improvement industry, Home Depot dominates the market share.

Home Depot acts as a competitor to Kingfisher, not only in its market share and expansion to similar markets, but also in its financial statistics, service, format and other offerings that set it apart from the company. The company operates 2,234 stores in total and had 2008 revenue of $77,349,000,000.[8] Revenues for Kingfisher on the other had were just over $17,000 (Mill).[8] Based on financial data and market share information, Home Depot is the leading competition for Kingfisher. However, its new offerings and format might be what set it apart from others in the industry. Home Depot introduced Expo Design Center stores and new layouts in its expansion efforts. The Design Center stores and extra services for home renovation are unmatched by the competition. In fact, Kingfisher plans to revamp its remaining stores in China,[11] and increase its services and update 60% of its overall product range.[12] Kingfisher, a decentralized retailer, will add new service training, customer service and smaller store formats to appeal to the changing markets. Instead of adjusting its format and offerings based on the market demands of the new locations, Kingfisher is at risk of losing its presence.[13] Home Depot, on the other hand is continually expanding and adapting to new markets such as its 12 Home Depot stores in China.

Another key competitor on the global scale for Kingfisher, is Lowe's Companies Inc. Lowe's is a large-scale home improvement retailer that operates 1,534 stores in the United States and Canada.[8] As previously stated, the company occupies 4.2 percent of the market share. Even though its presence posses less of a threat for Kingfisher currently, the company's expansion of it's DIY format in the future and its market share percentage make it a key competitor. Sales for Lowe's increased from 2007 to 2008 by 2.9 percent.[8] However, Lowe's saw decreases in its profitability over the last year and is primarily attributable to increase in selling, general, and administrative and depreciation costs as well as interest expenses.[8] Lowe's market share and sales figures are offset by its profitability and lack of international expansion.

Lastly, Focus(DIY) Limited is a competitor of Kingfisher, primarily in the UK. After the company sold its ownership in Wickes in 2005, the company dropped to the number three spot for this sector in the UK.[8] Its decline in sales, loss of assets, and poor performance have weakened the company as a whole. However, they still play a major role in decisions that Kingfisher makes as far is its expansion plans in the UK. Previously the second leading market share holder in the Home Improvement and DIY sector in the UK, the company is also trying to revamp its stores and adjust to the no longer stable market.

## Business Strategy

With store locations throughout Europe and Asia, it has a seemingly proven way of strategizing its corporation and retail operations. From its beginning, and continuing into its global expansion, Kingfisher has focused on three main broad strategies, as well as other specific business tactics, to keep its market share up and maintain a strong presence in the global DIY sector. The first broader strategy is that it places importance on its management. Rather than operating under a typical decentralized management structure, Kingfisher has adopted what they call a Retail Board.[14] The board, which consists of the group CEO, CFO, and three retail divisional heads[14] as well as other leaders within each department, meets on a monthly basis to assess the company's progress and determine further courses of action to ensure financial and operational success.[14] Second, Kingfisher focuses on its capital. With thought-out and specific goals regarding capital (Kingfisher has required spending limits and approval processes), the company has set a goal for its flat net debt (a specific figure has not been mentioned, though Kingfisher does refer to it as its new key evaluative criterion of manager's success.)[14] The third broad strategy Kingfisher utilizes is its returns. To ensure appropriate, realistic sales goals, Kingfisher has revamped its returns figures in accordance with the demand of its goods and services. For instance, the 2008/2009 annual budget reflects negative changes in anticipated sales growth, while earnings and net debts remain the same. In order to properly monitor returns and company performance, Kingfisher has appointed its Retail Board to focus on both weekly and monthly financial information. As Kingfisher anticipates expansion and growth, they have incorporated a standard financial and operational...scorecard[14] that will be used throughout the coming years and has already been secured as a way of monitoring corporate success through 2012. Though management, capital, and returns are three key components that Kingfisher focuses on as successful business strategies, it uses other unique tactics to ensure its success and customer satisfaction. By utilizing these three strategies, Kingfisher is able to focus on its greatest strategy, international expansion.

With the global demand for home improvement and DIY products continuously rising, Kingfisher views international expansion to be a major opportunity and its main business strategy. Kingfisher has taken note of such countries as Poland, China, and Russia, where wealth and disposable income is increasing, and has begun aggressively seeking out opportunities in these locations.[15] While expanding, Kingfisher has realized the importance of adapting to the countries and cultures it comes into contact with and, as a result, has seen great success in eleven countries throughout Europe and Asia.

Another unique business strategy that Kingfisher utilizes is a new, redesigned way of operating IT. Kingfisher has formed what it calls, KITS (Kingfisher Information Technology Services). With the creation of KITS, Kingfisher was able to eliminate its numerous IT locations and create just one data center located in the UK. All brands under Kingfisher, including Brico Depot, B&Q, Screwfix, and Castorama, are now included in the consolidated IT system, leading to greater efficiency and improved benefits of scale.[16]

As another specific strategy, Kingfisher offers its newly updated B&Q website. Rather than simply shopping for products, consumers can now utilize a free room design as well as a free bathroom planner for assistance in their DIY home improvement projects. Also, the website features 35,000 different products, 6,500 of which are available for home delivery.[16]

## Retail Culture

For Kingfisher, providing the service and knowledge to complete a home improvement project is how they operate. "Kingfisher enables customers to complete a full project, including 'finishing touches', such as lighting and soft furnishings."[17] "These stores offer traditional DIY products that are displayed alongside "room sets" displaying complete kitchens, bathrooms and bedrooms".[18] The finished in-store displays get the customer excited to start their projects because they can see how great it's going to look in the end.

In the late 90's Kingfisher knew it had to take its business online to capitalize on new and growing opportunities. Stephen Robertson, head of DIY e-commerce at

Kingfisher, is quoted saying "In the future, a retailer without online relationships will be as ineffective as a store without a telephone."[19] On July 1st, 2000 Kingfisher launched its very own website starting out focusing on core markets of DIY, electric goods, general merchandising and ventures.[19] The online business has been very successful for Kingfisher however, Kingfisher's CEO Sir Geoff Mulcahy later stated "As e-commerce develops it's becoming clear that simply being online isn't enough," he told a briefing two weeks ago. "While much talk of the Internet's impact on the retail market has emphasized price, quality of service and ease of use have emerged as even more important factors."[19]

The online store and brick and mortar stores sell a wide array of brands and within those brands a wide variety of products. Listed below are the brands and the product category breakdowns as well as the services offered by the retailer.

**Brands Include**

- B&Q

- Brico Depot

- Castorama

- ScrewFix

- Trade Depot

- Other own-brands

- Performance Power

- MacAllister

- Colours

- Airforce

- Bodner&Form

**Products Include**

- Building materials

- Cleaning supplies

- Electronics

- Flooring accessories and mats

- Furniture

- Gardening tools and equipment

- Heaters, coolers, fans, air filters and thermostats

- Kitchen and bath fixtures

- Lighting fixtures

- Plumbing tools and equipment

- Power tools

**Services Offered**

- Installation services

- Repair and remodeling services

- Online shopping[18]

Kingfisher is a large retailer and therefore has many suppliers. They use a company called SAS to leverage supplier performance and achieve greater profitability.[20] In 2003 they cut 3,000 suppliers. Kingfisher's reasoning was "to reduce our supply base was less about cutting costs and more about working far more closely with fewer suppliers. It's about buying more from them and forming more direct relationships rather than working through wholesalers. We want to avoid the middleman. Wholesalers can often add something in terms of value and service, but most of the time, they do not. We want to build exclusive own-brands and undertake more direct sourcing," he added.[21] The company focuses a great deal on streamlining their operations in all dimensions to obtain a very efficient business strategy.

## International Expansion

### United Kingdom

First Store Opened: 1982                    Number of Stores: 422

Kingfisher was originally established in the United Kingdom and named Woolworth Holdings PLC. The two brands operated in the United Kingdom today are B&Q and ScrewFix. The U.K. operates more Kingfisher stores than any other country. However, these stores in the United Kingdom are struggling in this poor global economic climate. Most recently in the U.K, B&Q made major changes to its business, not only refreshing much of its ranges with new products, but also revamping around 5.5 million square feet of its store space. This has been a demanding task, which has been carried out well at a difficult stage in the business cycle. These changes are delivering good results, ensuring B&Q is ready to take full advantage when the market improves.[22]

## France

First Store Opened: 1993

Number of Locations: 187
(98 Castorama and 89 Brico Depot)

After opening Castorama and Brico Depot stores in France, Kingfisher has been successful in becoming the market leader in the country.[22] Complimentary formats, high levels of home ownership, and low levels of consumer debt have been some of the few reasons that Kingfisher has continued to be successful in France even in times of economic downturn. In fact, total sales in France grew 7.2% for Kingfisher in 2008.[22] While the UK and China have been struggling, the French market continues to be an important market for Kingfisher. Expansion into France began in 1993 and their presence was increased in 1998 when it merged its B&Q chain with Castorama. Followed by this, Kingfisher launched its own free Internet service in France, which also helped to increase its presence.[5]

## Poland

First Store Opened: 1996

Number of Locations: 42
(40 Castorama and 2 Brico Depot)

Since entering Poland in 1996, Kingfisher has been extremely successful and plans to continue growing and expanding throughout the country. Polish sales exceeded initial expectations, leading Kingfisher to grow at a quicker rate than first planned.[23] A key reason for Poland's success is the smaller formatted stores that Kingfisher offers in the less populated cities of the country. Rather than building a full 12,000 square meter store, they have built smaller 5,000 square meter units to better serve smaller communities. The results of the small units were a strong indicator of the success Kingfisher would experience in Poland.[23] Management contributes to the success to the home improvement market in Poland, which accounts for five billion euros.[23] Also, the Polish market consists of residents with relatively high disposable income that pride themselves on home ownership and more specifically, DIY projects.[22]

## Taiwan

First Store Opened: 1996              Number of Locations: 21

Kingfisher entered Taiwan as a joint venture in 1996. While Kingfisher was in Taiwan they were quite successful but Taiwan had limited opportunities for future growth. Kingfisher left Taiwan in 2007.

## Italy

First Store Opened: 1998              Number of Locations: 31

Italy has the fourth largest market in Europe. Kingfisher entered the Italian market with the acquisition of Castorama. Kingfisher held the #2 spot in market share but lately sales in Italy have been weak and Kingfisher decided to pull out in 2008. They sold their stores to Groupe Adeo, which is currently the market leader in Italy with 4% of the DIY market.[24]

## Ireland

First Store Opened: 1999              Number of Locations: 9

With a population of only 4 million Ireland is one of the smallest markets in Europe.[1] Kingfisher entered Ireland in June of 1999 about 10 years after they had entered Northern Ireland. This B&Q outlet was Kingfishers 287th store. In Ireland, "B & Q is not a name readily familiar to Irish DIY enthusiasts but it is the UK's biggest home improvement retailer with nearly a fifth of the DIY market."[25] The concept of a warehouse was new to the Irish as well and much larger than they were used to in the small town of Newry.[25] Ireland has proved to be a strong market, growing faster than any other EU market in the last five years.[1]

## Turkey

First Store Opened: 2000              Number of Locations: 19

Kingfisher PLC has a joint venture between the UK DIY retailer and Turkish industrial and services giant Koc Group, the chain store called Koctas. The joint venture with Kingfisher PLC took place in May of 2000. The first Koctas as a joint venture entered Istanbul, Turkey in June of 2001. Kingfisher's Koctas decision to open its joint venture in Turkey has been very successful for them. Koctas is the largest home improvement retailer in Turkey. They haven't been affected by the recession, they have continued to have growth through it. Koctas has 19 different stores in 9 different cities and has a goal to have 50 stores by 2012, with hopes that the growth will be in the east.[26]

## China

First Store Opened: 2000            Number of Locations: 63

Kingfisher expanded to China in 2000 to take advantage of the fast-growing urban middle class market.[22] China is considered to be one of the fastest growing, and most important retail markets in the world. The company has opened 63 B&Q stores since 2000. However, new competition and a slow economy has affected sales for Kingfisher in China. As a result, Kingfisher is planning to close a third of its stores in China by 2010.[11] It also plans to revamp and cut its shop space by 40 percent over the next two years. While the Chinese market has been performing poorly, Kingfisher still sees the market as important and vital for its success internationally.

## Germany

Kingfisher has a strategic alliance with a 21% stake in Hornbach. Hornbach has over 120 stores throughout Europe.

## Spain

First Store Opened: 2003            Number of Locations: 13

Kingfisher PLC's company in Spain is called Brico Depot. It first opened its store in 2003 and now operates 13 different stores but in only 7 different regions. Brico Depot has a predicted 9.3% growth for 2008, which will lead to the opening of more stores. Brico Depot has been highly successful due to them mirroring how France formatted their store.

## South Korea

First Store Opened: 2005            Number of Locations: 2

Kingfisher entered Seoul, South Korea in 2005 as a test market. They kept a close watch and they found that with the rising property costs and lack of locations to expand that it wasn't likely to reach the necessary growth. Kingfisher left South Korea in 2007.

## Russia

First Store Opened: 2006                    Number of Locations: 6

In February 2006, Kingfisher expanded into the Russian market under its Castorama brand. Beginning with three stores in its opening year, Castorama expanded to a total of six retail locations by October 2008. Kingfisher decided to hire former IKEA executive, Peter Partma, as the head of Kingfisher's Russian expansion.[27] There were several factors that Kingfisher considered when predicting success in the Russian retailing sector. For example, Russia's rising GDP, strong retail growth, declining inflation, and consistent exchange rate all made Russia an attractive outlet for Kingfisher.[28] Upon entering the country, management noted the importance of adapting to Russian culture when opening new stores and bore in mind the unique Russian taste in home improvement goods when marketing its products.[29] Also, to maintain the Russian environment throughout its Castorama stores, Kingfisher offers high quality products that are locally made, as well as imported goods that Russians do not specialize in, such as drills and other tools.[29] Lastly, Russia's population played an important role in Kingfisher's decision to expand in the nation. Russia has thirteen major cities that are each home to as least one million residents.[28] Russia's housing market is growing and as a result, the demand for DIY products, such as the ones sold at Kingfisher, is rapidly increasing throughout the populous cities.

## Questions

**1.  Is the retailer classified as a global retailer or a multinational retailer? Explain its pattern of expansion. What expansion strategy did/is the retailer use/using?**

*Kingfisher is classified as a multinational company. The company expanded into France, a culturally similar market which is a common practice of a multinational company. Once they developed a proven expertise in their culturally similar markets, they took the opportunity to expand their brand into markets that differed from the Western European cultures and locations. As one can see, Kingfisher successfully followed the Stages Theory. Through their expansion, Kingfisher kept control by being a wholly owned corporation while utilizing a decentralized management strategy. Another expansion strategy of multinational retailers is to adapt products and services to the countries it expands to. For example, when Kingfisher first entered Russia, it noted the importance of adapting its product selection to the unique Russian culture.*

**2.  Based on Dunning's eclectic theory, how do ownership, locational and internalization factors play in your retailers' international expansion?**

*Dunning's theory plays a significant role in Kingfisher's international expansion. According to Sternquist, it is hard for multinational retailers to have private labels. Through research, we discovered Kingfisher does not have any private labels, possibly a result of its decentralized management. However, Kingfisher does possess some other asset-based advantages such as a unique product offering, including a website that B&Q customers can virtually customize a room and purchase over 6,500 products. Kingfisher has several transaction-based advantages such as direct sourcing that guarantees the lowest price for their customers while also offering superior, high quality products. Another transaction-based advantage is Kingfisher's consolidated IT system that streamlines efficiency and provides improved benefits of scale. Lastly, internationalization and decentralization are important transaction-based assets because they give managers extensive decision making experience.*

*Kingfisher's expansion demonstrates the importance of locational advantages. Cultural proximity is important for multinational retailers because they first expand close to home, where cultures are similar. Market size, another aspect of locational advantages, shows that Kingfisher saturated a great deal of their home market before expanding internationally. A third component of locational advantage is geographic proximity. Kingfisher first expanded at home in the U.K with a corporate office in London. Most recently, they opened another corporate office in Hong Kong to reduce costs and streamline corporate communication. Kingfisher learned firsthand that low cost land and labor are significant in locational advantages. After expanding to South Korea, property costs increased and availability of land decreased, leading to Kingfisher exiting the country.*

*Internalization is the final factor in Dunning's theory. By not franchising or licensing, Kingfisher has kept its business practices within the company.*

### 3. What role does cultural proximity and geographical proximity play in the retailers' international moves?

*Cultural proximities play significant roles in retailers' international moves. People in the U.K and of Western Europe share similar patterns of life. This made expanding to other European countries attainable for the beginning of Kingfisher's expansion. It has been proven that cultural proximity has led to great success for Kingfisher. They were well received in France, Ireland, and Poland.*

*Geographical proximity played a great role in Kingfisher's international success, however it was not as important as cultural proximity because the company is decentralized, which means they generally operate as independent units and don't need to be micromanaged from the corporate level. However, geographic proximity does cut costs and streamlines corporate communication.*

### 4. Can you predict the retailer's future international expansion?

*We predict that Kingfisher will continue expanding in Russia "to take full and timely advantage of this exciting and fast-growing economy."[22] Also, if wider market conditions continue to improve in China, Kingfisher plans to expand the chain again in 2011. They hope to combat Home Depot's efforts in the country by creating an even greater presence. Even though many of their expansion efforts have been postponed due to the global economic slump, we believe Kingfisher will continue to expand once conditions start to improve.*

## Propositions

**P1: The greater the ownership advantages for retailers, the less likely they will franchise or license.**

*We agree with this proposition. Unlike many retailers, "Kingfisher owns its stores and plans to be debt free...".[30] Kingfisher has control over all of its stores and have never franchised or licensed, indicating that they have great ownership advantages.*

**P2: The greater the available organizational slack the greater the likelihood of expanding internationally.**

Current Assets to Current Liabilities
3 Year Average = 1995-1997 (Oldest Available Dates on Mergent)

1995: CA= $1,573,000,000.00
CL= $1,420,900,000.00
Ratio: 1,573,000,000/1,420,900,000 = **1.12**

1996: CA= $1,704,000,000.00
CL= $1,418,900,000.00
Ratio: 1,704,000,000/1,418,900,000 = **1.20**

1997: CA= $2,043,800,000.00
CL= $1,678,100,000.00
Ratio: 2,043,800,000/1,678,100,100 = **1.22**

*We agree with this proposition because it is supported by the ratios for Kingfisher plc. In fact, if year a=1995, b=1996, and c=1997; it is shown that a<b<c. Because the ratio of current assets to current liabilities has continued to grow with each year, this supports the proposition.*

**P3: The greater the recoverable slack the greater the likelihood of expanding internationally.**

*We agree with this proposition. The greater the recoverable slack, the greater the likelihood of expanding internationally. Kingfisher plc had a large ratio of general and administrative expenses to sales between the years 1995 and 1997. After looking at Mergent, this shows that during early expansion, Kingfisher had a large ratio and if that ratio goes down, they will work less on international expansion.*

**P4: The greater the potential slack the greater the likelihood of expanding internationally.**

*We agree with this proposition. The greater the potential slack, the greater the likelihood of expanding internationally. When using the ratio of Equity to Capital, Mergent shows that the first three years of reports showed increases in equity. From 1995-1997, equity continued to increase for Kingfisher. When comparing equity to capital, the ratio was nearly 5.6:1. During these years, Kingfisher was beginning to focus more on international expansion. This shows that the greater the potential slack, the greater the likelihood of expanding internationally.*

**P5:Multinational retailers will move to countries with lower disposable income than their home country.**

*We do not agree with this proposition. Most of the countries that Kingfisher expanded to were of equal or higher disposable income. Since Kingfisher specializes in DIY home improvement projects, they look for consumers with high disposable income that can afford to spend a portion of their income on such products.*

**P6:Multinational retailers will move to countries that have a high positive change in GDP**

> 1988 = $1,006,624,000,000
> 1983 = $552,662,500,000
>
> 1,006,624,000,000 − 552,662,500,000 = 552,662,500,000 = 82%

*We agree with this proposition. In 1988, Kingfisher expanded to France and their GDP was 36,669,950,000. Five years earlier, their GDP was 20,154,740,000.[31] This shows an 82% raise following Kingfisher's entry into France, and therefore, it is true that when multinational retailers move into countries they have a positive change in GDP.*

**P7:Multinational retailers will move to countries that have a high positive change in service-value added as % of GDP.**

1988= 61.4%
1983= 58.5%

61.4%-58.5% = 4.96%

*We agree with this proposition. Kingfisher exported initially to France which had a positive change in service value added as a percent of GDP.*

**P8: Multinational retailers will first move to countries that are culturally the most similar to their home country. (Hofstede=s indicators Home country-Host country for four factors, MvsFHuvsLU; IndvsCol; HPDvsLPD)**

*We agree with Hofstede's Cultural Dimensions Model. Kingfisher's first two expansions were into France and Poland, both of which are culturally similar and in the same Western European region to the U.K.*

**P9: Multinational retailers will expand within the country and then will expand regionally within that area.**

*We agree with this proposition. Kingfisher started expansions in France and Poland before any of the other countries it would eventually expand to. These two countries are both located within Western Europe.*

**P10: Periodically the multinational retailers will "jump" to a new geographic area and begin the stages form of expansion.**

*We agree with this proposition. Kingfisher, after expanding to numerous European countries, decided to take an international "jump" into Asian countries such as South Korea and China.*

**P11: Multinational retailers will move to countries that are geographically close to the home country initially, then expand to more distant countries.**

*We agree with this proposition. In the previous two propositions, Kingfisher first expanded close to home into countries that were culturally similar to the U.K and then proceeded to expand to Asian countries where the culture differed greatly.*

**P12: Multinational retailers will move to countries with large population bases.**

*We do not agree with this proposition. Kingfisher first expanded to France where there is a population of only 4 million. Kingfisher was very successful in Ireland and discredits the theory that multinational retailers will move to countries with large populations.*

## Endnotes

1. Kingfisher Website, Copyright 2009 Kingfisher PLC, www.kingfisher.co.uk, Retrieved March 27, 2009

2. Hall, J. & Kleinman, M. (2008, September 21). B&Q owner kicks off review of tax domicile. The Sunday Telegraph. Retrieved March 27, 2009, from LexisNexis Academic database.

3. Finch, J. (2007, September 21). Kingfisher chief executive warns of tough times ahead. The Guardian. Retrieved March 27, 2009, from LexisNexis Academic database.

4. Kingfisher plc. (15 March). Hoover's Company Records,90233. Retrieved March 30, 2009, from Hoover's Company Records database. (Document ID: 168264741).

5. Kingfisher PLC. Hoover's Company Records - In-depth Records (2009). Retrieved March 28, 2009, from LexisNexis Academic.

6. (2009). Kingfisher PLC Snapshot. Company Dossier, Retrieved March 27, 2009, from http://www.lexisnexis.com.proxy1.cl.msu.edu/us/lnacademic/search/comp anyDossiersubmitForm.do

7. Kingfisher Plc. (2008, December). Retrieved March 29, 2009, from Datamonitor/Life Science Analytics Company Profiles database.

8. Home Improvement Retail Industry Profile: Global. (2009, March). Home Improvement Retail Industry Profile: Global, Retrieved March 26, 2009, from Business Source Complete database.

9. Killgren, Lucy. (2008, November 28). Mounting problems in China cast a cloud over Kingfisher. Financial Times, 17. Retrieved March 29, 2009 from ABI/INFORM Global database.

10. Braithwaite, Tom. (2008, September 19). Kingfisher bolstered by strength in Europe. Financial Times, 19. Retrieved March 27, 2009, from ABI/INFORM

Global database.

11. Rigby, Elizabeth. (2009, March 27). China losses force Kingfisher to pare back. Financial Times,17. Retrieved March 29, 2009, from ABI/INFORM Global database.

12. Kingfisher Website, Copyright 2009 Kingfisher plc, www.kingfisher.co.uk, Retrieved March 29, 2009

13. Hall, James. (2007, November 4). Kingfisher didn't have a Grand Design. The Sunday Telegraph; London, 5. Retrieved March 29, 2009, from LexisNexis Academic database.

14. (2008). Our Aims. Retrieved April 2, 2009, from Kingfisher Web site: http://www.kingfisher.co.uk/index.asp?pageid=226

15. (2006). Our Strategy. Retrieved March 20, 2009, from Kingfisher Web site: http://www.kingfisher.com/managed_content/files/reports/annual_report_2006/index.asp?pageid=38

16. The United Kingdom's Largest Users of IT. CIO, Retrieved March 20, 2009, from http://www.cio.co.uk/cio100/kingfisher/4193/

17. Kingfisher Synopsis. Retrieved April 5, 2009, from Mergentonline.com Web site: http://www.mergentonline.com.proxy1.cl.msu.edu/compdetail.asp?company=40295&Page=business

18. Kingfisher Products and Services. Retrieved April 5, 2009, from Marketlineinfo.com Web site: http://www.marketlineinfo.com.proxy2.cl.msu.edu/library/DisplayContent.aspx?R=30240375-E5B8-4C6C-9101-D9BF0362D440&N=4294841525&selectedChapter=IDAW3LH#IDAW3L

19. MCMAHON, Michael (2000,July,06). Kingfisher Looking to Build on high street Sucess. LexisNexis, Retrieved 4-4-09, from http://www.lexisnexis.com.proxy2.cl.msu.edu/us/lnacademic/results/docview/docview.do?docLinkInd=true&risb=21_T6233827322&format=GNBFI&sort=RELEVANCE&startDocNo=1&resultsUrlKey=29_T6233827325&cisb=22_T6233827324&treeMax=true&treeWidth=0&csi=153104&docNo=20

20. SAS. Retrieved April 5, 2009, from Supplier Intelligence Web site: http://www.sas.com/offices/europe/germany/download/files/success/SAS_Kingfisher_Asia.pdf

21. Binns, Simon (2003,November, 27). Kingfisher sets to cut 3000 suppliers. Pro-Quest, Retrieved 4-4-09, from http://proquest.umi.com.proxy2.cl.msu.edu/pqdweb?index=7&did=524446551&SrchMode=1&sid=1&Fmt=4&VInst=PROD&VType=PQD&RQT=309&VName=PQD&TS=1238965583&clientId=3552

22. Kingfisher PLC (2007/2008) (Annual Report) London, United Kingdom

23. Butler, Sarah (2004, October, 2). Kingfisher Steps Up Expansion in Poland. Times Online, Retrieved March 22, 2009, from http://pedagogie.ac-montpellier.fr/disciplines/anglais/bts/oraux/j2d8.pdf

24. Boyle, C. & Dearbail, J. (2008, August 2). Kingfisher sheds Italian business as part of revamp. The Times. Retrieved March 27, 2009, from LexisNexis Academic database.

25. Harrison, B. (1999, June 16). Giant DIY outlet aims for blanket coverage. The Irish Times. Retrieved March 27, 2009, from LexisNexis Academic database.

26. Turkey's Koctas opens warehouse. (2001, July). National Home Center News, 27(14), 6,11. Retrieved April 2, 2009, from Business Module database. (Document ID: 76052347).

27. Butler, Sarah (2006, October, 4). Kingfisher Enters Russia but is Forced to Mind Its P's and Q'a. Times Online, Retrieved March 22, 2009, from http://business.timesonline.co.uk/tol/business/markets/china/article610994.ece

28. (2004, June 10 ). Press Releases. Retrieved April 5, 2009, from Kingfisher PLC Appoints Management for Expansion in Russia Web site: http://www.kingfisher.co.uk/index.asp?PageID=164&subsection=&Year=20   04&NewsID=420

29. (2005, April, 19). Kingfisher to Dip Into Russia Via St. Petersburg. The St. Petersburg Time, Retrieved March 23, 2009, from http://www.sptimes.ru/index.php?action_id=2&story_id=3325

30. (2008, September, 19). Kingfisher bolstered by strength in europe. Opalesque, Retrieved March 21, 2009, from http://www.opalesque.com/Realestate_Briefing/?p=1778

31. (2009). Nationmaster. Retrieved March 23, 2009, from Nationmaster Web site: http://www.nationmaster.com/index.php

# Metro AG

*Emily Anderson, Molly Schaffner, Elissa Albert, Josephine Vendal,*
*Liz Lee*

## Metro AG

Powerful, dominant, and essentially one of the most versatile retailers in the industry are characteristics that a majority of retailers strive to have define their companies. Over forty-six years of trial and tribulations, successes and failures, these three attributes are what currently describe Metro AG. The company, known for their various sectors in retail including, hypermarkets, grocery stores, discount and specialty stores, and wholesale stores, has illustrated that through a defined expansion strategy and continuous motivation to enhance the company's business, such measures can be achieved. The European based retailer believes that success lies in not just one market, but in various markets around the world, and therefore will continue to grow their business through their expansion process.

This case study begins with an overview of the company, which will then lead into Metro AG's expansion strategies and the regions of the world the company has expanded into.

# FLOW CHART

| Country Stores | Open Date | Total |
|---|---|---|
| Germany | 1964 | 1017 |
| Netherlands | 1968 | 49 |
| Belgium | 1970 | 44 |
| Austria | 1971 | 46 |
| United Kingdom | 1971 | 30 |
| Denmark | 1971 | 5 |
| France | 1971 | 123 |
| Italy | 1972 | 147 |
| Spain | 1972 | 95 |
| Turkey | 1990 | 44 |
| Portugal | 1990 | 20 |
| Morocco | 1991 | 8 |
| Greece | 1991 | 19 |
| Hungary | 1994 | 35 |
| Switzerland | 1994 | 20 |
| Romania | 1996 | 48 |
| China | 1996 | 42 |
| Czech Republic | 1997 | 13 |
| Bulgaria | 1999 | 11 |
| Slovakia | 2000 | 5 |
| Russia | 2001 | 87 |
| Croatia | 2001 | 6 |
| Vietnam | 2002 | 9 |
| Japan | 2002 | 6 |
| India | 2003 | 5 |
| Ukraine | 2003 | 26 |
| Moldova | 2004 | 3 |
| Serbia | 2005 | 5 |
| Sweden | 2006 | 16 |
| Pakistan | 2007 | 5 |
| Luxembourg | 2008 | 1 |
| Kazakhstan | 2009 | 1 |

# Overview

Metro ranks as the world's third-largest retailer and as the largest retailer in Germany. They own and operate over 2,200 wholesale stores, supermarkets, hypermarkets, department stores, and Media Markt and Saturn consumer electronics shops.

Metro operates a majority of their stores in Germany, and also operates stores in 33 other countries throughout Europe, Africa, and Asia. The company employs over 300,000 employees worldwide.[1] The company initially began operating Metro Cash & Carry stores and further expanded their sales divisions to Real hypermarkets, Media Markt and Saturn specialty stores, and Galeria Kaufhof, the company's department store division. The company quickly developed and became the world's market leader in Cash and Carry outlets as well as Europe's leader in consumer electronic retailing.[1]

By offering a large amount of merchandise to their customers, Cash and Carry outlets have been the most successful and account for a large majority of stores owned by Metro AG. Cash and Carry stores offer over 20,000 different food items as well as over 30,000 non-food products in various countries. These products are all unique to the country the Cash and Carry outlet is located in. Metro Cash and Carry is focused on offering their customers the best value possible for the best quality products. This division currently thrives in over 30 countries and will continue to expand in the future.[2]

"Real: one store, you won't need more"[3] is the slogan Metro AG is using in their most current advertisements. Consumers who shop Real hypermarkets tend to shop here for convenience at the right price. As we may call it "a one stop shop", Metro Real Hypermarkets account for all products consumers may use on an everyday basis, including: "food, electronics, and clothes."[3] Real focuses on targeting consumers of all demographics, at a lower price point to ensure all customers remain satisfied and loyal. To secure loyalty along with the product offerings Real also offers a loyalty card known as *Payback*.

Metro AG's divisions that specialize in consumer electronics are Media Markt and Saturn. These divisions offer electronics at a competitively low price and various services that can be utilized by customers, such as repair, delivery, and installation. Media Markt has 540 locations as compared to the 240 locations Saturn offers. Both stores offer technological, innovative, and brand name products.[4]

Also known as the management company of all Metro AG department stores, Galeria Kaufhof offers "premium products, international brands, a matching product presentation and employees who are eager to serve their customers."[3]

Associated with what Americans may call luxury brands, Galeria focuses its brand image around trendy, higher end, international clothing products.

## Competition

Metro AG dominates the retail industry around the world, yet they must still compete with similar retailers to maintain their market share. Metro AG's main competition lies in companies such as Carrefour, Aldi, and REWE Group. All four, including Metro, of these retailers specialize in hypermarkets, grocery stores, discount retail stores, and specialty stores. These European based companies are significant to Metro AG because their headquarters are in close proximity to Germany, Metro AG's home country.[1]

Part of Metro AG's strategic positioning is internationalizing outside their home country of Germany. Metro AG was able to make a standardized model of their retail stores and replicate it into other countries. With only changing the product to fit different cultural needs, not the store operations format, Metro AG was able to increase their market share internationally. This gives Metro AG a competitive advantage.[5] Metro AG has a very clear and concise vision for their expansion strategy. They saturate regions that are somewhat culturally similar and in close proximity to one another. They choose regions based on market potential and other predetermined criteria that show them that a particular country is appealing and profitable for them to enter. Metro AG's main competitors are likely to follow them into the same markets that they enter. However, because of this strategy, Metro AG does hold first mover's advantage with the markets that they enter. For example, Metro AG was first of their competitors to enter the Russian market. Soon after, Carrefour and Wal-Mart followed suit by entering Russia.[6] Wal-Mart only opened an office while they explored an acquisition in Russia. Subsequently they determined that Russia was not an attractive market for them. They closed the office in 2009. Carrefour did not foresee gaining market share in Russia after Metro AG's success.[7] This is just one example of how having first movers advantage is vital at gaining market share for a multinational company.

REWE Group, a German based food retail company, recently acquired 245 Extra Stores from Metro AG. This acquisition greatly increased their quantity of stores in Berlin and North Rhine-Westphalia and Lower Saxony. This sale to REWE Group is allowing Metro AG to narrow their focus on hypermarkets and wholesalers where they feel there is more potential.[8] Saturn, one of their divisions in Metro AG, has their own competitive strategy they use when opening stores and keeping the merchandise flowing. Saturn provides exceptional customer service along with keeping prices as low as possible . Saturn makes sure that all of their employees are qualified and understand their products well so that they acquire knowledge to assist customers.[3]

A vital part of Metro AG and their competitor's strategic asset is their ability to integrate private label products into their stores. Metro AG is able to use their private label line to distinguish them from their competitors. The majority of Metro AG's Cash and Carry revenues are coming from their private label line. By creating competitive pricing and making sure the quality is just as good as branded products, Metro AG has been able to set themselves apart from their competitors.[9]

## Expansion Strategy

The company uses an organic expansion strategy meaning they build their own stores instead of acquiring stores.[10] This allows them to implement strategic internal operations. Metro focuses on expanding to markets that are similar to the culture of Germany, their home base, so that the company can make appropriate adaptations to their format as quickly as possible to ensure success in that country.[11] The company focuses their expansion process on the same development path and follows a specific format designed to allow for an easier adaption process in the newly entered country.[5]

Metro has a very organized and detailed strategy they follow in order to expand internationally. The company first analyzes prospective countries by scoring a country's market attractiveness. Once Metro has chosen the countries they want to pursue, they then have a team conduct and gather research about the "country's economic indicators, political stance, societal and legislative environments, its market, and competitive state."[5] After this step takes place, the company conducts another more detailed study of the country. This time the team researches and collects information about the management and operations that will be required for opening new stores. Once this information is analyzed, a final decision is made as to whether or not Metro will enter that country. If they decide to enter that country, Metro then determines the locations, store format, and store sizes. A new country management team is then selected to oversee the process of expansion and make decisions as to what merchandise to have in stock, price points, purchasing policies, and real estate decisions. This team is also required to create and establish a relationship with various levels of government in the particular country, such as the local government, tax regulators, and politicians.[5]

The company then recruits new employees to run their stores. Metro holds a strong belief in hiring local people because they will be able to have a more successful business due to their amplified knowledge of local customer purchasing methods.

Metro has an extensive training program that all new management employees must attend. There are four training center locations that are located around the world in Germany, France, China, and Russia. Metro employs 280 training coaches 45 of which are managers from around the world. The company trains employees on their business philosophy as well as their culture. The training program aims at "developing an international spirit in the organization, while remaining true to the basic concept of the business as it was originally conceived in Germany, and empowering trainees to easily transfer Metro's business concept to their home offices, in their own or another country.[5]

When initially expanding, Metro typically opens a Cash and Carry store. Utilizing a Cash and Carry format allows the company to quickly understand how to do business in that country. Once Metro feels comfortable operating their business in that country, they then begin to open different formats such as their hypermarket format; Real, specialty stores; Media Markt and Saturn, etc.

Metro's growth process has developed in waves. In the 1970s the company began its initial expansion into the Netherlands, followed by numerous countries in Western Europe. Once the desirable markets in Western Europe became saturated with Metro stores, the company expanded into the Mediterranean region of Europe in the 1990s. In the 2000s Metro began expansion into Eastern Europe and Asia. The company plans to continue expansion into these regions in the years to come.[5]

## Western Europe

"The Big Four, Germany, France, Italy, and United Kingdom account for over 80% of retail sales within the European Union".[10] According to the flow chart, Metro currently operates over 1,300 stores in these four Western European countries. Metro AG has gained great success over the past 46 years by expanding throughout Western Europe. Having almost completely saturated the Western European market, this has allowed Metro AG to capitalize on growing opportunities beyond its home base location.

While expanding further into Europe, this multinational company is going about positioning itself a little differently than it has in the West. A strategy Metro has thrived on throughout expansion in Western Europe is staying as decentralized as possible. Metro's executives have decided to give full power to managers in each sales division of all new store openings. This facilitates greater customer orientation, improved cost management, and gains in efficiency.[1]

## Mediterranean

Metro AG focused their international expansion into the Mediterranean countries during the 1990s. These countries included Turkey, Greece, and Morocco.[5] Metro AG entered into Turkey in 1990 in a joint venture with Migros, Turkey's largest food retailer. This Turkish based company dominates the supermarket industry with 154 stores.[12]

When Metro AG entered into Greece in a joint-venture with Westdeutsche Landesbank, 1992, their main focus was Cash and Carry operations. With recent interest in expanding their e-commerce chain, Metro AG has decided to put 290 properties on the market to be sold. Because of the success of their Cash and Carry locations, Metro AG and Westdeutsche Landesbank will maintain these stores.[13] Although the Mediterranean market shows potential for growth, currently Metro AG's expansion focus is on the Eastern European market.

## Eastern Europe

Metro began their expansion into Eastern Europe when they entered Romania in 1996. The company believes Eastern Europe is a desirable location for expansion due to its great deal of market potential and currently low number of competitors.[14] Metro also views this area as a profitable expansion possibility because it offers a desirable market coinciding with the company's store formats.[15]

In order to ensure success, Metro will adapt their store formats to better fit the markets of Eastern Europe. Metro AG will also focus on creating a strong brand image by sourcing 90% of the goods from local vendors. In Russia, specifically, Metro will adapt their stores to the region by having a sales area of approximately 3,500 square meters, create a new color concept because of shared colors among competition in the region, have an assortment of products that focus on white goods and smaller domestic appliances, and create a marketing campaign that focuses on the strengths of the company.[15]

Over the past eight years, Metro's stores in Eastern Europe have tripled in sales. In 2000, sales in Eastern Europe were recorded as $7.856 million. That amount increased to $24.380 million by 2008. Eastern European locations account for 18% of Metro's store locations, with the majority of store formats representing Cash and Carry outlets. The company's expansion in Eastern Europe was reliant to a large degree on the transferability and strength of the Cash & Carry business model, which can thrive in areas with relatively low per capita because of its self-financing nature.[16]

The stores in this region make up about 50% of Metro Group's earnings before interest and taxes. Poland, Russia, Romania, and the Czech Republic generate the most profit for the company in this region. Metro considers these countries the Big Four of Eastern Europe, which generate about 70% of their Eastern European sales.[15]

The company will continue expansion in the Eastern European market in the near future, and will target the areas with potential market growth and growing economic strength.[17] As Metro internationalizes into this region, they believe they have the aptitude of leadership and knowledge to open modern retail formats in these less developed retail markets.[18]

## Asia

The Asian market was first introduced to Metro in 1996 when the company opened its first store in China. Today, Metro operates 67 stores across the continent of Asia including stores in India, Vietnam, Japan, China, and Pakistan. Metro plans to use the Greenfield option for expansion into Asia, meaning the company will build their stores from scratch instead of acquiring currently existing stores.[10] When Metro initially enters an Asian country they begin their expansion with Cash and Carry stores in the country's capital and continue to build new Cash and Carry outlets into other major cities around the country.[19]

Metro decided to extend their stores to Asia because their home market and countries that experienced expansion in the years prior had become saturated. Asia is an appealing place to internationalize to because it offers many growth opportunities and economies of scale.

When entering Asia, Metro has faced the challenge of adapting their stores to appeal to the Asian market. The company has encountered difficulties such as governmental restrictions and packaging problems, but has critically assessed their business and solved many of these challenges. For instance, Metro has taught farmers that sell their crops to the company how to package food more efficiently to reduce spoilage in the distribution process.[20] More specifically, when adapting to the Japanese market, the company has had to learn to adapt their seafood selections and offer their customers the freshest and best quality seafood available in their Cash and Carry stores.

The future outlook for Metro's development into the Asian market is promising. The company sees the most potential in China and India and plans to continue expansion in these countries.

# Conclusion

Overall, Metro AG utilizes their experience, knowledge, and willingness to take risks to capitalize in all aspects of company expansion. Multinational companies begin by saturating their home markets, maintaining a decentralized management system, and learning from this process to continue expansion beyond their home region. Metro AG continues to succeed by focusing solely on their own expansion strategies and captivating the market potential where they see best fit. This has resulted in Metro AG becoming one of the leading retailers worldwide.

# Questions

**1. Is the retailer classified as a global retailer or a multinational retailer? Explain its pattern of expansion. What expansion strategy did/is the retailer use/using?**

*Metro AG is classified as a multinational retailer. Metro Cash & Carry, which is engaged in the Cash and Carry sector in the global market, operating under the Metro and Makro brands; Real, a hypermarket operator in Germany and Poland; Media Markt and Saturn, which is engaged in the consumer electronics retailing business; and Galeria Kaufhof, which is engaged in the concept and system department store sector in Belgium and Germany.[21] To continue growth into the future, Metro AG is concentrating on primarily expanding into European countries such as Poland, Russia and Asia.[22] Metro AG chooses the markets it enters based on economic status, purchasing power in the country, and the opportunities of growth in the market. Metro AG's plans to expand heavily in China and more specifically in China's electronics sector. Metro AG does not franchise nor license due to the constant redevelopment of the company to fit into the cultural dimensions of the market they are entering. In order to raise funds for expansion and renovation of the company, Metro AG became a joint venture in the 2000, shifting 290 hypermarkets. By becoming a joint venture, Metro is able to be more customer orientated and overall more efficient.*

**2. Based on Dunning eclectic theory, how do ownership, locational and internalization factors play in your retailers' international expansion?**

*According to Dunning's Eclectic Theory, ownership, locational and internalization factors are a significant part in going international with Metro AG. Metro focuses ownership advantages on both transaction based advantages and asset based advantages. Transaction based assets make the company difficult to copy and it is almost impossible to franchise or license. Metro group is a wholly owned business allowing all of their company secrets to remain confidential. This is an example of Metro's asset based advantages. Locational advantages that Metro aspires* to achieve are saturating the host country first, which was Germany, and then expanding into culturally similar countries like its first move into the Netherlands. Once the culturally similar countries become saturated, they move into less similar markets like China and India. Metro positions themselves in countries based on the market segment and economic status. Once the market segment is occupied, Metro uses the gained knowledge from the market as a tool to improve their sales strategy and their competitive advantage. Metro wishes to "continue developing [their] sales divisions, and enhancing [their] status as unmistakable retail brands that set themselves apart from the competition".[8] Metro is a wholly owned subsidiary which allows the company's method of operation and distribution to be successful. Metro does not strategize on entering markets that lack product similarity or competition, but capitalizes on gaining market share in order to sustain internalization.

### 3. What role does cultural proximity and geographical proximity play in the retailers' international moves?

Cultural proximity does play a role in Metro's international expansion. When comparing the countries that Metro first expanded to, the cultural dimensions, as according to Hofstede, are very similar. As the years progressed and countries close in cultural and geographical proximity became saturated with Metro stores, the company began expanding to countries that were less similar in cultural aspects and further in geographical distance from Germany. Metro's international expansion happened in three waves. In the 1970s the company focused on expanding into the western part of Europe. By the 1990s the company began expansion into Mediterranean countries such as Morocco and Greece. At the turn of the century, Metro began expansion into Eastern European and Asian countries.[5]

### 4. Can you predict the retailer's future international expansion?

Metro AG is expecting to expand their company more internationally in the next few years, planning on opening aproximatley 95 new stores. Metro plans on opening 40 Cash and Carry's, 15 Real, and 70 Media Markt and Saturn stores.[5] Metro AG plans to expand into China due to it's thriving market. They also play to expand in Eastern Europe. Egypt is another area that Metro AG is expanding their Cash and Carry into. Metro AG is well aware of decreasing sales in the past few years and realize with the expansion of new stores, they will be able to increase their market share by increasing their private labels in new store openings. With the history of Metro's expansion process we think that Metro will continue expansion into countries they feel can be profitable and have an impact on as a retailer. We feel Metro will continue to expand into Asian countries and soon to the Middle East because of the potential these markets illustrate.

## Propositions

**P1: The greater the ownership advantages for retailers, the less likely they will franchise or license.**

*This proposition is true for Metro. Metro AG does not franchise nor license due to the fact that they use shareholding in their company. The shareholding in the company is used to help stabilize and manage how the company is growing. They do not use franchising because they reinvent the products they carry, and have a growing organization, changing what their format to stores or their company is.[10] Metro AG has begun perfecting their private label brands to help them expand their market, beginning in India, as an experiment to see how consumers like their private label.[23] Private labels have generated 10% of the revenue before starting in India, but Metro wants to increase the revenue.*

**P2: The greater the available organizational slack the greater the likelihood of expanding internationally.**

*This proposition is not true for Metro. Organizational slack can be important to the company because with the excess resources going unused they can be utilized by expanding the company into a new market. One of Metro's thriving retail strategies as an international company is the incentive of continual growth and expansion. Looking at the current ratios for the years 2005-2007 the ratio is steadily increasing. While the organizational slack of Metro is decreasing, but the continuous growth of the company is still underway.*

**P3: The greater the recoverable slack the greater the likelihood of expanding internationally.**

*[Ratio of General and Administrative Expenses to Sales (3 year average before their first international expansion)]*

Before 2002 expansion into Japan

| In € millions | 1999 | 2000 | 2001 |
|---|---|---|---|
| Gen and admin expenses | 828 | 1,068 | 1,304 |
| Sales | 43,833 | 46,930 | 49,522 |
| Expenses to sales | .01889 | .0228 | .02088 |

*This proposition is not true for Metro. The ratio did not get larger as the propositionn predicted.*

**P4: The greater the potential slack the greater the likelihood of expanding internationally.**

*[Ratio of Equity to Capital (3 year average before their first international expansion)]*

Before 2002 expansion into Japan

| In € millions | 1999 | 2000 | 2001 |
|---|---|---|---|
| Equity | 4,022 | 4,146 | 4,242 |
| Capital | 1,446 | 1,620 | 1,572 |
| Equity to Capital | 2.781 | 2.559 | 2.698 |

*This proposition is not true for Metro because the numbers from 1999 - 2001 indicate that the company is not consistently going up or down. This draws us to conclude that the greater the potential slack there is no likelihood of expanding internationally.*

**P5: Multinational retailers will move to countries with lower disposable income than their home country**

*This proposition is not true for Metro. Beginning in the early 1990s, Metro AG Began expanding into less developed countries, such as Morocco (1991), Romania (1996), and Bulgaria (1999). The company expands into countries with less disposable income, and thereafter continues to keep business open even if the country's economy is worsening. For example, as competitors pull out of Russia, Metro AG continues to open stores although the market is crisis struck.*[14]

**P6: Multinational retailers will move to countries that have a high positive change in GDP**

*This proposition is true for Metro. Looking at Metros entry into Vietnam in 2002, their GDP was higher than 5 years previous. Metro is one of those retailers who sees the rising of GDP as an opportunity of expansion. The GDP has currently risen until the current year making the country more desirable for expansion of more locations for Metro to enter.*

<u>$35.1 billion- $26.8 billion</u>
$35.1 billion

**P7: Multinational retailers will move to countries that have a high positive change in service-value added as % of GDP.**

*This proposition is not true for Metro. Metro does not use the percent service GDP to consider moving into a country due to the fact that when they moved into Vietnam, Vietnam had a percent service GDP of 38.5 and 5 years before that had a percent of 41.7. Metro is more of a product based company rather then service based.[24]*

**P8: Multinational retailers will first move to countries that are culturally the most similar to their home country.**

*This proposition is true for Metro. According to Hofstede's Cultural Dimensions Theory, the countries that Metro AG first expanded into have very similar cultural dimensions to Metro AG's home country, Germany. The early years of Metro's expansion took place in the Netherlands, Belgium, and Austria. These three countries in the economies of scale can correlate with the cultural dimensions of Germany. Whereas future expansions began to take place in countries that were very dissimilar to that of Germany. For instance, in 2003 Metro AG expanded into India which has very few similarities to Germany.[25]*

**P9: Multinational retailers will expand within the country and then will expand   regionally within that area**

*This proposition is not true for Metro. According to our flow chart, Metro has expanded regionally within that area. Metro entered Hungary and Poland in 1994 and has continued expanding into the countries surrounding, including Czech Republic, Croatia, Ukraine, Romania, Bulgaria, Slovakia, and Serbia. Metro will find the opportunity to expand into a country if the opportunity is given, especially if it is a surrounding country of where a Metro is located.*

**P10: Periodically the multinational retailers will "jump" to a new geographic area and begin the stages form of expansion.**

*This proposition is true for Metro. After Metro has moved into most of Europe and Asia, they are now beginning to develop their company elsewhere. Vietnam is a country where Metro jumped into a geographic location unlike where they're mainly located. Other areas where Metro has developed their company would be in Pakistan, the only Middle Eastern country entered. Metro has decided to enter the African market opening 10 stores over the short term Egypt.*

**P11: Multinational retailers will move to countries that are geographically close to the home country initially, then expand to more distant countries. (Miles from Home Country to Host country)**

*This proposition is true for Metro. The first expansions consisted of expanding to countries that were geographically close to Germany, such as the Netherlands, Austria, and the United Kingdom. As time went on and countries close in geographical distance to Germany became saturated, Metro AG began to expand to countries further from their home base. Based on the number of store openings in each country, discussed in the flow chart, the pattern of openings becomes less and less focused on culture or geographical closeness to Germany.*

**P12: Multinational retailers will move to countries with large population bases.**

*This proposition is not true for Metro. Although large populations are favorable, Metro AG's strategic expansion method is based on other factors. The company does not limit expansion based on population size, rather, they base their expansion on potential growing markets with growing economic strength and favorable purchasing power trends.[26]*

## Endnotes

1. METRO AG. (1 April). Hoover's Company Records,52620. Retrieved February 28, 2010, from Hoover's Company Records. (Document ID: 1046966901).

2. "Metro Cash and Carry". Metro AG. 3/19/10 <http://www.metro cc.com/servlet/PB/menu/1014962_l2/index.html

3. "Metro Group". 2/27/2010 <http://www.metrogroup.de/servlet/PB/menu/1_l2/index.html>.

4. "Media-Saturn". Metro AG. 3/19/10 <http://www.media saturn.com/EN/Company/Pages/Default.aspx>.

5. Krafft, Manfred, Murali K. Mantrala, & Mierdorf Zygmunt (2006). In Retailing in the 21st Century. Retailing in the Global World: Case Study of Metro (pp. 27-38) Austin, TX: Springer Berlin Heidelberg.

6. (2008, September 23). Carrefour spending to expand into Russia. The Globe and Mail (Canada), p. B13. Retrieved March 3rd, 2010, from Lexis Nexis academic.

7. Kramer, Andrew and Saltmarsh, Matthew (2009, October 17). Final French Retailer to Close Its Russia Stores. The New York Times. Section B, p. 7.

Retrieved March 3rd 2010, from Lexis Nexis Academic. http://www.lexisnexis.
com.proxy1.cl.msu.edu/hottopics/lnacademic/

8. (2008, January 26). REWE buys 245 Extras from Metro. The Grocer. p. 14.
Retrieved March 10th, 2010, from Lexis Nexis Academic. http://www.lexisnexis.
com.proxy2.cl.msu.edu/hottopics/lnacademic/

9. "Metro Cash & Carry Reveals New Private Label Strategy." Spire
Advertising & Web Design, 9 Dec. 2009. Web. 20 March 2010. <http://www.
storebrandsdecisions.com/news/2009/12/09/metro-cash-and-carry-reveals-new-
private-label-strategy->.

10. Sternquist, Brenda. (2007). "Mexico and Canada." International Retailing (pp.
211). New York: Fairchild Books & Visuals.

11. Annual Report 2008. Retrieved March 24, 2010, from http://www.metrogroup.
de/multimedia/microsite/Geschaeftsbericht-2008/pdf/GB2008-en.pdf

12. Welt, Die. "METRO CO Enhanced Coverage Linking METRO CO -Search
using: * Company Profile * News, Most Recent 60 Days -OPERATES WITH
TURKEY'S LARGEST RETAILER (METRO KOOPERIERT MIT GROSTEM
TURKISCHEN EINZELHANDLER)". Lexus Nexis. 3/1/2010 <http://www.
lexisnexis.com.proxy2.cl.msu.edu/hottopics/lnacademic/>.

13. Beck, Ernest. (2000, January 5th). Germany's Metro to Sell Holdings In Real
Estate to Fuel Expansion. The Wallstreet Journal (Eastern edition). p.A19.
Retrieved March 15th, 2010. From ABI/INFORM Global. (Document ID
47653566).

14. Stych, Matthew. Analysis- Carrefour Backs Home Front While Metro Plays Away.
Retrieved April 2, 2010, from LexusNexis

15. Cordes, Dr. Eckhard. "METRO Group's Presence in Eastern Europe – Facts
and Figures." Commerzbank, 1 Oct. 2009. Web. 5 Apr. 2010. <http://www.
metrogroup.at/servlet/PB/show/1228240/IR-Events-Other-2009-Commerzbank-
en.pdf>.

16. Europe's grocers chase emerging consumers. Retrieved March 30, 2010, from
LexusNexis http://www.lexisnexis.com.proxy2.cl.msu.edu/us/lnacademic/
results/docview/docview.do?docLinkInd=true&risb=21_T8960762973&f
ormat=GNBFI&sort=RELEVANCE&startDocNo=1&resultsUrlKey=29_
T8960762981&cisb=22_T8960762977&treeMax=true&treeWidth=0&csi=23403
6&docNo=4

17. METRO Group-Company Corporate Strategy." Metro Group. N.p., 17 Mar. 2010.
Web. 20 Mar. 2010.<www.metrogroup.de/servlet/PB/menu/1000083_l2/index.
html>.

18. METRO Group - Corporate Principles." METRO Group . N.p., 11 Aug. 2006. Web. 25 Mar. 2010. <http://www.metrogroup.de/servlet/PB/menu/1004232_l2/index.html>

19. Wiedmann, Michael. "Metro Cash and Carry International." N.p., July 2006. Web. 20 March 2010. <http://www.metro-cc.com/servlet/PB/show/1020136/mcc-news-260606-CorpPresentation-long-eng.pdf>.

20. Wassener, Bettina. "Asia gives Metro haven from economic storm; German retailer embarks on aggressive expansion in rare region of growth; Spotlight." The International Herald Tribune, 13 June 2009. Web. 13 March 2010. <http://www.lexisnexis.com.proxy2.cl.msu.edu/us/lnacademic/results/docview/docview.do?docLinkInd=true&risb=21_T8996190686&format=GNBFI&sort=RELEVANCE&startDocNo=1&resultsUrlKey=29_T8996190693&cisb=22_T>.

21. "Metro AG Company". Mergent Online. Retrieved March 6th. <http://www.mergentonline.com/compdetail.asp?company=92135>.

22. METRO AG. (15 March). Hoover's Company Records,52620. Retrieved March 19, 2010, from Hoover's Company Records. (Document ID: 1046966901). http://www.metrogroup.de/servlet/PB/menu/1000083_l2/index.html)

23. "Metro Unveils Private Label Business For Mom 'n' Pop Shops." Economic Times, 23 October 2007. < http://www.india-reports.com/retail/Nov07.aspx>

24. "World Resources Institute". Earth Trends. 2/25/2010 <http://earthtrends.wri.org/searchable_db/index.php?step=countries&cID[]=195&theme=5&variable_ID=216&action=select_years>.

25. Hofstede, Geert . "Geert Hofstede Cultural Dimensions". Itim International. 3/25/2010 . <http://www.geert-hofstede.com/hofstede_india.shtml>.

26. METRO AG. (15 March). Hoover's Company Records,52620. Retrieved March 19, 2010, from Hoover's Company Records. (Document ID: 1046966901). http://www.metrogroup.de/servlet/PB/menu/1000083_l2/index.html)

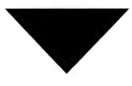

# Office Depot, Inc.

*Lindsey Alber, Sarah Blankenship, Laura Duffin, Bryan Selley,*
*Neils Moltmaker, Andrew Joslyn*

## Office Depot, Inc.

### Timeline

1986: United States (1,338 in 2008)
1992: Canada (29 in 2008)
1994: Israel (44 in 2008)
1994: Colombia (2 in 2007)
1995: Mexico (173 in 2007)
1995: Poland (exit in 2004)
1995: France (48 in 2008)
1995: Thailand (4 in 2007)
1997: Japan (28 in 2008; planned exit in 2009)
1997: Hungary (17 in 2008)
2002: Guatemala (5 in 2007)
2002: Costa Rica (4 in 2007)
2003: El Salvador (2 in 2002)
2003: Spain (6 in 2003)
2006: Panama (3 in 2007)
2006: Honduras (3 in 2007)
2006: South Korea (13 in 2008)
2007: Puerto Rico (6 in 2009)
2008: Sweden (13 in 2008)

## Opening Statement

Through rapid expansion by means of organic growth, licensing, joint ventures and acquisitions Office Depot, Inc. has managed to reach customers all over North America, Europe, Asia and Central America. Once named "Company of the Year" by the Miami Herald and at one time claiming the title of largest office supplies retailer in North America1, Office Depot, Inc. is now closing stores all over North America as well as exiting other countries completely. While the company continues to expand, growth has slowed as the worsening economy takes its toll on the office supply giant.

Established in 1986, Office Depot predominantly sell to small firms, home offices and individual consumers.[2] They employ a strategy of using low-profile fixtures, bins and steel shelving in order to achieve bulk inventory stacking and quick and efficient restocking.[3] Office Depot, Inc. offers national branded and private label merchandise with some of the private label brands being Office Depot, Niceday, Foray, Christopher Lowell, and Ative.[4] In recent years the company has made the move to place more emphasis on private label. Private brands represented nearly 20% of sales, but that figure was expected to increase, private-label penetration is a key component of the company's strategy to improve profits and achieve differentiation.[5]

Office Depot, Inc., a global supplier of office products and services, conducts its business through three main divisions: North American Retail, North American business solutions and international division. Their strategy is to achieve organic growth through store based expansion, additional private brand launches and development of multi-sales channels. When organic growth is not possible the company expands its presence in domestic and international markets by means of acquisition.[6] The company operates under the names Office Depot, Inc., Tech Depot, and Viking Direct.

While Office Depot, Inc. has managed to penetrate markets all over the world as well as open over a thousand stores in their home market, there are major obstacles that are beginning to surface. Office Depot, Inc. operates in a competitive and fragmented industry, consisting of retailer, dealers, and distributors. The company faces competition from office supply retailers like Staples and OfficeMax, along with global retail giants like Wal-Mart.[7] Risks to the company include vendor confidence, increased competitive activity, domestic store saturation, a weak labor environment, deterioration in small business optimism and potential for a further slowdown in mid and large size corporate spending on office and related products.[8]

## Domestic Expansion: (United States)

Office Depot, Inc. was founded by Pat Sher, Jack Kopkin and Stephen Dougherty in Fort Lauderdale, Florida in 1986. By the end of 1987 there are a total of 10 stores inbetween Florida and Georgia. Throughout the next two years Office Depot, Inc. continued its rapid expansion by adding over 50 stores in 12 states while also going public on June 1st, 1988. Shortly after, an extensive line of recycled paper products is introduced initiating the company's environmental focus which continues today. A merger with Office Club, Inc., the first in a long line of mergers and acquisitions is completed in April 1991. The same year sales broke the billion dollar mark making Office Depot, Inc. the largest office products retailer in North America. Growth continues during the years of 1993 and 1994 with the acquisition of 8 contract stationers in North America. 1998 brings the opening of 100 new stores in North America, the highest in the company's history as well as the launch of their first public website. By 2005 Office Depot, Inc. has opened its 1000th store and has achieved annual sales of over $13 billion.[9] In 2006, privately held Allied Office Products is acquired, the countries largest independent dealer of office products and services.[10] In July of 2008, Office Depot, Inc. opened its first "Green" store in Austin Texas. Hoping to appeal to customers who have been increasingly focused on environmental issues, the "Green" store will use less energy and water in its daily operations, increase recycling and leave a much smaller overall environmental footprint than the typical store of its size.[11] In contrast, store closings will be the theme for 2009 with 126 stores in North America closing their doors in order to cut capital spending and operational overhead.[12]

## International Expansion

Office Depot began their international expansion with Canada in 1992. A couple years later, in 1994, Office Depot, Inc. made the jump overseas into the Israeli market.[13] Their international growth initiatives include fueling profitability through cost management activities, making strategic acquisition of promising companies in emerging markets, driving private brand sales through expanded product assortments and increased marketing, as well as broadening their product and service offerings.[14] Growth continued through 1997 with moves into Central America, expansion through Europe as well as entry into Asian markets. In 1998 Office Depot, Inc. made one of its biggest strategic moves by merging with Viking Direct (Viking Office Products), a company that serves large business customers in Europe and Australia through direct mail. Viking Direct maintains one of the highest customer service and retention levels of any European office supplies company and is widely acclaimed for its dedication to the concept of "fanatical customer service" - impress a customer so much that they want to buy again and again.[15] Office Depot, Inc. has adopted this concept.[16] The merger with Viking allowed the company to have a strong foothold for eventual expansion throughout Europe. In 1999 their first international website was launched which marks the beginning of a strategy to enter new markets via non-store formats.[17] This strategy has proven successful in a number of countries. In 2003 the size of the company's European business doubled through the acquisition of Guilbert S.A., a leading European contract stationer. In 2006 Best Office Co., Ltd., Papirius s.r.o., and AsiaEC were aquired giving them access to South Korea, countries throughout Eastern Europe and China respectively.[18] While expansion still continues in other parts of the world, it was announced that Office Depot, Inc. will be shutting down its operations in Japan in 2009.[19]

## Canada

Canada presented a great market expansion opportunity with little competition.[20] Expansion was through acquisition, this time of an office supply chain called The Great Canadian Office Supplies Warehouse, whose parent company was called HQ Office International.[21] HQ Office International was an extension of an unsuccessful HQ warehouse company in California.[22] Recently in 2007, Office Depot, Inc. acquired Axidata, a company in Canada that sells office products.[23] When transitioning into Canada, Mark Begelman said of the move:

> "This agreement enables Office Depot to enter the important Canadian market with an established based of five existing stores, leases for two additional stores and a staff of office products professionals already experienced in doing business in Canada."[24]

Acquiring this company was a strategic move on Office Depot, Inc's part. It saves time and money when you buy an existing company that already has an established core of executives and employees who implement a proven system. In 2009, Office Depot, Inc. announced that it would be closing 3 stores throughout the Northeast part of the U.S. and Canada.[25]

## Israel

Less than 10 years after Office Depot, Inc's modest beginnings the company breaks out onto the international scene through a licensing agreement in 1994.[26] The Middle Eastern economy is one of the fastest expanding retail sectors.[27] Israel's economy is forecasted to raise almost a full percent and their retail industry is supposed to raise 10% in 2009 and continue to rise through 2013.[28] In 2006, Office

Depot, Inc. Israel increased their holding to a majority share. Two years later in 2008, the remaining shares were purchased making operations in Israel a wholly owned subsidiary.[29]

## Columbia

In 1994, the same year as international expansion into Israel, a licensing agreement was also struck in Columbia.[30] This move into Columbia has said to mean that there will be continued movement into Spanish speaking countries.[31] Although Office Depot, Inc. already has a retail presence in Colombia it was recently announced that the Joint Venture in Mexico will allow the company to enter Colombia with their partner, Grupo Gigante.[32]

## Mexico

In 1995, through a joint venture agreement with Grupo Gigante, Office Depot, Inc. made its move into Central America. The partnership was established to develop and operate a chain of office supply retail stores throughout Mexico. This partnership came to revolutionize not only the sale of office supplies, but created a new concept for selling school supplies, furniture, computers and electronics, bringing the benefits of buying in bulk to final consumers. Thus, the negotiations with global partners enabled Office Depot, Inc. customers to have access to prices that were previously only available to large wholesalers.[33] In recent years, this venture, Office Depot de Mexico, has grown in size and scope and now includes retail locations in Costa Rica, El Salvador, Guatemala, Honduras, and Panama.[34] A quote from David Fuente, chairmen and CEO of Office Depot, Inc. at the time describes this joint venture best:

> "The joint venture allows us to combine Office Depot's successful store format and marketing expertise with Grupo Gigante's solid operational structure and 32-year history of retailing in Mexico."[35]

Joining with Grupo Gigante allows the company to team up with a very prestigious retailer and get to know the international environment faster.[36]

In July 2008 Gigante offered Office Depot, Inc. $430 million dollars to buy out their 50% stake in the joint venture. The purchase would give Gigante complete control of Office Depot de Mexico SA and would be conditioned on Gigante gaining rights to expand the chain into Latin America.[37] In October, Office Depot, Inc. announced that it had rejected Gigantes bid to buy their 50% and the two companies would look for alternatives to expand into the region.[38]

## Poland

Under a licensing agreement retail locations were opened in Poland in 1995. However, in 2004 operations were discontinued because of a flawed expansion strategy. The problem arose when Office Depot, Inc. introduced their brick and mortar stores at the same time that the French office supplies company Lyreco introduced their catalog and online approach to the country. The French strategy proved to be more successful and Lyreco now controls the market. A few years later in 2007, Office Depot, Inc. announced that they would be re-entering the country with a remodeled strategy. They are planning to replicate that of Lyreco's with telesales and online sales, which will be less costly than their brick and mortar stores. Also, to avoid a negative association with the Office Depot, Inc. brand name they will be entering the country under the Viking Office products name.[39]

## France

In 1995, under a joint venture agreement with Carrefour SA Office Depot, Inc. expanded to France. In 1998 Office Depot, Inc. acquired the remaining 50% of its operations in France making it the sole owner. Shortly after, the decision was made to consolidate the Office Depot, Inc. and Viking Office Products headquarters into one that is more conveniently located.[40] In 2003, Office Depot, Inc. acquired French office furniture retailer Guilbert, expanding its presence in Europe.[41] Because of Vikings strength in France it continues to be one of Office Depots strongest markets with a total of 44 stores. Joint Ventures have also helped Office Depot get to know their consumers in different parts of the world.

## Thailand

To go along with their extensive expansion strategy, in 1995 an international licensing agreement was signed to open stores in Thailand. In recent years the company has been focusing on supporting sales growth in Asia to compensate for a sluggish home market caused by the financial and economic turmoil in the United States. Office Club, the licensed operator of Office Depot stores in Thailand, said the licensor (Office Depot, Inc.) is providing greater support in terms of product development and expansion, know-how in direct-selling, Internet site and e-procurement, as well as in logistics.[42]

## Japan

Under a joint venture agreement with Deo Deo in 1997 the first store in Japan was opened. Two years later the company announced that it acquired the remaining

50 % of its Japanese operations for approximately $28 million. The acquisition made Office Depot, Inc. the owner of 100% of its Japanese operations.[43] Originally the joint venture may have been necessary to enter Japan however, the relationship would be a valuable learning experience for any company entering a new market. By 2002 Office Depot, Inc. instituted a number of changes in its business model designed to make the Company more efficient and sales-driven in the high-risk, high-return market.[44] Unfortunately, the changes did not do enough to save the company and in 2009 it closed the doors of eight Japanese stores and announced that the other twenty were expected to be closed by the end of the year.[45] Closing these stores in Japan would end up costing Office Depot, Inc. around $13 million.[46]

## Hungary

Originally Office Depot, Inc. entered Hungary under a licensing agreement with Elso Iroda Superstore Kft, in 1997. However, in April 2004 it was announced that Elso Iroda Superstore Kft, which had been operating Office Depot, Inc. retail stores and direct sales businesses would be acquired by the office supply chain making this their first wholly owned subsidiary in Eastern Europe. The rest of their businesses in Eastern Europe were under licensing agreements. This move becomes increasingly important as new countries are joining the EU. Bruce Nelson, Chairman and CEO of Office Depot, Inc. said of the move:

> "This very strategic transaction represents further evidence of our commitment to being the leading office products supplier throughout Europe. We will continue to look for appropriate opportunities to grow in areas of Europe where we are not now represented, even as we consolidate our leading positions in the major markets of Western Europe."[47]

Due to the success of Office Depot, Inc's expansion throughout Hungary, in 2007 the company planned to eventually expand its retail network to 40 stores.[48] The majority of Office Depot, Inc's business in Hungary is generated through its retail stores, though it also has a health B2B business which is unique to this market.[49] As of January 2008 there are currently 17 retail locations throughout Hungary as well as an Internet sales facility.[50]

## Guatemala

Under its joint venture agreement with Grupo Gigante, one of the largest retailer in Mexico, Office Depot, Inc. opened two stores in Guatemala in 2002.[51] The entry mode in Guatemala was through a joint licensing agreement.[52] According to the Office Depot, Inc. website they now have a 5 store presence in the country.[53]

## Costa Rica

The joint venture with Grupo Gigante that led the way for expansion into Guatemala also aided with expansion efforts into Costa Rica. The entry mode into Costa Rica was through a joint licensing agreement.[54] By the end of 2002 the company had 2 retail locations in place.[55]

## El Salvador

As with the expansion into previous Central American countries Grupo Gigante also paved the way for Office Depot, Inc. to enter El Salvador in 2003. Today there are 2 retail locations in El Salvador.[56]

## Spain

In 2003 Office Depot, Inc. made its official debut in Spain with the introduction of 6 office supplies superstores. The stores are an adaptation of the retailer's European model, offering a broad range of products designed to meet the needs of Spanish small and medium-sized businesses. Previously Viking Office Products had been operating a direct mail order business in Madrid so there is a supply chain already in place.[57] To go along with their direct mail, Viking also established a catalog similar to the one in Switzerland and Portugal.[58] Launching the catalog operations assures that customers will be able to speak to employees that speak the same language, encouraging ordering.[59]

## South Korea

In 2006 Office Depot, Inc. entered South Korea by acquiring a controlling interest in Best Office Co., Ltd., one of the top office supply companies in South Korea. CEO at the time Steve Odland said this of the acquisition:

> "This transaction strengthens Office Depot's global presence in a rapidly growing area of the world. Our investment in Best Office, with its demonstrated history of sustainable and profitable growth, not only allows us to continue our geographic expansion, but extends our ability to deliver innovative products and services to customers of all sizes in the South Korean market."[60]

Best Office operated more than 70 stores and it is said that this acquisition helped Office Depot's international expansion efforts.[61]

## Panama

Eleven years after the joint venture agreement was made with Grupo Gigante of Mexico the same agreement helped Office Depot, Inc. enter Panama in 2006.[62]

## Honduras

Just like Grupo Gigante aided with the expansion into Guatemala, El Salvador, Costa Rica and Panama they also led the way into Honduras.[63] With the initiation of operations in Honduras in 2006, Office Depot, Inc. has successfully penetrated all States of the Mexican Republic. The growth they experienced throughout this region is the result of the pursuit of customer satisfaction and talent to operate with lower costs as well as offer a wider variety of price, quality and choice.[64]

## Puerto Rico

In 2007 Office Depot, Inc. opened its first store in Puerto Rico. This store was opened with the goal of "providing businesses here with exceptional value, a wide selection of products and services, and outstanding customer service." In November of 2009 the opening of the sixth store in Ponce was celebrated with a ribbon cutting ceremony.[65] Opening these stores in Puerto Rico has lead to positive consumer reaction and also produces around 25 jobs each time a store is opened. Office Depot has plans of opening more stores in this region.[66]

## Sweden

Since 2004 Office Depot, Inc. has had a strategic alliance with AGE, a Swedish office supplies company that is among the largest in the region. In 2008 the move was made to acquire a majority interest in the company, which marks the entry of the Office Depot brand in the Nordic market. This acquisition added 13 retail locations and a contract business to the companies growing portfolio. Among things gained by the relationship are more than 6,500 national and private brand office products and solutions as well as the market knowledge and resources of AGE.[67]

## Future Growth: The Middle East (Kuwait City & Dubai)

As of January 2009 Office Depot, Inc. signed an agreement with M.H. Alshaya Co., an international retailer operating over 40 international franchise brands throughout the Middle East, Eastern Europe and Russia, to sell office products and services under the Office Depot, Inc. name. This agreement will give M.H.

Alshaya Co. the franchise rights for all channels in the Kingdom of Saudi Arabia, the United Arab Emirates, Kuwait, the Kingdom of Bahrain, Qatar and Oman. The first 4 retail locations are scheduled to open in 2009 in Kuwait City and Dubai. Because of their lack of experience in the region Office Depot, Inc. is partnering with a company with greater expertise and knowledge of the Middle East to develop their retail business.[68] The Middle East is among one of the regions that have a positive outlook in terms of economic expansion.[69] Office Depot plans to take advantage of this high spending and increasing growth rate by being able to increase their market share as well as their revenues. Retail sales in the Middle East slumped during 2008 due to the ailing economy but have been forecasted to jump 13% in 2009.[70]

## Websites, Direct Mail, Catalogs

Besides acquisitions, licensing and organic growth Office Depot, Inc., with the help of Viking Office Products, reaches customers all over the world through direct mail, catalogs and websites. Catalogs are used to market directly to both existing and prospective customers throughout operations globally.[71] All together the company has over 40 public websites as well as over 15 corporate customized contract websites outside of North America.[72] Office Depot, Inc. uses the Internet to improve processes, reduce costs and expand services.[73] Other than having websites designed especially for all the countries in which there are retail locations, some other countries that Office Depot, Inc. reaches through these mediums are Belgium, Luxembourg, Slovakia, Switzerland, United Kingdom, Italy, Germany and The Netherlands.[74]

Through the merger with Viking Office Products, Office Depot, Inc. gained access to Australia one of Viking's largest markets. Viking has been mailing Australia since 1993 and in 2001 they acquired Sands & McDougall, an office supplies company based in Perth, however in 2002 the company was ready to sell its catalog and internet operations.[75] The company was in the unfamiliar position of being fourth in the market and due to industry consolidation felt there was limited opportunity for growth.[76] The growth rate and rate of return in the European division, has lead to the decision to reinvest proceeds into this division of the company.[77]

## Key Alliances (Non-Store):

### Singapore

As of August 13, 2008 Netbizz Office Supplies has agreed to enter into a strategic alliance with Office Depot. Netbizz is a leading office supplies provider in

Singapore.[78] The two joining together provides a well put together, more efficient supply system to cater to people's needs all over the nation. Singapore is a very good place for Office Depot to develop an alliance due to the country's consecutive ranking of the best place in the world to do business by the World Bank's annual Doing Business Report.[79] In this scenario to join in a strategic alliance both companies determined that they each have a common objective, Office Depot's International capabilities offset Netbizz's weaknesses in that area, reaching the common objective alone is either too costly, risky or takes too much time, and finally Office Depot's and Netbizz combine their strengths to accomplish their task which would otherwise be impossible.[80]

## China

During September 2006, Office Depot, Inc. acquired a majority stake in AsiaEC, China's leading dealer of office products and services. This acquisition gives Office Depot a presence in China.[81] This statement is supported by Charles Brown's, president of Office Depot, Inc. International, statement:

> "This acquisition gives Office Depot a significant presence in the fast growing Chinese market, and allows us to further leverage our operations in Japan and South Korea to enhance our competitive position within this increasingly important region."[82]

China's fast growing nation may mean huge growth for Office Depot. In 2008 Office Depot, Inc. acquired the remaining shares of AsiaEC giving them 100% ownership.[83]

## Eastern Europe

In August of 2006 Office Depot, Inc. announced that they had acquired Papirius s.r.o., one of the largest business-to-business suppliers of office products and services in Eastern Europe. Papirius s.r.o has operations in the Czech Republic, Lithuania, Hungary, and Slovakia, considerably extending Office Depot, Inc.'s international reach.[84] This partnership could lead to future retail locations as well as increased international sales.

## Questions

**1. Is the retailer classified as a global retailer or a multinational retailer? Explain its pattern of expansion. What expansion strategy did/is the retailer use/using?**

*Office Depot is classified as a global retailer. The distribution channels include direct mail, contract delivery, Internet website, and business to business e-commerce. In 2002 they implemented SAS Enterprise Miner to provide more advanced analytics and modeling. The objective was to create a web-based solution to evaluate the financial and logistical impacts of different communication plans, streamline campaign management and reduce costs. In 2004 Office Depot used a Millenium2 expansion vehicle which includes; differentiate from competitors, be less costly to open, more efficient to operate and offer great customer appeal. Through the mail order channel alone the company has more than 2.5 million active customers.*

**2. Based on Dunning's Eclectic Theory, how do ownership, locational, and internalization factors play in your retailers' international expansion?**

*The ownership advantage has a great influence on what type of expansion strategy suits best for companies willing to expand abroad. The amount of organizational slack and other physical recourses are important to finance expansion. The amount of tacit knowledge is also important, if there are many transactional advantages. It may be smart to expand organically rather than using franchises and licensing companies. A locational advantage is different depending on the type of company that is expanding. Global companies will choose major cities to reach a similar market segment while multinationals may prefer cheaper locations where there is less competition. The amount of secrets that the company wants to keep (internalization) is critically important when deciding on an expansion strategy. The more internalization, the more preference of wholly owned companies to make sure that company secrets remain within the company. Franchising is more risky and licensing is extremely risky.*

*Based on Dunning's Eclectic Theory it is clear that cultural and geographic proximity are no longer a factor in Office Depot's international expansion. Office Depot has expanded to nearly all corners of the globe including, North America, Latin America, South America, Europe, Asia, and the Middle East. With its asset-based advantages Office Depot will continue to look for a distinct segment of consumers who like and can relate to their product. It is also clear that Office Depot will continue to use joint ventures, licensing, and acquisition as their main form of international expansion as it has been so effective for them thus far.*

3.    **What role does cultural proximity and geographical proximity play in the retailers' international moves?**

*It is clear that cultural and more importantly geographic proximity played a huge role in Office Depot's international moves at the beginning. Office Depot's first expansion was in 1992 through acquisition of The Great Canadian Office Supplies Warehouse Chain. By doing so, Office Depot entered Canada. Both the United States and Canada are characterized by small power distance, high individualism, weak uncertainty avoidance, and high masculine orientation. Furthermore, Canada is one of two countries that share a border with the United States, making its geographical proximity extremely close.*

*The other country that shares a border with the United States is Mexico. Sequentially, entering Mexico through a joint venture was Office Depot's next international move in 1994. Mexico and the United States have low cultural proximity due to Mexico displaying large power distance, high collectivism, and strong uncertainty avoidance. However, it is evident that their close geographical proximity played a large role in Office Depot's expansion into Mexico.*

*After expanding into its neighboring countries, both cultural and geographic proximity played little role in Office Depot's next moves. In 1994, the same year Office Depot expanded into Mexico through a joint venture, Office Depot expanded into Israel, Colombia, and Poland through licensing agreements. Poland is relatively close in cultural proximity to the United States as both display small power distance, high individualism, and weak uncertainty avoidance. It is clear that cultural proximity played no role in the licensing agreements in Israel and Colombia as both countries have very little cultural similarities with the United States. From here, the trend continued, as it appears that little emphasis was placed on cultural proximity.*

4.    **Can you predict the retailer's future international expansion?**

*It can be predicted that Office Depot will continue international expansion mostly through joint ventures and licensing agreements, as they have done in the past. Where they will expand cannot be accurately predicted, but assuredly it will be in a large city. Just recently, Office Depot has announced that it will open new stores in Dubai and Kuwait City. Office Depot will continue to expand in places that like and can relate to their products. Apart from this, it is difficult to tell where exactly they will expand, but expansion is obvious.*

## Propositions

**P1:The greater the ownership advantages for retailers, the less likely they will franchise or license.**

*This proposition is refuted because one of Office Depot's main components in expanding internationally has been the use of licensing agreements. The ownership advantage does not only entail the tangible assets but also intangible assets. A unique product is an example of a tangible asset. The other advantage is transaction based, it's the knowledge gained from their experience. Based by the limited information available, it is not smart to franchise or license. The reason for this is that the company wants to keep their trade secrets to themselves; it is smarter for them to grow organically.*

*Office Depot uses licensing as well as organic growth through wholly owned subsidiaries. Rather than following this proposition, Office Depot chooses their entry strategy more on risks and knowledge of the market.*

**P2:The greater the organizational slack the greater the likelihood of expanding internationally.**

|  | 1989 | 1990 | 1991 |
|---|---|---|---|
| Current Assets | $50,867,000 | $144,110,000 | $206,759,000 |
| Current Liabilities | 35,747,000 | 81,126,000 | 147,079,000 |
|  |  |  |  |
| Organizational Slack | 1.423 | 1.776 | 1.406 |

*This proposition is refuted because although the organizational slack increased from 1989 to 1990, Office Depot's organizational clack decreased from 1990 to 1991.*

**P3: The greater the recoverable slack the greater the likelihood of expanding internationally.**

|  | 1989 | 1990 | 1991 |
|---|---|---|---|
| G & A Expenses | $6,451,000 | $12,892,000 | $20,286,000 |
| Sales | 132,035,000 | 314,587,000 | 625,764,000 |
|  |  |  |  |
| Recoverable Slack | 0.049 | 0.041 | 0.032 |

*This proposition is not supported because Office Depot's recoverable slack decreased from 1989 to 1990 to 1991. Although general and administrative expenses increased, sales increased as well, and at a higher rate.*

**P4: The greater the potential slack the greater the likelihood of expanding internationally.**

|  | 1989 | 1990 | 1991 |
|---|---|---|---|
| Equity | $28,845,000 | $100,695,000 | $111,192,000 |
| Capital | 15,120,000 | 62,984,000 | 59,680,000 |
|  |  |  |  |
| Potential Slack | 1.908 | 1.599 | 1.863 |

*This proposition is refuted because potential slack decreased from 1989 to 1990. However, Office Depot's potential slack increased by from 1990 to 1991.*

**P13: Global companies will move to the largest/capital cities in a country.**

*This proposition is supported because Office Depot has moved to mostly large and capital cities when expanding internationally. Currently, Office Depot has planned opening stores in Kuwait City and Dubai. Office Depot has stores in many other large cities such as Hong Kong, Toronto, and Ottawa. Global retailers move to major cities and world capitals in search of a globally similer customer, this is because the segment there is universally the same. They do not need to change their product offering when expanding into major cities.*

**P14: Global companies will not be attracted by population size, income, cultural proximity, or geographical proximity.**

*This proposition is refuted because in the case of their first international expansion, Office Depot acquired The Great Canadian Office Supplies Warehouse Chain in Canada. Canada, a bordering country, has extremely close geographical proximity to the United States. Canada also has a fairly high level of income, $39,100, on average (Canada Country Insight, 2009).*

*However, since Office Depot's first move, it has moved into several countries that have low cultural proximity such as China and Israel. Office Depot has also entered into countries with very low cultural proximity such as China, Japan, and Thailand. The distance from Washington, D.C. to Beijing, China is 6933 miles (City Distance Tool). The distance from Washington, D.C. to Tokyo, Japan is 6779 miles (City Distance Tool). The distance from Washington, D.C. to Bangkok, Thailand is 8804 miles (City Distance Tool). Likewise, Office Depot has entered several countries with low incomes such as Mexico and Colombia. Mexico has an average income of $14,200 (Mexico Country Insight, 2009). Similarly, Colombia has an average income of $8,800 (Colombia Country Insight, 2009). In conclusion, it is evident that Office Depot is neither attracted nor deterred by cultural proximity, geographical proximity, income, or population size.*

**P15: The greater the asset based ownership advantages of a global retailer, the more likely they are to franchise.**

*This proposition is refuted because Office Depot has not entered into any franchising agreements. Although many global retailers have significant asset based ownership advantages because they focus on private label merchandise, Office Depot has found more success with joint ventures and licensing over franchising.*

**P16: The greater the transaction based ownership advantages of a global retailer, the less likely they are to franchise.**

*This proposition is refuted because, as a global company, Office Depot has found it more beneficial to use licensing and joint ventures in their expansion strategy instead of franchising. Although this type of ownership is difficult to transfer to other countries, Office Depot has relied much of its expansion on joint ventures and licensing with other foreign companies that are similar to their own, creating success for the company. With a large successful company it is important to keep ownership advantages from being copied, which again makes it difficult to use franchising to transfer the knowledge.*

**P17: The greater the available organizational slack the greater the likelihood that global retailers will reacquire international franchisees.**

*This proposition is refuted. Although resource based theory suggests that a company franchises because they can't afford to expand on their own and after a certain amount of time the company will reacquire its stores, Office Depot has a majority of its stores still listed as joint ventures and licensing agreements in foreign countries. They have however reacquired stores in Japan because of the company's success in the region, but this reacquisition of stores is no pattern for the company and was a joint venture, not a franchise.*

**P18: The greater the recoverable slack the greater the likelihood that global retailers will reacquire international franchisees.**

*This proposition is refuted because Office Depot has not reacquired any international franchises.*

**P19: The greater the potential slack the greater the likelihood that global retailers will reacquire international franchisees.**

*This proposition is also refuted because, as mentioned before, Office Depot has not reacquired any international franchises.*

## Endnotes

1.  Office Depot Timeline. Retrieved October 10, 2009 from Office Depot Site website: http://www.officedepot.com/specialLinks.do?file=/companyinfo/companyfacts/timeline.jsp&template=companyinfo

2.  "Office Depot, Inc. Company Risk Report." (July 1, 2009). IBIS World. Retrieved October 15, 2009 from Investext Database

3.  Binder, Daniel. "Office Depot, Inc. Company Report." ( October, 27, 2009). Jeffries Company, Inc.  Retrieved November 1, 2009 from Investext Database

4.   "Office Depot, Inc. Company Report." (August 12, 2009). Datamonitor Independent Research. Retrieved October 15, 2009 from Investext Database

5.   DSN Retailing Today. (2006, March 13). Office Depot to Place More Emphasis on Private Label. Retrieved November 10, 2009 from BNET website: http://findarticles.com/p/articles/mi_m0FNP/is_5_45/ai_n16111725/

6.   "Office Depot, Inc. Company Report." (April 2009). Datamonitor Independent Research. Retrieved October 15, 2009 from Investext Database.

7.   "Office Depot, Inc. Company Report." (April 2009). Datamonitor Independent Research. Retrieved October 15, 2009 from Investext Database.

8.   Binder, Daniel. "Office Depot, Inc. Company Report." ( October, 27, 2009). Jeffries & Company, Inc. Retrieved November 1, 2009 from Investext Database

9.   Office Depot Timeline. Retrieved October 10, 2009 from Office Depot Site website: http://www.officedepot.com/specialLinks.do?file=/companyinfo/companyfacts/timeline.jsp&template=companyinfo

10.  Office Depot Acquires Allied Office Products. (2006, May 17). Retrieved November 1, 2009 from Recharger Magazine website: http://rechargermag.com/home.aspx

11.  Office Depot Celebrates Its First 'Green' Store. (2008, July 15). M2 Wireless News. Retrieved November 1, 2009 from LexisNexis Database

12.  Office Depot to close 126 store, 3 in Canada. (2008, December 10). CBC. Retrieved October 6, 2009 from LexisNexis Database

13.  Office Depot Timeline. Retrieved October 10, 2009 from Office Depot Site website: http://www.officedepot.com/specialLinks.do?file=/companyinfo/companyfacts/timeline.jsp&template=companyinfo

14.  Office Depot, Inc. 2006 Annual Report. Retrieved from Mergent Database

15.  Viking Office Products To Launch Direct Mail and E-Commerce Businesses In Spain. (2001, December 11). Internet Retailer. Retrieved on November 1, 2009 website: http://www.internetretailer.com/internet/marketing-conference/239939338-viking-office-products-launch-direct-mail-e-commerce-businesses-spain.html

16.  Office Depot Company Information. Retrieved November 5, 2009 from Office Depot Site website: http://www.officedepot.com/specialLinks.do?file=/companyinfo/careers/careers.jsp&template=companyinfo

17.  Office Depot Timeline. Retrieved October 10, 2009 from Office Depot Site website: http://www.officedepot.com/specialLinks.do?file=/companyinfo/companyfacts/timeline.jsp&template=companyinfo

18.  Office Depot Timeline. Retrieved October 10, 2009 from Office Depot Site website: http://www.officedepot.com/specialLinks.do?file=/companyinfo/companyfacts/timeline.jsp&template=companyinfo

19.  Office Depot to close all Japan stores: report. (2009, May 4). Marketwatch.com Retrieved October 6, 2009 from LexisNexis Database

20.  Liebeck, Laura. Office Depot ventures into Canada. (2002, February 3). Discount Store News. Retrieved November 17, 2009 from BNET website: http://findarticles.com/p/articles/mi_m3092/is_n3_v31/ai_11812296/

21.  Office Depot Timeline. Retrieved October 10, 2009 from Office Depot Site website: http://www.officedepot.com/specialLinks.do?file=/companyinfo/companyfacts/timeline.jsp&template=companyinfo

22.  Office Depot Company History. Connecting Angel Investors and Entrepreneurs. Retrieved November 17, 2009 website: http://www.fundinguniverse.com/company-histories/Office-Depot-Inc-Company-History.html

23.  Office Depot Inc, Overview. Retrieved November 13, 2009 from Marketline Database.

24.  Liebeck, Laura. Office Depot ventures into Canada. (2002, February 3). Discount Store News. Retrieved November 17, 2009 from BNET website: http://findarticles.com/p/articles/mi_m3092/is_n3_v31/ai_11812296/

25.  Office Depot to close 126 stores, 3 in Canada. (2008, December 10). CBC. Retrieved October 6, 2009 from LexisNexis Database

26.  Office Depot Timeline. Retrieved October 10, 2009 from Office Depot Site website: http://www.officedepot.com/specialLinks.do?file=/companyinfo/companyfacts/timeline.jsp&template=companyinfo

27.  Office Depot Inc, Overview. Retrieved November 13, 2009 from Marketline Database.

28.  Office Depot Inc, Overview. Retrieved November 13, 2009 from Marketline Database.

29.  Office Depot Company Information. Retrieved November 5, 2009 from Office Depot Site website: http://www.officedepot.com/renderStaticPage.do?file=/companyinfo/international/international.jsp&template=companyInfo

30.  Office Depot Timeline. Retrieved October 10, 2009 from Office Depot Site website: http://www.officedepot.com/specialLinks.do?file=/companyinfo/companyfacts/timeline.jsp&template=companyinfo

31.  Liebeck, Laura. Office Depot to open in Mexico; joint venture sees opportunity for 50 Stores – forms partnership with Grupo Gigante to open chain of office supplies

Superstores – Brief Article. (1994, October 17). Discount Store News. Retrieved November 17, 2009 from BNET website: http://findarticles.com/p/articles/mi_m3092/is_n20_v33/ai_15819163/

32. Mexico's Gigante, Office Depot to Enter Colombia. (2008, December 8). Retrieved November 15, 2009 from Reuters website: http://www.reuters.com/article/mergersNews/idUSN0832812920081208

33. Office Depot Mexico. Retrieved November 10, 2009 from Office Depot Mexico Site website:http://translate.google.com/translate?hl=en&sl=es&u=http://store.officedepot.com.hn/OnlineStore/&ei=Go4AS8WuCMfinAfil_yOCw&sa=X&oi=translate&ct=result&resnum=1&ved=0CAkQ7gEwAA&prev=/search%3Fq%3Doffice%2Bdepot%2Bin%2Bhonduras%26hl%3Den

34. Office Depot Company Information. Retrieved November 5, 2009 from Office Depot Site website: http://www.officedepot.com/specialLinks.do?file=/companyinfo/companyfacts/index.jsp&template=companyinfo

35. Liebeck, Laura. Office Depot to open in Mexico; joint venture sees opportunity for 50 Stores – forms partnership with Grupo Gigante to open chain of office supplies Superstores – Brief Article. (1994, October 17). Discount Store News. Retrieved November 17, 2009 from BNET website: http://findarticles.com/p/articles/mi_m3092/is_n20_v33/ai_15819163/

36. Sternquist, B. (2007). International Retailing. (Second Edition). Internationalization of Retailing (Page 8). New York: Fairchild Books.

37. Black, Thomas. (2008, July 30). Gigante Offers $430 Million for Office Depot's Stake in Venture. Retrieved November 15, 2009 from Bloomberg.com website: http://www.bloomberg.com/apps/news?pid=20601086&sid=aMAqXGHrCXeY&reger=news

38. *Mexico's Gigante, Office Depot to Enter Colombia.* (2008, December 8). Retrieved November 15, 2009 from Reuters website: http://www.reuters.com/article/mergersNews/idUSN0832812920081208

39. Office Depot to Shortly Re-Enter Poland with Remodeled Strategy. (2007, June 5). Eastbusiness.org. Retrieved November 1, 2009 from LexisNexis Database

40. Office Depot Joint Ventures. Retrieved from Mergent Database.

41. "Office Depot, Inc. Company Report." (April 2009). Datamonitor Independent Research. Retrieved October 15, 2009 from Investext Database.

42. Sales Focus Firmly on Asia. (2008, November 12). The Nation. Retrieved November 10, 2009 from LexisNexis Database.

43. Office Depot History. Retrieved from Mergent Database.

44. Office Depot, Inc. 2002 Annual Report. Retrieved from Mergent Database.

45. Office Depot to close all Japan stores: report. (2009, May 4). Marketwatch.com. Retrieved October 6, 2009 from LexisNexis Database

46. Office Depot Inc, Overview. Retrieved November 13, 2009 from Marketline Database.

47. Office Depot Acquires Business in Hungary: Former Licensee Becomes Wholly Owned Subsidiary: Expansion into Eastern Europe Significant as New Countries Join the EU. (2004, April 8). Press Release. Retrieved October 10, 2009 from the Office Depot site website: http://investor.officedepot.com/phoenix. zhtml?c=94746&p=irol-newsCorporateArticle&ID=513067&highlight=

48. Office Depot to Open 10 New Stores in Hungary. (2007, January 8). Eastbusiness. org.Retrieved November 12, 2009 from LexisNexis Database.

49. Office Depot Company Information. Retrieved October 25, 2009 from Office Depot Hungary Site website: http://www.officedepot.eu/aboutus/emea/hungary/

50. Office Depot 2008 Company Report. Retrieved from Mergent Database.

51. Office Depot Company Information. (2002, February 28). Business Wire. Retrieved November 5, 2009 from Office Depot Site website: http://investor.officedepot.com/ phoenix.zhtml?c=94746&p=irol-newsCorporateArticle&ID=263887&highlyght=

52. Office Depot Timeline. Retrieved October 10, 2009 from Office Depot Site website: http://www.officedepot.com/specialLinks.do?file=/companyinfo/companyfacts/ timeline.jsp&template=companyinfo

53. Office Depot Company Information. Retrieved November 8, 2009 from Office Depot Honduras Site website: http://translate.google.com/ translate?hl=en&sl=es&u=http://store.officedepot.com.hn/OnlineStore/&ei=Bur 8SsXYOYyCnQex4omgCw&sa=X&oi=translate&ct=result&resnum=1&ved=0C AsQ7gEwAA&prev=/search%3Fq%3Doffice%2Bdepot%2Bhonduras%26hl%3D en

54. Office Depot Timeline. Retrieved October 10, 2009 from Office Depot Site website: http://www.officedepot.com/specialLinks.do?file=/companyinfo/companyfacts/ timeline.jsp&template=companyinfo

55. Office Depot Company Information. (2002, February 28). Business Wire. Retrieved November 5, 2009 from Office Depot Site website: http://investor.officedepot.com/ phoenix.zhtml?c=94746&p=irol-newsCorporateArticle&ID=263887&highlyght=

56. Office Depot Company Information. Retrieved November 8, 2009 from Office Depot Honduras Site website: http://translate.google.com/ translate?hl=en&sl=es&u=http://store.officedepot.com.hn/OnlineStore/&ei=Bur

8SsXYOYyCnQex4omgCw&sa=X&oi=translate&ct=result&resnum=1&ved=0C AsQ7gEwAA&prev=/search%3Fq%3Doffice%2Bdepot%2Bhonduras%26hl%3D en

57. International News – Office Depot Set for Spain Outlets. (2003, February 21). Retail Week. Retrieved November 12, 2009 from LexisNexis Database.

58. Office Depot Inc, Overview. Retrieved November 13, 2009 from Marketline Database.

59. Viking Office Products to expand into Spain. (2001, December 11). Multi Channel Merchant. Retrieved November 18, 2009 website: http://multichannelmerchant. com/news/marketing_viking_office_products/

60. Office Depot Acquires Best Office, Sets 52-Week Closing High on Higher Volume (2006, February 16). M2 Financial Wire. Retrieved November 5, 2009 from LexisNexis Database.

61. Office Depot Inc, Overview. Retrieved November 13, 2009 from Marketline Database.

62. Office Depot Company Information. Retrieved November 8, 2009 from Office Depot Honduras Site website: http://translate.google.com/ translate?hl=en&sl=es&u=http://store.officedepot.com.hn/OnlineStore/&ei=Bur 8SsXYOYyCnQex4omgCw&sa=X&oi=translate&ct=result&resnum=1&ved=0C AsQ7gEwAA&prev=/search%3Fq%3Doffice%2Bdepot%2Bhonduras%26hl%3D en

63. Office Depot Company Information. Retrieved November 8, 2009 from Office Depot Honduras Site website: http://translate.google.com/ translate?hl=en&sl=es&u=http://store.officedepot.com.hn/OnlineStore/&ei=Bur 8SsXYOYyCnQex4omgCw&sa=X&oi=translate&ct=result&resnum=1&ved=0C AsQ7gEwAA&prev=/search%3Fq%3Doffice%2Bdepot%2Bhonduras%26hl%3D en

64. Office Depot Company Information. Retrieved November 10, 2009 from Office Depot Honduras Site website: http://translate.google.com/ translate?hl=en&sl=es&u=http://store.officedepot.com.hn/OnlineStore/&ei=Go4 AS8WuCMfinAfil_yOCw&sa=X&oi=translate&ct=result&resnum=1&ved=0CA kQ7gEwAA&prev=/search%3Fq%3Doffice%2Bdepot%2Bin%2Bhonduras%26hl %3Den

65. Office Depot Celebrates Sixth Store in Puerto Rico with Grand Opening Celebration Across Island. (2009, November 9). News Blaze. Retrieved November 15, 2009 website: http://newsblaze.com/story/20091109060229000003.bw/topstory.html

66. Liebeck, Laura. Office Depot to open in Mexico; joint venture sees opportunity for

50 Stores – forms partnership with Grupo Gigante to open chain of office supplies Superstores – Brief Article. (1994, October 17). Discount Store News. Retrieved November 17, 2009 from BNET website: http://findarticles.com/p/articles/mi_m3092/is_n20_v33/ai_15819163/

67. Office Depot Company Information. Retrieved November 5, 2009 from Office Depot European corporate site website: http://www.officedepot.eu/aboutus/emea/Sweden/

68. Office Depot and M.H. Alshaya Co. Sign Franchise Agreement. (2009, January 11). Comtex News Network, Inc. Retrieved October 6, 2009 from LexisNexis Database.

69. Office Depot Inc, Overview. Retrieved November 13, 2009 from Marketline Database.

70. Office Depot Inc, Overview. Retrieved November 13, 2009 from Marketline Database.

71. Office Depot 2008 Annual Report. Retrieved from Mergent Database.

72. Office Depot Company Information. Retrieved November 5, 2009 from Office Depot Site website: http://www.officedepot.com/renderStaticPage.do?file=/companyinfo/international/international.jsp&template=companyInfo

73. Office Depot 2001 Annual Report. Retrieved form Mergent Database.

74. Office Depot Company Information. Retrieved November 5, 2009 from Office Depot Site website: http://www.officedepot.com/renderStaticPage.do?file=/companyinfo/international/international.jsp&template=companyInfo

75. Office Depot to Sell Australian Operations. (2002, October 1). Multi Channel Merchant. Retrieved October 15, 2009 website: http://www.multichannelMerchant.com/news/marketing_office_depot_sell

76. Office Depot Sells Australian Ops to Coles Myer. (2002, December 1). CBS Market Watch. Retrieved November 7, 2009 from LexisNexis Database.

77. Office Depot to Sell Australian Operations. (2002, October 1). Multi Channel Merchant. Retrieved October 15, 2009 website: http://www.multichannelMerchant.com/news/marketing_office_depot_sell

78. Netbizz not Resting on its Laurels. (2008, November 11). The Business Times Singapore. Retrieved November 10, 2009 from LexisNexis Database.

79. Netbizz not Resting on its Laurels. (2008, November 11). The Business Times Singapore. Retrieved November 10, 2009 from LexisNexis Database.

80. Sternquist, B. (2007). International Retailing. (Second Edition). Licensing,

Franchising & Strategic Alliances (Page 148). New Year:Fairchild Books

81. Office Depot Inc, Overview. Retrieved November 13, 2009 from Marketline Database.

82. Kollath, Carlie. Office Depot to enter China. (2006, September 8). RetailNet. Retrieved November 17, 2009 website: http://www.retailnet.com/story. cfm?ID=31659

83. Office Depot Company Information. Retrieved November 7, 2009 from Office Depot Site website: http://www.officedepot.com/renderStaticPage.do?file=/ companyinfo/international/international.jsp&template=companyInfo

84. Office Depot Announces Acquisition of Papirius; Leading Eastern European Business-to-Business Office Supplier Expands Company's International Operations. (2006, August 31). Business Wire. Retrieved November 15, 2009 from Office Depot Site website: http://mediarelations.officedepot.com/phoenix. zhtml?c=140162&p=irol-newsArticle&ID=900915&highlight=

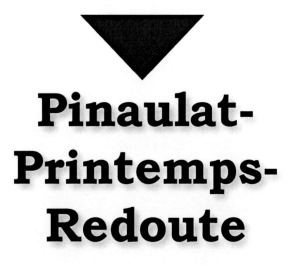

# Pinaulat-Printemps-Redoute

*Kaitlyn Brower, Chen Chen, Laura Marie Hammer, Elyse Hodges*
*Wan Jun Kim, Angela Napolitano*

## Pinaulat-Printemps-Redoute

Pinault-Printemps-Redoute's (PPR) portfolio of brands is the core of their strategy. Their acquisition of major retail brands and companies has given them a global presence in the luxury and consumer goods markets. By targeting various market segments, they have become the world's third largest luxury group. The company has five main subsidiaries: Fnac, Redcats, Gucci Group, Conforama, and Puma. They specialize in various consumer products such as books, leather goods, furniture, active wear, and shoes. Although, PPR is a major player in the luxury goods market; the company's foundation is in the timber business.

# FLOW CHART

| Entry Year | Entry Location | Exit Year |
|---|---|---|
| 1963 | France | 2009 |
| 1990 | Burkina Faso | 2009 |
| 1990 | Cameroon | 2009 |
| 1990 | Central African Republic | 2009 |
| 1990 | Chad | 2009 |
| 1990 | Democratic Republic of Congo | 2009 |
| 1990 | Gabon | 2009 |
| 1990 | Gambia | 2009 |
| 1990 | Guinea | 2009 |
| 1990 | Ivory Coast | 2009 |
| 1990 | Madagascar | 2009 |
| 1990 | Mali | 2009 |
| 1990 | Niger | 2009 |
| 1990 | Nigeria | 2009 |
| 1990 | Reunion | 2009 |
| 1990 | Senegal | 2009 |
| 1990 | Sierra Leone | 2009 |
| 1990 | Togo | 2009 |
| 1991 | Luxembourg | |
| 1991 | Portugal | |
| 1991 | Switzerland | |
| 1992 | Spain | |
| 1992 | Belgiium | |
| 1995 | Benin | 2009 |
| 1995 | Canada | |
| 1995 | Germany | |
| 1995 | United Kingdom | |
| 1997 | Denmark | |
| 1997 | Estonia | |
| 1997 | Finland | |
| 1997 | The Netherlands | |
| 1997 | Norway | |
| 1998 | Mauritius | 2009 |

| Entry Year | Entry Location | Exit Year |
|---|---|---|
| 1998 | United States | |
| 1998 | Sweden | |
| 1999 | Australia | |
| 1999 | Austria | |
| 1999 | Brazil | |
| 1999 | Equitorial New Guinea | 2009 |
| 1999 | French Polynesia | 2009 |
| 1999 | Malta | |
| 1999 | Greece | |
| 1999 | Czech Republic | |
| 1999 | Hungary | |
| 1999 | Ireland | |
| 1999 | Italy | |
| 1999 | Russia | |
| 1999 | New Zealand | |
| 1999 | Korea | |
| 1999 | United Arab Emirates | |
| 1999 | India | |
| 1999 | Japan | |
| 1999 | Malaysia | |
| 1999 | Taiwan | |
| 1999 | Thailand | |
| 1999 | Singapore | |
| 1999 | Guam | |
| 1999 | China | |
| 1999 | Mexico | |
| 2000 | Kenya | 2009 |
| 2000 | Morocco | 2009 |
| 2000 | New Caledonia | 2009 |
| 2000 | Tanzania | 2009 |
| 2001 | Croatia | |
| 2001 | Poland | |
| 2001 | Algeria | 2009 |
| 2001 | Zambia | 2009 |

| Entry Year | Entry Location | Exit Year |
|---|---|---|
| 2002 | Malawi | 2009 |
| 2003 | Lebanon | |
| 2003 | Slovenia | |
| 2006 | Mauritania | 2009 |
| 2006 | Saudi Arabia | |
| 2007 | Angola | 2009 |
| 2007 | Sao Tome | 2009 |
| 2007 | Vietnam | |
| 2007 | Zimbabwe | 2009 |
| 2007 | Cyprus | |
| 2007 | Lithuania | |
| 2007 | Romani | |
| 2007 | Chile | |
| 2007 | Argentina | |
| 2007 | Slovakia | |
| 2007 | Brtish Virgin Islands | |
| 2007 | South Africa | |
| 2007 | Uruguay | |
| 2007 | Peru | |
| 2007 | Turkey | |
| 2007 | Ukraine | |
| 2007 | Hong Kong | |
| 2007 | Bulgaria | |
| 2008 | Ghana | 2009 |

## Select Subsidiary Flow Charts

### Flow Chart -- Fnac

| Entry Year | Entry Location | Number of Stores in 2009 | Exit Year |
|---|---|---|---|
| 1980 | France | 80 | |
| 1981 | Belgium | 8 | |
| 1993 | Spain | 19 | |
| 1993 | Italy | 7 | |
| 1993 | Portugal | 16 | |
| 1993 | Switzerland | 4 | |
| 1999 | Brazil | 9 | |
| 2008 | Greece | 3 | |

### Flow Chart -- Conforama

| Entry Year | Entry Location | Number of Stores in 2009 | Exit Year |
|---|---|---|---|
| 1967 | France | 161 | |
| 1976 | Switzerland | 13 | |
| 1991 | Portugal | 4 | |
| 1991 | Luxembourg | 1 | |
| 1992 | Spain | 14 | |
| 2001 | Italy | 15 | |
| 2001 | Croatia | 3 | |
| 2001 | Poland | | 2008 |

*The entry and exit years for the subsidiary flow charts refer to when the individual subsidiary entered and exited the country, not PPR.

## History of PPR

With the death of his father in 1963, Francois Pinault took over the family timber trading business, renaming it Pinault Group. Pinault Group specialized in timber trading and building materials and became a prosperous enterprise with Pinault's exemplary negotiation skills. He was able to sell his company when he sensed the demand for his product was high, and re-bought it at a profit two years later. With his smart eye, he was able to make successful acquisitions of various timber businesses, eventually turning them around to create one vertically integrated timber distribution, trading and manufacturing company.[1] In 1988, Pinault Group had their initial public offering (IPO) on the Paris Stock Exchange.

In 1990 and 1991, Pinault Group made a major acquisition of the African trading group, Compagnie Francasie de l'Afrique Occidentale (CFAO) and entered the retail industry with the acquisition of French furniture chain, Conforama. In 1994, the Group acquired catalog company, La Redoute, through a merger with the Printempts Group and the Group renamed once more to Pinault-Printempts-Redoute. In the same year, Pinault-Printempts-Redoute acquired a majority stake in Fnac.[2] Seeing the importance of online presence, they launched their first website, laredoute.fr., in 1995, and later started websites for their companies, most notably, Fnac. With these acquisitions of retail companies, Pinault-Printempts-Redoute was beginning to become a major competitor in the international retail industry.

In 1999, the Group entered the luxury market with its minority acquisition of Gucci Group NV. They acquired 42% of Gucci Group from French luxury retail company LVMH for $2.6 billion. A legal investigation ensued two years after the purchase, testing the legality of the merger. Following this investigation, Pinault-Printempts-Redoute purchased LVMH's remaining stake in Gucci Group, and in 2004, finalized the acquisition by purchasing the rest of the company. By purchasing the remainder of Gucci Group, Pinault had a major stake in the luxury goods market, shifting its focus.[3] Gucci Group continued to expand with the acquisitions of luxury brands such as Bottega Veneta and Balenciaga, and partnerships with Alexander McQueen and Stella McCartney.[4] The 2007 acquisition of the sports-lifestyle brand, Puma, gave the company an additional growth opportunity to develop their markets.

## Expansion

Since its beginning, PPR has operated with an entrepreneurial spirit driving its acquisitions of various developed companies. PPR strategically chooses brands and companies that are already successful and well managed. They choose companies with different qualities and product offerings to diversify and add to their group of subsidiaries.[5] Through the anticipation of market trends, they are able to capitalize on future successes.

The company has outlined the criteria they use to decide whether to acquire a company or not. They will only choose companies that have the same overall strategy as the Group and that will potentially offer a sufficient return on investment for the company. Researching into the potential financial benefits of the company is essential to PPR's decision to acquire a company.

PPR operates through a decentralized structure with various brands present in different countries. The company operates through a mixture of retail formats and product offerings in each country. All of the companies are specialized in their offerings with Fnac focused on books and music, Puma focused on sportswear, and Conforama focused on furniture, for example. Each branch manages independently as a wholly owned subsidiary of their brand while still aligning with the strategic direction of the entire PPR group. Each of PPR's brands operate as global companies having centralized operations of their brands. Being close to their customers and market helps its subsidiaries make the best decisions possible regarding their businesses and their individual directions. Each of its subsidiaries can work together with their knowledge of the industry to improve performance as well as pool resources to decrease expenses. PPR capitalizes on the asset-based advantages of the companies it acquires, and provides its transaction-based assets to help the company continue success. PPR itself manages the overall group's strategic direction and decides on additional mergers and acquisitions according to this vision.[5] Currently, the group is focused on building a portfolio of luxury brands and looks to companies that fit this criteria.

PPR began international expansion with the acquisition of the French company, Compagnie Francasie de l'Afrique Occidentale (CFAO) in 1990. With this acquisition PPR expanded its presence into 17 African countries, including Cameroon, Chad, Gabon, Mali, and Nigeria. Through this acquisition, PPR entered the automotive distribution and retail industry. Since then, CFAO has expanded into additional countries in Africa as well as Vietnam.[6] Currently, PPR does not control retail operations of CFAO, so they have exited all of the African countries where they had a presence. They have sold their majority stake, and maintain minority stake strictly as an investment. They decided to let go of their majority investment because it does not align with their current fashion and luxury goods focus.[7]

The acquisition of Conforama brought PPR into the traditional retail market involving the sale of furniture and home furnishings. This led them to be present in several other European countries including Luxembourg, Spain, Portugal, and Switzerland. In 2009, sales from Conforama contributed 17.7% of PPR's total revenues.[5] Conforama brings a discount retailer into the luxury brands group.

The next major acquisition for PPR was the purchase of French companies Au Printempt and La Redoute later becoming Redcats. Redcats focuses on specialty merchandise such as men's and women's apparel, sporting goods, accessories, outdoor gear, and home furnishings through mail-order, e-commerce, and retail store formats. Catalog and Internet sales are very important for the company since store sales only account for 12% of their total sales.[1] Redcats contributed 20.5% of PPR's total revenue in 2009.[5]

Fnac, a PPR's subsidiary that is the leading seller of music and books in six European countries and Brazil, operates as a click-and-mortar business operating in specialty store and e-commerce channels. Their e-commerce channel is quite successful, being the number one visited e-commerce site. Fnac contributed 26.4% of PPR's total revenue in 2009; however, they return lower margins than other subsidiaries.[5]

The acquisition of Gucci Group helped PPR change its focus to the luxury goods market. Gucci Group itself has a great portfolio of brands and PPR saw the potential of these brands and the company. Gucci Group was attractive because of their very strong asset-based advantage in their global brands. The acquisition of Gucci Group in 1999 led PPR into many new international markets including the United Arab Emirates, Taiwan, China, and India. Gucci Group has contributed 20.5% of PPR's total revenue in 2009.[5]

The most recent international expansion for PPR was when they acquired sports lifestyle brand, Puma. This acquisition brought PPR into the South American market including Peru, Uruguay, Argentina, and Chile. In addition, they expanded to South Africa and Romania through this brand. This acquisition was a smart choice for PPR because Puma fits well in its portfolio of luxury and consumer goods brands. Jochen Zeitz, the CEO of Puma, said that the acquisition is strong because both companies balance each other with their European backgrounds and global perspectives.[8] Last year, Puma contributed 14.9% to PPR's total revenue.[5]

## Competition

The main competitor for PPR is LVMH (Louis Vuitton Moet Hennessey), which, through its collection of stores, sells some of the most well known luxury brands in the world.[9] The group has a unique portfolio of over 60 esteemed brands in the following sectors: wines and spirits, fashion goods, cosmetics, leather goods, perfumes, watches and jewelry, and selective retailing,[10] A few examples of the company's most famous acquisitions include: Louis Vuitton, Benefit Cosmetics, Emilio Pucci, Givency, Belvedere Vodka, Sephora, and Marc Jacobs.[10]

Currently, LVMH has holdings in fifty-eight countries, from Argentina to Vietnam.[10] With more than 2,400 stores worldwide and over 70,000 employees, 74% of whom are based outside of France, LVMH has proven to be a direct competitor for PPR in the luxury goods holding industry. The combination of the company's superior brand development strategy and the expansion of its international retail network have allowed LVMH to sustain a powerful growth dynamic since the company's inception in 1987.[10]

For these reasons, PPR must continually monitor LVMH in order to remain competitive in the industry. In 2009, PPR reported revenue of 16.5 billion Euros, 57% of which was generated outside of France.[11] Conversely, LVMH reported revenue of 17.1 billion Euros in 2009 with 86% generated outside of France.[12,13] While both companies have recently posted similar financial numbers, it is imperative to be the top company in such a small and unique industry. Therefore, PPR must find new and innovative ways to gain the competitive edge over LVMH in the luxury goods holding industry.

## SWOT Analysis[2]

### Strengths

- Strong brands that are market leaders
- Use of various retail formats
- International presence

### Weaknesses

- Weak performance of Conforama

### Opportunities

- Continued expansion of Gucci Group
- Growth of E-commerce
- Expansion of Puma

### Threats

- Increasing labor expenses
- Declining buyer confidence
- Counterfeit merchandise

## Strengths

### Strong Brands that are Market Leaders

PPR's greatest strengths as a retail holding company are its strong retail and luxury brands. Their main consumer retail brands include: Puma, Redcats, Conforama, and Fnac and their luxury brands include: Yves Saint Laurent, Balenciaga, Alexander McQueen, Stella McCartney, Gucci, Sergio Rossi, Bottega Veneta, and Boucheron. Most of these brands have leading positions in their own markets. For example, Redcats is the largest home shopping retailer in France, Scandinavia, and Portugal.[2] Having these strong asset-based advantages makes them a leader in the industry and makes international expansion for these brands much easier.

## Use of Various Retail Formats

PPR's various subsidiaries offer products through a variety of different retail formats. Their products are sold through department stores, specialty stores, duty-free boutiques, franchises, and company-owned stores. E-commerce has been a popular way of reaching additional customers for PPR. Each of its subsidiaries has strong online presence as well, creating click-and-mortar businesses.[2] Redcats holds the #1 position for home shopping in France and Scandinavia due to its success in the e-commerce channel.[1]

## International Presence

With operations across the Americas, Europe, Africa, Oceania, and Asia, PPR has vast geographic presence in over 94 countries. This expansive world presence allows the company to "target a larger customer base, which in turn supports the company's revenue growth rate."[2] This wide presence also helps the company vary its operations to spread out any risk associated with operating in a specific country. Therefore, the occurrence of any unforeseen circumstance in one country will be offset by the holdings in the remaining countries. As a result, the retailing risk-laden industry is made slightly more stable by PPR's wide geographic presence.

## Weaknesses

### Weak Performance of Conforama

Conforama reported weak financial performance in the area of sales revenue for the 2008 financial year, and in the first quarter of 2009, sales decreased by 10%.[5] While the substandard performance is partly due to the economic downturn and exchange rate fluctuations, a continued decrease in sales revenues will undoubtedly have a severe impact on the company's overall performance.[2] If the weak performance continues after the economy begins to recover, PPR will have to make a decision as to whether to keep the acquisition or remove it from its holdings. If PPR does not make the wisest decision or acts at the wrong time, it is likely that PPR as a whole will suffer. Therefore, the company must keep a close watch on Conforama to see if its financial performance will turn around or if the subsidiary is merely a money pit.

## Opportunities

### Continued Expansion of Gucci Group

Currently, Gucci develops through an organic growth strategy focusing on their brands' assortments.[2] Expansion into additional international markets through the building of Gucci's own stores would enable Gucci to benefit from the fast growth of rising markets and reduce the risk of focusing on one specific market. Because of Gucci's standard retail format and extensive use of private label, it is considered a global retailer. Therefore, it is expected that the company would expand internationally using its own stores. If Gucci acts quickly, it will be able to exploit its uniqueness by "colonizing a concept."[9]

## Growth of E-Commerce

The Internet is becoming a major retail format with consumers saving time and money by shopping at home. By increasing its Internet offerings, PPR would be able to further position itself as a modern lifestyle brand and also reach a larger target market. Also, growth in online retail spending would help PPR earn more revenues from its online websites.[2]

Online shopping is gaining popularity all over the globe.[9] With an increase in Internet penetration in foreign countries comes an increase in electronic retailing as a whole. In Australia, Internet penetration has reached 68.2%; Brazil is the ninth-largest Internet market in the world and the largest in Latin America[9] with three percent of users buying products and services on a regular basis. Germany is notably one of the leaders in retail technology with all of the country's top retail companies having websites. Furthermore, Internet sales in India are increasing by approximately 69 percent per year, and in the Netherlands, more than 38 percent of Internet users purchased something from an Internet retailer. There is high potential in the Korean Internet retailing market as it ranks third in the world for Internet use.[9] Considering the fact that all of the aforementioned countries are home to PPR subsidiaries, there is great potential for success in the online retail industry for PPR.

Despite the rising popularity of online shopping, PPR must ensure that it is able to overcome the problems related to electronic retailing. Specifically, the company must realize that the website is its physical presence in the e-commerce market. PPR must be able to adjust to different cultures and climates. They must efficiently distribute merchandise, collect sales taxes if required, and make sure their website is tailored to their customers in different countries.[9]

## Expansion of Puma

By expanding its product line and adding new categories, Puma can further strengthen its position in the sports lifestyle market. Through merchandising and marketing initiatives, Puma can increase brand awareness and reach new target markets in order to generate long-term growth.[2]

In addition, this strategy will allow both PPR and Puma to diversify as companies. PPR will be able to gain an important holding in the sports, lifestyle, and fashion category, a new venture for the firm. Conversely, Puma will be able to solidify its presence in its traditional category while exploring new opportunities and satisfying a larger customer base.

## Threats

### Increasing Labor Expenses

Labor costs in Europe have been increasing in recent years in addition to reduced labor availability and increased minimum wages and overtime. Furthermore, there has been an increase in full-time workers, which increases costs for the company. These increased expenses could negatively impact the group's profit. With the company employing over 90,000 employees, any increase in wages can really impact the bottom line.[2]

### Declining Buyer Confidence

The success of PPR depends extensively on the current macro-economic climate at both the local and international level. The recession in the United States and Europe has impacted the overall confidence of consumers. As a result, consumer spending has declined, adversely affecting the revenues and profitability of PPR.[2]

Because PPR's subsidiaries are retail companies that sell mostly durable goods, the firm has been especially hurt. The current economic condition has caused consumers to postpone the purchase of these goods. Instead, more of a consumer's disposable income is being allotted to non-durables and services. Until a strong economic recovery comes around, it is safe to say that the revenues and profits of PPR subsidiaries will continue to suffer.

### Counterfeit Merchandise

The abundance and prevalence of counterfeit goods is impacting PPR in an extremely negative way; counterfeit merchandise can weaken the exclusivity and brand image of PPR's brands.[2] This could, in turn, impact the company's sales and profits. Consumers will be less confident in PPR's products when they are unsure of the quality as they are exposed to counterfeit goods in the black market.

## Geographic Regions

### Asia

PPR currently is present in 12 Asian countries. The percent of PPR revenue that comes from Asian countries is 12.1 percent.[14] Mainly their subsidiaries in Asia are Gucci Group, which is a leading luxury retailer world-wide. The Gucci Group includes high-end designer labels including: Alexander McQueen, Balenciaga, Bottega Veneta, Gucci, Sergio Rossi, and Stella McCartney.[15] Another subsidiary PPR has presence in the Asian market with is Puma. Puma is one of the world's foremost sports lifestyle corporations with its focus on selling footwear, apparel and accessories.[16] Finally, the last subsidiary of PPR that is present in Asia is CFAO, a distribution specializing in automobile, pharmaceutical, technologies and the distribution of consumer products.[17]

PPR entered China, India, Japan, Korea, Malaysia, Singapore, Taiwan, and United Arab Emirates in 1999. In these eight countries Puma and Gucci Group are present subsidiaries of PPR. Finally, in 2007 PPR entered Vietnam with CFAO and Puma is now operating there.

### Australia and New Zealand

PPR does have a presence with their subsidiaries Gucci Group and Puma in Australia and New Zealand. In these two countries, Australia and New Zealand, they account for 0.5 percent of PPR total revenue.[14] In 1999, they expanded into Australia and New Zealand. Some concepts Puma emphasizes in Australia and New Zealand are motorsports, tekkies, kehinde wiley and Rudolf Dassler.[19]

### Africa

PPR has a dominant presence in Africa. CFAO is the subsidiary there. CFAO is present in 26 countries in Africa including: Algeria, Angola, Benin, Burkina Faso, Cameroon, Central Africa Republic, Democratic Republic of Congo, Equatorial Guinea, Gabon, Gambia, Ivory Coast, Kenya, Madagascar, Malawi, Mali, Mauritius, Morocco, Niger, Sao Tome, Senegal, Chad, Tanzania, Togo and Zambia

The expansion of PPR into Africa began in 1990 and the last countries they have entered with CFAO were in 2007, this included Angola and Sao Tome. The percent of total revenue for PPR that comes from the Africa region is 0.9 percent.[14] Therefore, although PPR is present in numerous countries in Africa, this is not a significant contribution considering other more lucrative regions.

### North America

PPR presence in North America includes subsidiaries in Canada, Mexico and the United States. The subsidiaries that are found in these regions include Redcats, Gucci Group, and Puma. Redcats, Gucci Group, and Puma are all present in

Canada and the United States, whereas only Gucci Group and Puma are present in Mexico. Redcats Group is an international online retailer that specializes in fashion and home furnishings; they operate over 60 e-commerce sites, with more than 27 million active customers in Europe and the United States. North and South America account for 15.8 percent of total revenue for PPR.[20] Redcats accounts for 20.5 percent, Gucci Group accounts for 20.5 percent and Puma accounts for 14.9 percent of revenue activity for PPR.[14]

## Europe

Excluding France, PPR first entered Europe in 1991. In that year, the company expanded into Luxembourg, Portugal, Spain and Switzerland. Over the next sixteen years, the company continued to move into twenty-five more countries, resulting in a total of twenty-nine European countries. The countries that PPR currently has holdings in include: Austria, Belgium, Bulgaria, Croatia, Cyprus, Czech Republic, Denmark, Estonia, Finland, France, Germany, Hungary, Italy, Lithuania, Luxembourg, Malta, Monaco, Netherlands, Poland, Portugal, Romania, Russia, Slovakia, Slovenia, Spain, Sweden, Switzerland, Ukraine, Turkey, and the United Kingdom.

Throughout the continent, the subsidiaries of Redcats, Gucci Group, Puma, Fnac, Conforama, and CFAO are present. Fnac is a retailer offering cultural and technological products. They have roughly 3.6 million members and their Web site fnac.com is the number one retailer website by visitor numbers.[21] Conforama is a key retailer in European home furnishings offering a multi-product and multi-style discount format.[22] Fnac accounts for the largest revenue activity of the subsidiaries contributing 26.6 percent to total sales for PPR.[14] Therefore, Europe is a key continent for PPR's operations as it accounts for over one quarter of its yearly sales.

## France

PPR began its operations in France in 1963 when the company was established. Currently, the subsidiaries Conforama, Redcats, Gucci Group, Puma, and CFAO are located in France. Due to its long history with PPR and its immense success in the home country, France accounts for 43.1% of PPR's total sales revenue.

The significance of Europe is unparalleled when it comes to the financial figures for PPR. Indeed, France and the rest of Europe combined accounts for approximately 71% of PPR's total sales revenue. Therefore, it is crucial for PPR to maintain its holdings in the thirty European countries in order to sustain its profits and its position as a market leader.

## South America

PPR first expanded into South America in 1999 with its move into Brazil, which is now home to Fnac, Redcats, Gucci Group and Puma. In 2007, they entered Argentina, Chile, and Uruguay; all three of these countries have only the Puma subsidiary of PPR. While PPR only occupies four countries in South America, it still contributes a strong revenue figure: North and South America combined account for 15.8% of total sales revenue.[11] This number is fourth only to France, the rest of Europe, and Asia.

## Conclusion

PPR is not a typical retailer and does not follow a specific or familiar format that other retailers do. Their secret is in acquiring well operated companies all over the world and expanding, spreading their company mission to them. They have a presence in six continents and over ninety countries. This may seem sporadic but everything they do is calculated with a very precise goal.

This goal has been accomplished, with five exceptional subsidiaries currently under their name. These companies include Fnac, Redcats, Conforama, Gucci Group and Puma. With all of them being top ranking companies within their industry, PPR has succeeded in operating such a vast portfolio. The future truly is endless for PPR and they have few boundaries as a company for they have entered into numerous sectors. This company is one of great allure and ultimate success that is fascinating to follow.

## Questions

**1. Is the retailer classified as a global retailer or a multinational retailer? Explain its pattern of expansion. What expansion strategy did/is the retailer use/using?**

*PPR is a multinational retailer in the sense that they are decentralized and use transaction based advantages. Their strong entrepreneurial culture led them to embrace decentralization. However, PPR is also an acquisition-based company, which refers to purchasing an existing company and allowing management to continue operations. PPR purchases companies like Gucci, Puma, and Redcats, who are well performing companies, and allows them to manage themselves with little involvement from PPR. They move into emerging economies first, and then more developed countries with locational advantages later. PPR expands in stages, which allows PPR to learn about each subsidiary and country, which in turn gives them a better portfolio of knowledge for each expansion made thereafter.*[23]

## 2.   Based on Dunning's eclectic theory, how do ownership, locational and internalization factors play in your retailers' international expansion?

*According to Dunning's theory, ownership, locational, and internalization factors have played an important role in PPR's expansion process. PPR does have an ownership advantage because they purchase companies that are already operating properly, they do not franchise or license. They have asset-based advantages because they own the rights to their subsidiaries. Their whole business strategy is based on acquiring existing businesses. PPR uses transaction-based advantages to expand its business. Transaction based advantages are based on tacit knowledge, which relates to PPR's methods of expansion because they focus on learning with the acquisition of each subsidiary and each country with great devotion in order to improve future expansion options. From the information learned throughout their expansion process they are able to implement this knowledge in future expansion opportunities. Locational factors are very important to the company when deciding to acquire new investments. Given that PPR is a multinational company, locational research has a significant effect on the success of the company. PPR first started their expansion in countries that were culturally similar to their home country, for example, Germany. When it was time to start expanding to areas that weren't so familiar, factors such as cultural proximity, market size, competitors' moves, and geographic proximity all became very relevant. For instance, one of their subsidiaries, Gucci, is a high-end retailer that sells outstanding quality and exclusivity. This implies that their expansion needs to be in more developed countries with a higher disposable income. Finally, internalization may not be such an important factor to the PPR Group. Internalization means keeping the information within the company, but considering that PPR purchases companies that are already in operation, there is no information that would need to be kept within the company. One aspect that may be useful to keep internalized is how PPR makes their purchasing decisions for expansion. The factors that influence their choices to involve themselves with certain companies, is knowledge that many other companies would like to know about.*

## 3.   What role does cultural proximity and geographical proximity play in the retailers' international moves?

*Cultural proximity plays more of a role in PPR's international retailing than geographical proximity does, simply because they do not have to be so selective in where they expand, but to whom they expand. For example, PPR's first expansion through the acquisition of CFAO was to Africa, which has close cultural ties to the European French.*[24] *Their subsidiaries on the other hand have to take the opposite route. Gucci and Puma are both centralized and global, which means that they need to pay particular attention to where they expand to and less attention to who they expand to because they do not change their products for each country that they enter. They perceive that they are culturally different than the cultures that they enter into, which means that they make continuous adaptations to the host country. This also correlates with their expansion methods; they expand to areas that are most similar to their country first and then branch out to dissimilar countries. The geographic proximity does not hold much value for PPR because they are allowed to operate as independent units and are able to source from within the host country.[9]*

### 4. Can you predict the retailer's future international expansion?

*Considering that PPR has been doing exceptionally well with their mode of expansion, we do not foresee them changing their format drastically. They are the third-largest luxury retail group in the world, and will continue with their success. They have saturated their markets in France and Switzerland, so they should continue searching for unsaturated markets such as the United States, the United Kingdom, Brazil, and Canada for expansion options.[23] Approximately 60% of PPR's sales are generated outside of its home country, which means that they will have more success expanding outside of their country.[25] They will continue to find successful companies that reach a unique market and grow these companies into something even greater.*

## Propositions

### P1: The greater the ownership advantages for retailers, the less likely they will franchise or license.

*Yes, PPR does support this proposition. The explanation states that companies with significant ownership advantages would not want to give away their secrets. Ownership advantages include innovative processes the company can use to obtain market power. There are asset-based advantages, which refer to tangible items such as patents or products. PPR has significant ownership advantages, and they do not franchise because they want each of their subsidiaries to maintain their own operations with the vision of PPR guiding them along their path towards innovation, creativity, and growth. PPR itself does not franchise or license, but they do own the rights to their subsidiaries, which is like a tangible asset. Also within ownership advantages are transaction-based advantages, which come about because of the way things are done within a business. Transaction-based knowledge is a tacit knowledge (learning by doing), which describes PPR perfectly. They search for companies or brands that are doing well and show promise for the future, purchase them, and give these subsidiaries the guidance they need to continue growing. Some companies or brands could be great investments, while others go in a different direction than PPR saw them going in. Slack is also another component of ownership advantages. Organizational slack includes three measures, which are available slack, recoverable slack, and potential slack. PPR has been successful throughout their acquisitions and purchases, which imply that they would have earnings to reinvest (available slack) in their company that have not yet been absorbed by the company. PPR already owns various companies and brands, which means that they have absorbed this capital, and that capital is adding to their earnings. PPR continues to acquire new companies and brands, which means that they are continuously reinvesting their earnings (potential slack). Each acquisition made is giving PPR more potential slack. PPR supports this proposition in all of these ways.*

**P2: The greater the available organizational slack the greater the likelihood of expanding internationally.**

*PPR.SA fails to support Proposition 2. This proposition suggests a sustainable growth of organizational slack will increase the likelihood of a company to expand internationally. It is mostly because organization slack, which refers to excess financial resources, is very important in supporting an organization's international expansion strategy. Chart1 illustrates the reason why PPR's does not support the propositions. Their organizational slack is fluctuating during the first three years with slight differences. Although it did not increase during consecutive years, PPR's organizational slack, which maintained at a certain level, could help them to expand internationally.*

**Chart1**

| | |
|---|---|
| 1995 | 0.809708176 |
| 1996 | 0.796187131 |
| 1997 | 0.817057429 |
| 1998 | 0.766072539 |
| 1999 | 0.84011269 |
| 2000 | 0.813969901 |

*\*The closest year we could find near PPR's international expansion with complete financial figures to compute organizational slack is 1995.*

**P3: The greater the recoverable slack the greater the likelihood of expanding internationally.**

*No, PPR does not support Proposition 3. However, from Chart 2, which shows PPR's recoverable slack from 1991 to 2003, we could tell PPR's case does not fit the proposition. Despite subtle differences, its recoverable slack was able to be kept at a stable level, which could support their expansion.*

**Chart 2**

| | |
|---|---|
| 1991 | 0.980278 |
| 1992 | 0.979212 |
| 1993 | 0.981754 |
| 1994 | 0.970281 |
| 1995 | 0.968588 |
| 1996 | 0.958716 |
| 1997 | 0.953633 |
| 1998 | 0.948658 |
| 1999 | 0.939709 |
| 2000 | 0.934381 |

*\*The closest year we could find near PPR's international expansion with complete financial figures to compute recoverable slack is 1991.*

**P4: The greater the potential slack the greater the likelihood of expanding internationally.**

*Yes, PPR supports the proposition. This proposition is stating that a company with increasing potential slack, which represents future ability to generate resources,[26] will be more likely to choose international expansion strategy. By having an increase, the company is able to accumulate the resources needed to help with the international expansion. Chart 3 shows the potential slack PPR had from 1995 to 2000, since 1995 is the latest year with available financial figures. When looking at the chart, we can directly see that PPR's potential slack kept steady growth during the six years. The increase has supported their international expansion.*

**Chart3**

| | |
|---|---|
| 1995 | 8.2300215 |
| 1996 | 8.9709879 |
| 1997 | 10.062007 |
| 1998 | 11.731348 |
| 1999 | 19.236652 |
| 2000 | 22.604945 |

*\*The closest year we could find near PPR's international expansion with complete financial figures to compute potential slack is 1995.*

**P5: Multinational retailers will move to countries with lower disposable income than their home country.**

*Since PPR is present in many countries, they sometimes fit this proposition and sometimes do not. Even though PPR is a multinational retailer it does not focus on moving to countries that have a lower disposable income than their home country. Their first expansion was to various African countries, which generally have lower disposable incomes than France. However, when comparing the disposable income of United States, Italy and Germany, this proposition does not fit. These countries have very similar disposable income or even greater than France. France has a GDP per capita of $32,800 which is much lower than in the case of United States which has a GDP per capita of $46,400, Italy has a GDP per capita of $30,200 and Germany has a GDP per capita of $34,200. This clearly shows that PPR does not focus their international strategy based on the lower disposable income of other countries.*

### P6: Multinational retailers will move to countries that have a high positive change in GDP

*PPR does fit with this proposition because most of the countries in which they expand to do show a high increase in their GDP from the year they expanded and 5 years back. In the case of United States, PPR expanded into this country in 1997 when the U.S had a GDP of $8,250,900,000,000.00 and five years back (1992) they showed a GDP of $6,286,800,000,000.00. In the case of Germany, PPR expanded to this country also in the year 1997 when Germany showed a GDP of $2,160,591,000,000.00 and five years back (1992) they had a GDP of $2,062,141,000,000.00. Another country that shows a similar pattern of growth is Italy. PPR expanded to Italy in 1991 when they showed a GDP of $1,195,265,000,000.00 and 5 years back (1986) they had a GDP of $617,003,100,000.00. This clearly shows the increment in GDP that these countries had over the years.*[27]

| Country | Formula |
|---|---|
| United States | ($8,250,900,000,000.00 - $6,286,800,000,000.00) / $6,286,800,000,000.00 = 0.31 or 31% |
| Germany | ($2,160,591,000,000.00 - $2,062,141,000,000.00) / $2,062,141,000,000.00 = 0.05 or 5% |
| Italy | ($1,195,265,000,000.00 - $617,003,100,000.00) / $617,003,100,000.00 = 0.94 or 94% |

**P7:  Multinational retailers will move to countries that have a high positive change in service-value added as % of GDP.**

*PPR does fit with this proposition because most of the countries in which they expand to do show a high increase in their Service % of GDP from the year they expanded and 5 years back. In the table below one can see the increase in percent that these countries had within the five years.*[28]

| Country | Formula |
|---|---|
| United States | (73-72) / 72 = 0.01 or 1% |
| Germany | (68-63) / 63= 0.08 or 8% |
| Italy | (71-68) / 68 = 0.04 or 4% |

**P8: Multinational retailers will first move to countries that are culturally the most similar to their home country.**

*Yes, PPR does support this proposition. The explanation states that since multinational retailers will alter their offerings in different countries, it is important for them to understand the countries' culture. The closer two cultures are, the more likely the company is to understand the second culture. PPR's initial expansion was to Africa. As stated earlier in the research, Parts of Africa were once a colonial empire of France.*[29] *Four out of PPR's six core subsidiaries are French based companies. In 1999 PPR acquired Gucci, which was the first of their six main subsidiaries that was based in a country that was not France; Gucci is an Italian company.*[30] *There are various similarities between France and Italy. For example, both countries have regulations on expansion in order to protect small businesses, and northern Italy can be evenly compared to France's urban areas.*[31] *This acquisition made by PPR helps support this proposition because of the similarities between the host country and the home country. PPR is a variation of a multinational retailer; hence, there are some exceptions to this proposition in particular. Since PPR acquires companies, PPR has presence in each country that the subsidiary has presence. For this company, we would propose that they expand through acquisition to culturally and strategically similar companies, which have expanded to various countries. This thought would then contradict the proposition due to the fact that PPR did not determine the countries that they were expanding to, only the company that they were acquiring.*

**P9: Multinational retailers will expand within the country and then will expand regionally within that area.**

*Yes, PPR does support this proposition. The proposition states that once a multinational retailer has moved into a country they will expand there before entering another country. In 1990, PPR internationalized to Africa and opened* up full retail activity. It was not until 1999 when PPR finally started purchasing subsidiaries that were not French based companies. PPR's initial purchases were all French based companies like Fnac, Redcats, Conforama, and CFAO. It was not until fairly recently that PPR purchased Gucci Group and Puma, which are Italian and German companies. PPR purchases businesses that have been sustainable and successful, so that they have more of a guarantee and more knowledge when purchasing companies in the future. PPR expanded throughout France and then continued on their expansion throughout Africa, Italy, and Germany.

**P10: Periodically the multinational retailers will "jump" to a new geographic area and begin the stages form of expansion.**

No, PPR does not support this proposition. This proposition states that when a multinational retailer has expanded within a region and is ready for further expansion, it will target a new geographic area and take a leap to expand there. PPR is a holding company, so the jumps that it does make are to new brands or companies, which in turn give them expansion into new countries. PPR focuses on the specific brand or company in place of focusing on the geographic area. When the subsidiary is successful, it is usually because of the geographic area they decided to expand to.

## Endnotes

1.  Biesada, Alexandra (2010). PPR S.A. *Hoovers Company Records*. Retrieved February 22, 2010, from Proquest (886858611).

2.  Datamonitor (2009). PPR S.A.. Retrieved February 22, 2010, from Marketline Business Information Center.

3.  Biesada, Alexandra (2010). PPR S.A. *Hoovers Company Records*. Retrieved February 22, 2010, from Proquest (886858611).

4.  www.ppr.com (2010)

5.  PPR Annual Report (2008). Retrieved February 22, 2010 from www.ppr.com

6.  CFAO automotive (2010) Retrieved March 26, 2010 from http://www.cfaogroup.com/automotive/

7.  Business: out of Africa; PPR spins off CFAO (2009). *The Economist*. Retrieved February 22, 2010 from Proquest (1910823221).

8.  Kerrigan, Andy (2007, May). PPR makes a bid for Puma. *SGB*. 40(5). Retrieved March 27, 2010 from Proquest.

9.   Sternquist, Brenda (2007). *International Retailing: Second Edition.* (pp.332) New York: Fairchild Publications

10.  LVMH Group. *LVMH.* Retrieved March 26, 2010 from http://www.lvmh.com/groupe/pg_mot.asp?rub=2&srub=0.

11.  Key figures. *PPR.* Retrieved March 26, 2010 from www.ppr.com

12.  Activities. *LVMH.* Retrieved March 26, 2010 from http://www.lvmh.com/comfi/pg_activites.asp?rub=8&srub=3.

13.  Key figures. *LVMH.* Retrieved March 26, 2010 from http://www.lvmh.com/comfi/pop_repere.asp?str_contenu_pop=3.

14.  *2009 Financial Document.* PPR. Retrieved 26 March 2010 from http://www.ppr.com/DataUploadFiles/publications/7003/VDEF_VA.pdf.

15.  *Company Profile.* Gucci Group. Retrieved 26 March 2010 from http://www.guccigroup.com/index.html

16.  *Puma At a Glance.* Puma. Retrieved 26 March 2010 from http://about.puma.com/?cat=4).

17.  *Profile.* CFAO. Retrieved 26 March 2010 from http://www.cfaogroup.com/index.php?t=p&id_rub1=1&id_rub2=1&col=1&col2=1.

18.  *2009 Financial Document.* PPR. Retrieved 26 March 2010 from http://www.ppr.com/DataUploadFiles/publications/7003/VDEF_VA.pdf

19.  Concepts. Puma. Retrieved 26 March 2010 from http://www.eshop.puma.com.au/eShop/Controller?page=index&levelOne=10&levelTwo=0&tab=&index=&sort=&search=

20.  *Redcats Group.* PPR. Retrieved 28 March 2010 from http://www.ppr.com/front_sectionId-246_Changelang-en.html

21.  *Fnac.com.* PPR. Retrieved March 28, 2010 from http://www.ppr.com/front_sectionId-243_Changelang-en.html

22.  *Conforama.* PPR. Retrieved 28 March 2010 from http://www.ppr.com/front_sectionId-244_Changelang-en.html

23.  Mergent Online: Company Details. PPR SA. Retrieved March 23, 2010 from Mergent online.

24.  The French Colonial Empire http://www.knowledgerush.com/kr/encyclopedia/French_Colonial_Empire/

25.  Hoover's Profile: PPR SA http://www.answers.com/topic/ppr-sa

26. Herold, D,M., Jayaraman, N., Narayanaswamy, C.R. (2006). "What is the relationship between organizational slack and innovation?" *Journal of managerial issues.*

27. GDP statistics. Retrieved March 28, 2010 from  http://www.nationmaster.com/graph/eco_gdp-economy-gdp&date=1997

28. The World Bank Group. Retrieved March 28, 2010 from http://ddp-ext.worldbank.org/ext/DDPQQ/member.do?method=getMembers&userid=1&queryId=135

29. "French Equatorial Africa." Retrieved on March 23, 2010 from http://www.discoverfrance.net/Colonies/Eq_Africa.shtml.

30. The Alacra Store. Retrieved on March 23, 2010 from http://www.alacrastore.com/mergers-acquisitions/PPR_SA-1028010.

31. Absolute Astronomy. Retrieved on March 23, 2010 from http://www.absoluteastronomy.com/topics/French-German_enmity.

# Seven and i Holdings

*Mollie Dargan, Susanne Faris, Kevin McElmurry, Michael Simbol,*
*Chelsea Smykowski*

## Seven and i Holdings

7-11 Company Flow Chart

| COUNTRY | YEAR | EXIT YEAR | STORE NUMBER |
|---------|------|-----------|--------------|
| United States | 1934 | | 6,726 |
| Canada | 1969 | | 465 |
| Mexico | 1971 | | 1,223 |
| Japan | 1974 | | 13,049 |
| Australia | 1977 | | 415 |
| Sweden | 1978 | | 189 |
| Taiwan | 1980 | | 4,790 |
| China | 1981 | | 1,717 |
| Singapore | 1983 | | 549 |
| Philippines | 1984 | | 567 |
| Malaysia | 1984 | | 1,250 |
| Norway | 1986 | | 173 |
| South Korea | 1989 | | 3,150 |
| Thailand | 1989 | | 5,840 |
| Denmark | 1993 | | 129 |
| Indonesia | 2009 | | 23 |

## Opening Statement

Although relatively new to the market, Seven and i Holdings is already becoming a leader in the retail industry. According to STORES Magazine, in 2009 Seven and i was ranked number 14 with $54,113 million in total sales, up from a previous ranking of 16 in 2008[1]. Seven and i Holdings operates in an assortment of retail formats including convenience stores, superstores, supermarkets, department stores, food services, financial services, and IT/ services[2] that accounts for a global total of 41,410 stores[3] that employ over 52,814 people[4]. Worldwide, Seven and i sees 38 million customer store visits per day[5]. Ultimately Seven and i Holdings main goal is to "focus energies on meeting global customer demand for quality, fashion and low-prices."[6] They plan to do this all while "striving to address the local needs of each country by molding our operations to the realities of each country, while utilizing key services and software developed in Japan. All of the above is carried out in order to enhance the strength of the brands and companies under Seven & i Holdings around the world."[7]

## Company Overview

Seven and i Holdings Co, Ltd. was established early September 2005[8]. This holding company was created through a stock transfer involving three other previously established companies; Seven-Eleven Japan Co., Ltd., Ito-Yokado Co., Ltd., and Denny's Japan Co., Ltd.[9] Ultimately the holding company was created for these three separate companies for two major reasons, the first being to maximize the group's enterprise value. Maximizing their value was made possible by leveraging synergies amongst operational areas as well as reducing overall costs by integrating administrative functions.[10] The second reason for establishment was to strengthen corporate governance.[11] This was done by delineating autonomy and the responsibilities of each segment of the company as well as evaluating profitability and efficiently allocating management resources based on monitoring.[12]

As previously mentioned Seven and i holdings Co. strives to attain 'a New, Comprehensive Lifestyle Industry' through their seven chief operational areas.[13] The core areas that make Seven and i Holdings so successful are convenience stores, superstores, supermarkets, department stores, food services, financial services, and IT/Services which were identified at the time of their establishment.[14]

One of the operational areas that make up the company Seven and i Holdings is convenience store. The main convenience store is 7-Eleven, which is the largest retail store chain in the world with over 40,255 stores worldwide in 16 countries.[15] The first convenience store that was established under Seven and i Holdings control was in January of 2004.[16] Their key strategy for the convenience store development is market dominance mainly in urban areas.[17] A second approach to increase store development is to expand small-type convenience stores as well as open standard roadside stores.[18] Of the seven different operations, convenience stores bring in 38.3% of all revenue with ¥1.968 trillion, second highest among all operations.[19] Since 2005, convenience stores have had a steady increase each year in total revenue until 2008 when total revenues started to decrease each year.[20] However, the outlook in 2011 looks promising. Seven and i is forecasting ¥2,040.0 billion of total revenue which is up 3.6% and an operating income of ¥185.5 billion which is a gain of 0.9%.[21]

The second retail format that Seven and i Holdings operate is superstores. These superstores are made up of stores that provide apparel, household goods, and food in Japan and China.[22] The main superstore is Ito-Yokado which has 174 stores and employs over 40,363 people.[23] The first superstore was established in December of 1996.[24] Ito-Yokado's store development strategy is market dominance.[25] They have recently changed their store format to a new lifestyle support discount store called The Price.[26] Superstores are the leading operation area in regards to total revenue with ¥2.017 trillion which comes out to be roughly 39.2%.[27] Since 2005, Ito-Yokado's revenue has fluctuated up and down but there has been a steady decrease since 2008.[28] The outlook for superstores in 2011 is estimating that there will be an increase in revenues of ¥2,030.0 billion, up 0.7%, and for operating income they are forecasting ¥22.0 billion in revenues which is a gain of 55.2%.[29]

Another operational area that is used by Seven and I Holdings is supermarkets. The core supermarket is York-Benimaru which has more than 164 stores.[30] Another supermarket is York Mart which has over 62 stores.[31] The establishment of superstores was first implemented in November of 2004.[32] Market dominance is once again the main store development strategy.[33] In 2010, York-Benimaru had a total of ¥348.7 billion in total revenues which was slightly lower than the previous year.[34] Since 2005 though, York-Benimaru has seen a steady increase in revenue each year.[35] In 2011, York-Benimaru plans to focus on improving the profitability of their existing stores rather than open up new stores. As far as merchandising goes they plan to add Group Merchandising and Team Merchandising.[36]

Seven and i Holdings also has department stores. The main department store is Sogo & Seibu which has over 28 stores that employs more than 11,003 people.[37] Sogo & Seibu uses two main store strategies, key stores and suburban stores.[38] Their key stores are the places that make large contributions to the company and suburban stores are places that need a whole new earnings structure.[39]

Key Stores will implement renovations to their stores as well as aggressive merchandising.[40] Suburban stores will use a multi-purpose commercial facility store format and get away from the traditional department store format.[41] Department stores made ¥922.8 billion in total revenue which is also 18.0% of Seven and i Holdings total revenue.[42] Sogo & Seibu's total revenue increased after their first year in 2007 but then has decreased each year since then.[43] The outlook for 2011 has a projected increase in total revenue of ¥928.0 billion which is an increase of 0.6%. Also their operating income is estimated to be ¥7.0 billion, an increase of 41.2%.[44]

Food services are another operational area that makes up Seven and i Holdings. The main food service is called Seven and i Food Systems which runs different restaurants, meal provision services, and fast food places.[45] There are in total 892 stores with 1,584 employees.[46] In 2007, Seven & i Food Systems merged the three different companies, Denny's Japan Co., Ltd., Famil Co., Ltd., and York Bussan K.K.[47] Food services made a total revenue of ¥86.4 billion in 2010.[48] This accounts for 1.1% of Seven and i Holdings total revenue.[49] Total revenues for food services have decreased every year since 2006.[50] Seven and i Holdings projects ¥79.0 billion in revenue, down 8.6% in 2011, and an operating loss of ¥0.5 billion, which is an improvement of ¥2.2 billion.[51]

The second to last retail format is financial services. Seven Bank is the main financial service that is used.[52] They have numerous ATMs around the world. As of 2010 there were 13,985 ATMs in Seven and i Holdings stores and 616 ATMs in non-Group locations.[53] Financial services department employs more than 329 people.[54] In 2010, there was a total of ¥110.4 billion in revenue which is also a total of 2.1% of Seven and i Holdings total revenue.[55] The total revenue for financial services has increased every year since 2005[56] but in 2011 Seven and i Holdings is projecting their first decrease in revenue.[57] They are forecasting total revenue to be ¥107.0 billion, down 3.1%, and operating income to be ¥26.5 billion, a decrease of 12.1%.[58]

The last operational area that Seven and i Holdings operate is IT/Services. Seven & i Netmedia, which was established in 2008, is the chief company that is in charge of reorganization and consolidation of IT/Services for Seven and i Holdings.[59] IT/Services is a unique service that helps implement the Internet to the different retail companies.[60] This service enables Seven and i Holdings to offer an Internet shopping service that helps their customers with their buying needs at their different convenience stores, superstores, supermarkets, and department stores.[61]

These seven operational areas play a vital role in Seven and i Holdings success. They are what makes up the entire company and have led the corporation to being one of the top retailers in the world. Seven and i Holdings plans to open new markets in order to meet customer needs.[62] Their purpose is to implement different strategies that will hopefully lead to long-term growth.[63] The two strategies are to increase profit of the existing operations and also open up new sectors in Japan's e-commerce market.[64] Their overall outlook for 2011 is very promising. They expect ¥5.140 trillion in total revenue which is an increase from the previous year. Also they expect a net income of ¥100 trillion which is a 222.8% YOY.[65]

## Competition

Seven & i Holdings Company is the 16th largest company in the world.[66] With their seven retail formats that include convenience stores, super stores, supermarkets, department stores, food services, financial services, and IT services, it makes their holdings company not only multifunctional but also profitable. However, like any business, Seven & i Holdings Company has three main competitors. The main competitors are AEON Co., Alimentation Couche-Tard, and LAWSON Inc.[67]

AEON Company is located in Chiba, Japan but is also expanding to Southeast Asia and China.[68] The Holding company franchises over 5,000 stores worldwide and has 169 subsidiaries.[69] AEON is mostly known for its life-style enhancing retail company but also operates supermarkets, financial services, amusement facilities, and conscious specialty stores like The Body Shop and The Laura Ashley stores to name a few.[70] Also, AEON runs 1,200 supermarket chains under the MaxValu name which is the largest in Japan.[71]

Alimentation Couche-Tard is located in Laval, Quebec Canada.[72] It is the second largest convenience store in North America operating in 43 states and the number one convenience store in Canada with almost 6,000 outlets over three regions.[73] Couche-Tard operates under the names, Mac's, Circle K, and On the Run.[74] Two-thirds, or 4,100, of its convenience stores sell gasoline.[75] Furthermore, 75% of Alimentation Couche-Tard's sales come from the United States alone.[76]

The last competitor for Seven & i Holdings Company is LAWSON Inc. LAWSON Inc. is located in Tokyo Japan.[77] LAWSON is known for on-the-go Japanese food.[78] It is the second largest convenience store following 7-Eleven Japan.[79] LAWSON Inc. operates almost 10,000 stores in total throughout Japan and Shanghai, China.[80] An astounding 85% of sales come from the food and groceries sector.[81]

## Expansion Strategy

Seven and i Holdings controls a variety of different operational areas which span across 16 countries. The expansion strategy of these retail formats depends on each of the different segments. These strategies include; stores operated directly by their subsidiaries, stores operated by companies in each country granted a defined area license from Seven-Eleven, Inc., and finally stores with a license to use the trademark of Sogo & Seibu Co., Ltd.[82] Until now, the licensee operations of 7-Eleven, Inc. (SEI), had primarily entailed the provision of trademark rights to licensees. Moving forward, however, SEI and SEJ (Seven-Eleven Japan) will work together to establish a support system for area licensees in each country. This includes the sharing of information with area licensees, primarily in regard to SEJ's operational infrastructure related to merchandising, store facilities, store operations, and information/distribution systems. With consideration for the specific situation in each country, such as employment conditions and the brand strength for 7-Eleven overall will be fostered by allowing area licensees to use SEJ's strong operational infrastructure.[83] In providing this information to all 7-Eleven licensees across the globe Seven and i holdings will be able to standardize their stores allowing for greater expansion in the countries that they are currently in as well as moving with ease into countries not currently on their map.[84]

In addition to these strategies for convenience stores Seven and i Holdings has developed an expansion strategy for their core operations which would also include food supermarkets and all overseas operations.[85] In convenience stores, food supermarkets, and overseas operations, which are positioned as core operations, Seven and i Holdings will implement aggressive expansion initiatives in order to raise the profitability of the Group as a whole. On the other hand, in domestic superstore operations, department store operations, and food services, which have been positioned as operations targeted for rebuilding, unprofitable stores will be converted to new formats or closed, and we will focus our management resources on stores in unfavorable locations.[86] In implementing this strategy Seven and i Holdings hopes to increase efficiency in the operational areas across the globe.[87]

Seven and i Holdings have designed two other strategies not necessarily for expansion purposes, but to increase business as a whole. The first is the group store opening strategy in which, the company develops stores in several formats and therefore opens stores of various sizes. Each format is clearly defined in terms of its motivations for store visits and has a different catchment area. Accordingly, Seven & i Holdings can achieve a higher density level in its store-opening strategy across the different format of stores.[88] The last global plan of attack is area dominance strategy in which Seven and i would position a dense population of stores in a single region.[89]

The largest source of global expansion for Seven and i Holdings is the convenience store sector consisting solely of 7-Eleven stores. As of 2010 the global 7-Eleven store network currently possesses 37,696[90] stores and is rapidly growing at a rate of 1800 -2000 new stores per year.[91] Seven and i's consolidated subsidiaries control the primary 7-Eleven stores across the world.[92] These chief convenience store locations are found in Japan, the United States, Canada, China (Beijing, Tianjin), and Hawaii.[93] The remaining countries; Sweden, Norway, Denmark, Thailand, Malaysia, Singapore, Mexico, South Korea, Taiwan, Austria, Philippines, and Indonesia operate their 7- Eleven convenience stores as an area licensee.[94] Dissimilar to the 6 additional areas of operations, 7-Eleven is the only entity that resides in all 16 countries.[95]

## Japan

Since Seven and i Holdings originated in Japan, they happen to be the only country in which all seven retail formats are operated directly by subsidiaries.[96] They also seem to be the sole country in which all seven areas of operations are represented. In Japan there are multiple 7-Elevens, the convenience store format; several Ito Yokados, the superstore format; numerous York-Berimarus, the super market format; quite a few Sogo & Seibus, the department store format; and a vast amount of Seven and i food services.[97] Seven and i Holdings also has two specialty stores, THE LOFT Co, Ltd which can be found inside their department stores as well as Akachan Honpo Co, Ltd which is located in their superstore format.[98] Several ATMs stemming from their financial area of operations can be found throughout Japan in most of Seven and i Holdings' entities.[99]

## China

Seven and i holdings utilized their area dominance strategy when it came to opening new stores in China.[100] Thus multiple formats such as restaurants, convenience stores, super stores, department stores, and super markets, were put into operation.[101] Though not every operational area is represented in China, they do happen to be the only other country besides Japan that runs more than two of

Seven and i Holdings' multiple entities.[102] China's expansion strategy is also a bit different than Japan's. The majority of the established 7-Elevens were granted a defined area license from Seven-Eleven Inc. as opposed to being operated directly by Seven and i Holding's subsidiaries.[103] The department store sector Sogo and Seibu fall into the same category by having obtained a license to use the trade mark of Sogo and Seibu Co. Ltd instead of being controlled directly by subsidiaries.[104] Finally, both the superstores Chengdu Ito-Yokado Co., Ltd. and Hua Tang Yokado

Commercial Co., Ltd., as well as their super market Beijing Wang fu jing Yokado Commercial Co., Ltd. and restaurant Seven & i Restaurant (Beijing) Co., Ltd. are all ran directly by Seven and i holdings subsidiaries much like the entirety of the operational areas in Japan.[105]

## Private Label

Many companies, including Seven & i's subsidiary, 7-Eleven, offer private labels to competitively contend with national brands. Private label is described as the label of a product, or the product itself, sold under the name of a wholesaler or retailer, by special arrangement with the manufacturer or producer.[119] 7-Eleven is the leading convenience store with on-the-go premade food for the consumer to easily grab morning, noon, night or even late night munchies.[120] 7-Eleven has a low cost private label called 7 Select.[121] It offers a wide array of items under 7 Select, including household items like paper plates, paper towels, and plastic cups, food and beverage items like water, cranberry juice, orange soda, powdered donuts, potato chips and salsa con queso. Along with 7-Eleven's private label, 7 Select, the company also has proprietary products. The products that are most widely known to the 7-Eleven stores are the Slurpee and Big Gulp beverage offerings.[122] Big Bite hot dogs and freshly brewed coffee are other products that 7-Eleven owns.[123] However, of the 38,000 stores worldwide[124], only the 7,200 stores in the United States and Canada carry the private label brand 7 Select.[125] Even though private label is predominately in the United States and Canada, other countries are slowly recognizing the importance of private label and implementing them into their 7-Eleven stores. For example, Malaysia is now offering private label water called Aktif in three different versions; Mineral water, Reverse Osmosis and Distilled water.[126]

Another private label brand that Seven and i Holdings have implemented is Seven Premium.[127] This is a high value and low priced brand.[128] Its quality is the same if not better than other national brands as well as having prices being the same if not lower than other national brands.[129] One can find the Seven Premium brand in superstores, supermarkets, convenience stores, and department stores.[130] The different Seven Premium product categories are processed foods, daily foods, processed fresh foods, and household goods.[131] In November 2009, they started sales of wine simultaneously in Japan and North America as Seven and i Holdings first private brand product for the global market.[132] As of May 2010 there were a total of 1,100 SKUs in these different operations.[133] Also their total sales in 2010 were ¥ 320 billion.[134]

# Questions

**1. Is the retailer classified as a global retailer or a multinational retailer? Explain its pattern of expansion. What expansion strategy did/is the retailer use/using?**

*7-Eleven would be classified as a global retailer. One reason is the fact that the company uses a standard retail format; this means that most stores are generally the same, and in 7-Eleven's case the main format that is used is convenience stores. 7-Eleven also generally has centralized management. Another characteristic of a global retailer is the extensive use of private label. As mentioned before, 7-Eleven's private label sector, created to compete with popular national brand products, is growing in the United States, Canada, and several other international countries. One last factor that defines global retailers is the fact that the stores are generally small-medium size. Since 7-Eleven stores only serve a limited supply of convenience products they do not need to have a large store setting. 7-Eleven stores are located in sixteen countries and the company's expansion strategy varies depending on the segment. Seven and i expands their stores by either operating directly by a subsidiary, operating through companies in each country that are granted a defined area license from 7-Eleven, Inc., or through a license to use trademark of Sogo & Seibu Co., Ltd. Seven and I's convenience store chain, 7-Eleven, is constantly expanding. The company is continuously opening new stores in all countries of operation. The franchisers are given a vast amount of information when opening a store which makes it easy for the company to expand. 7-Eleven also focuses on closing stores that are not profitable, while continuing to open stores in more successful locations.*

**2. Based on Dunning's eclectic theory, how do ownership, locational and internalization factors play in your retailers' international expansion?**

*Ownership, location, and internalization are the three concepts covered by Dunning's eclectic theory. 7-Eleven's international expansion is focused on asset based advantages rather than a transactional based ownership advantage. 7-Eleven helps franchisees tailor their businesses to the individuality of their selected market bases and customer needs and that means happier customers that come back.[135] The franchisor bears the cost of services including cost of the land, building and store equipment record keeping, bill paying and payroll services for store operations fees, and financing for all normal store operating expenses. They even pay water, sewer, gas and electric utilities. By providing all of the aforementioned to its new stores they are using its excess capital to provide all the essential start up assets to make sure all new stores have the right beginning to be profitable. Congruently being asset based typically makes an organization a successful franchise rather than a licensor. 7- Eleven's location advantage is important to its further expansion. As a global retailer it is important to use franchise operations as an advantage for continual growth. With locations in almost every corner of the globe it is vital to have a simplified operation system to run all the stores relatively the same. Finally, internalization is almost nonexistent with a huge global franchisor. By spreading stores all over and sharing its operation systems with all individual franchisees only the most important company information is retained by the managing holding company 7 and i.*

### 3. What role does cultural proximity and geographical proximity play in the retailers' international moves?

*Cultural proximity and geographical proximity do not play a huge role in 7-Eleven's international moves. 7-Eleven is a global retailer and according to the Strategic International Retail Expansion Model, multinational retailers focus on locational advantages, like cultural proximity and geographical proximity,[136] however, global retailers focus on ownership advantage. Since 7-Eleven gives most of their information to their franchiser's it is easy to keep standardized stores in all locations. Most 7-Eleven stores have the same format but contain different products based on the tastes of the country the store is operating in. Cultural proximity has not been a main focus for expansion because as a global retailer and franchising company it would not be beneficial or strategic for 7-Eleven.*

### 4. Can you predict the retailer's future international expansion?

*Based on the extreme growth of 7-Eleven stores it is easy to see that the company will continue to grow. From January 2010 to January 2011 of the sixteen countries that 7-Eleven operates in, only one country saw a decrease in store number and that was only by three stores. Store numbers grew by 626 in the United States, 124 in Japan, 110 in China, 80 in Malaysia, 445 in South Korea, and 180 in Thailand. From this information it is clear that 7-Eleven stores will continue to expand, especially in the United States, South Korea, and Thailand. Our prediction for Seven and i Holdings overall growth is an increase of 2,000 stores.*

# Propositions

**P2: The greater the available organizational slack the greater the likelihood of expanding internationally.**

| Year | Current Assets | Current Liabilities | Current Ratio |
|------|----------------|---------------------|---------------|
| 2008 | $1,354,417.00 | $1,177,493.00 | 1.15 |
| 2009 | $1,397,102.00 | $1,255,937.00 | 1.11 |
| 2010 | $1,460,186.00 | $1,263,370.00 | 1.16 |

*Seven and i does follow this proposition. Organizational slack refers to the excess money that can be used. A company with high organizational slack can use the excess resources to first saturate the home market then begin international expansion. Above from the years 2008-2010 the current ratio is provided by dividing current assets by current liabilities. By comparing the ratios annually we can see that the middle year 2009 took a small hit but bounced back strong above its 2008 number.*

**P3: The greater the recoverable slack the greater the likelihood of expanding internationally.**

| $ | 2008 | 2009 | 2010 |
|---|------|------|------|
| Gen & Admin Expenses | $415,566 | $406,264 | $405,498 |
| Sales | $5,223,832 | $5,094,757 | $4,549,867 |
| Expenses to Sales | 0.080 | 0.080 | 0.089 |

*Seven and i does support this proposition. The greater the recoverable slack the greater the likelihood of expansion.*

**P4: The greater the potential slack the greater the likelihood of expanding internationally.**

| | 2008 | 2009 | 2010 |
|---|------|------|------|
| Equity | $1,979,848.00 | $1,862,962.00 | $1,789,065.00 |
| Captial | $731,621.00 | $576,074.00 | $576,072.00 |
| Ratio | 2.71 | 3.23 | 3.11 |

**P13: Global companies will move to the largest/capital cities in a country.**

*7 and i through its 7-Eleven convenience stores have a presence almost everywhere inside its host nations. It is located in the largest markets in all the countries including all but one of the capital cities. So yes, global companies will move to the largest capital cities in a country.*

| Country | Capital | 7-Eleven (Y/N) |
|---|---|---|
| USA | Washington DC | Yes |
| Canada | Ottowa | Yes |
| Mexico | Mexico City | Yes |
| Japan | Tokyo | Yes |
| Australia | Canberra | No |
| Sweden | Stockholm | Yes |
| Taiwan | Taipei | Yes |
| China | Beijing | Yes |
| Singapore | Singapore | Yes |
| Philippines | Manila | Yes |
| Malaysia | Kuala Lumpur | Yes |
| Norway | Oslo | Yes |
| South Korea | Seoul | Yes |
| Thailand | Bangkok | Yes |
| Denmark | Copenhagen | Yes |
| Indonesia | Jakarta | Yes |

**P14: Global companies will not be attracted by population size, income, cultural proximity or geographical proximity.**

*In the case of 7-Eleven's expansion the company has not focused on cultural proximity or geographical proximity. Since stores are franchised the company does not need to focus on cultural proximity. 7-Eleven is also a global retailer. Global retailers do not typically concentrate on expanding within a geographic area.*

**P15: The greater the asset based ownership advantages of a global retailer, the more likely they are to franchise.**

*7-Eleven has been a leader in the franchise industry for more than 40 years. 7-Eleven helps Franchisees tailor their businesses to the individuality of their selected market bases and customer needs and that means happier customers that come back.[137] The franchisor bears the cost of services including cost of the land, building and store equipment record keeping, bill paying and payroll services for store operations fees, and financing for all normal store operating expenses. They even pay water, sewer, gas and electric utilities. In conclusion, yes the greater the asset based ownership advantages of a global retailer, the more likely they are to franchise.*

**P16: The greater the transaction based ownership advantages of a global retailer, the less likely they are to franchise.**

*Because of the small size of the store and relative sameness globally operation of 7-Eleven Stores are universal for the most part. The operations are not a huge secret that 7 and i holds close to the chest. This allows for low transaction based ownership advantages of this global retailer and a higher degree of franchising.*

## Endnotes

1.    Seven & i hldgs. co., ltd corporate outline 2010. (2010). Date retrieved March 20, 2011. Retrieved from http://www.7andi.com/en/ir/pdf/corporate/2010_all.pdf

2.    Seven & i holdings annual report 2010. (2010). Date retrieved March 20, 2011. Retrieved from http://www.7andi.com/en/ir/pdf/annual/2010_all.pdf

3.    Seven-Eleven Japan. (2011, January 31). Date retrieved March 20, 2011. Retrieved from http://www.sej.co.jp/company/en/g_stores.html AND Seven & i holdings annual report 2010. (2010). Date retrieved March 20, 2011. Retrieved from http://www.7andi.com/en/ir/pdf/annual/2010_all.pdf

4.    Seven & i holdings annual report 2010. (2010). Date retrieved March 20, 2011. Retrieved from http://www.7andi.com/en/ir/pdf/annual/2010_all.pdf

5.  Seven & i holdings annual report 2010. (2010). Date retrieved March 20, 2011. Retrieved from http://www.7andi.com/en/ir/pdf/annual/2010_all.pdf

6.  Seven & i holdings annual report 2010. (2010). Date retrieved March 20, 2011. Retrieved from http://www.7andi.com/en/ir/pdf/annual/2010_all.pdf

7.  Seven & i holdings annual report 2010. (2010). Date retrieved March 20, 2011. Retrieved from http://www.7andi.com/en/ir/pdf/annual/2010_all.pdf

8.  Seven & i holdings annual report 2010. (2010). Date retrieved March 20, 2011. Retrieved from http://www.7andi.com/en/ir/pdf/annual/2010_all.pdf

9.  Seven & i holdings annual report 2010. (2010). Date retrieved March 20, 2011. Retrieved from http://www.7andi.com/en/ir/pdf/annual/2010_all.pdf

10. Seven & i hldgs. co., ltd corporate outline 2010. (2010). Date retrieved March 20, 2011. Retrieved from http://www.7andi.com/en/ir/pdf/corporate/2010_all.pdf

11. Seven & i hldgs. co., ltd corporate outline 2010. (2010). Date retrieved March 20, 2011. Retrieved from http://www.7andi.com/en/ir/pdf/corporate/2010_all.pdf

12. Seven & i hldgs. co., ltd corporate outline 2010. (2010). Date retrieved March 20, 2011. Retrieved from http://www.7andi.com/en/ir/pdf/corporate/2010_all.pdf

13. Seven & i holdings annual report 2010. (2010). Date retrieved March 20, 2011. Retrieved from http://www.7andi.com/en/ir/pdf/annual/2010_all.pdf

14. Seven & i hldgs. co., ltd corporate outline 2010. (2010). Date retrieved March 20, 2011. Retrieved from http://www.7andi.com/en/ir/pdf/corporate/2010_all.pdf

15. Seven-Eleven Japan. (2011, January 31). Date retrieved March 20, 2011. Retrieved from http://www.sej.co.jp/company/en/g_stores.html

16. Seven & i hldgs. co., ltd corporate outline 2010. (2010). Date retrieved March 20, 2011. Retrieved from http://www.7andi.com/en/ir/pdf/corporate/2010_all.pdf

17. Seven & i hldgs. co., ltd corporate outline 2010. (2010). Date retrieved March 20, 2011. Retrieved from http://www.7andi.com/en/ir/pdf/corporate/2010_all.pdf

18. Seven & i hldgs. co., ltd corporate outline 2010. (2010). Date retrieved March 20, 2011. Retrieved from http://www.7andi.com/en/ir/pdf/corporate/2010_all.pdf

19. Seven & i holdings annual report 2010. (2010). Date retrieved March 20, 2011. Retrieved from http://www.7andi.com/en/ir/pdf/annual/2010_all.pdf

20. Seven & i hldgs. co., ltd corporate outline 2010. (2010). Date retrieved March 20, 2011. Retrieved from http://www.7andi.com/en/ir/pdf/corporate/2010_all.pdf

21. Seven & i holdings annual report 2010. (2010). Date retrieved March 20, 2011. Retrieved from http://www.7andi.com/en/ir/pdf/annual/2010_all.pdf

22. Seven & i holdings annual report 2010. (2010). Date retrieved March 20, 2011. Retrieved from http://www.7andi.com/en/ir/pdf/annual/2010_all.pdf

23. Seven & i hldgs. co., ltd corporate outline 2010. (2010). Date retrieved March 20, 2011. Retrieved from http://www.7andi.com/en/ir/pdf/corporate/2010_all.pdf

24. Seven & i hldgs. co., ltd corporate outline 2010. (2010). Date retrieved March 20, 2011. Retrieved from http://www.7andi.com/en/ir/pdf/corporate/2010_all.pdf

25. Seven & i hldgs. co., ltd corporate outline 2010. (2010). Date retrieved March 20, 2011. Retrieved from http://www.7andi.com/en/ir/pdf/corporate/2010_all.pdf

26. Seven & i hldgs. co., ltd corporate outline 2010. (2010). Date retrieved March 20, 2011. Retrieved from http://www.7andi.com/en/ir/pdf/corporate/2010_all.pdf

27. Seven & i holdings annual report 2010. (2010). Date retrieved March 20, 2011. Retrieved from http://www.7andi.com/en/ir/pdf/annual/2010_all.pdf

28. Seven & i hldgs. co., ltd corporate outline 2010. (2010). Date retrieved March 20, 2011. Retrieved from http://www.7andi.com/en/ir/pdf/corporate/2010_all.pdf

29. Seven & i holdings annual report 2010. (2010). Date retrieved March 20, 2011. Retrieved from http://www.7andi.com/en/ir/pdf/annual/2010_all.pdf

30. Seven & i holdings annual report 2010. (2010). Date retrieved March 20, 2011. Retrieved from http://www.7andi.com/en/ir/pdf/annual/2010_all.pdf

31. Seven & i holdings annual report 2010. (2010). Date retrieved March 20, 2011. Retrieved from http://www.7andi.com/en/ir/pdf/annual/2010_all.pdf

32. Seven & i hldgs. co., ltd corporate outline 2010. (2010). Date retrieved March 20, 2011. Retrieved from http://www.7andi.com/en/ir/pdf/corporate/2010_all.pdf

33. Seven & i hldgs. co., ltd corporate outline 2010. (2010). Date retrieved March 20, 2011. Retrieved from http://www.7andi.com/en/ir/pdf/corporate/2010_all.pdf

34. Seven & i holdings annual report 2010. (2010). Date retrieved March 20, 2011. Retrieved from http://www.7andi.com/en/ir/pdf/annual/2010_all.pdf

35. Seven & i hldgs. co., ltd corporate outline 2010. (2010). Date retrieved March 20, 2011. Retrieved from http://www.7andi.com/en/ir/pdf/corporate/2010_all.pdf

36. Seven & i holdings annual report 2010. (2010). Date retrieved March 20, 2011. Retrieved from http://www.7andi.com/en/ir/pdf/annual/2010_all.pdf

37. Seven & i hldgs. co., ltd corporate outline 2010. (2010). Date retrieved March 20, 2011. Retrieved from http://www.7andi.com/en/ir/pdf/corporate/2010_all.pdf

38. Seven & i hldgs. co., ltd corporate outline 2010. (2010). Date retrieved March 20, 2011. Retrieved from http://www.7andi.com/en/ir/pdf/corporate/2010_all.pdf

39. Seven & i hldgs. co., ltd corporate outline 2010. (2010). Date retrieved March 20, 2011. Retrieved from http://www.7andi.com/en/ir/pdf/corporate/2010_all.pdf

40. Seven & i hldgs. co., ltd corporate outline 2010. (2010). Date retrieved March 20, 2011. Retrieved from http://www.7andi.com/en/ir/pdf/corporate/2010_all.pdf

41. Seven & i hldgs. co., ltd corporate outline 2010. (2010). Date retrieved March 20, 2011. Retrieved from http://www.7andi.com/en/ir/pdf/corporate/2010_all.pdf

42. Seven & i holdings annual report 2010. (2010). Date retrieved March 20, 2011. Retrieved from http://www.7andi.com/en/ir/pdf/annual/2010_all.pdf

43. Seven & i hldgs. co., ltd corporate outline 2010. (2010). Date retrieved March 20, 2011. Retrieved from http://www.7andi.com/en/ir/pdf/corporate/2010_all.pdf

44. Seven & i holdings annual report 2010. (2010). Date retrieved March 20, 2011. Retrieved from http://www.7andi.com/en/ir/pdf/annual/2010_all.pdf

45. Seven & i hldgs. co., ltd corporate outline 2010. (2010). Date retrieved March 20, 2011. Retrieved from http://www.7andi.com/en/ir/pdf/corporate/2010_all.pdf

46. Seven & i hldgs. co., ltd corporate outline 2010. (2010). Date retrieved March 20, 2011. Retrieved from http://www.7andi.com/en/ir/pdf/corporate/2010_all.pdf

47. Seven & i hldgs. co., ltd corporate outline 2010. (2010). Date retrieved March 20, 2011. Retrieved from http://www.7andi.com/en/ir/pdf/corporate/2010_all.pdf

48. Seven & i holdings annual report 2010. (2010). Date retrieved March 13, 2011. Retrieved from http://www.7andi.com/en/ir/pdf/annual/2010_all.pdf

49. Seven & i holdings annual report 2010. (2010). Date retrieved March 13, 2011. Retrieved from http://www.7andi.com/en/ir/pdf/annual/2010_all.pdf

50. Seven & i hldgs. co., ltd corporate outline 2010. (2010). Date retrieved March 13, 2011. Retrieved from http://www.7andi.com/en/ir/pdf/corporate/2010_all.pdf

51. Seven & i holdings annual report 2010. (2010). Date retrieved March 13, 2011. Retrieved from http://www.7andi.com/en/ir/pdf/annual/2010_all.pdf

52. Seven & i holdings annual report 2010. (2010). Date retrieved March 13, 2011. Retrieved from http://www.7andi.com/en/ir/pdf/annual/2010_all.pdf

53. Seven & i hldgs. co., ltd corporate outline 2010. (2010). Date retrieved March 13, 2011. Retrieved from http://www.7andi.com/en/ir/pdf/corporate/2010_all.pdf

54. Seven & i hldgs. co., ltd corporate outline 2010. (2010). Date retrieved March 13, 2011. Retrieved from http://www.7andi.com/en/ir/pdf/corporate/2010_all.pdf

55. Seven & i holdings annual report 2010. (2010). Date retrieved March 13, 2011. Retrieved from http://www.7andi.com/en/ir/pdf/annual/2010_all.pdf

56. Seven & i hldgs. co., ltd corporate outline 2010. (2010). Date retrieved March 13, 2011. Retrieved from http://www.7andi.com/en/ir/pdf/corporate/2010_all.pdf

57. Seven & i holdings annual report 2010. (2010). Date retrieved March 13, 2011. Retrieved from http://www.7andi.com/en/ir/pdf/annual/2010_all.pdf

58. Seven & i holdings annual report 2010. (2010). Date retrieved March 13, 2011. Retrieved from http://www.7andi.com/en/ir/pdf/annual/2010_all.pdf

59. Seven & i hldgs. co., ltd corporate outline 2010. (2010). Date retrieved March 13, 2011. Retrieved from http://www.7andi.com/en/ir/pdf/corporate/2010_all.pdf

60. Seven & i hldgs. co., ltd corporate outline 2010. (2010). Date retrieved March 13, 2011. Retrieved from http://www.7andi.com/en/ir/pdf/corporate/2010_all.pdf

61. Seven & i hldgs. co., ltd corporate outline 2010. (2010). Date retrieved March 13, 2011. Retrieved from http://www.7andi.com/en/ir/pdf/corporate/2010_all.pdf

62. Seven & i holdings annual report 2010. (2010). Date retrieved March 13, 2011. Retrieved from http://www.7andi.com/en/ir/pdf/annual/2010_all.pdf

63. Seven & i holdings annual report 2010. (2010). Date retrieved March 13, 2011. Retrieved from http://www.7andi.com/en/ir/pdf/annual/2010_all.pdf

64. Seven & i holdings annual report 2010. (2010). Date retrieved March 13, 2011. Retrieved from http://www.7andi.com/en/ir/pdf/annual/2010_all.pdf

65. Overview of consolidated financial results. (2010). Date retrieved March 13, 2011. Retrieved from http://www.7andi.com/en/ir/fi/summary.html

66. Hoovers. (2011). Date retrieved March 29, 2011. Retrieved from http://www.hoovers.com/company/Seven__i_Holdings_Co_Ltd/rcfthci-1-1njea3.html

67. Hoovers. (2011). Date retrieved March 20, 2011. Retrieved from http://www.hoovers.com/company/Seven__i_Holdings_Co_Ltd/rcfthci-1-1njea3.html

68. Hoovers. (2011). Date retrieved March 20, 2011. Retrieved from http://www.hoovers.com/company/Seven__i_Holdings_Co_Ltd/rcfthci-1-1njea3.html

69. Aeon. (2008). Date retrieved March 20, 2011. Retrieved from http://www.aeon. info/en/aboutaeon/index.html

70. Hoovers. (2011). Date retrieved March 20, 2011. Retrieved from http://www. hoovers.com/company/Seven__i_Holdings_Co_Ltd/rcfthci-1-1njea3.html

71. Aeon. (2008). Date retrieved March 20, 2011. Retrieved from http://www.aeon. info/en/aboutaeon/index.html

72. Hoovers. (2011). Date retrieved March 20, 2011. Retrieved from http://www. hoovers.com/company/Seven__i_Holdings_Co_Ltd/rcfthci-1-1njea3.html

73. Couche-tard. (n.d.). Date retrieved March 20, 2011. Retrieved from http://www. couche-tard.com/corporate/the-network.html

74. Couche-tard. (n.d.). Date retrieved March 20, 2011. Retrieved from http://www. couche-tard.com/corporate/the-network.html

75. Hoovers. (2011). Date retrieved March 20, 2011. Retrieved from http://www. hoovers.com/company/Seven__i_Holdings_Co_Ltd/rcfthci-1-1njea3.html

76. Hoovers. (2011). Date retrieved March 20, 2011. Retrieved from http://www. hoovers.com/company/Seven__i_Holdings_Co_Ltd/rcfthci-1-1njea3.html

77. Hoovers. (2011). Date retrieved March 20, 2011. Retrieved from http://www. hoovers.com/company/Seven__i_Holdings_Co_Ltd/rcfthci-1-1njea3.html

78. Hoovers. (2011). Date retrieved March 20, 2011. Retrieved from http://www. hoovers.com/company/Seven__i_Holdings_Co_Ltd/rcfthci-1-1njea3.html

79. Hoovers. (2011). Date retrieved March 20, 2011. Retrieved from http://www. hoovers.com/company/Seven__i_Holdings_Co_Ltd/rcfthci-1-1njea3.html

80. Hoovers. (2011). Date retrieved March 20, 2011. Retrieved from http://www. hoovers.com/company/Seven__i_Holdings_Co_Ltd/rcfthci-1-1njea3.html

81. Hoovers. (2011). Date retrieved March 20, 2011. Retrieved from http://www. hoovers.com/company/Seven__i_Holdings_Co_Ltd/rcfthci-1-1njea3.html

82. Seven & i hldgs. co., ltd corporate outline 2010. (2010). Date retrieved March 27, 2011. Retrieved from http://www.7andi.com/en/ir/pdf/corporate/2010_all.pdf

83. Seven & i hldgs. co., ltd corporate outline 2010. (2010). Date retrieved March 27, 2011. Retrieved from http://www.7andi.com/en/ir/pdf/corporate/2010_all.pdf

84. Seven & i hldgs. co., ltd corporate outline 2010. (2010). Date retrieved March 27, 2011. Retrieved from http://www.7andi.com/en/ir/pdf/corporate/2010_all.pdf

85.  Seven & i holdings annual report 2010. (2010). Date retrieved March 27, 2011. Retrieved from http://www.7andi.com/en/ir/pdf/annual/2010_all.pdf

86.  Seven & i holdings annual report 2010. (2010). Date retrieved March 27, 2011. Retrieved from http://www.7andi.com/en/ir/pdf/annual/2010_all.pdf

87.  Seven & i holdings annual report 2010. (2010). Date retrieved March 27, 2011. Retrieved from http://www.7andi.com/en/ir/pdf/annual/2010_all.pdf

88.  Seven & i hldgs. co., ltd corporate outline 2010. (2010). Date retrieved March 27, 2011. Retrieved from http://www.7andi.com/en/ir/pdf/corporate/2010_all.pdf

89.  Seven-Eleven Japan. (2011, January 31). Date retrieved March 27, 2011. Retrieved from http://www.sej.co.jp/company/en/g_stores.html

90.  Seven & i hldgs. co., ltd corporate outline 2010. (2010). Date retrieved March 27, 2011. Retrieved from http://www.7andi.com/en/ir/pdf/corporate/2010_all.pdf

91.  Seven & i hldgs. co., ltd corporate outline 2010. (2010). Date retrieved March 27, 2011. Retrieved from http://www.7andi.com/en/ir/pdf/corporate/2010_all.pdf

92.  Seven & i hldgs. co., ltd corporate outline 2010. (2010). Date retrieved March 27, 2011. Retrieved from http://www.7andi.com/en/ir/pdf/corporate/2010_all.pdf

93.  Seven & i hldgs. co., ltd corporate outline 2010. (2010). Date retrieved March 27, 2011. Retrieved from http://www.7andi.com/en/ir/pdf/corporate/2010_all.pdf

94.  Seven & i hldgs. co., ltd corporate outline 2010. (2010). Date retrieved March 27, 2011. Retrieved from http://www.7andi.com/en/ir/pdf/corporate/2010_all.pdf

95.  Seven & i hldgs. co., ltd corporate outline 2010. (2010). Date retrieved March 27, 2011. Retrieved from http://www.7andi.com/en/ir/pdf/corporate/2010_all.pdf

96.  Seven & i hldgs. co., ltd corporate outline 2010. (2010). Date retrieved March 27, 2011. Retrieved from http://www.7andi.com/en/ir/pdf/corporate/2010_all.pdf

97.  Seven & i holdings annual report 2010. (2010). Date retrieved March 27, 2011. Retrieved from http://www.7andi.com/en/ir/pdf/annual/2010_all.pdf

98.  Seven & i hldgs. co., ltd corporate outline 2010. (2010). Date retrieved March 27, 2011. Retrieved from http://www.7andi.com/en/ir/pdf/corporate/2010_all.pdf

99.  Seven & i hldgs. co., ltd corporate outline 2010. (2010). Date retrieved March 27, 2011. Retrieved from http://www.7andi.com/en/ir/pdf/corporate/2010_all.pdf

100. Seven & i hldgs. co., ltd corporate outline 2010. (2010). Date retrieved March 27, 2011. Retrieved from http://www.7andi.com/en/ir/pdf/corporate/2010_all.pdf

101. Seven & i hldgs. co., ltd corporate outline 2010. (2010). Date retrieved March 27, 2011. Retrieved from http://www.7andi.com/en/ir/pdf/corporate/2010_all.pdf

102. Seven & i hldgs. co., ltd corporate outline 2010. (2010). Date retrieved March 27, 2011. Retrieved from http://www.7andi.com/en/ir/pdf/corporate/2010_all.pdf

103. Seven & i hldgs. co., ltd corporate outline 2010. (2010). Date retrieved March 27, 2011. Retrieved from http://www.7andi.com/en/ir/pdf/corporate/2010_all.pdf

104. Seven & i hldgs. co., ltd corporate outline 2010. (2010). Date retrieved March 27, 2011. Retrieved from http://www.7andi.com/en/ir/pdf/corporate/2010_all.pdf

105. Seven & i hldgs. co., ltd corporate outline 2010. (2010). Date retrieved March 27, 2011. Retrieved from http://www.7andi.com/en/ir/pdf/corporate/2010_all.pdf

106. Seven & i hldgs. co., ltd corporate outline 2010. (2010). Date retrieved March 27, 2011. Retrieved from http://www.7andi.com/en/ir/pdf/corporate/2010_all.pdf

107. Seven & i hldgs. co., ltd corporate outline 2010. (2010). Date retrieved March 27, 2011. Retrieved from http://www.7andi.com/en/ir/pdf/corporate/2010_all.pdf

108. Seven & i hldgs. co., ltd corporate outline 2010. (2010). Date retrieved March 27, 2011. Retrieved from http://www.7andi.com/en/ir/pdf/corporate/2010_all.pdf

109. Seven & i hldgs. co., ltd corporate outline 2010. (2010). Date retrieved March 27, 2011. Retrieved from http://www.7andi.com/en/ir/pdf/corporate/2010_all.pdf

110. Seven & i hldgs. co., ltd corporate outline 2010. (2010). Date retrieved March 27, 2011. Retrieved from http://www.7andi.com/en/ir/pdf/corporate/2010_all.pdf

111. Seven & i hldgs. co., ltd corporate outline 2010. (2010). Date retrieved March 27, 2011. Retrieved from http://www.7andi.com/en/ir/pdf/corporate/2010_all.pdf

112. Seven & i hldgs. co., ltd corporate outline 2010. (2010). Date retrieved March 27, 2011. Retrieved from http://www.7andi.com/en/ir/pdf/corporate/2010_all.pdf

113. Seven & i hldgs. co., ltd corporate outline 2010. (2010). Date retrieved March 27, 2011. Retrieved from http://www.7andi.com/en/ir/pdf/corporate/2010_all.pdf

114. Seven & i hldgs. co., ltd corporate outline 2010. (2010). Date retrieved March 27, 2011. Retrieved from http://www.7andi.com/en/ir/pdf/corporate/2010_all.pdf

115. Seven & i hldgs. co., ltd corporate outline 2010. (2010). Date retrieved March 27, 2011. Retrieved from http://www.7andi.com/en/ir/pdf/corporate/2010_all.pdf

116. Seven & i hldgs. co., ltd corporate outline 2010. (2010). Date retrieved March 27, 2011. Retrieved from http://www.7andi.com/en/ir/pdf/corporate/2010_all.pdf

117. Seven & i hldgs. co., ltd corporate outline 2010. (2010). Date retrieved March 27, 2011. Retrieved from http://www.7andi.com/en/ir/pdf/corporate/2010_all.pdf

118. Seven & i hldgs. co., ltd corporate outline 2010. (2010). Date retrieved March 27, 2011. Retrieved from http://www.7andi.com/en/ir/pdf/corporate/2010_all.pdf

119. Private label. (2011). Date retrieved March 27, 2011. Retrieved from http://dictionary.reference.com/browse/private+label

120. 7-select. (n.d.). Date retrieved March 27, 2011. Retrieved from http://www.7-eleven.com/Only-at-7-Eleven/7-Select/Default.aspx

121. 7-select. (n.d.). Date retrieved March 27, 2011. Retrieved from http://www.7-eleven.com/Only-at-7-Eleven/7-Select/Default.aspx

122. 7-select. (n.d.). Date retrieved March 27, 2011. Retrieved from http://www.7-eleven.com/Only-at-7-Eleven/7-Select/Default.aspx

123. 7-select. (n.d.). Date retrieved March 27, 2011. Retrieved from http://www.7-eleven.com/Only-at-7-Eleven/7-Select/Default.aspx

124. Seven-Eleven Japan. (2011, January 31). Date retrieved March 27, 2011. Retrieved from http://www.sej.co.jp/company/en/g_stores.html

125. Corporate Headquarters Phone Call; Main Phone Number: (972) 828 – 0711

126. Aktif,(n,d.). Date retrieved March 27, 2011. Retrieved from http://www.7eleven.com.my/html/default.aspx?ID=3&PID=18

127. Seven & i hldgs. co., ltd corporate outline 2010. (2010). Date retrieved March 29, 2011. Retrieved from http://www.7andi.com/en/ir/pdf/corporate/2010_all.pdf

128. Seven & i hldgs. co., ltd corporate outline 2010. (2010). Date retrieved March 29, 2011. Retrieved from http://www.7andi.com/en/ir/pdf/corporate/2010_all.pdf

129. Seven & i hldgs. co., ltd corporate outline 2010. (2010). Date retrieved March 29, 2011. Retrieved from http://www.7andi.com/en/ir/pdf/corporate/2010_all.pdf

130. Seven & i hldgs. co., ltd corporate outline 2010. (2010). Date retrieved March 29, 2011. Retrieved from http://www.7andi.com/en/ir/pdf/corporate/2010_all.pdf

131. Seven & i hldgs. co., ltd corporate outline 2010. (2010). Date retrieved March 29, 2011. Retrieved from http://www.7andi.com/en/ir/pdf/corporate/2010_all.pdf

132. Seven & i hldgs. co., ltd corporate outline 2010. (2010). Date retrieved March 29, 2011. Retrieved from http://www.7andi.com/en/ir/pdf/corporate/2010_all.pdf

133. Seven & i hldgs. co., ltd corporate outline 2010. (2010). Date retrieved March 29,

2011. Retrieved from http://www.7andi.com/en/ir/pdf/corporate/2010_all.pdf

134. Seven & i hldgs. co., ltd corporate outline 2010. (2010). Date retrieved March 29, 2011. Retrieved from http://www.7andi.com/en/ir/pdf/corporate/2010_all.pdf

135. 7-11 Franchise Review . (2010). Date retrieved March 27, 2011. Retrieved from http://franchises.about.com/od/foodrestaurant/fr/7elevenfranchis.htm

136. Sternquist, Brenda. Retailers' Strategic International Expansion Lecture. (2011). Slide 56. Date retrieved March 27, 2011.

137. 7-11 Franchise Review . (2010). Date retrieved March 27, 2011. Retrieved from http://franchises.about.com/od/foodrestaurant/fr/7elevenfranchis.htm

# Shoprite Holdings Ltd.

*Molly Brown*

## Shoprite Holdings

Shoprite Holdings was started from a modest eight-supermarket chain acquisition, but has since become the leading food retailer in southern Africa. Various acquisitions have strengthened the group's brand portfolio and product offerings. This multinational retailer has seen success in southern Africa and along its western coast and met hard times after internationalizing to northern Africa and the Middle East.

Shoprite has a strong focus on contributing to the economic and social growth of Africa and its people. This community focus benefits the people as well as intra-African business by developing the economy and consumers' buying power. The company is able to target specific income groups with their different formats and price ranges. This has helped them internationalize because they have so many ways to adapt to the country in which they are expanding.

This case study will analyze Shoprite's international expansion strategy after a briefing of the company's history and their brand composition.

# FLOW CHART

| Year of Entry | Location | Total Stores in 2010 | Exit Year |
|---|---|---|---|
| 1979 | South Africa | 1,425 | |
| 1990 | Namibia | 93 | |
| 1995 | Zambia | 27 | |
| 1997 | Botswana | 16 | |
| 1997 | Mozambique | 7 | |
| 1997 | Swaziland | 11 | |
| 2000 | Zimbabwe | 1 | |
| 2000 | Uganda | 2 | |
| 2001 | Egypt | 0 | 2006 |
| 2001 | Malawi | 5 | |
| 2001 | Lesotho | 14 | |
| 2001 | Tanzania | 3 | |
| 2002 | Madagascar | 7 | |
| 2002 | Mauritius | 1 | |
| 2003 | Ghana | 3 | |
| 2003 | Angola | 9 | |
| 2004 | India | 1 | |
| 2005 | Nigeria | 2 | |

## History

The Shoprite Group started as a small company in 1979 with the purchase of a chain of eight Cape-based supermarkets for R1 million. Throughout the company's expansion over the following 30 years, they acquired many stores and internationalized strategically to help shape them into the successful company they are today.

Before 1990, the company was unable to expand internationally due to governmental restrictions in their home country. They spent the time from 1979-1990 expanding within the different regions of South Africa. With such a large population and vast size, this country was ideal for practicing their expansion strategy before it was time to internationalize. Also during this time, Shoprite was able to observe other companies who sought to expand internationally and analyze their tactics and redefine their own plan. Finally, when the restrictions were lifted in 1990, Shoprite had its strategy polished and was ready to move into Namibia.

Shortly after their entry into Namibia, the Shoprite group acquired Grand Bazaars and Checkers, increasing its size tremendously. These brands also helped establish the group quickly and gain further access within regions. Although the acquired stores were experiencing financial tumult at the time they were added to the group, Shoprite was able to quickly restore them to profitability.

By 1995, the company was able to open in Zambia, Central Africa. During this same year, Shoprite acquired Sentra, gaining entry into the franchising field, allowing the group to compete with small-scale retailers. Next, the group acquired OK Bazaars in the infamous 'R1 deal' that added 157 super and hyper sized supermarkets and 146 furniture stores to the rapidly expanding Shoprite family.[1] In 2000, Shoprite Holdings was selected as one of South Africa's Most Promising Companies by The Corporate Research Foundation and was the only supermarket retailer to receive this distinction.[1] The group continued to receive countless awards and distinctions through the course of their operations, including a ranking on financial Mail and Human Capital Corporation's (Deloitte & Touche) 40 Best Companies to work for, they were also voted South Africa's number one supermarket in the annual Ipsos Markinor Top Brands business-to-consumer survey in 2008, and in 2009 was added to Merrill Lynch & Co's list of most preferred stocks, with the bank citing excellent growth in sub-Saharan Africa.[1]

In 2001, the company broke into the North African Market when they opened their first of seven stores in Egypt. The following year, the group acquired Champion supermarket in Madagascar, adding five new branded stores. The new Usave warehouse format was established in 2003, right after expansion into Ghana and Angola. Shoprite was able to enter into the Indian market in 2004 as a license agreement in order to operate within the country. Laws in India restrict foreign direct investment; therefore the license strategy was employed by Shoprite to allow them access into the market. They used their Egyptian expansion as a stepping-stone for India so they could analyze the culture and market before expanding to multiple countries relatively far away from South Africa. Also in 2004, the company made major investments in technology, linking all of their African stores into a central database and replenishment system.[2] This has helped the company be more efficient and even more profitable as it saves time and money.

Many acquisitions took place in 2005 such as Foodword and Computicket. Also, the Shoprite Liquor Shop was introduced during the same year. In a big move by Shoprite, the group entered Nigeria, a new emerging market full of growth potential. Unfortunately, a year later it was forced to withdraw operations from Egypt due to lack of governmental cooperation and difficulty in operations.

Recently Shoprite Holdings has announced that they will begin to expand into the Democratic Republic of the Congo, hopefully opening stores by 2011. During March 2011, the company announced that they had purchased Metcash, which will be added to the OK Franchise division and have various formats including convenience stores and supermarkets. This will add to the company's value and help their franchise division grow to be even more successful.

Over the years the group has acquired many brands that have strengthened the Shoprite name and helped expand the group into various parts of Africa. Future growth through acquisitions is expected from the Shoprite group in order to strengthen their portfolio of stores. The company will continue to focus on providing low prices to customers with the high quality and reliability associated with the Shoprite name.

## Company Structure

Shoprite Holdings has five main segments to their brand structure: Shoprite, Checkers, OK Furniture, a Franchising division, and Hungry Lion. I will explain each of the segments and formats.

### Shoprite

Their main operational format includes Shoprite, Shoprite Hyper, and Usave. The original store of the company, Shoprite, constitutes the majority of their store formats while Usave is quickly becoming a major asset to the company. Shoprite promises that customers can be sure to pay the lowest prices on their basic food and household requirements and the consumers have developed the trust necessary to believe the integrity of the company's promise.[3] The target markets for the group's main brand are middle to lower-income consumers. This format is also the main format used in international expansion.

The Shoprite Hyper format is not used often but is used in locations where there is a great amount of space and consumer demand for a hypermarket to meet the everyday needs of consumers. This format also incorporates multiple service departments including Money Market, bakery, deli, fish, wine section, meat market and Medirite pharmacies. These service departments offer a specialized experience for customers who seek more than the usual assortment of goods.

Finally, the Usave format is a no-frills warehouse store that has become a preferred format in many communities. This format is ideal for expansion within African borders because there are a large number of underdeveloped locations that benefit from having low cost alternatives to other supermarkets.[4] Offering a limited selection of goods, this format caters towards low-income consumers by assigning the lowest possible prices to their merchandise, providing the customers with bulk value without having to actually buy in bulk. As of 2010, the company had established 212 Usave warehouses across Africa, mainly in South Africa and Namibia.

## Checkers

The chain of Checkers stores was acquired in 1991, expanding the Shoprite brand six-fold throughout South Africa.[1] Although it has a much different target customer than most of the Shoprite formats, Checkers has proven worthy of the brand association. Shoprite Holdings managed to raise revenue for the brand and restate the position. The store now targets upper-income customers- a great addition to the Shoprite group to diversify their stores and target different segments of people. The Checkers brand remains the second major brand after Shoprite. Checkers is located throughout South Africa (150 stores) and has one store in Namibia. Their strategy is to focus on providing fresh produce and a wide range of food products. There are lifestyle departments within the store such as wine, cheese, and meat, which cater to time-sensitive shoppers.

The Checkers Hyper format is used only in cities with large population densities. Although the positioning strategy is very similar to the main Checkers brand, the Hyper format offers a wider range of products and is more centered on bulk purchases in contrast to Checkers' convenience shopping. It serves as a complementary brand to Shoprite and is geared towards higher income groups.[5] All 26 of the Checkers stores are in South Africa.

## OK Furniture

OK Furniture is the largest segment to this division that also includes House & Home and OK Power Express. OK Furniture has 231 stores and branches located as far as Namibia, Lesotho, Mozambique, Swaziland, and Botswana.[6] Its offerings include furniture, appliances, carpet, and bedding to customers at a reasonable price.[7] Additionally, they possess one of the most extensive selections of wall-to-wall carpet services in the country with a free quotation service to customers. The company has succeeded in achieving sizeable sales growth with their competitive pricing strategy paired with improvements in customer service that included offering a supportive buying experience. They have also recently added a short-term insurance company within the furniture division, which has expanded the service portfolio of Shoprite Holdings.

House & Home targets higher income consumers by providing the best quality local and imported goods. They offer the same types of goods as OK Furniture but with higher emphasis on quality. OK Power Express was established in 2000 and since then, 16 stores have opened in South Africa in addition to one in Lesotho. The focus is on offering major appliances, home entertainment, cell phones, bedding, and carpeting. Targeting middle-income customers, OK Power Express is a small format retailer located primarily in high-density areas.[8]

## Franchising

The brands franchised by Shoprite include OK Foods, OK Grocer, OK MiniMark, OK Value, Sentra, Enjoy, and Megasave. These stores are Shoprite's smallest formats and are therefore easier to codify in order to franchise and maintain brand continuity. Most of these franchises have been gained through acquisition and added to the Shoprite brands with reimaging. OK and Sentra have been added to form a new franchise group that combines the expertise of all companies to take the franchising department to the next level.

These small-scale franchise outlets adapt to the environment that they are located and target the customers of the specific community in which they are present. This specialized division also offers tremendous value to investors and expands their brand portfolio while allowing them to continually add to or reshape this department.[9] To maintain continuity of excellence among their franchise operations, the company holds monthly meetings for all franchisees to come and report the progress of their shop and discuss ideas for improvement. This is crucial for the group to do because if these locations are not performing to the expectations of Shoprite customers, they risk losing people to the competition.[10]

## Hungry Lion

Established in 1997, Hungry Lion was born from CEO Whitey Basson's perception of a gap in the market for fast-food chicken. This was their first endeavor in the quick service restaurant market and the concept has grown into a chain of 132 stores throughout seven countries.[11] The chain has increased in popularity over the years, gaining a customer following that has helped support their rapid growth throughout South Africa. The chain is constantly seeking ways to innovate and provide customers with new products that have the same great quality they expect from Hungry Lion.

## Competition

The main competition for Shoprite is Massmart and Pick 'n Pay. These stores compete with the main Shoprite formats because they are all the same size and format. Potential competition includes stores such as Wal-Mart, Carrefour, and Tesco because they are all considering purchasing companies in African countries. Wal-Mart plans to enter South Africa through purchase of the majority stake of Massmart. This region has attracted foreign investors because during the ten years between 2000 and 2010, six of the world's ten fastest growing economies were in sub-Saharan Africa.[12] People who have middle-class buying power is rising on a scale comparable to India.

Foreign investment in Africa has been in natural resources and mining practices, but now there is a turn towards investment in consumer-oriented trades. This could stimulate spending within Africa and create countless jobs. There has been a major rise in the middle class that is linked to the strong economic performances since the end of the 1990's. In addition, average economic growth has been around 5 percent a year, while average inflation rates declined to 8 percent from an earlier high of 22 percent.[12]

If Wal-Mart or any other large foreign retailer were to enter the African market Shoprite would have to adapt their strategy. Shoprite would welcome the rise in jobs and consumer spending because they are confident that their competitive pricing strategy could match Wal-Mart. Wal-Mart's acquisition of Massmart would allow them to learn African business and get comfortable with the culture while Massmart benefits from Wal-Mart's expertise, especially in fresh food.[13] This does not compare to Shoprite's advantage of having been operating as a major supermarket in Africa for over 30 years with well-established distribution centers and logistics systems. Also, many companies won't be able to overcome challenges such as Africa's infrastructure. Massmart chief financial officer, Guy Howard, insists that the group is not directly competing with Shoprite, given their market size and dominance, but financial analysts of the industry disagree.[13]

Nevertheless, Shoprite Holdings is being considered for purchase by stores such as Carrefour and Tesco. This would be a major move by these European retailers and a major expansion for them into Africa. Shoprite's profits have been increasing as Africa's economies grow and the group expects to see continued growth as the governments and economies continue to develop. Although a potential buyout was discussed for the company in 2007 by Brait Private Equity, these negotiations fell through after Shoprite dropped the offer. It does not seem that they would be receptive to selling ownership of their successful company in the near future.

## International Expansion

Legislation in South Africa prohibited international expansion up until 1990 due to restrictions associated with the apartheid. This did not allow Shoprite to expand into other countries, but it allowed them time to watch as their competitors and other retailers expand into other countries of interest to the group. They analyzed these moves to formulate their own strategy for expansion.

Shoprite Holdings international expansion stages theory follows their strategy is centered on entering countries with lower disposable income than South Africa and that are geographically close and culturally similar to their home country. After they have gained experience within a country, they are able to move and expand to other countries. The group focuses on expanding throughout the continent in an effort to avoid being stuck in a saturated market. They try to spread out their brand geographically to provide the best return to investors and the best shopping experience to customers.

Whitey Basson, CEO of Shoprite Holdings insists that Africa has wealth and that its lack of infrastructure is an advantage to the company because they are able to expand without competition.[5] He also denies that doing business outside of their home country is a different concept by saying, "Basically, the people have to take in the same amount of calories whether it's here or Ghana."[5] This attitude demonstrates his company's perceptions of other countries while internationalizing. The group perceives these other countries as being culturally similar to their home country and feels that they only need to make minor modifications in order to serve their customers with the ultimate shopping experience. Shoprite insists that their business model is able to operate anywhere in the world with the only limitations being capital and supply lines.[14] The group aspires to expand beyond the geographic proximity of Africa and establish presence worldwide in the future.

## South Africa

After acquiring an eight-store chain in 1979, South Africa became the birthplace of Shoprite. The company expanded throughout the expansive and diverse country into different regions before furthering their expansion all over Africa. Currently the group has 1,425 stores and employs about 78,000 employees in their home country. The main format is the original and most popular Shoprite supermarket, followed by OK Furniture.

## Namibia

Shoprite supermarkets are the primary format used in Namibia; however OK Furniture also has a large presence here. Also, there are a large number of franchised outlets in Namibia. Another retailer in South Africa, OK Bazaar, was acquired by the Shoprite group in 2007. Many locations in South Africa and Namibia were converted to Shoprite brands, which expanded the group's portfolio immensely and put them in position to be the leading food retailer in both Namibia and South Africa.[15]

## Zambia

The Shoprite group has experienced success within Zambia since its entry in 1995. However, there have been some tumultuous encounters. In 2009 the workers of Shoprite Checkers nationwide went on strike, promising not to return to work until the company granted them a pay raise. Shoprite was temporarily paralyzed by the employees' refusal to work, but quickly began negotiations to reach the best solution.[16]

Hungry Lion food (the chicken and burger eatery) in Zambia is doing well. The concept for this fast-food chicken offering was conceived to fill a gap where no-one was offering discounted fast-food chicken. Although this brand does not largely contribute to Shoprite, plans are being made for expansion.[17] In addition to Hungry Lion stores, the Shoprite format is used extensively here where the group operates 27 stores. Shoprite continues planning for expansion within Zambia as it is one of their most profitable locations outside South Africa.[18]

## Botswana

Shoprite gained a presence in Botswana prior to 1997 using organic expansion. In 1998 the OK stores acquired through the infamous R1 deal were converted into Shoprite stores. This increased the company's presence here significantly. Botswana continues to be a great contributor to Shoprite's success where they currently have 16 stores. The main format used is OK Furniture specialty format, followed by the Shoprite supermarkets. There are also franchised outlets, Megasave and Sentra here.

The group expanded here early in their internationalization mainly because of the geographical proximity to South Africa. These countries are very culturally similar; therefore Shoprite felt comfortable expanding here and continued expanding to geographically close countries, such as Mozambique and Swaziland, immediately after establishing presence in Botswana. Plans for further expansion are in place for the country because customer spending is stable as a result of government protection of the economy. The further expansion through Botswana will increase the company's revenues and presence.

## Mozambique

Shoprite entered Mozambique in 1997 through organic expansion. The main format employed here is Shoprite supermarket followed by OK Furniture. Both of these formats target middle to low-income groups, found in Mozambique. This country has performed well economically, for example, prior to 2002, Mozambique had a five-year annual compound growth rate of 10% while South Africa's was a mere 2%.[5] As a result of showing good results at the end of last year, Shoprite will invest more into further expansion throughout Mozambique.

## Swaziland

With 1997 came entry into Swaziland. With a population of almost double that of South Africa, this country brought great opportunity to the group. Fitting with the group's expansion strategy, Swaziland has a very low GDP that enables the group to target low-income consumers, which is why they use their Usave warehouse format here in addition to their anchor, Shoprite. Because South Africa has such a significantly higher GDP than Swaziland, $354.4 vs. $3.154 billion respectively, the group is less likely to be affected by economic turmoil in the country.[19]

## Egypt

Shoprite entered Egypt in 2001 by teaming up with the Egyptian retailer, EK Holdings, in order to expand their operations in the northern region of Africa. As a result of South Africa's close potential for market saturation, many companies are also making expansion efforts towards northern Africa.[20]

Poor understanding of the local culture and logistical problems hindered the company's growth in the country. They went wrong by flying in executives from South Africa instead of utilizing the entrepreneurial resources available in Egypt.[20] Lack of support for foreign investors from the Egyptian government and the innumerable restrictions encountered in the country also barred Shoprite from optimizing the market here.[21] There are food regulations that force companies to source localy causing supply-line problems for Shoprite.[25] Because they did not foresee any changes in governmental action favoring foreign retailers, they thought it would be in the best interest of the company to invest its resources in more profitable sectors and withdraw from Egypt. From this experience, Shoprite learned many things and as is the case with many retailers, they analyze failures more thoroughly than successes and gain valuable insight about their company. They were able to realize that their research of the country's policies and culture was inadequate to support expansion throughout the country. They focused on the market potential and ignored signs of adversity in an attempt to take risks to be successful in northern Africa.

In the end, Shoprite lost about R19.9 million with the closing of their seven stores in Egypt in 2006. Although they have left Egypt, the distribution center and buying department remain in operation there to serve other potential North African operations and countries that benefit from importing goods from the country.[21] Upon leaving Egypt, the company announced that it would pursue further expansion through Nigeria because of superior performance from the Nigerian store opened the previous year.[22] This is a great way for Shoprite to keep the momentum of expansion moving throughout the northern region of Africa by expanding within markets that have already proved to be successful.

## Zimbabwe

Shoprite expanded organically to Zimbabwe in 2000, establishing its first and only store (as of 2011) in Bulawayo.[23] Further expansion has been reconsidered as high taxes and political rhetoric threaten the success of future endeavors. Policy inconsistencies and government regulations, such as excessive profits tax crackdown, are likely to slow the forecasted growth of the country in 2011.[24]

There have been some problems regarding the economy in the country that has made it difficult to reach profits and has minimized the value of the operations.[25] Despite this adversity, Shoprite plans to maintain its store here but halt further expansion plans within the country.

## Uganda

The group expanded into Uganda in 2000 through an organic expansion of a single Shoprite supermarket. As of 2003, Shoprite hadn't seen much success in this country and profits had been poor in their two stores.[14] In an effort to stimulate intra-African trade, the company started to sell coffee bought directly from Ugandan farmers in 2004. The Ruwenzori Coffee Company's products were to be sold in 110 Checkers Hyper stores in South Africa. According to their positioning statement, the group, inextricably linked to Africa, contributes to the nurturing of stable economies and the social upliftment of its people.[26] The effort to increase trade among African countries follows this goal by helping its own farmers be successful regardless of the red tape regulations it has to overcome in order to provide these local products.

## Malawi

Shoprite expanded into Malawi in 2002 through an organic expansion of their

Usave warehouse format. They currently operate three Usave warehouses and two Shoprite supermarkets. This country is mostly represented by lower-income individuals; a majority living on less than one US dollar a day.[27] This is why Shoprite has placed a number of their Usave warehouses here, in order to target these low-income customers.

## Lesotho

The first stores were opened here in 2001 through organic expansion of the OK Furniture specialty retailer and the Shoprite supermarket. The group currently operates 13 stores here. Lesotho has a very low GDP, which translates into diminished consumer spending power throughout the country. This affects the group's ability to be as successful as they would like, however because they are seen as the leader in everyday low pricing, people trust that their money will go farthest at Shoprite and continue to shop there and remain loyal customers.

## Tanzania

Shoprite entered Tanzania in December of 2002 through the acquisition of Score Supermarkets. Three supermarkets and a distribution center were added to the company's portfolio and they were converted into Shoprite stores. Since then, the group has been forced to close many of the operations in the country. Although supermarkets are still able to be profitable in the country, Shoprite has found it difficult to support such a large format and to break even with these stores. The smaller stores are not able to support themselves and are being closed accordingly. Shoprite has been taking many factors into consideration such as the global recession and sales across all outlets in Tanzania.[28] The company currently operates five Shoprite supermarkets here.

## Madagascar

The Shoprite stores have been able to succeed on the island by targeting low and middle-income shoppers and adapting the stores to the customers' preference. People of Madagascar like shopping in the largely open and well-lit atmosphere created by Shoprite. The stores here on the island offer 8,500 different products to customers ranging from cheap rice to meats and bottled water.[25] Local tastes are a large driving force of the product offerings in Madagascar. The company understands that there's no reason to sell goods that the local people will not want to buy. In 2005, the currency of Madagascar collapsed, which had a negative effect of the group's profits. This experience taught the group that it was important to have local suppliers in the countries of expansion and not try to source all products from South Africa where the value of the rand has soared.[25]

## Mauritius

Shoprite acquired 51% stake to enter a joint venture with Ireland Blyth in order to gain a presence in Mauritius. They opened Shoprite Mauritius in November of 2002 in Quatre Bones because it is one of the three largest towns on the island.[29] They used Shoprite Hyper to expand here because this is the largest format that they use and it is able to best serve the customer demand on the island. The 8,000 m[2] provides all household items and food in addition to various service departments within the store. These services include things such as a bakery, deli, wine shop, and a meat market. The free harbor in Mauritius also benefits the group as a distribution point because of its excellent storage facilities.[2]

## Ghana

Shoprite expanded to Ghana in response to President Kufuor's "call for international businesses to invest in the heart of West Africa."[30] The company eagerly accepted this challenge and opened their first store in Ghana in 2003 where 98% of their employees are Ghanaians. The main format used here is the Usave hypermarket concept that offers everything that customers would need in terms of living necessities with reduced prices because of their packaging cost reductions. They believe that when the company saves money, the consumer saves money.

## Angola

Entry into Angola was in the form of organic expansion in 2003. There are currently nine stores operating in the country with the Usave warehouse format being the most popular. These stores target the lower-income consumers present in Angola's low GDP country. Because they are able to target the right set of people, Shoprite Holdings has seen great performance from Angola and continues to invest there.

## India

Shoprite entered into its first market outside of Africa through a license agreement as a loophole strategy to the country's foreign retailer laws. These laws state that foreign retailers selling multiple brands must enter through a franchise or licensing agreement. This enabled them to get a feel for the country and learn from the culture. Shoprite was one of the first foreign food-retailers to be admitted into the country.[25] CEO Whitey Basson explains that the group's interest in India was because the market in Mumbai alone is bigger than the whole of SA.[31] These Indian consumers were seen as having a hunger for new, foreign stores.[25] However, the company quickly faced opposition from competitors after they started a price war on goods selling them below cost. Indian retailers were frustrated with this company strategy because they are unable to compete in this way.

Nevertheless, in 2010, Shoprite made the announcement that they were planning a divestment in India. This was largely attributed to the governmental regulations that prohibited them from achieving economies of scale and consequently resulted in the company's inability to reach break-even results.[10] Instead, the company is focusing on their western African opportunities which are more in line with their long-term growth plan.[1]

## Nigeria

After careful research and risk assessment, Shoprite Holdings entered Nigeria in 2005 through an organic expansion of their Shoprite supermarket. The shop is located in Lagos' first ever shopping mall. Nigeria is attractive to retailers because of its oil-producing capabilities, large middle-class markets, and the high-growth markets. South African stores such as Pick 'n Pay are also considering moves into the Nigerian region of Africa. Also, northern African countries are being considered for expansion by European supermarket chains now that the economy is doing well and retailers have been seeing success. Nigeria is along the northeast coast of Africa with access to the Gulf of Guinea, which makes it even more desirable because of its access to the water and ports there.

After meeting success with their Lagos Shoprite, the company is planning to add seventy stores in the next ten years with twenty of them being in Lagos.[20]

## Conclusion

Shoprite Holdings has expanded throughout Africa swiftly and rapidly in the past 20 years. Utilizing the stages theory, the company began their international expansion by entering countries that were both close geographically and similar culturally. The company has managed to acquire different store formats to strengthen its portfolio to allow it to expand into so many African nations.

The success in southern Africa did not translate as hoped in northern Africa. The company was forced to withdraw operations in Egypt and begin divestment in India. This was a result of a combination of problems, mainly a disconnect between the government's willingness to accommodate foreign retailers and the retailer's inability to help these countries grow due to the government's restrictions. Although these northern African expansions have not achieved ultimate success, the company was able to redefine and reshape their expansion strategy to react to these failures. The company is now focusing its efforts in Nigeria as its economy is growing at a tremendous rate.

Future expansions are planned for the Democratic Republic of Congo sometime in the next two years. It's been about six years since the company entered a completely new country and this expansion would mark the next phase of growth for Shoprite Holdings. This is just the beginning, for the potential trade on this continent is vast, provided governments are prepared to accommodate the needs of those who can assist growth.[2]

## Questions

**1.  Is the retailer classified as a global retailer or a multinational retailer? Explain its pattern of expansion.**

*Overall, Shoprite Holdings is classified as a multinational retailer. Although they have a separate segment of their company dedicated to franchising, the company's main stores do not franchise because their large format makes codifying their information difficult. Also, the company offers multiple store formats, all offering different merchandise that is tailored to the community in which they are present.*

*Shoprite started expanding throughout southern Africa into countries similar to their home country in terms of culture. Characteristic of multinational retailers, the group tries to source merchandise locally when possible and hire management from the local area.[32] Typically, Shoprite enters into new countries through organic expansion or acquiring existing stores within a country and transforming them into Shoprite stores. This allows the company to acquire good store locations and also operation knowledge of the country and culture. Unlike most multinational companies, Shoprite had not saturated their home market completely before internationalizing. Instead, they could foresee saturation and expanded before they had all of their investment placed in a saturated market. The company continues to expand throughout the African region and hopes to successfully move beyond Africa's borders in the future.*

**2.  Based on Dunning's eclectic theory, how do ownership, locational and internalization factors play in your retailers' international expansion?**

*Dunning's eclectic theory is comprised of three parts: ownership factors, locational factors, and internalization. All three of these components are very important in the analysis of Shoprite's internationization. Most important are the locational factors of cultural and geographic proximity. This is the foundation for Shoprite's expansion model in the sense that they started expanding through geographically close countries that had similar cultures to their home country. This gives them an advantage in the market because they operate in so many markets similar to their home market. Low cost land and labor is also a considerable part of their strategy because the strength of the rand is so high compared to other African currencies, they are able to get more for the money in less developed countries which makes it easier to acquire prime locations.*

*Ownership advantages are also important to Shoprite in the form of their private label (asset-based) but more importantly in their knowledge of southern African markets and distribution therein (transaction-based). These advantages make it hard for competition to achieve the same status that Shoprite holds within these countries. They are able to offer low prices because of their well-developed supply chain and distribution and their house brand products are very popular among consumers seeking low prices. Finally, because the company does not franchise their main stores, internalization is obviously important. They seek to protect their ownership advantages and do not want to release their knowledge through franchising.*

### 3. What role does cultural proximity and geographical proximity play in the retailers' international moves?

*Geographical and cultural proximity are paramount to Shoprite's expansion strategy. They choose to expand to countries close to their home in South Africa that have a similar culture atmosphere. This allows them to only have to make minor adaptations to each new country they enter. The company is able to expand with less risk because they can better analyze the market and understand the consumers there. To target these country-specific customers, they alter their product offerings to match the preferences of consumers in that area.*

### 4. Can you predict the retailer's future international expansion?

*Shoprite plans on expanding within Nigeria by opening 16 additional stores in addition to entering three new African countries.[33] The company is now competing against the giant retailer, Wal-Mart, and must either expand rapidly or risk being bought out by this huge competitor.*

## Propositions

### P1: The greater the ownership advantages for retailers, the less likely they will franchise or license.

*There are two types of ownership advantages, asset-based and transaction-based. Asset-based advantages include tangible items or unique products such as private label or patents. Transaction-based advantages refer to the tacit learning that is difficult to transfer to other people. An example of this could be a certain logistical process employed by the company. Shoprite does follow this proposition because* they do not franchise their main formats. This is mostly because they have high transaction-based advantages, including an advanced distribution system and knowledge of African markets. These transaction-based advantages are established from tacit knowledge, learning by doing. Also, Shoprite has a strong private label, Ritebrand, which is identified as an asset-based advantage.[34] This makes them less likely to franchise because they want to internalize this information instead of sharing it with other people.

**P2: The greater the available organizational slack the greater the likelihood of expanding internationally.**

| USD in millions | 2001 | 2002 | 2003 |
|---|---|---|---|
| Current Assets | $564 | $435 | $651 |
| Current Liabilities | $532 | $437 | $647 |
| Organizational Slack | 1.006 | .995 | 1.006 |

Shoprite does not support this proposition. Although they continued international expansion throughout 2001-2003, their organizational slack decreased from 2001 to 2002. Organizational slack is comprised of three components: available, recoverable, and potential. This slack refers to excess resources that can be used at a company's discretion.

**P3: The greater the recoverable slack the greater the likelihood of expanding internationally.**

| USD in millions | 2007 | 2008 | 2009 |
|---|---|---|---|
| General & Admin Expenses | $612.6 | $714.5 | $864.1 |
| Sales | $5,792.2 | $7,086.3 | $8,821.3 |
| Recoverable Slack | .1057629 | .1008284 | .0979561 |

The data for the years of Shoprite's international expansion was not available, but the statistics from recent years has been retrieved. Although the recoverable slack decreases each year during a period of time that the company did not internationalize, the proposition is not supported.

**P4: The greater the potential slack the greater the likelihood of expanding internationally.**

| USD in millions | 2005 | 2006 | 2007 | 2008 |
|---|---|---|---|---|
| Equity | $340 | $430 | $524 | $614 |
| Capital | $1,256 | $1,387 | $1,688 | $1,893 |
| Potential Slack | .27070 | .31002 | .31043 | .32435 |

*Although the potential slack continues to increase from 2005-2008, Shoprite did not expand internationally during this time. Instead, they divested from India and Egypt during this time. For these reasons, Shoprite does not support this proposition.*

**P5: Multinational retailers will move to countries with lower disposable income than their home country.**

*Shoprite supports this proposition. Every country that they have entered, with the exception of India, has had a lower disposable income than their home country of South Africa. This follows the company's policy that they try to enter into economically disadvantaged communities so they can help the country grow by providing employment and which also helps the company as well. As stated in their annual report, the support of economic growth of the many economically-disadvantaged communities where the Group operates outside of South Africa improves the trading environment and supports development of new markets, growth in demand and, ultimately, new stores. If local markets were to stagnate, the business would see loss of skills in the workforce accompanied by diminishing local supply and little or no growth. Better local supply and labor can result in better operational efficiencies and lower prices to customers.[26] Being present in countries with lower disposable income than their home country provides the opportunity to achieve double digit growth within the country. This is also because the South African rand is currently very stable and is maintaining high value.*

**P6: Multinational retailers will move to countries that have a high positive change in GDP.**

$$\frac{(GDP\ at\ the\ time\ of\ expansion - GDP\ 5\ years\ before\ expansion)}{GDP\ 5\ years\ before\ expansion}$$

*Shoprite does not support this proposition. Although Nigeria saw a 113.6% growth from 2000 to 2005, other countries decreased prior to the company's expansion. For example, Zimbabwe's GDP decreased by 15.7% from 1995 to*

*2000 and Namibia also shouldered a decreasing GDP. Nevertheless, Shoprite*
*expanded into these countries with a strong rand backing for support.*

**P7: Multinational retailers will move to countries that have a high positive**
     **change in service-value added as % of GDP.**

*(Service% of GDP at time of Expansion - Service% of GDP 5 years before)*
*Service% of GDP 5 years before expansion*

*Shoprite does not support this proposition. When reviewing the data for Angola,*
*from 1998 to 2003 they experienced a 22.44% decrease in their service % of GDP.*
*However from 2000 to 2005, Nigeria had a 16.63% increase in their services.*
*Shoprite does not consider these statistics when internationalizing. Instead, they*
*primarily focus on locational factors.*

**P8: Multinational retailers will first move to countries that are culturally the**
**most similar to their home country.**

*Shoprite supports this proposition. According to the stages theory, a company will*
*expand to countries culturally similar and then expand to countries that are less*
*similar.[35] The majority of the countries that the group has expanded to have been*
*culturally similar to South Africa. The group started expanding through southern*
*Africa where the countries are very culturally similar. With the exception of India*
*and Egypt, all of the countries had extremely similar cultures to the home country*
*of South Africa.*

**P9: Multinational retailers will expand within the country and then will**
**expand regionally within that area.**

*Shoprite supports this proposition. The first six countries that they expanded to*
*shared borders with one another. As they expanded throughout Africa, they began*
*to fill in the gaps between countries and usually expand to adjacent countries after*
*they had expanded throughout that country. This allows them to adapt slowly as*
*the culture changes slightly from one region to another. They are also able to perfect*
*their supply chain and warehouse system and make it as efficient as possible by*
*keeping their locations relatively close. The company tries to reduce supply chain*
*inefficiency in order to reduce their carbon footprint and remain a sustainable*
*company.[26]*

**P10: Periodically the multinational retailers will "jump" to a new geographic**
**area and begin the stages form of expansion.**

*Shoprite supports this proposition. They expanded throughout southern Africa*
*before they "jumped" to Egypt in northern Africa. They then looked to expand*

into India, relatively close to Egypt. This lets them experiment in a country before expanding through the geographic region. Before the group saturated the southern African markets it needed to test another region and Egypt seemed perfect because of their large population. However, the company eventually pulled out of the country because it found the legal restrictions and lack of government cooperation too burdensome to be able to operate profitably. The company would not consider this a failure because they were able to analyze the northern African markets and consider possible future expansions.

**P11: Multinational retailers will move to countries that are geographically close to the home country initially, and then expand to more distant countries.**

Shoprite supports this proposition. As previously stated, the first six countries that the group expanded to shared borders with one another. Shoprite then proceeded to expand to Egypt, which is on the opposite side of the continent in northern Africa. Geographic proximity also benefits Shoprite because it increases their brand awareness and it helps consumers trust their brand. This is very important to the group because they offer low prices and they need to convince customers that they actually do have the lowest prices and this occurs when the customers trust the brand. As more people are exposed to the Shoprite stores and have the opportunity to shop there, the more people will be able to spread the word about their everyday low prices and high quality products.

**P12: Multinational retailers will move to countries with large population bases.**

Shoprite does not support this proposition. The countries that the company expands to do not boast significant population bases. Instead, Shoprite looks for areas where their brand would fit with the community and have positive impacts there. Usually their focus is to expand to areas with a lower disposable income than South Africa.

**Endnotes**

1.  Shoprite. (2011, March 1). About our Company- History. Retrieved April 2, 2011, from Shoprite Holdings: http://www.shopriteholdings.co.za/pages/1019812640/about-our-company/history.asp

2.  Business Day. (2004, October 11). South Africa; Shoprite Holdings CEO Paid R12,5m. Business Day .

3.  Shoprite Holdings. (2011, March 1). Our Brands- Shoprite. Retrieved April 2, 2011, from Shoprite Holdings: http://www.shopriteholdings.co.za/pages/1019812640/

our-brands/Shoprite.asp

4. Shoprite Holdings. (2010). Annual Report 2010. Brackenfell: Corporate.

5. Lipson, G. (2002, December 8). African safari brings the lure of prize game for Shoprite. Sunday Times (South Africa) , 4.

6. Shoprite Holdings. (2008). Our Brands- OK Furniture. Retrieved April 3, 2011, from Shoprite Holdings: http://www.shopriteholdings.co.za/pages/1019812640/our-brands/OK-Furniture.asp

7. Shoprite Holdings. (2008). Our Brands- House & Home. Retrieved April 3, 2011, from Shoprite Holdings: http://www.shopriteholdings.co.za/pages/1019812640/our-brands/House-And-Home.asp

8. Shoprite Holdings. (2008). Our Brands- OK Power Express. Retrieved April 3, 2011, from Shoprite Holdings: http://www.shopriteholdings.co.za/pages/1019812640/our-brands/OK-Power-Express.asp

9. Shoprite Holdings. (2008). Our Brands- OK Franchise. Retrieved April 3, 2011, from Shoprite Holdings: http://www.shopriteholdings.co.za/pages/1019812640/our-brands/OK-Franchise.asp

10. Shoprite Holdings. (2009). Annual Report 2009. Brackenfell: Corporate.

11. Shoprite Holdings. (2008). Our Brands- Hungry Lion. Retrieved April 3, 2011, from Shoprite Holdings: http://www.shopriteholdings.co.za/pages/1019812640/our-brands/Hungry-Lion.asp

12. Africa Renewal (United Nations). (2011, March 31). South Africa; A New Scramble for African Riches - Its Consumers. Africa Renewal (United Nations) .

13. Shevel, A. (2011, February 26). Massmart takes on Shoprite. Retrieved April 3, 2011, from Business Live: http://www.businesslive.co.za/Feeds/businesstimes/2011/02/26/massmart-takes-on-shoprite

14. Matthews, C. (2003, February 18). South Africa: Shoprite May List Furniture Business. Retrieved April 3, 2011, from All Africa: http://allafrica.com/stories/200302180377.html

15. Maletsky, C. (1997, November 4). Everything Not OK At OK. Retrieved April 3, 2011, from All Africa: http://allafrica.com/stories/199711040017.html

16. Times of Zambia. (2009, August 12). Zambia: Shoprite Paralysed. Retrieved April 3, 2011, from All Africa: http://allafrica.com/stories/200908120213.html

17. Matthews, C. (2004, November 30). South Africa: There's No Taste Like Home When You're Abroad. Retrieved April 3, 2011, from All Africa: http://allafrica.

com/stories/200411301723.html

18. Hall, W. (2007). Shoprite not quitting Zambia, says Basson. Business Day (South Africa) , 7.

19. CIA World Factbook. (2011, March 10). Swaziland. Retrieved April 4, 2011, from CIA World Factbook: https://www.cia.gov/library/publications/the-world-factbook/geos/wz.html

20. Rundell, S. (2010, July 8). Massive profits follow S Africa's northern 'invasion'. African Business , 40,42,44.

21. Shoprite Holdings. (2006). Annual Report 2006. Brackenfell: Corporate.

22. Blom, N. (2006, February 23). Shoprite to try again. Business Day (South Africa) , 22.

23. Madera, B. (2009, August 28). Zimbabwe: Shoprite Eyes Controlling Stake in Ok Zim. Retrieved April 3, 2011, from All Africa: http://allafrica.com/stories/200908280068.html

24. Mugari, E. (2011, March 13). Uncertainty threatens future investment in Zim. Sunday Times (South Africa) . N.P.

25. The Economist. (2005). Business: Africa's Wal-Mart heads east; Shoprite. The Economist , 62.

26. Shoprite Holdings. (2010). About our Company- Positioning Statement. Retrieved April 4, 2011, from Shoprite Holdings: http://www.shopriteholdings.co.za/pages/1019812640/about-our-company/positioning-statement.asp

27. IRIN. (2006, October 23). SOUTHERN AFRICA: Retail chains accused of shunning local producers. Retrieved April 3, 2011, from IRIN: Humanitarian News and Analysis: http://www.irinnews.org/report.aspx?reportid=61396

28. The East African. (2009, October 26). Tanzania; Help Businesses to Survive Recession. The East African . N.P.

29. Business Day. (2011, November 1). South Africa: Shoprite Heads For Mauritius. Retrieved April 3, 2011, from All Africa: http://allafrica.com/stories/200011010177.html

30. Coomson, J. (2003, December 3). Ghana: Shoprite Holdings Breaks Into Ghanaian Market. Retrieved April 3, 2011, from All Africa: http://allafrica.com/stories/200312030538.html

31. Matthews, C. (2004, February 14). South Africa: Shoprite Has Eye On India, With R1,6bn to Spend. Retrieved April 4, 2011, from All Africa: http://allafrica.com/

stories/200402180224.html

32. Sternquist, B. (2007). International Retailing (2 ed.). New York: Fairchild Publications, Inc. (43)

33. Thomas, S. (2011, March 18). Expansion in Africa becoming adventurous. Retrieved April 3, 2011, from howzit msn: http://news.za.msn.com/article. aspx?cp-documentid=156550989

34. Sternquist, B. (2007). International Retailing (2 ed.). New York: Fairchild Publications, Inc. (49)

35. Sternquist, B. (2007). International Retailing (2 ed.). New York: Fairchild Publications, Inc. (44)

# Starbucks Coffee

*Kristy Cano, Angela Lindberg, Marie Nagle*
*Alyssa Nee, Emily Rubin, Ryann Tubert*

## Starbucks Coffee

Café Au Laits, Cinnamon Dolce Lattes, Tazo Chai Frappuccinos and Banana Chocolate Vivanno Smoothies; these are only a few of the vast assortment of beverages offered at Starbucks. The world's best coffee comes from Starbucks. As of 2009 Starbucks had 16,729 stores in 50 countries. Starbucks generated revenues of $10.4 billion in fiscal year 2008.[1] Howard Schultz, chairman of Starbucks, was awarded the prestigious First Magazine Award for Responsible Capitalism 2007, which recognizes social responsibility at the core of commercial strategy.[2] With the help of this influential leader, the company continues to provide the world with the highest quality coffee.

# FLOW CHART

| Entry Time | Entry Location | Total Stores in 2009 | Exit Year |
|---|---|---|---|
| 1971 | United States | 11,266 | |
| 1987 | Canada | 768 | |
| 1996 | Japan | 854 | |
| 1996 | Singapore | 64 | |
| 1997 | Philippines | 150 | |
| 1998 | United Kingdom | 717 | |
| 1998 | Taiwan | 221 | |
| 1998 | Thailand | 13 | |
| 1998 | New Zealand | 43 | |
| 1998 | Malaysia | 131 | |
| 1999 | China | 504 | |
| 1999 | Kuwait | 65 | |
| 1999 | South Korea | 254 | |
| 1999 | Lebanon | 16 | |
| 2000 | Dubai | 90 | |
| 2000 | Hong Kong | 114 | |
| 2000 | Qatar | 9 | |
| 2000 | Bahrain | 10 | |
| 2000 | Saudi Arabia | 70 | |
| 2000 | Australia | 23 | |
| 2001 | Switzerland | 46 | |
| 2001 | Israel | 0 | 2003 |
| 2001 | Austria | 11 | |
| 2002 | Oman | 7 | |
| 2002 | Indonesia | 69 | |
| 2002 | Germany | 142 | |
| 2002 | Spain | 76 | |
| 2002 | Puerto Rico | 22 | |
| 2002 | Mexico | 259 | |
| 2002 | Greece | 74 | |
| 2003 | Netherlands | 3 | |
| 2003 | Turkey | 121 | |
| 2003 | Chile | 30 | |
| 2003 | Peru | 23 | |
| 2003 | Cyprus | 9 | |
| 2004 | Costa Rica | farmers support center | |
| 2004 | France | 51 | |
| 2005 | Bahamas | 8 | |
| 2005 | Ireland | 29 | |

| Entry Time | Entry Location | Total Stores in 2009 | Exit Year |
|---|---|---|---|
| 2005 | Jordan | 10 | |
| 2006 | Brazil | 18 | |
| 2006 | Egypt | 20 | |
| 2007 | Romania | 6 | |
| 2007 | Denmark | 2 | |
| 2007 | Russia | 16 | |
| 2008 | Argentina | 3 | |
| 2008 | Bulgaria | 3 | |
| 2008 | Czech Republic | 9 | |
| 2008 | Belgium | 2 | |
| 2008 | Portugal | 4 | |
| 2009 | Poland | 3 | |

## History of Starbucks

Starbucks began in Seattle in 1971 when three friends, Jerry Baldwin, Zev Siegl and Gordon Bowker opened the first store in Seattle's Pike Place Market because of their shared love for coffee and tea. The goal to supply Seattle with the best coffee and tea around prompted the trio to develop the shop. They named the store after a character in Herman Melville's *Moby Dick*, a classic American novel about the 19th century whaling industry. The seafaring name seems appropriate for a store that imports the world's finest coffees to the cold, thirsty people of Seattle. The three opened up a small shop selling fresh roasted gourmet coffee beans. The shop did well, but things changed for Starbucks in the 1980's. Even though it was the largest coffee bean seller in Washington, with six outlet stores in total, Zev Siegl decided to leave the company in 1980. Howard Schultz was eventually hired as the new head of marketing in 1982. Soon after being hired, Schultz was sent to attend an international housewares show in Milan, Italy. In Italy, Schultz was captivated by the exciting coffee culture and tried his very first café latte. While he sipped his latte in the small café he noticed all the customers chatting and enjoying companionship. At that moment he had the idea of creating that same coffee atmosphere back in the United States. This idea did not go over well with Baldwin because he was very content with selling whole beans and had no intention of getting involved with the restaurant industry. He did, however, let Schultz test his idea in the corner of one of his shops. This small corner of the store was a huge success. Feeling limited by space, Schultz decided to open his own coffee house that he named *The Daily* or *Il Giornale*, after Italy's largest newspaper.

Two months later, the new store was serving more than 700 customers a day, and was selling 300 percent more than the Starbucks locations. In 1987 the Starbucks Coffee Company owners sold their coffee business along with the name to a group of local investors for $3.7 million. The money paid by the investors had been raised by Schultz, who had convinced the investors that he could open 125 outlets in the next five years. His original coffee shop, Il Giornale, was changed to the Starbucks name, and the bare-breasted mermaid logo was turned into something a little more socially acceptable. The six existing Starbucks shops were turned into elegant, comfortable coffee houses. Eventually making it a "Third Place" in customers' minds, the first two being home and work as a comfortable place in which to find oneself.[3] In 1987 Starbucks started with 17 stores, but the company rapidly expanded into Vancouver, Portland, and Chicago. By 1991 the company had expanded to mail order catalogs, licensed airports stores and into California. The company went public in 1992, after becoming one of the first companies to offer stock options to its part-time employees, and by 1997 Starbucks had grown tenfold with locations in the US, Japan, and Singapore. Initially, the move to go international was motivated by the company's three objectives; to have first mover advantage against its competitors, gain from the growing desire for Western brands, and to cater to the very high coffee consumption rates in different countries.[4] Today they continue to expand to build their brand by using the distinct experience their stores deliver, or the Starbucks Experience; to become a global company that cultivates human connections through its products and experiences delivered, and to develop a presence in new markets, but at the same time adapting their strategies to better match each new culture they enter.[5]

Today Starbucks not only sells assorted coffee drinks but also premium teas, whole beans at supermarkets, premium ice cream with Dreyer's and CDs. Mostly through word of mouth advertising, Starbucks has become a global success with more than 16,000 locations in 50 countries serving 40 million customers or more a week. [6,7]

## Expansion

Over the past 22 years, Starbucks has had great success expanding into international markets. As a global company they are able to license, create joint ventures, and operate wholly owned subsidiaries.

Starbucks forms joint ventures in various international markets. They look for their international partners to fit a list of criteria. According to Starbucks website their partners must share their same values and fit into the corporate culture. Management needs to be committed, experienced and involved in every business aspect, while adequate financials and human resources are important, too. They must have knowledge and access to where the best real estate locations are, be local business leaders, and have a positive record with partnership developments. The partner must also have experience with licensing and be in the food and beverage industry. Lastly the company needs to have a leveragable infrastructure in order to become an international partner with Starbucks. They look for partners that already have a similar store set up so not many changes need to be made.[8] To avoid bearing all the risks in expansion, Starbucks will enter a partnership so another company is there to share the losses if the operation fails. These companies have a higher knowledge and experience about the market Starbucks is entering and can provide the proper guidance and support to make the partnership succeed. Starbucks has acquired some of its joint ventures by buying-out their partners share in the company to gain full ownership and control of the stores. This has happened in countries such as France, Canada, China, and Germany, as well as a few others.[8]

Another way Starbucks expands is through licensing their company in both the United States and international markets. With licensing, Starbucks is able to gain the most desirable locations and share their company knowledge to create the best possible store. Starbucks licenses its branded products through various partnership agreements. The International Coffee Partnership, North American Coffee Partnership, Starbucks Discoveries agreement and Starbucks Tazo Tea agreement are among the various license agreements Starbucks is involved in.[9]

Starbucks prefers to maintain majority control of their stores. This is why they continue to operate a large number of company owned stores and subsidiaries in foreign markets. By sustaining full ownership of many of their locations they are able to implement their business strategies into different markets more easily and retain higher profits.

Once Starbucks chooses an expansion method, they need to find the best location to have the most success. Locations for stores include areas that generate a great deal of traffic and are highly visible. University campuses, office buildings, shopping malls, and suburban and downtown shopping centers are typical locations for Starbucks outlets. Shopping centers are not the most desired locations due to the unavailability of a drive-thru. Stores with drive-thru operations have become more popular and are an important factor in determining store locations. Starbucks wants foot and motor traffic to be able to easily access its stores. By locating in malls, Starbucks is losing the commuting customer who would stop on their way to work if a drive-thru were available.[9, 10]

Israel is the only country Starbucks exited. This occurred in 2003 due to changes in operations and conflicts within the country that threatened the company.[11] Due to the presence of suicide bombers, Starbucks became a potential target and felt it was unsafe to stay in Israel.[12]

Until 2008 Starbucks had been expanding rapidly, opening approximately 8 new stores a day and entering into new markets.[10] With the downturn in the economy Starbucks closed over 660 stores between the United States and Australia, while also slowing down expansion.[9] Instead of expanding into new markets, Starbucks is looking into markets in which they already have stores.[10] This way they already have knowledge about that country and can eliminate many costs associated with entering a new area. The company is now looking for markets with younger customers for the greatest expansion potential.

When looking into international expansion, Starbucks does not try to change the culture to match that of the United States. They respect the traditions and unique aspects of these new areas in order to gain customers everyday.[8] As a company, they seek to bring a unique and special experience to every customer that enters though their doorway.

The *Starbucks Experience* is intended to be the same in all stores, no matter where or how they are operated. Regarding expansion, all stores are operated the same way, follow the same procedures, and offer almost the same menu. The *Starbucks Experience* has lost its specialty by expanding too quickly and losing aspects that make it unique. Other less expensive coffee options are becoming available and at the same quality as a Starbucks cup of coffee. This creates the issue of losing customers to these companies that offer cheaper alternatives.[10] Starbucks faces competition from various other companies, including many lower priced brands.

## Competitive Advantages

Starbucks has many different competitive advantages which are based on their commitment to global responsibility. Starbucks' Shared Planet is their commitment to doing business responsibly. The company partners with different organizations that help them take the steps necessary to achieve their goal of improving their environmental footprint. One of their partnerships with Conservation International helps the company design the environmentally, socially and economically responsible guidelines that drive their coffee purchases under Shared Plant.[13] Conservation International collaborates with Starbucks on the effort to improve ethical sourcing by promoting responsible farming practices. Starbucks uses Fair Trade Certified Coffee and is the largest purchaser, buying 40 million pounds of coffee in 2009.[14] In 2000 Starbucks created a partnership with Fair Trade Coffee, which supports fair working conditions and price paid for coffee.

Starbucks launched the Coffee and Farmer Equity program (C.A.F.E.) in 2004. C.A.F.E is a set of standards that fulfill the principles of Starbucks' Shared Planet Program. In 2008 Starbucks bought seventy-seven percent of their coffee from farmers who had followed all of the twenty-four criteria under the C.A.F.E. practices and guidelines.[12]

One of their biggest advantages and their primary focus is on ethically sourcing coffee beans. Starbucks controls its coffee purchasing, roasting, packaging and the distribution of coffee used in its operations. The company purchases green coffee beans from coffee-producing regions around the world. They custom roast them to its exacting standards for its many blends and single origin coffees.[9] The company is so involved with the processing of coffee beans because they want to ensure sustainability and future supply of high-quality green coffees in Central America and to reinforce their leadership in the coffee industry. Starbucks operates Coffee Agronomy Company S.R.L., a wholly owned subsidiary located in Costa Rica. This location, known as a farmer support center is staffed with agronomists and sustainability experts. It is designed to proactively respond to changes in coffee producing countries that impact farmers and the supply of green coffee. Along with the support center in Costa Rica, there is an additional one in Rwanda, Africa and the company is committed to opening a center in Ethiopia in the future. There are four areas of focus in order to achieve the goal of ethically traded coffee. The first is product quality; all coffee must meet Starbucks standards of high quality. The second is economic accountability; suppliers must submit evidence of payments made throughout the coffee supply chain to demonstrate how much of the price Starbucks pays for green (unroasted) coffee gets to the farmer.[13] The third is social responsibility, which requires safe, fair and humane working conditions are in place for their workers. Some of the responsibilities include protecting the rights of workers and providing adequate living conditions, compliance with the indicators for minimum-wage requirements and addressing child labor. The last is environmental leadership, with measures in place to manage waste, protect water quality, conserve water and energy, and preserve biodiversity. Starbucks has set a goal that by 2015 100% of their coffee will be responsibly grown and ethically traded.

Another environmental issue that Starbucks has really been developing is their 'go green' initiative. Starbucks is committed to building greener stores, which are a big part of their environmental preservation. According to Starbucks, "greening" their stores means designing, building and operating them in ways that reduce their impact on the planet.[15] Sustainable building materials and furnishings are combined with energy and water-efficient measures into store design. The first step toward greener stores is to have all company-owned stores worldwide become certified green by using the LEED green building program, which will begin in late 2010. The U.S. Green Building Council will oversee LEED. Some of the design elements include conserving energy by allowing air-conditioned stores to reach 75 degrees Fahrenheit instead of 72 on warm days, saving water by using high-blast nozzles to clean pitchers instead of running water, installing cabinets made from 90% post-industrial material with no added formaldehyde, using recycled flooring tiles and using paints with lower amounts of volatile organic chemicals. Currently, Starbucks is working on certifying new company-owned stores and in the spring of 2010 they are planning to open 10 pilot stores that will be registered LEED certified in 6 bioregions. The test stores will use a variety of strategies to reduce energy and water use without adding construction costs.[15] Starbucks has the ability to control a few specific things within the environment which include: adjustable low-energy lighting systems, continuing to use green materials and finishes, recycled construction, dual-flush toilets and low-use water faucets. Other major environmental factors that Starbucks is improving on is reducing energy use, which they have set a goal that they will reduce 50% of the energy used in company-owned stores and it will come from renewable sources, working on a 100% recyclable coffee cup, innovating a paper cup and ways to improve the plastic cup. The goal is to have 100% of their cups both be reusable or recyclable by 2015 and will provide recycling in every store.[15] Many other retailers are improving their environmental footprint but have not gone to the extreme measures that Starbucks has.

Starbucks also owns Ethos water, which focuses on donating a portion of the profit to provide clean water to children around the world. For each bottle of water that is sold, five cents are donated to the humanitarian water programs in Latin America, Asia, and Africa. To date, the Starbucks Foundation has donated over six million dollars.

Starbucks has also teamed up with Product RED to increase the donations to people living with HIV in Africa. Starbucks RED also finances programs to fight tuberculosis and malaria. Starbucks makes a contribution to the Starbucks RED fund every time customers use their Starbucks RED card or purchase Starbucks RED products and drinks created exclusively for the RED campaign. Through Starbucks RED, contributions there have been more than four million doses of HIV medication dispensed.[16]

## International Expansion

### The Americas

In 1971 Starbucks opened its first location in Seattle, Washington. As of 2009 they operate over 11,000 stores in all fifty states. Starbucks operates these stores as both company operated and licensed outlets. In 2008, Starbucks closed 600 stores due to a downturn in the economy and underperformance from these locations.[17]

Starbucks' first international location was in Vancouver, British Columbia, Canada in 1987. As of 2009 they operate almost 770 stores throughout Canada. They entered as company operated stores and continue to run them that way today.

Starbucks first entered Latin America in 2002 through a joint venture in Mexico with SC de Mexico, S.A. de C.V., which is an affiliate of Alsea. With this move Starbucks began purchasing coffee from local farmers and has created over 2,000 jobs. There are currently 259 Starbucks locations in Mexico.[18]

## Japan

On August 2, 1996, Starbucks opened its first location outside of North America in Ginza, a district of Tokyo, Japan. Starbucks entered into the Japanese market by establishing a joint venture between Sazaby League and Starbucks Coffee International in October 1995 thus creating Starbucks Coffee Japan, Ltd.[19] When Starbucks entered the market the company differentiated themselves from competitors by offering special coffee-based drinks, perviously unknown to the Japanese consumers.[20] Today Starbucks Japan offers their specialty coffees as well as confectionery gifts and specialty food items.[21] Since entering Japan, Starbucks has been rapidly growing throughout the country. As of March 2009 the total store count in Japan is 854 and Starbucks holds 40 percent ownership with this joint venture. Recently, Fukuoka, Japan was named as one of the pilot stores to reduce their carbon footprint.

## Southeast Asia

Starbucks entered Jakarta, Indonesia in 2002 through a licensing agreement with PT Mitra Adiperkasa. Taipei, Taiwan has been selected as a pilot store for the LEED initiative to build natural, green stores. There are currently 69 stores in Indonesia. The company entered South Korea in July 1999 when they opened the first store in Edae district of Seoul through a licensing agreement with Shinsegae Dept. Stores Co, Ltd. In 2000, Starbucks acquired 50 percent equity of South Korean operations from Shinsegae Department Stores, which created a joint venture partnership. In 2003, Starbucks opened their 100th store in Itaewon, which is one of the most popular tourist and shopping districts in the city. Starbucks has established itself as the leading specialty coffee brand in Korea. The traditional social culture of consuming food and drink indoors in Korea has led to some of the largest store developments in the world.[23] Currently, there are 254 stores in South Korea.

In 1997, Starbucks entered into the Philippines with the first store opening in Makati City through a licensing agreement with Rustan Corporation. Today, there are 150 stores in the Philippines licenced by Starbucks.

Singapore is the next location after Japan that Starbucks entered in 1996, making it the third international location the company entered. They strategically placed the first store in the nation's famous shopping district in the Liat Towers. They came into the nation with a partnership with Bonvest Holdings Limited and eventually reacquired in 2004 to support their growth in the Southeast Asia region.[24] Currently their total store number in Singapore is 64 and has no current plans to close any locations in the country.

In Thailand, the company operates through a wholly owned subsidiary, Starbucks Coffee Thailand. They currently have 131 locations in the nation and maintain a stable expansion rate. The first store was opened in Central Chidlom in 1997 and has now expanded to a total of 12 cities and 29 neighborhoods in the nation.[25]

## China

Starbucks International entered the China market in 1998 when the first store opened in Taipei, Taiwan through a joint venture with President Group, which Starbucks holds 50% of ownership. The first mainland store in China opened in January of 1999 through a licensing agreement with Mei Da Coffee Co. Ltd. In May of 2000, Starbucks entered Shanghai at the Lippo Tower, through a joint-venture agreement with President Cayman Holdings, Ltd. Also in 2000, Starbucks entered Hong Kong through a joint venture with Maxim's Caterers Ltd and currently holds five percent ownership. In July 2003, Starbucks increased its equity position in Shanghai and Taiwanese operations, acquiring 50 percent ownership interest in the joint ventures.

In February of 2008, Starbucks expansion reached to 26 mainland cities. Currently, Starbucks has more than 690 locations throughout greater China, including the People's Republic of China, Hong Kong, Macau and Taiwan. Company-operated stores in China are located in Beijing and Tianjin of which they have 100 percent ownership and Shenzhen and Guangdong which they have 70 percent ownership. Starbucks extends its services to reach customers in cities other than metropolitan markets. In order to support their rapid expansion, in 2005 Starbucks established the Starbucks Greater China support center located in Shanghai. The support center oversees the overall business strategies and operations. Starbucks in China has established itself as the premium coffee leader with high brand recognition and customer satisfaction.[22]

## Australia

Australia first got a taste of the *Starbucks Experience* in 2000 when the first store opened in Sydney. Presently, Starbucks has 23 locations in the country located in Sydney, Melbourne, and Brisbane.[26] Back in 2008 the company did major restructuring of the Australia businesses and decided to close 61 stores that were underperforming, cutting down the total number from 84 to 23, along with reducing the major areas that Starbucks was located in from seven cities to three.[27] The company operates through a wholly owned subsidiary, Starbucks Coffee International.

Starbucks opened their first store in New Zealand in 1998 in Auckland. The company entered the country by licensee agreement with a local company called Restaurant Brands New Zealand Ltd. with plans to open 10 stores within two years of its first location.[28] Today Starbucks is found in 43 locations in the country and continues its licensee agreement with Restaurant Brands Ltd.

## Europe Middle East and Africa (EMEA)

Beginning in 1998 and continuing through 2009, Starbucks has opened 1,617 stores in Europe, the Middle East and Africa. Starbucks employs approximately 24,255 employees in countries within these regions as of 2009. When Starbucks enters into these areas they generally use licensing and/or joint ventures, and a small number of these international locations are entered as wholly owned stores.

Starbucks has opened licensed and/ or joint ventured stores in EMEA countries including Kuwait, Lebanon, the United Arab Emirates, Qatar, Saudi Arabia, Israel, Oman, Greece, Turkey, Jordan, Denmark, Russia, Belgium, Portugal, Netherlands, Bahrain, Switzerland, Austria, Germany, Spain, Cyprus, France, Egypt, Romania, Bulgaria, Czech Republic, and Poland. Ireland is the only country that is wholly owned and the United Kingdom is the only majority acquisitioned country in the EMEA region.

Within the EMEA are the sub-regions of Europe, the Middle East and Africa who have individual countries that have the largest markets of Starbuck's stores as of 2009. In Europe these countries are the UK and Ireland, who together have 750 stores. For the Middle East, Turkey is the leader with 121 stores. As of today the EMEA is the fourth largest market for Starbuck's and they are continuing to grow.[29]

## Conclusion

Starbucks has potential to continue to grow in the upcoming years, but at a slower pace than before. They have expanded into 50 countries and saturated many markets already, so they will have to look elsewhere to continue their growth.

Starbucks is focusing their money on the 'go green' initiative instead of opening new stores. This movement is beginning to take off in stores and will be a large part of Starbucks' future. Being environmentally friendly and reducing the stores footprint will be critical in upcoming years.

## Questions

**1. Is the retailer classified as a global retailer or a multinational retailer? Explain its pattern of expansion. What expansion strategy did/is the retailer use/using?**

*Starbucks Corporation is a global retailer. Most of their product offerings are private label and are uniform throughout all the countries they operate in. The company prefers to have a majority control of their stores in each country to maintain a firm hold on business operations and standardized image all over the world. Although they claim that they do not franchise, Starbucks' international expansion pattern mimics that of a franchising firm because of their strictly enforced standard format and goal to feel exactly the same all over the world, which propelled their rapid growth in the international market. The company's three main business structures when expanding overseas are joint ventures, licensing, and wholly-owned subsidiaries.[8] They use these strategies when entering new regions in the world so they maintain control of operation directly. If necessary they will partner up with a local company who shares the same business structure and has much experience in the industry allowing these partners the right to operate and build stores in their region. An executive who heads Starbucks Coffee International claims that it helps in discovering prime locations and deal with complicated government paperwork by teaming up with experienced partners in local areas.[12] Also, it's appealing to the community to have a local firm operating an international firm within their region. In the majority of the partnerships, Starbucks' has more than a 50 percent hold and has a history of reacquiring a lot of the remaining shares to maintain a high number of company-owned stores.[8]*

**2. Based on Dunning's eclectic theory, how do ownership, locational and internalization factors play in your retailers' international expansion**

*According to Dunning's eclectic theory ownership, locational, and internalization factors have played an important role in Starbucks international expansion. There are many ownership advantages the company possesses that have helped with their internationalization. An asset-based advantage that is very important to the company is their private label. By having a private label, the company is able to keep cost down which allows them to use the money to enter into new markets and have a standardized product that they bring with them. A transaction-based* advantage the company has is their tacit knowledge they have gained over the years of expanding. Over the years the company has gained the know-how of what the customer wants and expects out of a coffee store and they use this knowledge when opening up new stores in new markets. The company is very big on customer service and giving each customer the best experience while in the store. They use their customer service as another transaction based advantage. Location factors are important for the company. Pull factors are very important. The first mover advantage as a factor seems to play an important role when the company enters into a new market. Starbucks looks for markets where there are people who drink coffee and want to be the first company to get to the market. When doing this they are able to get their name there and retain consumers' mind space. Another locational factor for why the company has expanded internationally is that they have saturated their home market. This is a push factor giving Starbucks reasons to go outside the home market and achieve more sales in new markets. One way the company uses its internalization factors is by sending experts out to the foreign markets to help supervise the opening the new stores. The company sends experts who posses the knowledge and know how of the company and make sure the new business is built up to the Starbucks standards. The internalization factor may not be the strongest for the company due to the fact that coffee stores are not new, and everyone knows how to make coffee. What Starbucks does bring is a specific way of doing business and this is helping them internationalize.

### 3. What role does cultural proximity and geographical proximity play in the retailers' international moves?

Geographical proximity was a factor when Starbucks expanded into their first international location of Vancouver, Canada. Vancouver is only 119 miles from Starbucks home in Seattle.[30] After expanding into Canada, Starbucks first international location outside of North America was Tokyo, Japan. Geographical proximity does not play a factor for Starbucks to expand into Japan because it was entered because of similar cultural lifestyles. Starbucks saw Japan as an opportunity for their coffee because Japan is a country that loves coffee and is the third largest coffee consuming country in the world.[31] Starbucks uses a rapid expansion strategy to move into a country's market first to gain a competitive advantage. Starbucks factors many qualities whether to expand into countries. One of the most important factors is if the country shares Starbucks values and culture. Starbucks searches for a country that fits in with their mission, which is, "to inspire and nurture the human spirit -- one person, one cup, and one neighborhood at a time."[32] For example, Starbucks believed China was a good one to enter because China's culture shares Starbucks' coffee passion and expertise with customers by encouraging them to sample, savor and enjoy its premium coffee.[33]

*Starbucks looks for countries and neighborhoods that they will be invited into and will have a positive impact on the community, customers, and partners every day.*[34] *Starbucks stores are typically located in high traffic areas. The company locates retail stores in select rural and off-highway locations to serve a broader array of customers who live outside of the metropolitan markets.*[9] *Another way that Starbucks provides better service to customers is that they expand development of drive-thru retail stores to accommodate non-pedestrians. The partners provide improved access to desirable retail space.*

*Further important qualities that Starbucks looks for in international partnerships is seasoned operator of small box, multi-unit retailer, sufficient financial and HR, involved and committed top management, local business leader, strong track record with developing new ventures and food and beverage experience.*[35]

### 4. Can you predict the retailer's future international expansion?

*Yes, it is certain what Starbucks will do in the future. So far Starbucks has saturated most markets that were potentially successful to them and have begun cutting back on some locations due to over expansion. They will continue to cut back on locations in which they are not as profitable, which will also eliminate the costs for those stores. As of 2008 Starbucks has been facing a dim future due to foreclosures, high food prices, and less generous credit card limits. Their stock is at a low and continues to decrease today. All of the respectable gains of the past seven years have been wiped away. At the start of 2009 Howard Schultz, CEO of Starbucks Corp., announced plans to cut jobs, close stores and slow growth around the world. Starbucks will close 300 underperforming company-operated stores worldwide with about 200 in the U.S. These closings are in addition to the 600 U.S. stores and 61 in Australia announced last year. Overall, that's nearly 1,000 announced store closings in less than two years. In the U.S. market in 2009, the company will open 140 stores, which is 60 fewer than its previous target of 200. Internationally, it will open 170 stores that is 100 fewer than its previous target of 270.*[36]

*The company is not bringing in the profits that they once were and they should be focusing more time and money in the stores that will give them the best long-term profit, instead of opening up more stores that may or may not do well. If they invest their time in the most profitable stores they may be able to expand to more places further ahead in the future.*

## Propositions

P1: **The greater the ownership advantages for retailers, the less likely they will franchise or license.**

No, Starbucks does not support this proposition. This proposition states that a company with many ownership advantages would not want to franchise or license their business. Starbucks does have ownership advantages and uses them when internationalizing in new markets. The use of private label is very important for the company and helps make the international process a lot easier. Starbucks licenses their business in international markets and when they do, their tacit knowledge gained from previous expansion is very important to the company. "Employees working in licensed retail locations are required to follow Starbucks detailed store operating procedures and attend training classes similar to company operated stores"⁵ Starbucks wants their customers to have the same experience wheather they are at a company owned store or licensed store. All their stores should feel the same to a customer, regardless of the location.

**P2: The greater the available organizational slack the greater the likelihood of expanding internationally.**

| | |
|---|---|
| 1999 | 1.536 |
| 2000 | 1.468 |
| 2001 | 1.334 |

No, Starbucks does not support this proposition. The proposition states that for a company to expand internationally their organizational slack should increase each year. Organizational slack is important to a company because they have excess resources that can be used to help expand the company. The chart shows Starbucks' organizational slack over three years. This chart illustrates why Starbucks does not support the proposition. Starbucks' organizational slack is decreasing over these three years and even with this, Starbucks was able to expand internationally. In fact, over these three years Starbucks expanded to 13 different countries.

**P3: The greater the recoverable slack the greater the likelihood of expanding internationally.**

| | |
|---|---|
| 2001 | 0.388 |
| 2002 | 0.402 |
| 2003 | 0.399 |
| 2004 | 0.417 |
| 2005 | 0.416 |
| 2006 | 0.425 |
| 2007 | 0.411 |
| 2008 | 0.422 |

No, Starbucks does not support this proposition. This proposition is stating that the recoverable slack needs to increase over the years in order for the company to expand internationally. Starbucks does not fit this pattern. The chart shows how Starbucks' slack has changed over the years. From this chart there is no definite pattern to be found, but knowing Starbucks history even without a definite pattern they were still able to expand internationally.

**P4: The greater the potential slack the greater the likelihood of expanding internationally.**

| | |
|---|---|
| 1999 | .767267 |
| 2000 | .769121 |
| 2001 | .743327 |
| 2002 | .753091 |
| 2003 | .762865 |
| 2004 | .747184 |
| 2005 | .594933 |
| 2006 | .503169 |
| 2007 | .427427 |
| 2008 | .439111 |

No, Starbucks does not support this proposition. This proposition is stating that a company's potential slack needs to increase every year in order for a company to expand internationally. By having an increase the company is able to use the excess resources to help with the international expansion. Starbucks does not fit this pattern. The chart on the left shows the potential slack Starbucks has over the years. When looking at the chart there is not a pattern to be seen with the potential slack Starbucks has. Even though there is no increase from year to year, Starbucks was still be able to expand internationally.

**P13: Global companies will move to the largest/ capital cities in a country.**

Yes, Starbucks supports this proposition. When Starbucks first enters a country it moves to the capital or largest city in that country. Some examples of this movement include moving into Zurich, Switzerland, which is the largest city in Switzerland, Buenos Aires, Argentina, which is the capital and largest city in Argentina, Vienna, Austria that is the capital city of Austria and Tokyo, Japan, which is the capital of Japan. The company decided to move to these cities first because it felt these locations would be the most profitable for the company. As compared with smaller cities a larger city has a lot more people and shopping locations to earn revenue. As the central place theory states, it is best for a company to position itself within a larger amount of retailers similar to theirs.

*This will provide the greatest potential profit revenue for the company.*[37, 38, 39, 40]

### P14: Global companies will not be attracted by population size, income, cultural proximity or geographical proximity

*No, Starbucks does not support this proposition. Starbucks' first international ventures included Tokyo, a large city in Japan with a current population of 12.790 million that is 10 percent of the population in the country.*[41] *When the company chooses a new country to enter, they have specific requirements that include having a focal point city that has a large population to build the presence from then move outwards from that point to other parts of that specific region.*[42] *Japan is around 5,133.13 miles from the US, making geographical proximity an unlikely reason for moving to Tokyo initially.*[30] *If they were strongly focused on moving into geographical proximity countries, their move should have been to Mexico after Canada, not across the ocean to Japan and other Asian nations. When it comes to cultural proximity, Japan being the third highest coffee consumming country, definitely supports the similarities when it comes to coffee consumption patterns supporting Starbucks' decision to move to Japan early on.*

### P15: The greater the asset based ownership advantages of a global retailer, the more likely they are to franchise.

*No, Starbucks does not support this proposition. According to Starbucks' website, they do not franchise which makes this proposition false. Licensing, joint ventures and company owned are the only ways they expand. An asset-based advantage Starbucks has is their extensive use of private label. The majority of Starbucks' sales are from their private label and this generates more revenue for the company. With the revenue they take in they are able to further expand to more international locations. Another way Starbucks uses private label to their advantage is being able to standardize the products available at their stores. This is a way for Starbucks to keep costs down as well as make it easier to expand into international markets.*

### P16: The greater the transaction based ownership advantages of a global retailer, the less likely they are to franchise.

*No, Starbucks does not support this proposition. According to Starbucks' website, they do not franchise which makes this proposition false. Licensing, joint venture and company owned are the only ways they expand. When looking further into licensing, it is actually the same as franchising according to International Retailing. Therefore, when looking at this using our licensing definition the proposition is true. One of the notable transaction based ownership advantages the company has is their customer service. They strive to have exemplary customer service in order to gain long-term customers. Another advantage is the tacit learning that the company gains from entering various markets. The company learns the best ways to run their business, what works and what does not by entering new markets. Through these transaction-based advantages, Starbucks is able to grow as a company and license their stores to various markets.*

**P17: The greater the available organizational slack the greater the likelihood that global retailers will reacquire international franchisees.**

| | |
|---|---|
| 1999 | 1.536 |
| 2000 | 1.468 |
| 2001 | 1.334 |

*No, Starbucks does not support this proposition. According to Starbucks' website, they do not franchise which makes this proposition false. Licensing, joint venture and company owned are the only ways they expand. The resource-based theory can help explain the expansion of Starbucks. The chart shows their liquid cash is decreasing and therefore they need funds from other companies to help expand. Since the cash is decreasing for the company it would only make sense to receive help from other companies to bring the retailer to foreign markets. When Starbucks has the funds they will actually reacquire the stores in the foreign markets. This helps illustrate why Starbucks uses the resource-based theory to help achieve its goals.*

**P18: The greater the recoverable slack the greater the likelihood that global retailers will reacquire international franchisees.**

| | |
|---|---|
| 2001 | 0.388 |
| 2002 | 0.402 |
| 2003 | 0.399 |
| 2004 | 0.417 |
| 2005 | 0.416 |
| 2006 | 0.425 |
| 2007 | 0.411 |
| 2008 | 0.422 |

*No, Starbucks does not support this proposition. According to Starbucks' website, they do not franchise which makes this proposition false. Licensing, joint venture and company owned are the only ways they expand. When looking at the chart it shows Starbucks' recoverable slack has increased and decreased over the years. This proposition states that the more recoverable slack a company has, the more likely they will reacquire their stores. In Starbucks' case even though they did not have a continuous increase of recoverable slack they were still able to reacquire stores, which proves this proposition wrong.*

**P19: The greater the potential slack the greater the likelihood that global retailers will reacquire international franchisees.**

| | |
|---|---|
| 1999 | .767267 |
| 2000 | .769121 |
| 2001 | .743327 |
| 2002 | .753091 |
| 2003 | .762865 |
| 2004 | .747184 |
| 2005 | .594933 |
| 2006 | .503169 |
| 2007 | .427427 |
| 2008 | .439111 |

*No, Starbucks does not support this proposition. According to Starbucks' website, they do not franchise which makes this proposition false. The proposition is stating that the more potential slack a company has the more likely it will reacquire its international stores. In the case of Starbucks there is no real pattern of potential slack the company has over the years. Even with no pattern or increase of potential slack the company was still able to reacquire stores from international markets.*

## Endnotes

1.  Mergentonlinemergent. (2008) company details: Starbucks Corp. retrieved November 3, 2009 from mergentonline database.

2.  Starbucks Newsroom: Starbucks Chairman Receives First Magazine Award For Responsible Capitalism. (2007, November 20). Starbucks Newsroom: Home. Retrieved November 19, 2009, from http://news.starbucks.com/article_display. cfm?article_id=83

3.  Howard Schultz and Dori Jones Yang, *Pour Your Heart Into It* (New York: Hyperion, 1997) p5

4.  Hwang, Jen-Lin. (2005). Coffee Goes to China: An Examination of Starbucks' Market Entry Strategy, Journal of Undergraduate Research, 6, 1-2.

5.  "Starbucks Coffee" 17 Nov. 2009 < http://www.starbucks.com/aboutus/ internationaldev.asp>

6.  Garza, George. "The history of Starbucks." Catalogs.com. Retrieved November 14, 2009 from http://www.catalogs.com/info/food/the-history-of-starbucks.html.

7. "A Brief History of Starbucks." Retrieved November 14, 2009 from http://me.starbucks.com/en-US/_About+Starbucks/History+of+Starbucks.htm.

8. www.starbucks.com (2009)

9. Starbucks Annual Report 2008. (n.d.) Retrieved November 10, 2009 from http://phx.corporate-ir.net/External.File?item=UGFyZW50SUQ9MTExNzN8Q2hpbGRJRD0tMXxUeXBlPTM=&t=1

10. Mitchell, D. (2009, March 22). Big Money: State of Starbucks: Inside Its Existential Crisis - washingtonpost.com. washingtonpost.com - nation, world, technology and Washington area news and headlines. Retrieved November 19, 2009, from http://www.washingtonpost.com/wp-dyn/content/article/2009/03/21/AR2009032100066.html

11. Starbucks Newsroom: Facts about Starbucks in the Middle East. (2009, January 16). Starbucks Newsroom: Home. Retrieved November 19, 2009, from http://news.starbucks.com/article_display.cfm?article_id=200

12. Jung, H. (2003, April 20). Lattes for all: Starbucks plans global expansion. Global Exchange - Building People-to-People Ties. Retrieved November 10, 2009, from http://www.globalexchange.org/campaigns/fairtrade/coffee/662.html

13. Ethical Sourcing-Starbucks Shared Planet Principles. (n.d.) Retrieved November 1, 2009, from http://www.starbucks.com/sharedplanet/ethicalInternal.aspx?story=sspPrinciples

14. Starbucks Newsroom: Starbucks, TransFair USA and Fairtrade Labelling Organizations International Announce Groundbreaking Initiative to Support Small-Scale Coffee Farmers. (n.d.). Starbucks Newsroom: Home. Retrieved November 13, 2009, from http://news.starbucks.com/article_display.cfm?article_id=17

15. FY 2008 Starbucks Global Responsibility Report. (n.d.) Retrieved November 12, 2009 from http://www.starbucks.com/sharedplanet/customGRPage.aspx

16. (STARBUCKS) RED. (n.d.). (STARBUCKS) RED. Retrieved November 19, 2009, from http://red.starbucks.com/red/default.aspx#num=01&id=red

17. Petrecca, L., & Krantz, M. (2008, July 2). When the cups are down: 600 Starbucks to close; Company-owned stores aren't profitable enough . Lexis Nexis. Retrieved November 16, 2009, from www.lexisnexis.com.proxy2.cl.msu.edu/us/lnacademic/search/homesubmitForm.do

18. The Americas Timeline. (n.d.). Starbucks. Retrieved November 5, 2009, from http://news.starbucks.com/images/10041/Timeline-TheAmericas_Q3FY09.pdf

19. Starbucks Japan-About Us. (n.d.) Retrieved November 14, 2009 from http://www.

starbucks.co.jp/en/company.html

20. Tokyo wakes up to Seattle taste (1998). Retrieved from http://ezproxy.msu.edu:2047/login?url=http://proquest.umi.com/pqdweb?did=37849932&Fmt=2&clientId=3552&RQT=309&VName=PQD

21. Mergent Online. (2008). Starbucks Japan. Retrieved November 2, 2009 from Mergent Online database.

22. Starbucks in China. (n.d.) Retrieved November 3, 2009 from http://www.starbucks.com.cn/en/aboutus/inchina.html

23. Starbucks Celebrates Five Years in South Korea With the Opening of its 100th Store (2004). Retrieved from http://ezproxy.msu.edu:2047/login?url=http://proquest.umi.com/pqdweb?did=670249691&Fmt=3&clientId=3552&RQT=309&VName=PQD

24. Starbucks to Acquire Operations in Singapore. (2004). Retrieved November 18, 2009, from http://www.allbusiness.com/company-activities-management/company-structures-ownership/5618874-1.html

25. Starbucks Coffee Company Thailand Website http://www.starbucks.co.th/en-US/_About+Starbucks/Starbucks+Coffee+Thailand.htm

26. Starbucks Australia Website, Starbucks in Australia http://www.starbucks.com.au/en-AU/_About+Starbucks/

27. Starbucks website Press Room Article. Starbucks Restructure Australian Operations to Position Business for Long-Term Growth. http://www.starbucks.com/aboutus/pressdesc.asp?id=883

28. Starbucks Coffee Company Opens First Store in New Zealand (1998). Retrieved from http://proquest.umi.com.proxy1.cl.msu.edu/pqdweb?did=35292955&Fmt=3&clientId=3552&RQT=309&VName=PQD

29. Golding, A. (2009, November 6). Starbucks launches heritage branding in the UK - Marketing news - Marketing magazine. Marketing news & marketing jobs - Marketing magazine - Resource for marketers. Retrieved November 9, 2009, from http://www.marketingmagazine.co.uk/News/MostDiscussed/964788/Starbucks-launches-heritage-branding-UK/

30. www.mapcrow.info

31. Starbucks to open coffee stores in Japan with local partner (2005). Retrieved from http://ezproxy.msu.edu:2047/login?url=http://proquest.umi.com/pqdweb?did=742481&Fmt=3&clientId=3552&RQT=309&VName=PQD

32. Our Starbucks mission. (n.d.) Retrieved November 7, 2009 from http://www.starbucks.com/mission/default.asp

33. Starbucks Newsroom-Greater China. (n.d.) Retrieved November 12, 2009 from http://news.starbucks.com/about+starbucks/starbucks+coffee+international/greater+china/

34. Our Starbucks mission. (n.d.) Retrieved November 7, 2009 from http://www.starbucks.com/mission/default.asp

35. Starbucks Coffee International. (n.d.) Retrieved November 13, 2009 from http://www.starbucks.com/aboutus/international.asp

36. Gilbert, S. (2008, November 25). Starbucks: Our future is dimmer than your future! - BloggingStocks. BloggingStocks. Retrieved November 12, 2009, from http://www.bloggingstocks.c

37. "Starbucks Opens its First Coffee House in Austria's Coffee Capital; Plans to open 10-15 coffee houses in Austria over the next 12-18 months." (2001, December 7). Business Wire. Retrieved November 11, 20009 from http://www.highbeam.com/doc/1G1-80623246.html.

38. "Starbucks Opens the Doors to Its First Coffeehouse in Argentina (Company overview)." (2008, May 29). Business Wire. Retrieved November 11, 2009 from http://www.encyclopedia.com/doc/1G1-179484298.html.

39. "Starbucks Opens First Store in Zurich, Switzerland; Expects Solid Growth for Years to Come in Continental Europe." (2001, March 7). Business Wire. Retrieved November 11, 2009 from http://www.encyclopedia.com/doc/1G1-71307822.html.

40. "Starbucks Opens 200th Store in Japan...in Record Time." (2001, January 24). Starbucks Corporation Press Room. Retrieved November 11, 2009 from http://www.starbucks.com/aboutus/pressdesc.asp?id=156.

41. Population of Tokyo - Tokyo Metropolitan Government. (n.d.).. Retrieved November 2, 2009, from http://www.metro.tokyo.jp/ENGLISH/PROFILE/overview03.htm

42. Starbucks Outlines International Growth Strategy; Focus on Retail Expansion and Profitability. | Asia > East Asia from AllBusiness.com. (2004, October 14). Business Resources, Advice and Forms for Large and Small Businesses. Retrieved November 4, 2009, from http://www.allbusiness.com/company-activities-management/financial-performance/5557397-1.html

# Tesco

*Mallory Chargot, Danielle Harve, Rachael Hennessey,*
*Amy Jackson, Hilary Pogarch*

## Tesco

Tesco has taken the term grocery retailer to a new level. The UK group, which is UK's largest retailer, currently operates in thirteen different countries in Europe, Asia and North America. Since going public in 1947, Tesco has had a whirlwind of growth within the UK and internationally.[1] The company is the third largest grocer retailer in the world so it is no wonder that they are able to serve millions of customers each week and employ over 440,000 people![2]

Throughout this case study, we will discuss the strategy Tesco has taken in order to become the dominate retailer that they are today. The supermarket group has expanded drastically over the last decade by providing a format for every type of customer such as hypermarkets, supermarkets, convenience stores, and department stores. We will also discuss the locations to which Tesco choose to expand in and the types of formats chosen for those locations. However, the market selection process is not as simple as it looks.

Although Tesco prefers to grow organically, the company mainly used small acquisitions and joint ventures when initially expanding into Europe and Asia.[3] However, their most recent expansion in the western part of the United States was solely done through organic expansion. Tesco's expansion strategy originally focused on countries with geographic proximity to the UK and a lack of modern retailers. They did this to capture the number one market position without competing against other major retailers such as Wal-mart and Carrefour. After their Central and Eastern European expansion efforts, the company mainly developed joint ventures when expanding into Asian countries such as Taiwan, South Korea, China and Malaysia. While spreading the Tesco name, there have been challenges and successes that make one wonder what is their next step? So get ready as we dive into the details of Tesco's international journey!

Tesco looks for several qualities in countries during their international expansion process. First, the ability for long term growth is key, therefore, the country should have a stable, consumer driven market. Second, since the company focuses on price cutting and discounts, they look for a growing middle class and a market filled with an increasing young population. Third, once the country passes the first two qualifications, Tesco uses a joint venture or small acquisition to decrease the risk when entering a foreign market. Finally, potential countries for Tesco's expansion should ideally be liberal when is comes to planning and lack contemporary retail competition. [4]

## Tesco Flow Chart

| Entry Year | Country | Number of Stores |
|---|---|---|
| 1992 | France (exits in 1997) | |
| 1994 | Hungary | 123 |
| 1995 | Poland | 301 |
| 1996 | Czech Republic | 96 |
| 1996 | Slovakia | 60 |
| 1997 | Ireland | 100 |
| 1998 | Taiwan (exits in 2005) | |
| 1998 | Thailand | 476 |
| 1999 | South Korea | 137 |
| 2002 | Malaysia | 20 |
| 2003 | Japan | 125 |
| 2003 | Turkey | 66 |
| 2004 | China | 56 |
| 2007 | United States | 53 |

Information from Hoovers, International Retailing Book, and Tescoplc.com

# France

Tesco entered France in 1992 as part of its initial geographic expansion phase. The retailer entered France via the majority "acquisition of the medium-sized supermarket chain Catteau". High profitability and the support of financial analysts made the chain an attractive opportunity, resulting in Tesco's plans to grow the chain nationally.[5]

Tesco abandoned its operations in France in 1997. "The business did not have the critical mass it needed to compete against the discounters so prevalent in the north of France and the might of the big hypermarket operators".[6]

The divestment of locations in the French market led to a number of learnings for Tesco that affected its future expansion strategy. First, the divestment resulted in the firm ensuring that they establish a strong market-leading position in new markets. A strong market position can obscure relatively small mistakes, whereas for small-scale operations such mistakes might prove to be fatal. Second, Tesco learned not to trust anybody they are buying assets from. Dissatisfaction with French operations generated negative press commentary, but also weakened management and investor confidence and visibly undermined the strategic credibility of the company. Third, Tesco realized its lack of understanding for how it would integrate and control the business.[5] The company's acquisition of Catteau in France did not prove to be the platform from which to inspire experimentation abroad.[5]

# Hungary

Tesco's first sucessful Eastern European expansion was to Hungary in 1994. They currently have 123 stores in Hungary, predominately hypermarkets, which has allowed the company to become the market leader with a market share of 15 percent.[4] However, since the hypermarket industry is becoming saturated, they started opening mostly 1k supermarkets to stay competitive against Carrefour.[4, 2] Tesco entered Hungary by acquiring 43 small convenience stores from the Global supermarket chain.[5] This acquisition provided Tesco with the experience needed for their expansion into other Eastern European Markets.

Tesco's operation in Hungary has not been easy. It has been difficult to remain the market leader in an unpleasant economic and retail setting, however, the company stayed strong by developing infrastructure, decreasing prices, and increasing store space during 2005 and 2006.[53] In 2007, a decrease in sales growth was blamed on the poor Hungarian economy.

Today, the Tesco in Hungary is doing well due to the company's increases in returns and increase in space by 12 percent during 2008. More specifically, the supermarket group has expanded by acquiring four hypermarkets, five 3k compact stores, twelve 1k stores, and one Tesco Express. By the end of 2009, Tesco hopes to have distributed a Clubcard in Hungary which will help them understand their customers by evaluating their purchase data.[2] Despite Hungary's difficult market, Tesco's hard work has paid off.

## Poland

Tesco has had recent success in Poland since expanding there in 1995.[7] This expansion took time to become successful because the country is very fragmented and has recently moved from a socialist system to a capitalist economy. However, the supermarket group is the market leader with a four percent market share.[3]

Tesco entered the Polish market through the acquisition of 36 supermarkets from the Savia SA Company. Their intention of the acquisition was to achieve knowledge of the Polish grocer retail market. This knowledge would allow them to successfully break into the hypermarket industry in the future. Years later in 2002, Tesco used their domestic store earnings to acquire HIT in Poland.[5] This expansion effort put them at 53 Tesco stores by the beginning of 2003.

In 2006, Tesco was able to strengthen their presence in Poland by purchasing 279 Leader Price convenience stores from the French competitor, Casino.[8] The supermarket operator believed that this purchase will help Tesco grow its business in the highly fragmented and competitive Polish market.[9] This acquisition tripled the number of stores Tesco owned in Poland.[7] Overall, Tesco's early business insight from their expansion into Hungary and Poland in the mid 90's led to their current number one market position in Poland.

## Czech Republic

Tesco entered into Central Europe for second time in 1996 by purchasing 13 department stores in the Czech and Slovak Republics.[10] Tesco's expansion in the country has shown to be successful from the number of innovations the company has implemented. As of 2007 Tesco was covering four million square feet of selling space. Tesco's main store formats in the Czech Republic are hypermarkets and supermarkets. The supermarket group has built up its Czech business through an asset swap with Carrefour, its French rival, and the acquisition of twenty-seven stores from the German Company Edeka.[11] Currently, Tesco is third in the market and is struggling to compete with the market leaders, Metro and Lidl.[4] One of Tesco's major setbacks in the Czech market is differentiating themselves between a supermarket and discount store. They have found it to be crucial to focus on value rather than just price to please consumers.[4] Most recently Tesco has found triumph with the innovative express stores that they are operating in the Czech Republic. The company opened their first express store in London 1994 and decided to move into other markets to continue their expansion. By acquiring the thirteen Kmart stores, it has increased Tesco's stake in Global to 97%, which shows that their long term strategy to expand outside of the UK to be valuable.[12] As of 2008, in the Czech Republic, Tesco is operating in 96 stores and employing 12,886 individuals.

## Slovakia

The expansion of Tesco into Slovakia took place in 1996. On February 6, 1996, Tesco announced that it would buy 100% stakes in Kmart's retail branches in Slovakia as well as the Czech Republic.[13] In October 2008, the Business Environment Ranking table of Food and Drink Ratings ranked Slovakia in the bottom place out of the 14 markets in Central and Eastern Europe. This was due to the expected decline of food consumption within the country. The company has recovered from the recent set-back of competition authorities blocking its acquisition of stores presently owned by French Carrefour, and has announced a new wave of expansions.[14] In Slovakia, Tesco plans to introduce their convenience store format, will open 15 new stores. They also recently established a new distribution center, which will supply its Central and Eastern Europe ventures with non-food products.[14]

## Ireland

Tesco, is the largest supermarket chain in Ireland with 26 percent market share.[1] [15] Tesco paid "$1.1 billion for Associated British Foods P.L.C.'s three supermarket chains" including Stewarts in Northern Ireland, Quinnsworth in the Irish Republic and Crazy Prices located in both regions.[16] The 111 locations collectively "employed about 7,500 in the Republic and a further 5,500 in Northern Ireland".[17]

By 2007, Tesco was opening six new stores within the year, bringing its total locations to 101.[18] The total number of stores in 2007 was less than originally acquired due to store closings in Northern Ireland in 1998.[19] The new stores accounted for one-third of its almost ten percent sales growth that year.[18] "Tesco increased sales... to EUR 2.99 billion" despite a hindrance in performance due to costs for its new central distribution center in Donabate, Co Dublin.[18]

In 2007, an industry survey of 4,000 Tesco products revealed that the supermarket giant [charged] Irish customers an average of 15% more than in the UK.[20] Tesco responded that the higher prices were due directly to higher costs from taxes, wages, rents and land prices in Ireland. [20]

In 2008 the supermarket chain advertised the sale of a number of [its] undeveloped sites" in order to open 16 new stores in Ireland by the end of its fiscal year in February 2009 as part of a EUR 150 million expansion.[15]

As most recently reported, Tesco operates 100 locations in Ireland, employing 12,474.[1] The retailer has twenty-six percent market share,[15] with 33.7% of its sales accounted for by private-label merchandise.[21]

## Thailand

Tesco entered Thailand in 1998 with the acquisition of Lotus, a chain of 13 hypermarkets.[28][23] In the same year, Tesco formed a holding company named Tesco Thailand Co Ltd in which Tesco Plc holds 49 percent against 51 percent by the CP Group, one of the biggest retail chains in Thailand.[23] Additionally, Tesco Thailand purchased 75 percent of CP-owned Ekachai Distribution System, the owner of Lotus.[23] The joint venture between Tesco and Ekachai Distribution System benefits both partners by combining synergy allowing each to learn sales techniques for dry and fresh food products respectively.[24]

Tesco's entrance into the market came during a period of economic downturn, allowing the company to capitalize on CP's economic woes and granting it quicker access to a future growth market than would be feasible via organic expansion.[25] It also gave Tesco the opportunity to develop new marketing skills which could later be applied in other locations, especially as it expanded in other parts of Asia.[26] In return, Tesco brought jobs and employee development to Thailand, continuing as a significant purchaser of its agricultural products.[26] Tesco encourages locals to manage the company, originally sending only six executives from England to serve as senior vice presidents of the Thai company.[24]

By 2001 Tesco had expanded its original 13 locations to 33 hypermarkets throughout the country. The rapid expansion of hypermarkets and decline of traditional grocery shops forced the government to reconsider the issuing of regulations to protect small retailers whose businesses were severely affected. A potential retail-zoning law made rapid expansion a critical priority.[27]

Not only does Thailand represent Tesco's entrance into Asia, it also serves as the first market for the retailer's Value Store formats. The format, introduced in 2002, was reduced in size compared to previous locations, and invited local suppliers in to sell products, in an effort to better suit the needs of local communities. The retail environment retains consumer spending within the community, developing the economy.[28]

In 2004 Tesco began efforts to introduce new store formats that would meet local regulations, smaller communities and different consumers' requirements. Formats include Express shops located at petrol stations and shop-house locations, Talad Lotus which offers dry and fresh food at Lotus hypermarket prices, and Khum Kha compact stores located in upcountry communities.[29] The same year, Tesco increased its stake in Lotus to 100%.[30] By 2006 Tesco had approximately 56 hypermarkets, 20 Talad Lotus centers and two or three Value Stores, as well as about 100 Lotus Express outlets.[31] As most recently reported, Tesco operates 476 stores in Thailand, employing 35,269.[1]

## Taiwan

Tesco entered Taiwan in 1998 through the acquisition of the Dutch group Makro Asia, which was shifting its attention from retailing to wholesaling. It opened its first store in 2000, a 10,000 square foot superstore, with the expectation of opening an additional 19 stores within the next 5 years.[32]

After five challenging years in Taiwan, Tesco traded six of its sites in the country for eleven Carrefour outlets in Czech Republic and Slovakia after the retailer failed to make inroads in a country that is dominated by supermarket chain Carrefour. The asset swap showed that both retailers were prepared to be realistic and avoid going head to head in markets that are not big enough for the two of them.[33] The swap resulted in an increase in market-share from fifth to fourth in the Czech Republic for Tesco.[34]

## South Korea

Through an acquisition, Tesco entered South Korea in 1999. They are currently operating in 137 stores with 12,641 employees.[1] South Korea has proven to be a key market for Tesco, although the expansion has taken nine years. South Korea has a large market with a growing young population which will continue to strengthen its operations there. Recently Tesco has expanded within the country by acquiring a 36-strong discount chain. South Korea is Tesco's largest international market in both profits and sales.[35] The attainment of such high-quality assets is an important strategic move that will allow Tesco to continue growth in South Korea's key market.[35] This expansion will put Tesco close behind the number one company in the market, E-mart. Throughout Tesco's international expansion the number and value of trading profit has continually increased, and will continue to do so with how well the company is doing. Tesco has been successful because they are offering the right sort of services, products at affordable prices, and pleasant, convenient environments.[36] Tesco has taken steps to re-brand many of their home-plus format stores in early 2008, in hopes of increasing success in the country. Tesco now operates 66 Home-plus hypermarkets and 72 Home plus Express stores.[37] After Great Britain, South Korea is Tesco's most successful market.

## Malaysia

Tesco entered the Malaysian market in 2002 and is currently operating 20 stores with 8,045 employees.[1] The initial acquisition was a strategic alliance with local conglomerate Sime Darby Berhad. In Malaysia the main retail format is a hypermarket. Many outlets in the country are re-opens and are managed by a combination of freehold and leasehold properties. In 2005 Tesco also launched Tesco Banting, Tesco Express Selayang, Ipoh & Kuantan. A Spokesperson for Tesco responded to a rumor that the company was moving into the convenience sector saying, Our current focus in Malaysia is to deliver a great offering for customers through our hypermarkets.[38] Stated on the Tesco PLC website, The new businesses which have been created and developed over the last decade as part of this strategy now have scale, they are competitive and profitable – in fact, the International business alone makes about the same profit as the entire group did a decade ago.[1] Overall, Tesco has worked hard to strengthen their presence in the Malaysian market.

## Japan

Tesco entered the Japanese market in 2003 through the acquisition of seventy-eight C Two-Network stores. These stores were local discount supermarkets located in the Tokyo area.[39] The deal cost Tesco $255 million dollars, and helped them further their knowledge about the Japanese retail market.[40] Tesco had been considering Japan for many years and did very in depth research before deciding to make this move into the market. They sent a group of individuals to Japan to learn Japanese shopping patterns and habits.[40] They found that Japanese consumers shop frequently and look for the freshest food available. This helped them determine that their normal hypermarket format would not be successful in this area. For this reason, Tesco developed a smaller store supermarket and convenience formats and placed them in busy city areas to better serve the customers in this region.[39]

Tesco continued to acquire additional stores in order to gain market share as well as a better understanding of the Japanese retail market. In 2004, 27 Frec's stores were acquired, a supermarket chain specializing in fresh food typically located in the more crowded suburban areas.[41] Then in 2005, Tesco gained an additional eight stores through the acquisition of Tanekin.[39]

According to Tesco's 2008 Annual Report, they continue to have a more difficult time operating in the Japanese market, but are confident that the new formats will produce positive results. By the end of 2007, they completed the building and development of the new Tesco Express format, with 7 of these stores now being present in Japan. Currently, Tesco is improving the management teams in Japan as well as developing a plan to revamp certain stores in the area. In 2008 Tesco operated 125 stores employing 3,604 individuals.[2]

## Turkey

Tesco began operating in Turkey in 2003, the same year they expanded into Japan. They entered the market by acquiring Kipa, a hypermarket chain in Turkey. They started out small that year by opening only five stores, with the deal costing around $125 million.[42] In order to gain knowledge about the Turkish market, Tesco made the decision to keep the Kipa name because this is a name recognized and trusted by Turkish consumers. Tesco allowed Kipa's current management team to remain in place, while changing certain systems used by the company, like the stock control system.[43] Tesco had been working on this deal since 2002 and was eager to enter the Turkish market because of Turkey's consistent economic growth and dense population.[42] By the end of 2005, Tesco maintained eight stores in Turkey, and by February of 2007 made plans of opening a total of 22 new stores.[44]

Tesco's 2008 annual report anticipates positive results for their growing business in Turkey. As of 2008 Tesco was operating 26 hypermarkets and 40 Express Tesco and supermarket formats in Turkey. They have plans to open 40 additional stores, as well as expanding the distribution center located in Yasibasi. They are doing all of this while looking to operate new stores in different areas, including Istanbul and Ankara.[2]

## China

In 2004, Tesco entered China as a joint venture. Tesco purchased half of the Hymall chain from Ting Hsin. Having a fifty percent stake in this Taiwanese-owned Hypermarket chain was expensive, but it gave Tesco immediate scales in China. This joint venture allowed Tesco to compete against other companies that already had established themselves in the Chinese market, for example Wal-Mart and Carrefour.[45] Chief executive Sir Terry Leahy stated "expanding into China was an important strategic step to becoming a 'truly international retailer'. "[45] Then in 2006 Tesco announced that they would be buying out their Taiwanese partner and taking control of 90 percent of the Chinese supermarket chain Hymall.[46]

Today Tesco stores in China operate under active management with the primary expansion strategy being organic growth which was fueled by China's decrease in retail government regulations.[4] They had around 56 stores as of 2008 with their primary focus on hypermarkets. "Hypermarkets will contribute hugely to future retail growth. The convenience of the one-stop-shop is growing in appeal to Chinese shoppers…"[47] Furthermore, Tesco is "on the lookout for a creative agency in China,"[48] and they want to expand their clothing division.

## United States

Tesco entered into the United States in 2007, debuting on the West Coast. This was the first international market they entered through organic expansion rather than acquisition or joint venture (Insights and implications of Tesco's entry into the US market, 2009).[49] This was one of the most important retail invasions of the U.S. market. Tesco launched their 'Fresh and Easy' convenience store division which is smaller than their average supermarket and focuses on centralized shopping and low prices. This convenience store format follows Tesco's profitable Tesco Express format, offering a large variety of take out and healthy prepared foods. They also have several private label lines, along with a healthy food line.[50] The Company makes every effort to keep shelves stocked with fresh ripe products ready for purchase, allowing for a low price point.[51] As of 2008, Tesco had 61 stores[43] and was making plans for continuous growth. They operate through dormant management now, rather than through active management when they first entered the country.[2]

A manager in training talked about his outlook on Tesco and stated "so far it's been a fantastic experience, and the company offers so many opportunities for growth. I appreciate how we try to make things easy for our customers…Most of our customers view Fresh & Easy as a Trader Joe's with Wal-Mart pricing".[52] However others have a different opinion. For example Fred Shaker, a former independent grocer owner states "based on my experience as a storeowner, I feel that Fresh & Easy stores are really struggling…Fresh & Easy stores don't offer the variety and service that you'd find in traditional supermarkets. Plus the people I've talked to who've shopped at the stores despise having to use self-checkouts…People still expect service. Long term, you can't operate a successful business without it."[52]

# Questions

**1. Is the retailer classified as a global retailer or a multinational retailer? Explain its pattern of expansion. What expansion strategy did/is the retailer use/using?**

*Tesco is classified as a multinational retailer. The company generally adjusts their product offerings and store formats to the society they are serving. This is why Tesco does not franchise because it would be too difficult to copy their store format. Also, Tesco saturated their home country of the United Kingdom before expanding internationally. The expansion outside of the UK was financed by the success of Tesco in their home market.*

*Tesco's pattern of expansion was to acquire small existing businesses in Central and Eastern European Countries, followed by establishing joint ventures with most of the Asian countries in which the retailer entered. Finally, Tesco made its way to North America by growing organically in the United States. The entry format varied depending on the country, ranging from hypermarkets in Hungary, Thailand, South Korea, Malaysia, China, and Turkey; supermarkets in Ireland, Japan, Poland, France and Taiwan; department stores in Czech Republic and Slovakia; and convenience stores in the United States.*

**2. Based on Dunning's eclectic theory, how do ownership, locational and internalization factors play in your retailers' international expansion?**

*"Dunning's eclectic theory focuses on Ownership, Location, and Internationalization, (OLI) factors that influence a company's decision to internationalize."[4] Tesco has strong ownership advantages because of its international experience in up-and-coming markets where hypermarket concepts are well adapted.[4] Also, since Tesco has strong brand recognition, they have the power to negotiate with suppliers. Locational advantages do play a significant role when Tesco expands internationally. Typically, multinational retailers are concerned with cultural proximity and less concerned with geographic proximity. Focusing more on large formats, Tesco initially entered markets that were culturally similar and would be more accepting of their large scale formats. Market size was important when Tesco entered emerging countries because the company had to adapt its products. Lastly, internalization is to keep the company's secret within the company. Tesco's corporate secrets are important to the retailer, which is why their main entry mode was majority acquisition. This allowed them to purchase existing businesses and own the majority of the company. The United States is a good example of Tesco's desire to keep their ownership assets internalized. Tesco entered the United States through organic growth; therefore they kept all of their secrets internal.*

### 3.  What role does cultural proximity and geographical proximity play in the retailers' international moves?

*Cultural and geographical proximity played a role during the beginning of Tesco's international expansion.  The grocery retailer initially believed these two factors were important, which is why they entered France in 1992 and Ireland in 1979.  However, they learned that these culturally similar and nearby countries would not provide Tesco with the success they hoped for.  It appears they took this into consideration by expanding into nearby CEE countries with emerging markets which have proved to be successful.  However, after exiting France and Ireland, Tesco learned that geographic proximity is not a major factor because they source within the host country anyway.*

*Tesco's main overall expansion approach was acquiring existing stores in Central and Eastern Europe, then expanding into Asian countries mostly through joint ventures, and finally through organic growth in the western states of North America.  This pattern clearly shows that cultural proximity is not a significant factor anymore because CEE countries and Asian countries have very different cultures than the UK.  Therefore, Tesco's strategy was to "initially enter countries that have the smallest cultural distance to the home market, but over time they will expand to countries that are culturally distant."[4]*

*Regardless of its cultural differences from most CEE countries, Tesco first expansion efforts started there.  The dominate retailer moved into Central and Eastern Europe beginning with Hungary in 1994 and Poland in 1995.  Unlike the United Kingdom, "Poland has had a sluggish economy and high unemployment"[4] which makes it difficult for a retailers success.  Two decades ago Hungary converted from a planned economy to a free market after eliminating Communist rule.  Retailers like Tesco were rare in Hungary during the mid 90s; however Tesco saw the country's privatization efforts to be an opportunity for success.  Hungary then became a leading market for Tesco in Central and Eastern Europe. Even though the United Kingdom is geographically separated from the rest of Europe, if geographic proximity was an important factor Tesco would have expanded into closer European countries.*

### 4.  Can you predict the retailer's future international expansion?

*Tesco's future international expansion will most likely be into other Asian countries such as India.  According to the corporate website, "Tesco PLC has announced that it intends to develop a wholesale cash-and-carry business in India."[1]  After finishing market research on India, the supermarket chain plans to offer food and non-food items to retailers, restaurants, and other business owners.  The current CEO thinks this move will be a success by stating, "this is another exciting development for Tesco. It complements our entries into China and the United States, giving us access to another of the most important economies in the world. Our wholesale cash-and-carry format will bring improved value, range and service to thousands of Indian businesses."*[1]

## Propositions

**P1: The greater the ownership advantages for retailers, the less likely they will franchise or license.**

*Yes, Tesco has significant ownership advantages that make the retailer less likely to franchise or license. Instead, Tesco prefers wholly-owned investments that internalize their ownership advantages, entering into new markets via acquisition or through organic expansion.*[22]

*The company's knowledge of how to enter international markets is a tacit-based advantage that it has developed over time, expanding from its home base into twelve other countries, ranking it as "the world's largest supermarket operator."*[22]

*Despite Tesco's significant ownership advantages, its potential decision to franchise in the near future could result with positive or negative effects. "The current [Ministry of Domestic Trade and Consumer Affairs] guidelines prohibit foreign hypermarket operators from opening convenience stores" in Malaysia, forcing Tesco to consider entering the market through franchising, just as its competitor Carrefour has done, to align with a different set of regulations. This would be the first time Tesco franchised its operations, and the company must consider whether the benefits from expanding into Malaysia will outweigh the costs of externalizing its company secrets.*

**P2: The greater the available organizational slack the greater the likelihood of expanding internationally.**

1994: $27,952/62482 = .447$
1995: $30,457/27,251 = 1.12$
1996: $23,923/30,303 = .789$

*No, Tesco does not support this proposition. The ratios of current assets to current liabilities for their first three years are .447 in February 1994, 1.12 in February 1995, and .789 in February 1996. Although the ratio increased from 1994 to 1995, it decreased from 1995 to 1996. Since the excess liquid cash is decreasing it must mean the company is borrowing money from outside capital costs.*

**P3:The greater the recoverable slack the greater the likelihood of expanding internationally.**

2005:  (1,405)/64,981= -.022
2006:  (1,440)/68,846= -.021
2007:  (1,780)/83,683= -.021

*Yes, Tesco would support the proposition. Recoverable slack includes the resources used by the organization, but can be recovered through increased efficiencies. Administrative expenses were of a negative value, as sales increased each year.*

**P4:The greater the potential slack the greater the likelihood of expanding internationally.**

1998:  229,217/9,200,000= .025
1999:  309,583/9,632,000= .032
2000:  390,348/9,632,000= .041

*Yes, Tesco would support the proposition for potential slack. Equity and capital both increased, except in 2000 when capital remained the same. Potential slack is positively related to risk.*[54]

**P5: Multinational companies will move to countries with lower disposable income than their home country.**

*Tesco is a multinational company that services and manages production in more than one country, most recently Tesco is operating in over 13 countries worldwide. Tesco would find it most beneficial to move to a country with a higher disposable income than that of the disposable income in London. The customers would have more money to be spending on luxury or "want" goods rather than just purchasing "need" goods. Moving to a country with a lower disposable income than the home country of operation for a multinational retailer would not be a smart move. Expansion into new markets is to continue growth and expand the company's success. Moving from a country with a lower disposable income would mean that the customers would have less disposable money to spend on anything, so a company like Tesco would have a harder time drawing customers into the store to purchase goods, due to the customer's lack of a disposable income. Moving to a country with a lower disposable income would not help, but would hinder the performance of the company, which would lead to less growth and profits for Tesco as a whole.*

**P6: Multinational retailers will move to countries that have a high positive change in GDP:**

*A country's gross domestic product is the dollar value of all the goods and services produced in a country in a year.*[4] *A multinational company will move to a country with a high positive GDP. A country that has large mass markets will benefit a retailer like Tesco because they have an advantage of purchasing merchandise; Tesco is like a mass merchandiser or discounter that benefits greatly from its multinational markets. An increase in demand in a country will increase the GDP, given that the producers can meet quality and price requirements of the buyers in the country. Having a high positive rate of GDP shows a company like Tesco that a country has a high demand for goods and services. If the goods and services are able to meet the demands of the customers in the country, they will ultimately have a high positive GDP. If the country previously had a lower negative GDP rate, a change to a higher positive GDP would be most beneficial to the company.*

GDP @ time of expansion – GDP 5 years prior to expansion
GDP 5 years prior to expansion

**P7: Multinational retailers will move to a country that has a high positive change in service value added as a percentage of GDP:**

*A country with a high positive change in service value added as a percentage of GDP is a country that has increased its percentage of services being provided within the country. Tesco along with other multinational retailers would benefit from making this type of expansion into a market where the country has an increase in the percentage of service value added of the GDP.*[4] *Tesco has expanded into markets where there is a young growing population who will continue to use goods and services within the country. By expanding into these types of countries/ markets Tesco has a huge amount of potential for growth and continual success. These strategic types of moves made by Tesco make it very easy to be successful in the countries where there is a high positive change in service value added as a percent of GDP.*

Service% GDP @ time of Expansion - Service% GDP 5 years before expansion
Service% GDP 5 years before expansion

**P8: Multinational retailers will first move to countries that are culturally the most similar to their home country.**

*Yes, Tesco "initially expanded into the geographically close markets of Ireland and France", which, similar to the U.K., were "structurally mature."*[5] *It is likely that Tesco sought to align with Hofstede's cultural dimension of uncertainty avoidance, seeking less risk by purchasing a small chain in a nearby country, as opposed to entering riskier emerging markets. Although Tesco's initial and pre-mature expansion was supportive of this proposition, Tesco withdrew from both countries before embarking on a well-developed expansion strategy later on.*

*"With more recent expansion the company has been more disposed toward emerging markets."⁵ Given the potential economic and political uncertainty that Tesco would face in these less culturally-similar Eastern European countries, the retailer "used 'seed' acquisitions to develop knowledge of the market before expanding organically through store-by-store development to minimize their own human and financial capital."⁵ This expansion strategy competes with the proposition, showing that Tesco was looking not to go head-to-head with competitors in culturally-similar countries, but instead to gain knowledge in emerging markets where they could eventually amplify their presence into market leadership.*

### P9: Multinational retailers will expand within the country and then will expand regionally within that area

*Yes, typically Tesco has focused on one particular area before moving to a different country.⁴ They have chosen to enter one or two markets at once instead of several in order to assist them in their "aim for leadership in markets and strong regional presence."⁵ They find it more important to maintain a strong presence in one particular region before moving on to another area. They also do this in order to further their knowledge about the particular country, "they are in the process of learning the culture of the new country so continuing to expand within this environment is helpful."⁴*

*It appears that Tesco is more concerned with expanding in a particular region rather then just a particular country before moving on. Tesco's expansion into Hungary can be seen as a relevant example of this. Tesco entered Hungary in 1994 by acquiring 43 stores.⁵ This was Tesco's first expansion into an Eastern European country and after a year of gaining knowledge about countries such as this, Tesco further expanded into the nearby country of Poland. They did not necessarily expand all throughout Hungary before moving onto another country, but they gained experience and understanding about the region before taking the next step into another country.*

### P10: Periodically the multinational retailers will "jump" to a new geographic area and begin the stages form of expansion.

*Yes, Tesco has made the "jump" into many new areas throughout the world. They have developed a strong presence in both their home country of the UK and also in the markets of Hungary and Poland that they entered into during their early* years of expansion. After they do this, they move onto other areas that may not be as similar and conduct research on the country and its citizens before making the final move.

An example of this is Tesco's expansion into Japan. Tesco moved into Japan through the acquisition of an already well-known existing company operating in the Japanese market.[39] Tesco did not have much knowledge of the Japanese market, therefore they sent in teams of individuals to learn about the shopping patterns and habits of the citizens there.[40] After Tesco gained information about this market, they learned that a different store format carrying special food items was vital in order to succeed. Tesco enters most of their other countries in similar ways such as this. When Tesco has "expanded within a region and is ready for further expansion, it will target a new geographic area and take leap to expand there."[4]

**P11: Multinational retailers will move to countries that are geographically close to the home country initially, then expand to more distant countries. (Miles from Home Country to Host country)**

Yes, Tesco initially moved into markets that are geographically close to the United Kingdom. Although as time went on, Tesco expanded into several countries that are much further away. Tesco's international expansion began by opening stores in the neighboring countries of Ireland and France. Soon after leaving these unsuccessful markets, they moved into the nearby countries of Hungary and Poland in 1994 and 1995. The proceeding years involved moves into the Czech Republic, Slovakia, back into Ireland, and Turkey.[4] Next, Tesco entered into the distant continent of Asia in 1998, starting in Thailand and Taiwan.[1] They proceeded by opening stores in South Korea, Malaysia, Japan, Turkey and China. Lastly, in 2007, Tesco finally made their move into North America by opening Fresh and Easy stores along the Western side of the United States.[49]

By following Tesco's expansion strategy it is evident that they began expanding into countries that were geographically closer to their home market. As time went on and more knowledge was gained, they extended their presence into the more distant Asian and North American markets. Therefore it appears that geographic proximity has not played an extremely important role in their expansion, because of the fact that they have expanded into so many different regions. The actions taken by Tesco follow along with the Stages Theory of expansion.[4] Tesco has done an excellent job of opening numerous stores and maintaining a large presence in an area before moving into a new region.

## P12: Multinational retailers will move to countries with large population bases.

*No, pertaining to Tesco's most recent phase of expansion, the retailer initially entered into Hungary, Poland, Czech and Slovakia, small Eastern European markets. The company's strategy was to dominate "smaller markets which were unlikely to attract much attention from the large retail multinational peers such as Carrefour and Wal-Mart who preferred to focus on the larger markets." "A strong market position can obscure relatively small mistakes, whereas for small-scale operations such mistakes might prove to be fatal." Its strategy has proven successful, increasing its market share in Poland and Hungary to over 40% by 2005.*[5]

*Most recently, Tesco has expanded into China and the United States, entering markets with very large populations. It is no longer in its initial stages of expansion, and has developed a tacit-based advantage surrounding its knowledge of how to successfully internationalize. The advantage allows it to seek opportunities in emerging markets as opposed to needing to focus on small countries for trial-and-error exercises.*

## Endnotes

1. Tesco Corporate Website. www.Tescoplc.com. Retrieved March 5, 2009

2. Tesco Annual Report (2008). Retrieved March 17, 2009, from Mergent Online.

3. Steiner, Rupert. (July 9, 2006). Tesco considers E800m bid for Polish supermarket chain. Knight-Ridder Tribune Business News. Retrieved March 23, 2009, from Lexis-Nexis database

4. Sternquist, B. (2007). International retailing. (Second Ed.), Retailing in the United Kingdom, the Netherlands, and Belgium (pp. 277). New York: Fairchild Books.

5. Palmer, M. (2005). Retail multinational learning: a case study of Tesco. International Journal of Retail & Distribution Management, 33 (1), 1-26. Retrieved April 1, 2009 from ProQuest.

6. Hollinger, P. (1997, December 10). A French blot on Tesco's copybook; [London Edition]. Financial Times, London, U.K, 30. Retrieved April 5, 2009 from ProQuest.

7. Tesco pays [pounds sterling] 72m for more outlets in Polish push. (July 17, 2006). Knight-Ridder Tribune Business New. Retrieved March 16, 2009, from Lexis-Nexis database

8.  Whitfield, Paul. (July 18, 2006). GE prowls in central Europe. Daily Deal/
    The Deal, Middle Market; M and A; Auction Book. Retrieved March 24, 2009,
    from Lexis-Nexis database http://www.lexisnexis.com.proxy2.cl.msu.edu/us/
    lnacademic/results/docview/docview.do?docLinkInd=true&risb=21_T6229611
    064&format=GNBFI&sort=RELEVANCE&startDocNo=1&resultsUrlKey=29_
    T6229611067&cisb=22

9.  Germany's Metro, Britain's Tesco expand in Poland. (July 17, 2006). The
    Associated Press, Business News. Retrieved March15, 2009, from Lexis-Nexis
    database

10. *Tesco-PLC* (2008). Retrieved March 28, 2009, http://www.tescoplc.com

11. Rohwedder, C. (2009). Tesco expands discount goods in bid to fend off
    rivals. The Wall Street Journal, p. b10. Retrieved April 1, 2009, http://www.
    lexisnexis.com.proxy2.cl.msu.edu/us/lnacademic/results/docview/docview.
    do?docLinkInd=true&risb=21_T6229555849&format=GNBFI&sort=RELEVAN
    CE&startDocNo=1&resultsUrlKey=29_T6229555852&cisb=22

12. Martin, B. (2008). Czech it out; It's the Business. Daily Star. Retrieved April 2,
    2009, http://www.lexisnexis.com.proxy2.cl.msu.edu/us/lnacademic/results/
    docview/docview.do?docLinkInd=true&risb=21_T6229603761&format=GNBFI
    &sort=RELEVANCE&startDocNo=1&resultsUrlKey=29_T6229603765&cisb=22

13. UK firm Tesco buys Kmart shops in Czech Republic and Slovakia. (6 February
    1996). Access Czech Republic Business Bulletin,2. Retrieved March 30, 2009,
    from ABI/INFORM Trade & Industry database.

14. Research and Markets Ltd.; Slovakia Food and Drink Report Q3 2008 - In
    Slovakia, Tesco Is Looking To Open 15 New Stores and Plans to Debut Its
    Convenience Store Format. (2008, October). Food Business Week,74. Retrieved
    March 30, 2009, from Sciences Module database.

15. Hancock, C. (2008, August 22). Tesco Ireland seeks to raise EUR 70m in property
    sell-off. The Irish Times, 1. Retrieved March 28, 2009 from LexisNexis.

16. (1997, March 22). International Briefs; Tesco of Britain to Buy Irish
    Supermarkets. The New York Times, 38. Retrieved March 28, 2009 from
    LexisNexis.

17. McGrath, B. (1997, March 20). Tesco targets Irish supermarket chains in
    Pounds 600m takeover deal. The Irish Times, 1. Retrieved March 28, 2009 from
    LexisNexis.

18. Brennan, C. (2008, April 16). Tesco sales in Ireland increased by almost 10% last
    year. The Irish Times, 23. Retrieved March 28, 2009 from LexisNexis.

19. (1998, December 8). Major store groups close Northern shops. Irish

Independent. Retrieved March 31, 2009 from LexisNexis.

20. Tighe, M., Davey, J. (2007, September 30). Every little helps: Tesco charges Irish 15% extra.. The Sunday Times (London), 1. Retrieved March 28, 2009 from LexisNexis.

21. Blaney, F. (2008, April 16). Tesco set to open 16 new stores as Irish turnover hits k3bn. Daily Mail (London), 4. Retrieved March 28, 2009 from LexisNexis.

22. Zwiebach, E. (2008, March 31). Tesco's International Expertise. Supermarket News, 22. Retrieved March 29, 2009 from LexisNexis.

23. (1998, May 19). Tesco targets Asia through Lotus stake, NATION. Emerging Markets Datafile, NATION. Retrieved March 29, 2009 from LexisNexis.

24. Rungfapaisarn, K. (1998, December 12). Tesco gets aggressive with Lotus. The Nation (Thailand). Retrieved March 30, 2009 from LexisNexis.

25. Yin, L. (1998, May 19). Tesco buys 75% of Thai retail chain for (pound) 200m. Business Times (Singapore). Retrieved March 29, 2009 from LexisNexis.

26. Rungfapaisarn, K. (2000, April 25). Firms see opportunity in Thailand. The Nation (Thailand). Retrieved March 29, 2009 from LexisNexis.

27. Rungfapaisarn, K. (2001, December 26). Tesco chief reshaped retail landscape. The Nation (Thailand). Retrieved March 30, 2009 from LexisNexis.

28. Rungfapaisarn, K. (2002, November 19). Tesco cuts store size, links to community. The Nation (Thailand). Retrieved March 29, 2009 from LexisNexis.

29. Rungfapaisarn, K. (2006, April 15). Hypermarkets scale down, go upcountry. The Nation (Thailand). Retrieved March 30, 2009 from LexisNexis.

30. Pongvutitham, A.(2004, February 6). UK's Tesco to take 100% control of Lotus. The Nation (Thailand). Retrieved March 30, 2009 from LexisNexis.

31. Pratruangkrai, P. (2006, October 5). Tesco Lotus forges ahead with its expansion plans. The Nation (Thailand). Retrieved March 30, 2009 from LexisNexis.

32. (2000, August 19). Tesco speeds up in Taiwan. The Grocer, 12. Retrieved March 31, 2009 from LexisNexis.

33. Farndon, L. (2005, October 1). Tesco quits Taiwan after French rival proves unbeatable. Daily Mail (London), 1. Retrieved March 31, 2009 from LexisNexis.

34. Butler, Sarah. (2005, October 1). Tesco checks out of Taiwan in Carrefour swap. The Times (London), 56. Retrieved March 31, 2009 from LexisNexis.

35. Fletcher, R. (2008). Retail Tesco buys Korean chain for pounds 950m. The Daily

Telegraph (LONDON). Retrieved March 28, 2009,

36.  *TESCO Home plus to modernize stores in South Korea* (2007, September 7). Retrieved April 2, 2009, http://www.fastmoving.co.za/news-archive/international-news/tesco-homeplus-to-modernise-stores-in-south-korea

37.  Tesco turns its gaze on South Korea with 36 new stores. Birmingham Post. Retrieved March 29, 2009, from lexisnexis.com.

38.  *MALAYSIA: Tesco focused on hypermarket growth* (2009, March 11). Retrieved March 27, 2009, http://www.just-food.com/article.aspx?id=105791

39.  Tesco-Japan Co.,LTD. Corporate Info. About Us. Retrieved March 25, 2009, from http://www.tesco-japan.com/eng/aboutus/

40.  Rahman, Bayan. (2004, January 16). Tesco's Japanese shopping without the hype: UK retailer checks out a marriage of convenience, writes Bayan Rahman :[LONDON 1ST EDITION]. Financial Times,p. 28. Retrieved March 25, 2009, from ABI/INFORM Global database.

41.  Tesco PLC: Retailer Seeks to Grow in Japan By Acquiring Stores From Fre'c. (2004, April 28). Wall Street Journal (Eastern Edition), p. 1. Retrieved March 25, 2009, from ABI/INFORM Global database.

42.  Board, Laura. (2003, November). Tesco gobbles up Turkey grocer. The Deal.com,1. Retrieved March 29, 2009, from ABI/INFORM Trade & Industry database.

43.  Tesco steps into Turkey via Kipa. (2003, November). Grocer, 226(7630), 13. Retrieved March 29, 2009, from ABI/INFORM Trade & Industry database.

44.  O'Doherty, John & Rigby, Elizabeth. (2006, December 6). Tesco in no rush but still thinking big and global INTERNATIONAL STAGE :[LONDON 1ST EDITION]. Financial Times,p. 23. Retrieved March 29, 2009, from ABI/INFORM Global database.

45.  Burgess, K., Guerrera, F., & Mcgregor, R. (2004, July 15). Tesco spends Pounds 140m on Chinese partnership:[LONDON 1ST EDITION]. Financial Times, pp. 22. Retrieved March 30, 2009, from ABI/INFORM Global database.

46.  Tieman, R. (12 December 2006). Tesco gains strength in China with store buyout. Knight Ridder Tribune Business News,1. Retrieved March 30, 2009, from ABI/INFORM Dateline database.

47.  Lewis, H. (1 November 2008). Branded foods in China - forecasts to 2013: Mass grocery retail market in China. Just - Food: Branded foods in China - forecasts to 2013: 2008 edition, 15-22. Retrieved March 30, 2009, from ABI/INFORM Global database.

48. Lim, K. (2008, October). Tesco seeks agency for China clothing. Media,2. Retrieved March 30, 2009, from ABI/INFORM Global database.

49. Research and Markets. (February 24, 2009). Insights and implications of Tesco's entry into the U.S. market. Business Wire, Retrieved March 23, 2009, from Lexis-Nexis database.

50. McTaggart, J. (2006, March). Industry awaits Tesco's invasion. Progressive Grocer, 85(4), 8,10. Retrieved March 30, 2009, from ABI/INFORM Global database

51. Wiedemann, L. (2008, August). Fresh & Easy Opens in Point Loma. San Diego Business Journal, 29(33), 3. Retrieved March 29, 2009, from ABI/INFORM Dateline database.

52. Tortola, J. (2008, September). Uneasy transition. Progressive Grocer: Toolbox for Independents, 4-5. Retrieved March 30, 2009, from ABI/INFORM Global database.

53. Tesco Annual Report, 2005

54. Anonymous, (2005). Company Financials. Retrieved November 6, 2007 from Mergent Online Database: http://www.mergentonline.com/compdetail. asp?company=-1&company_mer=8179&type=financials&DataType=AsReporte d&DataPeriod=AnnualsIFRS&DataArea=BS&DataRange=15&Currency=AsRep &Scale=AsRep&Submit=Refresh

# Toys "R" Us

*Jeannine Lyons, Kim Zditosky, Audrey Croswell,*
*Asil Canakci, Julie Sage, Cumali Cetinkaya,*
*Brandye Grant, Brian Monts, Ryan O'dea*

## Toys "R" Us

Toys "R" Us (TRU) is known in the United States as a discount toy store that has been through triumphs and trials. Through hard work and perseverance, the company has grown both nationally and internationally since its beginning in 1948.[12] The success of TRU's expansion is due to the use of different entrance strategies and extensive knowledge of the target markets. In addition, TRU establishes differentiation within the toy market, which is a critical asset to this specialty retailer. With a presence in over 30 countries, TRU is a highly valued company with great expansion strategies and a strong hold on the international toy market.[12]

In this case study, we will focus on how TRU began its international expansion and how it continues to grow as a global specialty retailer. We will go into detail about the history, business strategies and the industry of Toys "R" Us.

# Flow Chart

| | |
|---|---|
| 1948 | Toys R Us is established by Charles Lazarus |
| 1984 | Toys R Us expands internationally to Singapore and Canada |
| 1984 | TRU expands into Saudi Arabia |
| 1985 | TRU expands into The United Kingdom & Hong Kong |
| 1987 | TRU expands into Germany |
| 1989 | TRU expands into France & Austria |
| 1991 | TRU expands into Japan & Spain |
| 1993 | TRU expands into Austrialia, Switzerland, Netherlands & Portugal |
| 1995 | TRU expands Denmark, Sweden & United Arab Emirates |
| 1996 | TRU expands into Malaysia & Turkey |
| 2001 | TRU expands into Egypt |
| 2002 | TRU expands into China |
| 2003 | TRU expands into Norway & Oman |
| 2005 | TRU expands into Thailand |
| 2006 | TRU expands into Findland, Iceland & China |
| 2007 | TRU expands into The Philippines & South Korea |

## History

Charles Lazarus founded Toys "R" Us in 1948.[27] The company's first store opened its doors in 1957; it was a private company until going public in 1978 when it was listed on the NYSE. This was when the company changed its name to Toys "R" Us Inc.[27] Toys "R" Us extended its concept in 1983 and established the new store format; Kids "R" Us. One year later, the first international stores started their operations in Singapore and Canada. In 1996, Toys "R" Us added a new store format known as Babies "R" Us, which is still operating in the US and other countries.[26] In addition, the acquisition of Babystores in 1997 strengthened specialty baby store format.[26] In the following years, the company increased its sales volume and product offering by new acquisitions and the start of e-commerce operations (Imaginarium in

1998; Educational and Learning toys business, SB toys in 2000, RedRocket.com in 2000).[26]

Toys "R" Us outsourced its e-commerce operations to GSI Commerce Inc. and its logistics to Exel in 2006.[27] Recently, the company is trying to increase its private label sales by introducing new store brands. Moreover, it signs agreements with giant companies like Disney and designers like Amy Coe to start up new product lines like its new Halloween costume line in 2008 and a new baby's clothing line. They exited the market in Turkey and Netherlands. However, Toys "R" Us is a global company and continues its international expansion. Its new store format side by side stores and "R" superstores offer a one stop shopping experience to its customers by combining all different formats and products.[18] Today, the company operates 1,559 stores worldwide in different formats which are mostly traditional toy stores (846 domestic stores and 713 international stores).[18] In 22 out of 33 countries, the company has licensees and franchisees.

## Industry Description And Competition

### Market Definition

The toys and games market can be divided into three primary sectors: game consoles, game software and traditional toys and games.[14] Game consoles and software are all the interactive computer entertainment or electronic devices. Traditional toys would include all the rest (dolls, infant/pre-school toys, puzzles...). The traditional toy sector represents the largest percentage share, with 61.8 %. The game console sector accounts for 14.6% and the game software sector for 23.6%.[14]

The global toy and game market is dominated by large global enterprises that are seeking performant economies of scale in order to reduce their costs and enhance profit margins.[14] Competition within the toys and games industry is done through extensive product differentiation. It is a way to lower the threat of rivalry and new entrants in the industry. In addition, it weakens the bargaining power of buyers.[14] The bargaining power of the supplier is generally high in the toy and game industry. In effect, suppliers are generally involved in several stages of production and manufacturing. This establishes a high degree of dependency.[14]

### Market Segmentation

- The traditional toy market generates 61.8% of the global toy and game market's value.

- America's toy and game market accounts for 42.7% of the global toy and game market's value.[13]

## External Analysis

An external analysis can be realized by determining the opportunities and threats of the industry environment that Toys "R" Us faces. A five forces model gives further information concerning the company's position and competitiveness within its industry.

## Opportunities

### Geographic Expansion

US and Japan have become declining markets in the Toys and Games industry. TRU is therefore seeking to reduce its dependency in these markets through international expansion and entrance in other, more profitable countries such as China (first store opened in November 2006). The Chinese market is set to grow strongly over the forecast period. In addition, the single-child policy is favorable to TRU since it privileges massive amount of spending in the Toys and Games industry.[14]

### Increasing Online Sales

TRU entered the online retailing in 1998, with the Internet subsidiary www.toysrus.com and www.babiesrus.com.[14] From 2007 to estimated 2012, online sales in the US are expected to increase at 9.2% average annual growth rate.[14] Online sales offer an extra convenience to customers and improves the company's margins by lowering its operating costs. TRU is therefore well positioned to benefit from the expected growth in online sales.[14]

### Positive Demographic Factors

The number of children in US aged 0-4 years is expected to rise 11% from 2000 to 2010. This is faster than the 9.5% growth in total population. To take advantage of this trend, TRU has increased the number of Babies "R" Us specialty baby-juvenile retail stores in the US up to 260.

With this dedicated infant business division TRU is once again well positioned to meet the customer's satisfaction and needs of the growing infant segment and benefit from the ensuing revenue growth.[14]

### Format Flexibility

TRU is increasingly seeking new store formats, such as Internet retailing and small-size units (such as the Toy Box concept used in Albertson's grocery stores) in order to reduce the year-round costs.[14] Meanwhile, larger store formats can be adjusted to provide a wider range of services (such as entertainment facilities for children's parties), as a way to increase the economy of scope and therefore be more profitable.[14]

## Weaknesses

### Intense Competition

TRU operates in an increasingly competitive retail market. In its industry, TRU competes with mass merchandisers (such as Wal-Mart, Target and Kmart), consumer electronics retailers (such as Best Buy, Circuit City and Gamestop), national and regional chains and local retailers in the geographic areas it serves.[14] Mass merchandisers generally use aggressive pricing policies and enlarged toy-selling areas during the holiday season. Such a fierce competition impacts negatively the operations of TRU in the US. This tendency is also encountered in countries TRU entered, even if the competitors are different.[14]

Amazon opposition – having lost the deal to operate the Internet sales of TRU, amazon.com has relaunched its toys section as well as a baby section. It now offers products from a wide range of manufacturers. It remains to be seen whether Toys "R" Us can build a strong enough online identity to compete with Amazon.[14]

### Weak Consumer Spending in the US

Due to rising unemployment and higher food prices, consumer spending is expected to slow down in domains such as toys and games or travel. Since TRU's financial performance relies on changes in overall economic conditions affecting consumer spending, we can consider it an important threat.[14]

### Reduction in the Value of the Market

Over the 2006-2011 period, the global toy and game market is expected to shrink at a compound annual growth rate of nearly 1 percent as a result of the massive contraction in the US. The massive contraction is expected to create a decline by a CAGR of 7 percent. As a result, TRU is facing a lot of pressure on its domestic market.[14]

### Rising Labor Wages in the US

Lately, labor costs on the US market has been increasing significantly. Several reasons that can explain the tight labor markets are; increased overtime, government regulations and higher proportion of full-time employees or government mandated increases in minimum wages. These overall costs contribute to increases in the company's margin.[14]

**Porter's Five Forces Model**

1.    Threats of new entrants

The Albertsons (*) exclusive distribution agreement in the US may provide the template for future similar agreements with drugstore or supermarket chains. The fierce competition within the toy and game industry makes it unattractive to enter.[13]

2.    Bargaining power of buyers: high

Here, buyers are the end-users, or consumers. In retailing, customers generally have a strong bargaining power.[13] Their satisfaction determines how well a firm does within its industry. In terms of toys and games, buyers tend to be quite price-sensitive. In addition, the competitiveness of the industry lowers the switching cost of consumers.[13]

3.    Bargaining power of suppliers: moderate to high

In order to obtain exclusivity deals on top products, TRU must nurture strong relationships with manufacturers; however, the company also needs to ensure adequate profit margins by negotiating low wholesale prices, which could be a source of possible conflict.[13]

4.    Threats of substitutes: low

Since TRU operates in the three primary sectors: game consoles, game software and traditional toys and games, the threat of substitute products to the toy and game industry is relatively low. However the phenomenon of "kids grow older younger" jeopardizes the toy and game industry since their target may seek other types of entertainment such as hi-tech items.[13]

5.    Rivals within the industry: high

TRU functions within a highly competitive market, with increasing competition from Western companies such as Mothercare or Amazon.com. Also competition comes from mass merchandisers, such as Wal-Mart, Target and Kmart. These companies promote toys and games at a very competitive price, on a discounted basis. During holiday seasons, mass merchandisers offer low prices and sales.[13]

## Competitive Advantages and Business Strategy

With the massive competition that takes place between TRU and its major competitors, it has to have a strong business strategy and numerous competitive advantages that help set it apart and make it both the strong global and multinational market that it is. TRU competes directly in its US market with mass merchandisers such as Wal-Mart, Target and Kmart and with consumer retailers, such as Best Buy, Circuit City and GameStop. It also competes with national and regional retail chains. Within international markets, the company's principal competition is from mass merchandisers, discounters and hypermarkets such as Argos, Woolworths, Carrefour, Auchan, El Corte Inglés, Wal-Mart and Zellers.[14] As the pressure mounts from its competitors, TRU withstands with its more than 1,500 toy and baby stores worldwide offering multiple advantages such as its market leading position, strong vendor relationship, international positioning, increasing online sales, positive demographic factors, format flexibility, increasing year round sales and its new gift card exchange program.

TRU's market position creates an advantage for its company by having a comprehensive range of merchandise. This merchandise varies from toys, plush, games, bicycles, sporting goods, movies, video games, software and electronics, outdoor play equipment, books, educational and development products, clothing, infant and juvenile furniture as well as educational and entertainment computer software for children.[12] With all these products offered it is no wonder TRU holds between 8,000-10,000 products throughout the year, this amount being twice as much than any mass merchandisers or other specialty stores that sell toys within the same industry. To create a strong market position for itself TRU creates a highly recognized brand through many marketing strategies. The company advertises its product range through mass marketing programs, such as catalogues and inserts in local and national newspapers, and also on national television. The emphasis of its advertising campaign is targeted at peak holiday buying periods, such as Christmas, Thanksgiving and Halloween. In-store advertising is also linked to current television campaigns to provide continuity of the message. These advertising campaigns feature the Geoffrey the Giraffe character, described as the "spokesanimal" for the company. Toys "R" Us regularly publishes information about new toy products, usually on a seasonal or holiday basis. As a way of extending its expertise, Toys "R" Us entered an agreement with the Albertsons Inc retail group in 2003, which makes it the exclusive toy provider for some 2,000

Albertsons stores across the US.[12] From the information stated above, TRU's wide product range and extensive store network support the fact that TRU is the largest retailer of toys in the US and Puerto Rico. At the end of 2008, the company owned or operated 1,560 stores, including 585 domestic stores, 715 international stores and 260 baby-children stores.[12] The company also started selling merchandise through the internet in all US divisions, which helps create a stronger market position.

TRU's strong vendor relationships are yet another factor that creates a competitive advantage among its other competitors. The company has approximately 2,100 vendors from which they obtain their vast array of merchandise. For 2007, the company's top 20 vendors worldwide, based on TRU's purchase volume in dollars, represented approximately 40% of the total products it purchased.[12] One strategy that increases TRU's bargaining power and reduces its business risk associated with adverse changes in vendor relationships is the idea of sourcing from multiple vendors. When TRU does this it allows them to not be dependent on only a few vendors. As an advantage of its greater bargaining power, TRU is able to offer its products at competitive prices which are difficult to match, again creating a strong competitive advantage.[12]

TRU's international involvement is spanned largely across numerous countries and contributes largely to the success of this company. TRU's operations are internationally diversified across Japan, Europe (including the UK), Australia and Canada. The company operates 715 international retail stores across 34 foreign countries.[12] With the US economy in a downturn, TRU is taking steps to acknowledge exactly where to focus their brand name. More than ever TRU is looking to not be as dependent on declining markets such as the US and focus on international expansion. Take for example China. TRU expanded into the Chinese market in 2006. This market is set to grow rapidly over the forecast period, with the single-child policy resulting in a generation of well-financed "Little Emperors" controlling a massive amount of spending power.[12] Through expansions such as this, TRU can control its international operations to reduce exposure to the US and protect its brand name. TRU is very competitive in international involvement, creating a stronger brand name globally and giving them an advantage over many other retailers that choose not to expand as aggressively as TRU does.

Selling merchandise through the internet has been increasing at a rapid rate through numerous retailers, including TRU. As stated above, TRU has a company Internet subsidiary entitled Toysrus.com. This subsidiary sells merchandise through the following sites: www.toysrus.com and www.babiesrus.com. TRU can and does grow largely from this convenience to customers because it improves company's margins and cuts the costs of operation expenses. It also makes it a large convenience for TRU's customers to be able to shop online whenever they desire.

Positive demographic factors are also another competitive advantage that help make TRU the large retailer it is today. According to the US Census Bureau, the number of children aged 0-4 years are expected to rise 11% from 2000 to 2010, faster than the 9.5% growth in total population. That percentage favors TRU, considering it operates 260 Babies "R" Us specialty baby-juvenile retail stores in the US.[13] With the information stated above, it's apparent that TRU is supported with a dedicated infant business division. TRU is well positioned to meet the needs of the growing infant segment and benefit from the arising revenue growth, creating a large competitive advantage over other retailers not specializing in baby products.

Format flexibility is a crucial factor that helps create a strong competitive advantage for TRU. The idea of being able to sell TRU's products in other formats other than their large discount stores is something that is very crucial in differentiation (which is a strategy TRU focuses on heavily). With year-round costs of upholding large discount retailers such as TRU, especially in harder economic times, it becomes a struggle to do so at a consistent rate. That is why it is a benefit to have other store formats, such as TRU's internet retailing and small-size units such as the retail concept used in Alberton's grocery stores[13] that can offer the company a chance to reduce its costs. While decreasing the costs in one area, it allows TRU to re-calculate and provide a wider range of services such as entertainment facilities for children's parties.[13]

Increasing year-round sales is another advantage that TRU specializes in. It is yet another factor that helps make it a more unique retailer. With its multiple services, this company can create higher year-round sales and boost their profits. Services such as babiesrus.com baby registry, toysrus.com's Geoffrey's Birthday Club and in-store offers such as hosting birthday parties or baby showers are some that create a unique, enticing image for TRU.[13] These services can help create a wider based consumer network which roots interest and loyalty for the company all throughout the year. This helps set TRU apart from many other toy retailers because it helps keep consumers' interests through out the year and not just during the holiday seasons, where many other retailers in the toy industry succeed.

TRU has a program called the gift card exchange program that allows customers with KB Toys gift cards the chance to take advantage of special savings at TRU stores.[13] This program allows TRU to attract new consumers and expand its growing customer base. Considering KB Toys is one of TRU's major competitors, this is a large step of expansion with the aid of other retailers- a very bold move that other toy retailers would be extremely hesitant of, creating a competitive advantage for TRU.

Another business strategy that is largely implemented within the business of TRU is differentiation. TRU's chairman and CEO, Jerry Storch, believes that the only way for a specialty retailer to compete with discounters is to sell different items than its main competitors. TRU believes that selling products at the same or higher price than its large competing retailers such as Target and Wal-Mart is a losing game when attempting to succeed. Differentiation is the key to success with TRU's company. With more than 1,500 toy and baby stores worldwide, TRU has chosen to take a different step within the toy industry. They are focused on creating a more specialized and distinguished merchandise selection, bringing in a unique product mix on the floor. For example, this past holiday season TRU shelves were stocked with popular toy categories such as music-oriented merchandise and instruments. To add to that, TRU also added its own trend, Pink Play. This included Monopoly Boutique Edition, Twister Pink Edition and Pink Touch Tablet Notebook Computer. Storch believes that they don't need multiple discount chains but a true specialty retailer. To meet this new outlook, TRU is focusing its strategy around the idea of differentiating its offerings. The first step in this long process is fixing TRU's former image, which involved massive clean-up, which included the removal of merchandise from boxes in backroom aisles. The store formatting is one the TRU's main concerns when looking to create a sharper edge. First off, the store is adding specialized features such as stores within the TRU stores. The TRU retailer in Times Square has a Sony store within its store that specializes in high tech products such as digital cameras, laptop computer and even flat-screen televisions. In attempts to create this idea of a cleaner, brighter, well merchandised store, TRU is also straightening store aisles by removing non-linear, X-shaped configurations, which opens the floor space for easier navigation. This idea made customers think that the stores were larger. Creating more room for a larger assortment of products is huge for TRU differentiation strategy. One product line TRU is focusing on is their juvenile merchandise. By going back to its roots, TRU is once again pairing with Babies "R" Us for a combination formula that the company is very optimistic about- this idea creates an accelerating rate for the rollout of large stores. Quoted by the CEO of TRU, "This will certainly be our greatest year of growth Toys "R" Us has seen in a long time, both here in the US and internationally." TRU has four "R" Super Stores now, which hold both toys and juvenile products located in New Jersey, Arizona, California and Florida. These store formats maintain both the expertise in toys and baby products together in an adjacent space. Both of these formats are separated by keeping their own physical space, but are also easy to access from one side of the store to the other. To conclude with the store format, TRU is focused on the "side-by-side" format or the "two-for-one" store which include both Toys "R" Us and Babies "R" Us together. Older TRU retail stores are being re-modeled to include this idea of a smaller-sized prototype of Babies "R" Us within a store- all within a 45,000 square foot box. This is why the slight separation is very crucial, as mentioned above. This strategy minimizes the chances of customers detouring to other competitors, because they have both categories in one store. The largest growth for the near future lies within these stores for TRU, and creates a large competitive advantage to help TRU get ahead.

Toys "R" Us has stated that the principal competitive factors in the toy market are "product variety; quality and availability; price; advertising and promotion; convenience or store location; support and service". The company believes that it competes effectively by offering the broadest range of merchandise and high levels of customer support and service. The seasonal nature of the toy market is reflected in the fact that Toys "R" Us derives more than 40% of its sales (in both its US and international toy businesses), and a substantial portion of operating profits, from the fourth quarter of the year.[14] Toys "R" Us is making substantial strides within its market industry with its strong business strategies and new, evolving competitive advantages that helps set this company apart from others, as it grows and succeeds over time.

## Global Expansion

### Asia Pacific

TRUs first international expansion included Singapore in 1984; the company continued its growth in Asia. The next major move in Asia was to the untapped toy market of Japan.

The interest in moving to Japan began in the late 1980's. The company was challenged when entering this market with barriers such as store-size regulation, application procedures and a long-standing multilayered distribution system.[1] They overcame this challenge by joining with the McDonald's Company Japan to open stores in the country. TRU would have an 80 percent share in all stores opened in the country while McDonald's Japan would own the other 20 percent with the option to have a McDonald's restaurant in the TRU site.[2] United States officials helped the process of opening the first TRU stores in Japan move at a quicker pace by urging Japanese officials to speed the approval process on the application.[2] TRU became a test situation for other large U.S. retailers interested in opening stores in Japan and in 1991 opened their first of the planned 100 stores to be opened in Japan by the end of the decade.[2] To date, TRU has 168 stores in Japan. Other presence in Asia includes China, Hong Kong and Macau, Taiwan,

Thailand, Malaysia and Korea. China and Thailand are newer countries for the TRU company with entrance into the each in 2006 and 2005 respectfully. TRU entered Australia in 1993 and now has 32 TRU stores with two Babies "R" Us stores totaling 34 stores. The newest addition to TRU in the Asia Pacific area was to the Philippines in 2007. The future of TRU in the Asia Pacific area looks strong; the toys and games market in Asia Pacific is forecasted to have a value of $31.3 billion, an increase of 40.8 percent since 2008.[3]

## North America and Puerto Rico

According to United States Securities and Exchange Commission, Toys "R" Us' 2008 annual report states, that this company was incorporated into the United States in 1948, in Delaware. Currently, Toys "R" Us has 846 stores located in the United States including Puerto Rico. Puerto Rico is considered a part of the United States, meaning their financials are already included. As of January 31, 2009, this company operates in 49 states within the United States, Puerto Rico and through its internet sites.[9] The stores that are operated in the U.S. offer on average 8,000 to 10,000 active items all year round. This company has achieved their primary market position mainly due to building a well known brand name and conveying great customer service. With this being said, this specialty retailer has been rewarded for their remarkable performance.

As of the year 2008, this company was rewarded the "specialty retailer of the year" award due to the differentiation from competitors. The strategies that differentiate this company from their competitors help expand and strengthen their business and are enhancing their product offering and adding more exclusive products to their mix. Meaning, products that are offered only with their company will lead to higher margins and cannot be found elsewhere. This modernizes their store properties in the United States to revive their stores and improve the shopping experience, and rearranging their management teams for the toy stores to improve customer service. While Toys "R" Us seeks to differentiate themselves from competitors they are focused on a number of core areas, including product selection, product presentation, service, in-store experience, and marketing. Toys "R" Us trys to stand out from their competitors without losing the concentration on their target market which is grandparents and parents making toy and youthful purchases for children. This company has an all around focus on how to keep their existing customers satisfied and how to entice new ones even though it may mean minimizing unprofitable locations.

In the past two years, Toys "R" Us has closed 86 locations in the United States. This was for the better because they were looking to expand stores to superstores to lure in more customers so it would be more convenient for them to shop at one location instead of driving from store to store because not every Toys "R" Us is near a Babies "R" Us.[8] Toys "R" Us considers this as a weakness compared to their competition such as Target and Wal-Mart because mothers visit those stores on a regular basis and Toys "R" Us is not visited as often. They decided to combine the two stores to bring in more traffic. Toys "R" Us is making progress domestically and internationally on giving the customers a one-stop shopping experience. Having a new strategy for the company is what brought this expansion into the U.S. Given the economic conditions, pushing this integrated strategy will cost less by combining "R" superstore formats and side-by-side formats. Another method that helped the growth of this company is that they placed advanced orders on the most popular items such as Walt Disney's Hannah Montana dolls and Nintendo's Wii videogame systems. Not all customers can afford to buy expensive items due to the United States customer's spending decreasing so Toys "R" Us created a strategy that would reach out to all parents.

According to Lexis-Nexis, due to the recession existing in the United States, Toys "R" Us has adjusted to customer spending by seeking opportunities such as offering a $1-3 dollar fun section in the locations for those customers that cannot afford to make large purchases. The products are offered with themes such as dinosaurs, games, princess dress-up accessories, musical instruments and art supplies.

One of Toys "R" Us wholly owned operations is located in Canada. The company expanded into Canada in 1986, They now have 68 stores and 2,500 employees within the country.[6] A typical international store carries approximately 8,500 active items all year round.[9] The strategies that are used in the domestic stores are very similar to strategies used in Canada. Recent global growth has resulted in increased customer traffic, especially in combination with their integrated store format strategy. Toys "R" Us presents their international customers with a one-stop shopping environment and provide an immense product assortment unrivaled by their competitors through their "R" Us branded stores and through the Internet.[10]

## Africa

Toys "R" Us first expanded into Africa in 1997 opening 6 franchise stores in South Africa.[21] They also opened their first store in Egypt in 2001.[22] Since then they have opened one more store in Egypt and several more in South Africa to bring a total of 25 stores. The culture in Africa is quite different from the United States. Out of all the countries in Africa, South Africa has one of the most similar cultures compared to the United States. This is a good reason why they chose to open several stores there and not in many other countries. They chose to franchise and use dormant management which is a good tactic because the people of Africa know how to run a business in Africa the best.

## Europe

Toys "R" Us expanded their company into Europe in 1987. The countries that Toys "R" Us currently operates in are Germany, Spain, France, Netherlands, Austria, Denmark, Sweden, Portugal, Norway, Switzerland, Finland, Iceland and the United Kingdom. Toys "R" Us first expanded into Germany in 1987 and there are currently 58 stores in operation today, which may be the reason why Germany has the largest amount of stores in operation today.[28] Nearly two years later they expanded into France in 1989, then the Netherlands and Portugal in 1993. In 1995 Denmark was added to Toys "R" Us' expansion plan.[29] Throughout the century they continued their expansion into Europe and appealed to their target market by designing toys that they sell to their market's cultural background. For example in Germany Toys "R" Us stores sell wooden toys which have been found to attract many buyers.[28] The last country to be added to the Toys "R" Us Europe was Finland, the company continues to expand into Europe and assimilate their toys into the European culture today.[29]

## Questions

**1.   Is the retailer classified as a global retailer or a multinational retailer? Explain its pattern of expansion. What expansion strategy did/is the retailer use/using?**

*TRU is classified as a global retailer. In general, when TRU enters a new country they open stores in heavily populated areas or capital cities. They do not saturate the market before moving on to a new country. TRU uses subsidiaries, licensing or franchising when entering into a new market. For all these reasons they are considered a global retailer, but TRU also considers themselves multi-national in that they take a percentage of inventory in their foreign stores and focus it towards the local consumer.*

**2.   Based on Dunning's eclectic theory, how do ownership, locational and internalization factors play in your retailers' international expansion?**

*TRU uses multiple ways of expansion into international countries. These include franchising, which shows that internalization does not play a large role in the process of expansion. This is true because with franchising internal secrets are passed on to the management running the stores in the foreign countries. When talking about ownership advantage, TRU is beginning to have asset-based advantages with the addition of Pink Play, a line of pink edition products that works with different suppliers such as Monopoly and Twister to differentiate products from other toy* retailers. TRU also offers toy exclusives on its website, Toysrus.com. TRU is not affected by locational factors such as market pull or psychic distance because TRU is a global retailer they focus on entering world cities where customers are essentially the same in all markets and are not moved to enter because of economic development.

### 3. What role does cultural proximity and geographical proximity play in the retailers' international moves?

Geographic proximity is not a factor is TRU's expansion. TRUs first expansion was to Canada and Singapore, Singapore being on the other side of the globe, the proximity to its counterparts in the U.S. and Canada are very large and not a factor in expansion even with TRU being a centralized retailer. Because of TRUs classification as a global retailer and its entrance into major cities around the world, it is shown that cultural proximity is not extremely important for TRU because they focus on a similar consumer in all markets entered.

### 4. Can you predict the retailer's future international expansion?

Toys "R" Us' international division is growing every day. They already have stores in over 34 countries worldwide. They are the world's largest toy retailer and future plans for international expansion seem promising. Just like any retailer Toys "R" Us likes to expand into untapped markets where the company can be successful. They also franchise their stores into countries and buyout already existing toy stores. It is hard to say exactly where they will expand next, but the environment of the area must fit their expansion plan. Toys "R" Us wants to expand into countries with little political barriers, low competition from existing retailers, and low real estate costs. Though these characteristics would help expansion be successful, Toys "R" Us has said that many of their challenges in international expansion have come internally. Some internal challenges they have faced are misjudgments in finance systems, product selection, marketing and management selection.[4] Toys "R" Us will most likely close several international stores due to the lack of sales and profits, and also the large amount of debt they have obtained. In the past month they have ended their franchise deal with the Netherlands and have that country.[5] This could be the future for other countries where sales have been falling. In the future, Toys "R" Us will continue their strategy of opening stores in promising markets and closing stores that are lacking sales and hurting the company.

## Propositions Related to Ownership Advantages

**P1: The greater the ownership advantages for retailers, the less likely they will franchise or license.**

Toys "R" Us is not a company that holds many secrets nor are they willing to *expand internationally with licensees and franchisees in addition to their wholly owned operations like they have in the United Kingdom and Canada.[11] Toys "R" Us preferred expanding internationally very rapidly and did not want to miss out on the opportunities in other countries. Since their idea was unique but not their operation, they acted quickly and watched colonizing as a concept. Being a global company and having the opportunity to optimize their scale of operations as well as expanding their mixture of operations to reduce cost and increasing their efficiency worked well for Toys "R" Us and helped them expand internationally in early 1980.[11]*

**P2: The greater the available organizational slack the greater the likelihood of expanding internationally.**

*In the three years before Toys R Us expanded into Canada and Singapore in 1984, their ratio of current assets to current liabilities were (in millions);*

| Years | 1981 | 1982 | 1983 |
|---|---|---|---|
| **Current Assets** | $ 209,452 | $ 282,394 | $ 344,679 |
| **Current Liabilities** | $ 118,027 | $ 145,394 | $ 187,274 |
| **Ratio in between** | 1.77 | 1.94 | 1.84 |

Their Average of three years = 1.84 + 1.94 + 1.77 = 1.85[17]

*It is a fact that the more invested in a company; the more it will give back in return. It is like a snowball that starts rolling down the hill. It starts off small, and keeps building until it becomes huge. Many well established businesses have to face the matter of finding where to invest their excess money so that it will provide more revenue. Also, many companies seem to invest their money to gain the most. While investing in their current company, they are opening other stores in the main country or expanding internationally, like Toys "R" Us. After investing their current assets, their current liability ratio grew 1.85 in the 3 year average before their first international expansion. Their first international expansion was in Canada in the Greater Toronto Area when they opened four of their typical 45,000-sq.-ft. stores and a 150,000-sq.-ft. distribution center and business offices.[11]*

*In the early stages of the international expansion strategy, they acquired whole ownership within the country of entry. Now, they prefer expanding by franchisees and licensees because they did not want to risk as much assets, and they could expand at a much more rapid pace.*

**P3:The greater the recoverable slack the greater the likelihood of expanding internationally.**

*In the 3 years before the expansion of Toys R Us into Canada and Singapore in 1984, the ratio of percent of General and Administrative Expenses to sales was (in millions);*

| Year | 1981 | 1982 | 1983 |
|---|---|---|---|
| Expenses | $ 131,430 | $ 166,930 | $206,378 |
| Sales | $ 597,332 | $ 783,285 | $ 1,041,735 |
| Ratio Percent | 22.00% | 21.31% | 19.81% |

The Average of 3 years = 21.04%[17]

*The ratio went from 22 to 21 to 19 so this proposition is not true. The more capital available to cover the expenses the better for the company. Moreover, it is best to have smaller expenses over sales ratio. To provide this circumstance, it is necessary to expand with a current country. If expanding internationally it is best to read the cost of expenses in between more stores and get the more sales from the greater number of stores. This would affect the volume of expenses and it would have a smaller share of the pie as long as the sales keep increasing within the increasing number of stores, while expenses could be kept under control. As a result of this situation the ratio in between the sales and expenses would keep decreasing, which means expenses would not be as noticeable, which is something the shareholders would like to see as their investments grow.*

**P4.The greater the potential slack the greater the likelihood of expanding internationally.**

*Being unable to access or find annual reports for the three years previous to TRU's first international expansion, we will look at their entrance into China in 2006. The three years before this expansion, TRU's ratio of equity to capital was (in millions) 4,325/1,806 or 2.39 in 2005, 3,974/1,865 or 2.13 in 2004, and 3,815/1,185 or 3.22 in 2003, making a three year average of 2.58.[18]*

*Potential slack is a main concern for all companies. Most companies rely on their stockholders to help fund expansion into new markets and in turn know that they have to produce profits to keep their stockholders equity in good standing. Also, showing continous profit and gaining more equity will appeal to future and potential stockholders, the investments a company like TRU needs to continue expansion. By successfully expanding to new international markets, TRU is showing that not only are they obtaining more sales, but they are also becoming the major toy retailer in* most markets they enter. *This is an asset that most investors want to know before becoming a stockholder in a company. If a company is content with their position in a certain market and has no intentions of growing or expanding, possible investors may be deterred by this simplicity. It shows to investors that the owner(s) is/are pleased with its profitability and do not plan on gaining more profit. Toys R Us is always looking for opportunities to expand into foreign markets and maintain the most profits possible for its company. Since their first expansion into Canada in 1984, TRU has continued their dominance in foreign markets and has continued to show profits to please their stockholders. TRU knows the importance of pleasing its owners and current stockholders, as well as the need to intrigue future investors with their positive equity.*

### P13. Global companies will move to the largest/capital cities in a country.

*TRU's first entrance into international business started with its movement in 1984 into largely populated areas in the countries; Canada, UK, Singapore, and Hong Kong.*[23] *In October 2005, the royal family of Dubai paid $101 million for a suburban shopping mall in Rostock with tenants including a Toys "R" Us and a McDonald's.*[24] *TRU has a vision to enter areas that are highly populated with both money and families. Large cities are the places with the highest populations, and major specialty retailers like TRU need to be located in such areas. This proposition does not fit our retailer.*

### P14. Global companies will not be attracted by population size, income, cultural proximity or geographical proximity.

*The reason for expansion for any business is to gain a market share and obtain a profit. TRU, as stated in the previous proposition, concentrates its store near large populations. It is obvious that TRU relies on the most dominated areas for their stores to succeed. TRU started in Seattle, Washington, and now its largest store is located in New York City, New York. This can be attributed to the vast population in this city. As for international expansion, one of its first locations was in Hong Kong, a country that has the second largest retail spending in the world. TRU knew the need for their store in these large cities and they found the means to enter a market. They did not limit themselves to wholly owned stores in the foreign markets, they found it necessary to establish presence through franchises and licenses.*

### P15: The greater the asset based ownership advantages of a global retailer, the more likely they are to franchise.

*Asset- based ownership advantages of a retailer are patents, unique products and* other tangible assets that differentiate the company from its competitors. Toys "R" Us preferred to franchise in the countries where there are different business climates and risks.[18] They preferred to wholly own their stores even though in most of the countries (23 out of 32 countries) they have franchises. Toys "R" Us have proportionately higher private label or exclusively licensed product offerings, which means they have great asset based ownership.[18] Even though this makes a franchising offer of Toys "R" Us more attractive, they prefer to franchise primarily based on business climate of the host country and risk factors.

**P16: The greater the transaction based ownership advantages of a global retailer, the less likely they are to franchise.**

Transaction based ownership advantages of a retailer are the knowledge of internationalization, know-how and intangible assets that are difficult to transfer. A company which has great transaction based ownership might not want to franchise so as to protect its know how and secrets of operation. Toys R Us is a company that franchises in the most of its host countries and it doesn't consider transaction-based ownership as a criterion to choose its ownership format in the host countries. Its operations are very transparent and as in the case of South Korea, they let franchisees adopt its product offering up to the host countries culture and customer wants.[19] Despite its format selection criteria, Toys "R" Us prefers to own its stores in stable economies, which would avoid giving away its know-how.

**P17: The greater the available organizational slack the greater the likelihood that global retailers will reacquire international franchisees.**

As of today, Toys "R" Us hasn't reacquired any of its franchisees stores. Perhaps it would have been better for the company to reacquire some because of the incident that occurred between Toys "R" Us and their Turkish licensee. After their 12 years of agreement, the Turkish licensee told Toys "R" Us that they were going to stay in the same industry but with their own brand, Toyiki.[20]

**P18: The greater the recoverable slack the greater the likelihood that global retailers will reacquire international franchisees.**

*[Ratio of General and Administrative Expenses to Sales (3 year average before they begin reacquisition)]*

Sales and General and Administrative expenses continue to grow over the years, but sales are growing at a slower rate. This means that the ratio continues to increase, therefore recoverable slack gets bigger every year. This gives the retailer a window of opportunity to use this extra money to reinvest back into the company.

If Toys "R" Us wanted to reduce expenses, they could do this by reacquiring their international franchises. In short term this would have a big effect, but for long term it could be a good strategy to reduce expenses.

|  | 2008 | 2007 | 2006 |
|---|---|---|---|
| Net Sales | $13,724 | $ 13,794 | $ 13,050 |
| SGA Expenses | 3,856 | 3,801 | 3,506 |
| Ratio | .28 | .2755 | .268 |

**P19: The greater the potential slack the greater the likelihood that global retailers will reacquire international franchisees.**

*[Ratio of Equity to Capital (3 year average before they begin reacquisition)]*

*If Toys "R" Us has the possibility of gaining more slack then they have a bigger possibility of reinvesting that money into the company and expanding. By reacquiring their international franchises they would gain back control of the operational procedures of the stores. Since most of the international stores that Toys "R" Us has opened are franchises it could reduce their expenses to reacquire those stores. Toys "R" Us is currently in a state where their equity is in a deficit. This would be a problem for Toys "R" Us to reacquire their stores. They would want to wipe out all of their debt and reduce the amount of potential slack before reacquiring these franchises.*

|  | 2008 | 2007 | 2006 |
|---|---|---|---|
| Capital | 8,411 | 8,952 | 8,295 |
| Equity | (389) | (675) | (724) |
| Ratio | .046 | .075 | .87 |

**Endnotes**

1.    Spar, D., (1995) Toys "R" Us Japan (Electronic Version). Harvard Business Publishing, 9-796-077 http://harvardbusinessonline.hbsp.harvard.edu/b02/en/common/item_detail.jhtml;jsessionid=HPDNUQL15XHGMAKRGWDR5VQB KE0YIISW?id=796077

2.    Toys "R" Us, Inc. - Company Profile, Information, Business Description, History, Background Information on Toys "R" Us, Inc. http://www.referenceforbusiness.

com/history2/2/Toys-R-Us-Inc.html

3.  Toys & Games in Asia- Pacific: INDUSTRY PROFILE Reference Code: 0200-0778 Publication date: December 2008

4.  Findarticles.com

5.  Playthings.com

6.  Spensieri Emily. (March 13, 2009). Toys"R"Us, Canada opens new store in Mississauga.Canada NewsWire. Retrieved April 6, 2009, from Lexis- Nexis database.

7.  Anonymous. (Dec. 8, 2008) Specialty Retailer of the Year Toys'R'Us. Retailing Today. Retrieved April 1, 2009, from ProQuest database.

8.  Pereira Joseph. (May 22, 2008). Toys 'R' Us Unwraps Plans for Expansion; Company Bets Pairing With Baby-Ware Chain Will Lure More Shoppers. Wall Street Journal. Retrieved March 28, 2009, from ProQuest database.

9.  United States Securities & Exchange Commission. ( March 31, 2009).10-K Toys "R" Us Annual Report Ending January 31, 2009. Retrieved on April 3, 2008, from http://phx.corporate-ir.net/phoenix.zhtml?c=120622&p=irol-sec

10. United States Securities & Exchange Commission. ( February 3, 2007).10-K Toys "R" Us Annual Report Ending February 3, 2007. Retrieved on April 3, 2008, from Mergent Online database.

11. Moroz, Y. (2008). Toys R Us: Back In Growth Mode Comps Bode Well for Future (electronic version). 1-2.

12. Market Line, Datamonitor, *Toys «R» Us, Inc.* (June 2007)http:// www.marketlineinfo.com.proxy2.cl.msu.edu/library/DisplayContent aspx?R=E07857C1-BCAF-48B6-8716-34C0569D04B8&N=4294834595

13. Global Marketing Information Database, Euromonitor International, *Toys «R» Us Inc.-Retailing-World.* http://www.portal.euromonitor.com.proxy2.cl.msu.edu/ passport/ResultsList.aspx

14. Market Line, Datamonitor, *Global Toys&Games- Industry profile* (December 2008)Reference Code: 0199-0778 http://www.marketlineinfo.com.proxy2.cl.msu. edu/library/DisplayContent.aspx?Ntt=toys&N=210&Ntx=mode%2bmatchall&N ty=1&D=toys&Ntk=All&Ns=

15. ProQuest http://proquest.umi.com.proxy2.cl.msu.edu/pqdweb?index=1&did=15 78349661&SrchMode=1&sid=7&Fmt=3&VInst=PROD&VType=PQD&RQT=3 09&VName=PQD&TS=1238180522&clientId=3552

16. http://www5.toysrus.com/our/intl/

17. Hanson, Robert (1982). Moody's Industrial Manual. New York, NY: The Dun & Redstreet Corporation.

18. Toys R Us Inc. (2009) Annual Report. Retrieved April 6, 2009, from http://www. sec.gov/Archives/edgar/data/1005414/000095012309005856/y75530e10vk.htm

19. Ihlwan, Moon (2008, 05, 20). Why Toys 'R' Us, Tesco Are Hits in Korea. BusinessWeek, Retrieved 04/06/2009, from http://www.businessweek.com/ globalbiz/content/may2008/gb20080520_130610_page_2.htm

20. Toys R Us Don't Have Any Input on Our Business, We'll Continue With Our Brand "Toyiki". (2008,03,26). SABAH, p. Economy, Retrieved 04/06/2009, from http://arsiv.sabah.com.tr/2008/03/26/haber,6EAD44541F694BA79358CDE48393 631A.html

21. Toys R Us. (1997) Annual Report 1997, Retrieved from Mergent Online Database

22. Toys R Us. (2001) 2001 Annual Report, Retrieved from Mergent Online Database

23. 2006 Annual Report. Toys R Us Inc, Retrieved April 2, 2009, from Mergent database.

24. Christine, H., & Edward, T. (2006, February 15). Now on Sale: Real Estate In Germany; Europe's Largest Economy   Attracts International Bargain Hunters Hoping to Buy at   Bottom of Cycle. Retrieved May 3, 2009, from proquest.umi.com.proxy1.cl.msu.edu/pqdweb?index=0&did=986963291&SrchM ode=1&  sid=2&Fmt=3&VInst=PROD&VType=PQD&RQT=309&VName=PQ D&TS=12388227   35&clientId=355

25. Mark, M., Dori, Y., & Amy, D. (1987, January 26). Toys 'R' Us Goes Overseas -- And Finds That Toys 'R' Them, Too. Retrieved May 3, 2009, from proquest.umi.com.proxy1.cl.msu.edu/pqdweb?index=2&did=890996&SrchMode

26. Mergent, (2009). Mergent Online. Retrieved April 7, 2009, from www. mergentonline.co Website: http://www.mergentonline.com.proxy1.cl.msu.edu/ compdetail.asp?company=10451&Page=history (Mergent, 2009)

27. Datamonitor, (2009,02,02). Business Complete. Retrieved April 7, 2009, from http://web.ebscohost.com.proxy1.cl.msu.edu/ehost/detail?vid=4&hid=115&sid= fdc83b8c-103b-460b-b269-17a9b4ee9306%40sessionmgr102&bdata=JnNpdGU 9ZWhvc3QtbGl2ZQ%3d%3d#db=bth&authdb=dmhls&AN=E07857C1-BCAF- 48B6-8716-34C0569D04B8

28. http://www.marketlineinfo.com.proxy1.cl.msu.edu/library/iProduct_product. aspx?R=E07857C1-BCAF-48B6-8716-34C0569D04B8&s=IDATTQNB

29.  http://www.fundinguniverse.com/company-histories/Toys-R-Us-Inc-Company-History.html

# Uniqlo, Co., Ltd.

*Meaghan Lee Dalton & Anna Fisher*

## Uniqlo, Co., Ltd.

Uniqlo Co., Ltd., the Japanese clothing retailer, is fast fashion's next superstar. The company is redefining what it means to produce fast fashion with cheap-chic basics that value high quality over excessive trend. Uniqlo's garments remain relevant in the marketplace with elements of style, but being the trendiest in the industry is not the retailer's foremost focus. Rather, the retailer places greater emphasis on the creation of superior products, such as its revolutionary HEATTECH fabric, to help change the consumer's lifestyle, not just his or her image. In addition to the advantage provided by its innovative private label merchandise, Uniqlo has been able to achieve its rapidly growing success within the apparel industry through a number of other transaction-based advantages. The clothier's distinctive methods of production, strict quality control over production, and execution of a no-logo branding strategy all contribute to Unqilo's success. Along with the company's ability to learn quickly from its past experiences, Uniqlo maintains the ability to complete its transformation into a leading global retailer. Its expansion throughout the world to major cities will allow fashion, budget, and quality conscious consumers of all ages to find their ideal product in Uniqlo's assortment.

## Flow Chart

1984:   Japan (799 Direct-Run Stores, 20 Franchise Stores)
2001:   United Kingdom (15 Stores)
2002:   China (58 Stores)
2005:   Hong Kong (13 Stores)
        South Korea (52 Stores)
2006:   United States (1 Store)
2007:   France (2 Stores)
2008:   Singapore (3 Stores)
2010:   Taiwan (1 Store)
        Russia (1 Store)
        Malaysia (1 Store)

## Company Overview

Fast Retailing Co., Ltd., the parent company of Uniqlo Co., Ltd., was established in May of 1963 as Ogori Shoji Co., Ltd (the company would adopt its current moniker in 1991).[1] Unique Clothing Warehouse, later shortened to Uniqlo, opened in Hiroshima City in 1984, operating as a retailer of casual apparel for both men and women.[2] Over the course of its 47 year history, Fast Retailing has morphed into a portfolio of specialty apparel brands, including Uniqlo, Comptoir des Cotonniers, Princesse tam-tam, g.u., Cabin (carrying the brands Zazie and enraciné), and Theory.[3] With more than 85% of the group's earnings coming from its retailer hawking innovative basics, Fast Retailing owes its success story to its Uniqlo brand.[4]

After obtaining control of the company founded by his parents, Uniqlo's current President and CEO, Tadashi Yanai, studied the business model used by the successful American retailer, Gap. In 1998, the Chairman subsequently opened the first downtown outlet in Tokyo, on the same street as the Gap's Japanese flagship store, initiating a discount battle and indicating his future plans to become one of the retailer's biggest competitors.[5]

Tadashi Yanai's hard-driving perfectionist management and invariable goal to turn Uniqlo into a global brand has helped provide Japanese retailing with a new reputation.[6] The brand of casual, basic clothing symbolizes a novel variety of globally minded, entrepreneurial companies in Japan. Setting the company apart is its continued success during the global financial crisis.[7] In reality, the retailer owes a great deal of its success to the economic downturn which highlighted the appeal of the reasonably priced basics brand to an ever-growing market of price-conscious consumers.

In its home market of Japan, Uniqlo is known for a cheap, democratic image. As a discount-oriented retailer focused on pushing volume through its stores, slashing prices and distributing sales flyers via newspapers is common practice.[8] The retailer works to differentiate itself, however, from other merchants of fast fashion such as H&M, Zara, and Forever 21 through its innovative retail concepts, high-quality products, unique production strategy, and aggressive growth plans.

Through Uniqlo's production of apparel basics of a high quality, Tadashi Yanai is attempting to utilize truly great clothing to change the world.[9] The retailer achieves this goal through the use of its SPA (Specialty store retailer of Private label Apparel) business model, which allows for "control of the entire business process, from planning and design to material and procurement sales".[10] Along with Uniqlo's private label strategy, the company's innovative endeavors, precise inventory control, and accommodating manufacturing model facilitates the retailer's production of superior affordable clothing. Co-Chief Operating Officer of Uniqlo USA said of the company's unique method, "We approach clothes as an industrial product. We figured that since Japan is good at making things like cars and electronics, we should use that knowledge."[11]

Despite Uniqlo's competitive advantages and its history of success, recent uneven sales performance and the retailer's announcement of its first annual profit decline in four business years has peaked the concern of some investors.[12] The troubling profit forecast, however, should be viewed in the context of the company's recent strong performance (especially overseas) along with its healthy operating margins.[13] In truth, the volatile demand spurred by the apparel business lends itself to these types of ebbs and flows in a clothing retailer's business. What remains relevant is the fact that Uniqlo maintains the ability to learn from its setbacks. Moreover, the company's solid business strategy and Tadashi Yanai's forthright analysis of Uniqlo's challenges allows the company to remain a good bet.[14]

## International Expansion

For the past 26 years, Uniqlo has operated as a retailer of casual, value-driven apparel in its home market of Japan, becoming one of the country's fastest growing companies.[15] Hiroshima City, in Western Japan, was home to the first Uniqlo store in 1984, followed by the opening of multiple suburban roadside stores, positioning the retailer as Japan's top casual wear chain by 1997. Within the next year, the retailer gained popularity in urban areas such as Tokyo and Osaka, with a store opening in the trendy Harijuku district in Japan's capital city. The early years of the millennium witnessed the opening of the UNIQLO Design Studio and the development of large-format stores (at least 17,760 square feet). In 2005, Uniqlo embarked on the use of franchises to continue expansion within its home market. Through the use of a unique franchise formula, passionate employees are provided with the opportunity to operate their own Uniqlo stores. Unlike many other franchise methods, the franchisee must be experienced, with more than 10 years of service at the company and management experience at multiple Uniqlo outlets.[16] The use of a formula with such specific requirements indicates evidence of the Agency Theory as reasoning behind Uniqlo's decision to franchise. This theory predicts that individuals who own their own stores will likely perform at a higher level than hired managers and is characterized by a lack of reacquisition of the franchised outlets.[17] Since the start of its franchise operations, Uniqlo has not reacquired the shops, signaling use of the Agency Theory. The global retailer began this method of expansion following the implementation of an in-house system to oversee inventories and finances at each shop, standardizing the way in which the Uniqlo business is conducted.[18] More recently, the retailer initiated the use of concessions to grow within its home market through the opening of a Uniqlo shops inside the Takashimaya department store in Tokyo's Shinjuku district and in two branches of Sogo department store. This method is aimed at benefitting both the specialty and department store retailers. Uniqlo is able to utilize the department store's reputation to increase sales in a saturated market, while the department store gains profits as a kind of real estate company as it struggles to remain competitive.[19] As of 2010, the company has mushroomed into a total of 819 stores throughout Japan, 799 of which are direct-run and the other 20 function as franchise operations.[20]

Uniqlo began international diffusion of its cheap-chic brand in 2001 with the opening of its first store in the United Kingdom on London's Brompton Road. The Japanese retailer hoped to create a new class of British retailing; well-designed, casual basics that form the cornerstone of any wardrobe. In an increasingly fragmented market, consumers of British high street fashion, often fail to respond to a mass-market approach.[21] As such, despite the initial frenzy of interest in the retailer, Uniqlo suffered serious losses and disappointing sales within 18 months of its arrival in the UK, prompting the closing of 18 stores. High rents and sizeable staffing costs, along with the retailer's struggle to differentiate itself from rivals such as Gap, Zara, and H&M contributed to Uniqlo's difficulties in its first international market experience. Its attempts at decentralized management also failed for the global merchant, resulting in the control of remaining UK operations being returned to the head office in Japan.[22] In 2007, however, Uniqlo demonstrated its distinctive ability to learn from its mistakes with the launch of a flagship store on Oxford Street in London. Tadashi Yanai noted the company's failure to perfect the offer before building a network of stores in the United Kingdom. Prior to reopening new units, the sizing and the cut of the garments were modified for the European market.[23] Similar to Uniqlo's expansion in Japan, the retailer chose to open a concession shop in the UK's famed Selfridges department store in 2009. The relatively small space (1,000 square feet) will be home to the premium menswear collections and its opening will coincide with Selfridges' 100th anniversary.[24] Utilizing concessions is likely an attempt by Uniqlo to benefit from the department store's first-class reputation in order to gain share in the previously hesitant UK market. The company currently (as of 2010) boasts 15 stores in the United Kingdom, all of which are 100% consolidated subsidiaries.[25]

Following its rush of openings in the United Kingdom, Uniqlo entered the Chinese market in 2002 with the opening of its first store in Shanghai. At present, Uniqlo aspires for China to be the retailer's biggest market and the best-selling brand within the country. As the retailer's manufacturing center, China represents a region of incredible importance to the Japanese company. In 2010, Uniqlo opened a 39,000 square foot flagship store on Nanjing West Road, a luxury shopping avenue in Shanghai. The new store represents its first flagship store in Asia and the fourth in the world after New York, Paris, and London. Plans for a second flagship store in Beijing are also in the works.[26] As of 2010, the company operates 58 stores in China, all of which are 100% consolidated subsidiaries.[27]

A few years after its expansion to China, Uniqlo entered the country's special administrative region (SAR), Hong Kong, in 2005. The store opened in the Miramar Shopping Center in Tsim Sha Tsui, one of Hong Kong's busiest downtown shopping districts. Over the past five years, the retailer has steadily and organically increased its store count in the city to a total of 13, each claimed as a 100% consolidated subsidiary.[28] Throughout its time in the market, Uniqlo Hong Kong, Ltd. has experienced outstanding operating efficiency and high sales per store. Consumers have responded well to the +J collection, the result of a cooperative venture with German designer Jil Sander.[29]

In the same year that Uniqlo chose to expand in Hong Kong, the retailer also utilized a method of expansion new to the company by entering into a joint venture with Lotte Shopping Co. Ltd., South Korea's largest retailing enterprise. The venture lead to the opening of Uniqlo shops in Lotte department stores and Lotte Marts, as well as the launch of a large-format store in the Myong Dong district of Seoul.[30] As a *chaebol*, or a large, conglomerate family-controlled business group, Lotte exists as one of three major players in the highly concentrated Korean retail market.[31] Entering into such an environment as a foreign retailer would likely make obtaining any percent of market share immensely challenging. As a result, FRL Korea Co., Ltd., the new entity formed by the two Asian retailers, will allow Uniqlo to utilize Lotte's brand recognition and reputation to secure a stable share in the Korean market. FRL Korea Co., Ltd. exists as 51.0% consolidated subsidiary in Uniqlo's portfolio with 52 stores open in the country as of 2010.[32] The company largely owes its swift expansion throughout South Korea to its SPA (private label) business model, which allows Uniqlo to produce and exclusively sell its own clothing.[33] For a market in which consumers are notorious for being incredibly demanding and trend-conscious, maintaining control over the design and production of Uniqlo's inventory exists as a crucial advantage for the retailer.[34]

Uniqlo made its American debut in 2006 when it entered the US market through the opening of three stores in New Jersey.[35] Later that year, the retailer debuted its first global flagship store in New York City's Soho neighborhood. The original US Uniqlo stores were subsequently closed in April of 2007.[36] Alternatively, Soho, a breeding ground for youth fashion, provided a prime location for the cheap-chic retailer, with Uniqlo obtaining one of the highest levels of sales in the district. Cashmere sweaters, merino wool sweaters, denim wear, print T-shirts, and polo shirts, the traditional foundation of specialty basic apparel, has yielded the highest sales in the retailer's US location.[37] Uniqlo's foray into the world's largest retail market with the launch of its 36,000 square foot flagship store was a crucial move in the retailer's goal to finagle a takeover of the Gap, the American retailer that the Japanese company's model emulates.[38] To aid this endeavor, a second US global flagship store to open on New York City's 5th Avenue is in the works. Meanwhile, Uniqlo maintains one store in the United States, operated as a 100% consolidated subsidiary.[39]

Two years after its debut in the western hemisphere, Uniqlo refocused its efforts on European expansion with the opening of a compact "concept shop" (2153 square feet) in the Parisian suburb of La Defense. Perhaps in an attempt to learn from its troubling, premier European market entry into the UK, the retailer utilized the small store in order to communicate Uniqlo's brand message to the intensely fashion-conscious French consumer.[40] Despite the retailer's desires to open a flagship shortly after the concept outlet, Uniqlo encountered France's tough regulation laws and authorization took longer than expected. *Roi Loyer*, the French retail planning law, requires retailers, especially foreign discounters, to obtain a permit in order to open a store within the country.[41] After obtaining permission from the government, Uniqlo unveiled its third flagship store in 2009. The shop has been dubbed the "Paris Opera Store" for its strategic location next to the Garnier Opera house in the center of a busy tourist and shopping district that is also boasts the famed French department stores Galeries Lafayette and Printemps.[42] Given that nearly 75% of France's population live in urban areas, with 9.3 million people in Paris, the capital city is also likely the best location for the retailer to obtain recognition among French consumers. Moreover, specialty chains are stealing the traditional department store's market share due to their ability to address the distinct French lifestyle, creating a promising environment for Uniqlo's further expansion throughout the country.[43] Men's shirts, denim wear, HEATTECH, the +J collection with high-end designer Jil Sander, and UT *manga* T-shirts represent the best sellers among French consumers, revealing their desire for high quality, on trend merchandise.[44] The concept shop and the flagship store comprise the retailer's two-store presence in France as of 2010, with both as 100% consolidated subsidiaries.[45]

Uniqlo entered into its second joint venture in 2008 with its expansion into Singapore to form UNIQLO (Singapore) Pte. Ltd. The retailer's partnership with the country's leading retailer, Wing Tai Retail, has yielded three stores as of 2010, all 51% consolidated subsidiaries. Thus far, the units opened within the country maintain locations in predominant shopping centers and upscale, urban areas.[46] Singapore represents a country of incredible importance from a strategic perspective; Uniqlo views it as the gateway to the south-east Asian region.[47] With the current labor struggles throughout China, one might speculate that expansion into Singapore signals the possibility of producing merchandise there in the future. Regardless, the first two Uniqlo locations enjoyed such immense success within the country that numerous regional partners have expressed interest in the brand, opening the door for further expansion throughout the Asian market.[48]

Recent times have seen Uniqlo's most rapid succession of international expansion yet with store openings in Taiwan, Russia, and Malaysia in 2010. The retailer entered Taiwan and Russia via organic growth, with each country boasting one store each, both as 100% consolidated subsidiaries. Uniqlo entered into its third joint venture with its expansion into Malaysia, striking a deal with the Malaysian apparel company DNP Clothing Sdn Bhd to create UNIQLO (Malaysia) Sdn. Bhn.[49] The Japanese retailer owns 55% of the joint venture, maintaining a controlling interest in its one Malaysian shop.[50] Adhering to its previous patterns of expansion, Uniqlo has placed its new stores in prominent, upscale and urban shopping areas. The Taiwan outlet is located on the first basement level of the new Uni-President Hankyu Department Store in the central shopping district of Xinyi in Taipei.[51] Similarly, the retailer opened its first Russian shop, measuring 13,000 square feet, in Moscow's upscale Atrium shopping mall.[52] Uniqlo's joint venture in Malaysia follows the same trend with the retailer's store opening in Bukit Bintang, the most vibrant commercial district in Kuala Lumpur.[53] Despite being a retailer of "cheap-chic" fashions, Uniqlo tends to align itself with more upscale merchandise offerings by locating its outlets in prominent, high-end shopping districts in major world cities. Such a strategy exposes the retailer to a greater number of consumers, many of whom possess greater spending power, and contributes to the "quality" feature of Uniqlo's brand image. The company's most recent string of expansions is representative of its aggressive global expansion, particularly in Asia.[54]

## Marketing/Branding Strategy

Given the growing international popularity of fast fashion retailers such as Sweden's H&M and Spain's Zara, marketing and brand positioning exist as crucial elements to a specialty retailer's success. In an increasingly fragmented and competitive retail industry, differentiation is crucial to a firm's success, especially as it enters foreign markets. For a company whose initial business plan modeled the strategy of a US specialty retailer (the Gap), Uniqlo depends on the effective communication of its brand and innovative retail concepts to set it apart.

Perhaps Uniqlo's most important competitive advantage is also its most basic characteristic: the retailer's so-called "Japan-ness". Besides aiming to produce merchandise that is both trendier and less expensive than its competitors, Uniqlo takes advantage of consumer interest (particularly in the United States) in Japan and of the country's mounting reputation as a ringleader of popular culture. The retailer develops its merchandise from high-tech Japanese textiles, resulting in such garments as wrinkle-free shirts and sweat-resistant pants. Its in-store displays flaunt words in both English and Japanese, with prices listed in both dollars and yen in order to contribute to the outlets' international flair. As a greater number of fashion designers look to the über-trendy street fashions found in Tokyo's Harijuku district, Uniqlo will likely be able to continue touting its Japanese heritage as a benefit to consumers.[55]

Through its early experiences in the United States and the United Kingdom, Uniqlo has come to recognize that communicating the retailer's brand values is a vital component to its marketing strategy. Japan's answer to fast fashion depends on a limited breadth of assortment, allowing prices to stay low while quality remains high. This contributes to the Uniqlo consumer's increased levels of confidence, providing purchase reassurance not often found in the discount sector.[56] "Democracy is at the core of the brand; a product that everyone can wear."[57] The company's decision to forgo the use of logos on its garments aims to challenge the "culture of clothing propaganda" that uses consumers as advertisements. Uniqlo targets one distinct shopper—the individual seeking quality basics at reasonable prices with a hint of trend—but recognizes that this consumer can be found in either gender, in a wide range of ages. The unbranded stance, therefore, allows the company to justify the necessary ubiquity of its merchandise.[58]

Despite Uniqlo's adherence to the production of casual, basic garments, it acknowledges that skillful design is necessary to create a superior product. As such, the retailer teamed up with notorious German designer Jil Sander in late 2008 to produce the "+J" brand. Known for her attention to detail, Sander's minimalist approach and reputation as a luxury designer lends itself well to Uniqlo's stance as a retailer of basic, but quality, apparel. The partnership, which is slated to continue indefinitely, provides Uniqlo with an advantage over other specialty retailers. In the case of competing firms with design partnerships of their own, it at least places the Japanese retailer on a level playing field.[59] In 2006, shortly after its entrance into the United States, the retailer is also began collaborating with artists and students at Parsons School of Design in New York City. This allowed Uniqlo to obtain a better understanding of the US market by working directly with American consumers, ultimately helping to build its consumer-conscious reputation. The designers worked to develop Uniqlo's popular selection of graphic T-shirts.[60]

## Production

Uniqlo is currently making a name for itself through the use of an efficient, unique production strategy. The Japanese retailer's business model affords it control over the entire apparel production process, from planning and design to material procurement and sales. The groundwork for a Uniqlo item is laid at the R&D (Research & Development) Centers, located in Tokyo and New York City. Employees at each location compile trend information from around the world, create a concept for the season, generate garment designs, and assemble product ranges. Separating the R&D centers from the rest of the production process, and positioning them in the world's foremost fashion hubs, helps Uniqlo to stay relevant in the increasingly competitive retail market. The remainder of the production and management initiatives occurs at the Head Office, located in Japan, where executives work to perfect Uniqlo's store location development and store design; distribution management and inventory control; merchandising and marketing; and materials development.[61]

The retailer's most distinctive advantage lies in its materials procurement and apparel production strategy. Ninety percent of Uniqlo products are manufactured in China. Representative of typical Japanese retailing practices, Uniqlo views its business transactions with 70 companies as long-term relationships and commits to purchase up 100% of the raw materials that a particular supplier is able to provide to help decrease material costs. To maintain healthy, lasting supplier associations, the retailer offers positive technical support, but continues to insist on very thorough quality management.[62] Uniqlo maintains a significant supply chain advantage in the use of its *Takumi Team*, a group of engineers with over 30 years experience in the Japanese textile industry. The experts operate to offer the retailer's business partners steady and constructive technical support through the transfer of their knowledge to factory management. Uniqlo's International Production Management Section, a collection of 170 production management personnel operate in Product Management Offices in Shanghai and Shenzhen, China; Ho Chi Minh, Vietnam; and Dhaka, Bangladesh. Through weekly visits to the contract factories, these employees are able to monitor product quality on a consistent basis.[63] The combined efforts of the two teams allow for the maintenance of a high quality product.

Tadashi Yanai, Uniqlo's CEO, also regularly brings in outsider advisers to aid in the development of product ideas. During such brainstorming session with executives from the Japanese chemical giant Toray Industries, Uniqlo's immensely popular HEATTECH fabric was born.[64] The fabric, used to create a number of Uniqlo garments, resulted in a strategic partnership with the chemical manufacturer to co-develop new fabrics and products.[65] In order to maintain the collaborative and mutually beneficial components of a strategic alliance,[66] however, Uniqlo modified its production schedule to accommodate manufacturers like Toray, who usually keep their factories operating year-round. Moving to annual, rather than seasonal, commitments with its suppliers and production facilities ended up being incredibly advantageous for the Japanese retailer, who is now able to change its production plans swiftly and with short notice. The "just-in-time" inventory procurement allows Uniqlo to monitor weekly sales patterns and decrease excess inventory. If an employee tracking sales notes a sharp decline in the sales of a particular product, the retailer would then be able to contact its suppliers and request that the product's fabric be used to make an alternative garment.[67] The alliance, which began in 2006, was recently renewed to extend into 2015.[68] Ultimately, both companies are set to reap the benefits from their partnership. The high-performance products resulting from the new materials helps Uniqlo to increase sales while Toray is able maximize its product's added value, shifting its role as a fiber supplier to a producer of consumer goods.[69] The retailer maintains another strategic alliance with the Kaihara Corporation, the world's best supplier of denim materials boasting both quality and originality.[70] Uniqlo's method of vertical integration backwards manufacturing allows the global retailer's production to respond to demand within a few days.

Operating within the apparel sector of the retail industry propels Uniqlo to gravitate toward countries, such as China, with a strong labor factor of production. Diseconomies of scale, or the decrease in production efficiency as the organization grows, have caused Uniqlo to produce nearly all of its merchandise in Chinese factories.[71] Recently, the retailer announced plans to reduce its proportion of goods crafted in China from 90% to 65% over the next three years due to an increase in Chinese labor unrest.[72] Uniqlo has chosen Vietnam and Bangladesh as its new manufacturing bases. Both countries are located in south Asia, which represents a new market for their point of sale stores as well.[73]

## Future Growth

As consumers become increasingly trend aware and improved infrastructure increases the access to information, maintaining relevance in the retail market will also become progressively difficult. Although the global retailer began with a slow start, Uniqlo's need for faster growth is evident as competitors such as H&M and Zara multiply across the planet. Tadashi Yanai, Uniqlo's CEO, recognizes this need for rapid growth in order to colonize the company's concept of fast fashion basics, with both high quality and low prices, produced through a unique manufacturing process.

During a recent trip to New York, Yanai confirmed plans to increase the number of stores in the United States and to enter new European markets such as Germany and Spain.[74] The CEO has also previously stressed the importance of focusing further expansions on major urban areas that are more accepting of foreign brands.[75] Such a strategy is representative of the retailer's global tendencies, including the choice to internationalize to world cities rather than countries where a uniform customer segment exists, allowing for a consistent merchandise assortment, no matter the country.[76] Uniqlo also maintains high expectations for the retailer's growth potential within the Asian market. With recent store openings in south Asia, the Japanese company plans to continue expanding throughout the region with entrance into Vietnam, Thailand, Indonesia, and the Philippines.[77]

The use of varied entrance methods based on the market of entry is important as the retailer expands internationally in the coming years. Tadashi Yanai has never been shy about his plans for Uniqlo to develop as a global player and is eager to apply the company's $4 billion cash pile to acquisitions. "We want to be a brand that really changes the world."[78] Yanai's desire to change the world via his company's chic-cheap basics hints at global imperialism, or the alteration of material culture in any markets the retailer chooses to enter.[79] Uniqlo plans to implement its M&A strategy to further expand into the US and European markets, while organic growth will be reserved for Asia. Due to the high number of competitors present in the US and European markets, it would take an incredibly long time to grow organically in these regions. As an underdeveloped market, Asia provides better opportunities for organic expansion.[80] In assessing possible M&A deals, the company being considered must have growth potential and profitability, along with a sharing of Uniqlo's values, especially a strong "spirit of innovation and challenge."[81] These requirements allow for the active sharing of infrastructure and a meeting of the minds as far as the standards under which a Fast Retailing company operates, both of which are necessary to achieve financial gains under this type of growth. Providing franchise options to Uniqlo management employees represents an important opportunity for growth in the retailer's saturated home market of Japan. This method will also serve to increase the retailer's productivity through Agency Theory, under which owner-operators perform at a higher level than hired managers.[82] Concessions will also remain important in markets such as the United Kingdom which have struggled to accept the brand by providing Uniqlo with ties to an established, reputable domestic retailer to increase positive perception of the foreign label. The retailer's expansion of its women's apparel line will be crucial to sustaining Uniqlo's growth in whichever markets it chooses to enter. Given that approximately half of total sales are generated by women's wear, it would be foolish for the retailer not to recognize the segments growth potential. Uniqlo emphasize the importance, however, of developing garments capable of changing women's lifestyles, not simply their appearance.[83] Finally, with the growing dominance of the Internet as a credible channel in retailing, Tadashi Yanai's plans to offer Uniqlo products world-wide via e-commerce within the next year or two is exceedingly important.[84] Ultimately, in order to achieve success in any international market the Japanese retailer chooses to enter, Uniqlo must remain true to its core value: the creation of truly great clothing with exceptional value to delight its customers.[85]

## Questions

**1. Is the retailer classified as a global or a multinational retailer? Explain its pattern of expansion. What expansion strategy did/is the retailer use/using?**

*Uniqlo Co., Ltd. is classified as a global retailer. The retailer maintains a head office in Japan in which all production and management initiatives occur. Executives at headquarters work to perfect Uniqlo's store location development and store design; distribution management and inventory control; merchandising and marketing; and materials development.[61] The retailer is also vertically integrated backward, as demonstrated by its strategic alliance with Japanese textile manufacturer Toray Industries, Inc. and through its relationship with Kaihara Corporation, the renowned Japanese denim producer.[70] Uniqlo follows a SPA, or Specialty store retailer of Private label Apparel, business model, affording Uniqlo with control over the entire apparel production process, from planning and design to material procurement and sales.[61] With the recent implementation of a franchise formula in its home market of Japan, Uniqlo has demonstrated its ability to create a business format franchise. This was made possible following the implementation of an in-house system to oversee inventories and finances at each shop, standardizing the way in which the Uniqlo business is conducted.[18] Uniqlo targets one distinct shopper—the individual seeking quality basics at reasonable prices with a hint of* trend—but recognizes that this consumer can be found in either gender, in a wide range of ages. As a result, the retailer offers one assortment of merchandise in each market it enters.[58] In a move to better meet the needs of its international customers, the company slightly altered the sizing and display of its garments for customers in the United States and the United Kingdom. The actual item offering (i.e., colors, styles), however, remains the same across the world.[86] The CEO has also previously stressed the importance of focusing further expansions on major urban areas that are more accepting of foreign brands.[75] Such a strategy is representative of the retailer's global tendencies, including the choice to internationalize to world cities rather than countries where a uniform customer segment exists, allowing for a consistent merchandise assortment regardless of the country entered.[76] Furthermore, Tadashi Yanai has been quoted as saying, "We want to be a brand that really changes the world."[78] The desire of the company's leader to change the world via his company's cheap chic basics hints at global imperialism, or the alteration of material culture in any markets the retailer chooses to enter.[79] Uniqlo's CEO also recognizes the company's need for rapid growth in order to colonize the company's concept of fast fashion basics, with both high quality and low prices, produced through a unique manufacturing process.

To facilitate the company's international expansion, Uniqlo has used organic growth, joint ventures, and franchising; methods which all fall under the active management. The company plans to employ acquisitions to continue further growth in the American and European markets.[80]

## 2. Based on Dunning's Eclectic Theory, how do ownership, locational, and internalization factors play in your retailer's international expansion?

Uniqlo Co., Ltd. maintains a number of ownership advantages, or innovative or unique products or processes that the company can use to obtain market power, as it expands internationally. The retailer's asset-based advantages include its use of exclusive SPA, or Specialty store retailer of Private label Apparel, merchandise.[61] Included in this line of goods are the materials (including HEATTECH) created in Uniqlo's strategic alliance with Toray Industries.[64] Transaction-based advantages are found in the retailer's distinctive methods of production, including Uniqlo's use of direct negotiations; implementation of backwards vertical integration (in its strategic alliances with Toray Industries[65] and Kaihara Corporation[70]); strict quality control over production (through the use of its Takumi Team and International Production Management Section[63]); and execution of a no-logo branding strategy.[58]

Concerning locational advantages, or how suitable a host country is with respect to the firm's strategies, geographic proximity plays an important role in Uniqlo's expansion strategy. Expanding into regions that are closer to a retailer's home market reduces transportation and executive costs.[87] Given that Uniqlo maintains a centralized management strategy, sourcing merchandise to countries across the world becomes more difficult. Other locational advantages, such as cultural proximity, market pull factors, competitors' moves, and low cost land and labor, are less important for Uniqlo as the company is a global retailer.

Due to the vast ownership assets maintained by Uniqlo, internalization, or keeping information within the company, holds great importance.[88] The Japanese retailer displays its understanding of this concept in its choice to expand predominantly through the use of organic growth. Although Uniqlo does operate a limited number of franchise operations, they are based only in the company's home market of Japan. Furthermore, Uniqlo allows only current store managers with 10 or more years of experience. Agency theory, or the idea that under which owner-operators perform at a higher level than hired managers explains this situation.[82] Although the company does hold a few joint ventures (FRL Korea Co., LTD., UNIQLO (Singapore) Pte. Ltd., and UNIQLO (Malaysia) Sdn. Bhd.) within their portfolio, they maintain controlling interest in each.[89]

### 3. What role does cultural proximity and geographical proximity play in the retailers' international move?

Cultural proximity is less important for Uniqlo as it expands internationally due to the fact that the company operates chiefly as a global retailer and maintains a more narrowly defined customer segment. As a result, Uniqlo is also less prone to falling prey to the psychic distance paradox, or the idea that two countries of close geographic proximity are very similar, causing a retailer to make little to no changes to their offering.[90]

Geographic proximity plays an important role in Uniqlo's expansion strategy. Expanding into regions that are closer to a retailer's home market reduces transportation and executive costs.[87] Given that Uniqlo maintains a centralized management strategy, sourcing merchandise to countries across the world becomes more difficult.

### 4. Can you predict the retailer's future international expansion?

As consumers become increasingly trend aware and the access to information is easier as a result of improved infrastructure throughout the world, maintaining relevance in the retail market will also become progressively difficult. Although the global retailer began with a slow start, Uniqlo's need for faster growth is evident as competitors such as H&M and Zara multiply across the planet. Tadashi Yanai, Uniqlo's CEO, recognizes this need for rapid growth in order to colonize the company's concept of fast fashion basics, with both high quality and low prices, *produced through a unique manufacturing process.*

*During a recent trip to New York, Yanai confirmed plans to increase the number of stores in the United States and to enter new European markets such as Germany and Spain.[74] The CEO has also previously stressed the importance of focusing further expansions on major urban areas that are more accepting of foreign brands.[75] Such a strategy is representative of the retailer's global tendencies. The choice to internationalize to world cities in which a uniform customer segment exists allows for a consistent merchandise assortment in every country.[76] Uniqlo also maintains high expectations for the retailer's growth potential within the Asian market. With recent store openings in south Asia, the Japanese company plans to continue expanding throughout the region with entrance into Vietnam, Thailand, Indonesia, and the Philippines.[77]*

*The use of varied entrance methods based on the market of entry is important as the retailer expands internationally in the coming years. Tadashi Yanai has never been shy about his plans for Uniqlo to develop as a global player and is eager to apply the company's $4 billion cash pile to acquisitions. "We want to be a brand that really changes the world."[78] Yanai's desire to change the world via his company's chic-cheap basics hints at global imperialism, or the alteration of material culture in any markets the retailer chooses to enter.[79] Uniqlo plans to implement its M&A strategy to further expand into the US and European markets, while organic growth will be reserved for Asia. Due to the high number of competitors present in the US and European markets, it would take an incredibly long time to grow organically in these regions. As an underdeveloped market, Asia provides better opportunities for organic expansion.[80] In assessing possible M&A deals, the company being considered must have growth potential and profitability, along with a sharing of Uniqlo's values, especially a strong "spirit of innovation and challenge."[81] These requirements allow for the active sharing of infrastructure and a meeting of the minds as far as the standards under which a Fast Retailing company operates, both of which are necessary to achieve financial gains under this type of growth. Providing franchise options to Uniqlo management employees represents an important opportunity for growth in the retailer's saturated home market of Japan. This method will also serve to increase the retailer's productivity through Agency Theory, under which owner-operators perform at a higher level than hired managers.[82] Concessions will also remain important in markets such as the United Kingdom which have struggled to accept the brand by providing Uniqlo with ties to an established, reputable domestic retailer to increase positive perception of the foreign label. The retailer's expansion of its women's apparel line will be crucial to sustaining Uniqlo's growth in whichever markets it chooses to enter. Given that approximately half of total sales are generated by women's wear, it would be foolish* for the retailer not to recognize the segment's growth potential. Uniqlo emphasizes the importance, however, of developing garments capable of changing women's lifestyles, not simply their appearance.[83] Finally, with the growing dominance of the Internet as a credible channel in retailing, Tadashi Yanai's plans to offer Uniqlo products world-wide via e-commerce within the next year or two is exceedingly important.[84] Ultimately, in order to achieve success in any international market the Japanese retailer chooses to enter, Uniqlo must remain true to its core value: the creation of truly great clothing with exceptional value to delight its customers.[85]

## Propositions

**P1: The greater the ownership advantages for retailers, the less likely they will franchise or license.**

UNIQLO only operates franchise locations in Japan all other international locations are directly-run stores. UNIQLO operates no licensee locations. Due to the company's high performance and impressive sales results, ownership advantages, the company has little need or incentive to license/franchise stores.[91]

**P2: The greater the available organizational slack the greater the likelihood of expanding internationally.**

UNIQLO was first internationalized in the United Kingdom in 2001. Given this entrance date ratios were computed for 1998 (1.20), 1999 (1.78), and 2000 (1.65) regarding organizational slack.[92] Since no apparent trend is found, one can conclude that organizational slack does not increase the likelihood of expanding internationally for UNIQLO.

**P3: The greater the recoverable slack the greater the likelihood of expanding internationally.**

Given the entrance date of 2001 for the United Kingdom ratios for 1998 (0.34), 1999, (0.27), and 2000 (0.22) were computed regarding recoverable slack.[93] The ratios gradually decreased up to the time of internationalization. Due to this information, one can conclude that the opposite of this proposition is true: the lower the recoverable slack the greater the likelihood of expanding internationally.

**P4: The greater the potential slack the greater the likelihood of expanding internationally.**

Given the entrance date of 2001 for the United Kingdom ratios for 1998 (1.83), 1999 (2.19), and 2000 (2.30) were computed regarding potential slack.[94] The ratios gradually increased over the three year time period before UNIQLO's first internationalization opportunity so one can conclude that this proposition holds true for the company: the greater the potential slack the greater the likelihood of expanding internationally.

**P5:Multinational retailers will move to countries with lower disposable income than their home country.**

*Uniqlo Co., Ltd. is predominantly a global retailer, and as such, this proposition does not apply. The following is an alternative proposition.*

**P5: Global retailers will move to countries with higher disposable income than their home country.**

*In 2005, Japan's annual disposable income was $11,842. The United Kingdom, UNIQLO's first international move, had disposable income of $16,710 in 2005. The company later entered the United States, which had a disposable income of $19,776 for the same year. Based on the higher dollar amounts, one can conclude that this proposition is true and that global retailers will move to countries with higher disposable income than their home country.[95]*

*Note: Figures given in thousands of International Dollars using the IMF PPP Exchange Rates and adjusted with the US inflation rate and represent income per person.*

**P13: Global companies will move to the largest/capital cities in a country.**

*UNIQLO has, and will continue, to expand in to the world's major cities. They began focusing on major U.S. and European fashion cities, and will continue to expand in to large cities around the globe.*

**P14: Global companies will not be attracted by population size, income, cultural proximity or geographical proximity.**

*UNIQLO is not attracted by population size, income, cultural proximity or geographical proximity. UNIQLO's objective is to become "...the world's leading retailer of private label apparel...".[96] However, first, they aspire to become the leader of retailing in Asia. For example, they began their expansion into Singapore in order to further expand in to Thailand, Indonesia, The Philippines, India, Vietnam and Australia. UNIQLO's first international expansion was to the United Kingdom, which is almost 6,000 miles away and extremely different in cultural proximity.*

**P15: The greater the asset based ownership advantages of a global retailer, the more likely they are to franchise.**

UNIQLO *focuses on their private label merchandise, giving them a significant asset based ownership advantage. They have franchised in Japan, focusing on agency theory, however they have used organic growth and joint ventures in their international expansions.*

**P16: The greater the transaction based ownership advantages of a global retailer, the less likely they are to franchise.**

*The transaction based ownership advantages of UNIQLO lie in the resources and systems that they have in place to conduct business. As the company describes, "we have done this by establishing a SPA manufacturer/retailer business model that enables us to control all stages of the supply process--from product design to the procurement of materials, quality control, inventory adjustments and end sales."[97] Based on these advantages we conclude that UNIQLO is unlikely to franchise globally.*

**P17: The greater the available organizational slack the greater the likelihood that global retailers will reacquire international franchisees.**

*Currently the only franchised locations are locations within Japan. Since they have had organic or joint venture growth in all their other global markets there is no need to reacquire them. From this we can conclude that greater organizational slack will have no affect on UNIQLO.*

**P18: The greater the recoverable slack the greater the likelihood that global retailers will reacquire international franchisees.**

*Currently the only franchised locations are locations within Japan. Since they have had organic or joint venture growth in all their other global markets there is no need to reacquire them. From this we can conclude that greater recoverable slack will have no affect on UNIQLO.*

**P19: The greater the potential slack the greater the likelihood that global retailers will reacquire international franchisees.**

*Currently the only franchised locations are locations within Japan. Since they have had organic or joint venture growth in all their other global markets there is no need to reacquire them. From this we can conclude that greater potential slack will have no affect on UNIQLO.*

# Endnotes

1.  Fast Retailing Co., Ltd. (2010). *Fast Retailing Company Profile: History.* Retrieved from http://www.fastretailing.com/eng/about/history/.

2.  Uniqlo; a history. (January 2, 2008). *Creative Review,* 36. Retrieved November 12, 2010 from Lexis-Nexis database.

3.  Fast Retailing Co., Ltd. (2010). *Fast Retailing Company Profile: Group Companies.* Retrieved from http://www.fastretailing.com/eng/group/.

4.  Alford, Peter. (January 15, 2009). Barneys the best bay that Fast never made. *The Australian,* 21. Retrieved November 13, 2010 from Lexis Nexis Database.

5.  Alford, Peter. (January 15, 2009). Barneys the best bay that Fast never made. *The Australian,* 21. Retrieved November 13, 2010 from Lexis Nexis Database.

6.  Anonymous. (July 18, 2010). A Japaneses Steve Jobs? *Japan Times via McClatchy—Tribune Business News (Washington).* Retrieved from http://p2047-ezproxy.msu.edu.proxy1.cl.msu.edu/login?url=http://proquest.umi.com.proxy1.cl.msu.edu/pqdweb?did=2083168341&sid=1&Fmt=3&clientId=3552&RQT=309&VName=PQD.

7.  Nakamoto, Michiyo. (October 8, 2010). Expansion strategy and awkward fit for Fsat Retialing. *Financial Times (London, UK),* p. 18.

8.  Profiling the Value Retailers. (August 20, 2010). *Women's Wear Daily (Online).* Retrieved from http://www.wwd.com/retail-news/profiling-the-value-retailers-3225455?full=true#/article/retail-news/profiling-the-value-retailers-3225455?full=true.

9.  Fast Retailing Co., Ltd. (2010). *Investor Relations: CEO Message.* Retrieved from http://www.fastretailing.com/eng/ir/direction/message.html.

10. Fast Retailing Co., Ltd. (2010). *Investor Relations: UNIQLO Business Strategy.* Retrieved from http://www.fastretailing.com/eng/ir/direction/tactics.html.

11. Alexander, Jan. (November 19, 2009). *Japan's Just-in-Time Clothes.* Retrieved from http://www.bnet.com/article/japans-just-in-time-clothes/366509.

12. Kachi, Hiroyuki & Tomisawa, Ayai. (October 8, 2010). Fast Retailing Expects Profit Drop. *Wall Street Journal (Online).* Retrieved from http://p2047-ezproxy.msu.edu.proxy1.cl.msu.edu/login?url=http://proquest.umi.com.proxy1.cl.msu.edu/pqdweb?did=2156915001&sid=2&Fmt=3&clientId=3552&RQT=309&VName=PQD.

13. Dickie, Mure. (October 20, 2010). Fast Retailing sees quality as a good fit for Uniqlo. *Financial Times (London, UK),* p. 18.

14. Dickie, Mure. (October 20, 2010). Fast Retailing sees quality as a good fit for Uniqlo. *Financial Times (London, UK)*, p. 18.

15. Nakamoto, Michiyo. (October 8, 2010). Expansion strategy and awkward fit for Fsat Retialing. *Financial Times (London, UK)*, p. 18.

16. Uniqlo managers to get support in turning franchisee. (February 9, 2004). *The Nikkei Weekly (Japan)*. Retrieved on November 13, 2010 from Lexis Nexis Database.

17. Sternquist, Brenda. (2007). *International Retailing*. (pp. 139). New York, New York: Fairchild Publications.

18. Uniqlo managers to get support in turning franchisee. (February 9, 2004). *The Nikkei Weekly (Japan)*. Retrieved on November 13, 2010 from Lexis Nexis Database.

19. Wetherille, Kelly. (April 29, 2010). Forever 21, Uniqlo Open Units. *Women's Wear Daily (Online)*. Retrieved from http://www.wwd.com/retail-news/forever-21-uniqlo-open-units-3054491.

20. Fast Retailing Co., Ltd. (2010). *Fast Retailing UNIQLO Business: Japan*. Retrieved from http://www.fastretailing.com/eng/group/strategy/japan.html.

21. Bashford, Suzy. (November 22, 2001). Democratic dressing. *Marketing*, p. 22.

22. Butler, Sarah. (March 8, 2003). Losses prompt Uniqlo to close 16 stores. *The Times (London)*, 50. Retrieved November 12, 2010 from Lexis Nexis Database.

23. Rigby, Elizabeth. (November 6, 2007). Uniqlo chief sets out plans for global cover. *Financial Times (London, England)*, 20. Retrieved November 12, 2010 from Lexis Nexis Database.

24. Uniqlo readies for concession debut in Selfridges. (January 23, 2009). *Retail Week*. Retrieved on November 12, 2010 from Lexis Nexis Database.

25. Fast Retailing Co., Ltd. (2010). *Fast Retailing UNIQLO Business: UK*. Retrieved from http://www.fastretailing.com/eng/group/strategy/uk.html.

26. WWD Staff. (May 14, 2010). Uniqlo to Open Shanghai Flagship. *Women's Wear Daily (Online)*. Retrieved from http://www.wwd.com/retail-news/uniqlo-to-open-shanghai-flagship-3072833.

27. Fast Retailing Co., Ltd. (2010). *Fast Retailing UNIQLO Business: China*. Retrieved from http://www.fastretailing.com/eng/group/strategy/china.html.

28. Fast Retailing Co., Ltd. (2010). *Fast Retailing UNIQLO Business: Hong Kong*. Retrieved from http://www.fastretailing.com/eng/group/strategy/hongkong.html.

29.  Fast Retailing Co., Ltd. (2010). *Investor Relations: UNIQLO Business Strategy.* Retrieved from http://www.fastretailing.com/eng/ir/direction/tactics.html.

30.  Fast Retailing Co., Ltd. (2010). *Investor Relations: UNIQLO Business Strategy.* Retrieved from http://www.fastretailing.com/eng/ir/direction/tactics.html.

31.  Sternquist, Brenda. (2007). *International Retailing.* (pp. 496). New York, New York: Fairchild Publications.

32.  Fast Retailing Co., Ltd. (2010) *Fast Retailing UNIQLO Business: South Korea.* Retrieved from http://www.fastretailing.com/eng/group/strategy/southkorea.html.

33.  Hyun-cheol, Kim. (July 27, 2009). Cool in Tokyo, Hot in Seoul. *Korea Times.* Retrieved November 13, 2010 from Lexis Nexis Database.

34.  Sternquist, Brenda. (2007). *International Retailing.* (pp. 500-501). New York, New York: Fairchild Publications.

35.  Sanchanta, Mariko. (Steptember 7, 2006). Fast Retailing ready to expand in US. *Financial Times (London, England),* 26. Retrieved on November 12, 2010 from Lexis Nexis Database.

36.  Fast Retailing Co., Ltd. (2010). *Fast Retailing Company Profile: History.* Retrieved from http://www.fastretailing.com/eng/about/history/

37.  Fast Retailing Co., Ltd. (2010). *Investor Relations: UNIQLO Business Strategy.* Retrieved from http://www.fastretailing.com/eng/ir/direction/tactics.html.

38.  Sanchanta, Mariko. (November 8, 2006). Japanese 'Gap' tries on the US market for size. *Financial Times (London, England),* 31. Retrieved on November 14, 2010 from Lexis Nexis Database.

39.  Fast Retailing Co., Ltd. (2010). *Fast Retailing UNIQLO Business: US.* Retrived from http://www.fastretailing.com/eng/group/strategy/usa.html.

40.  Fast Retailing Co., Ltd. (December 14, 2007). Uniqlo opens its first French store!! *Fast Retailing Group News.* Retrieved from http://www.fastretailing.com/eng/group/news/0712141600.html.

41.  Sternquist, Brenda. (2007). *International Retailing.* (pp. 325). New York, New York: Fairchild Publications.

42.  Uniqlo opens flagship store in Paris. (October 1, 2009). *Japan Today.* Retrieved from http://www.japantoday.com/category/business/view/uniqlo-opens-flagship-store-in-paris.

43.  Sternquist, Brenda. (2007). *International Retailing.* (pp. 319-323). New York, New

York: Fairchild Publications.

44. Fast Retailing Co., Ltd. (2010). *Investor Relations: UNIQLO Business Strategy.* Retrieved from http://www.fastretailing.com/eng/ir/direction/tactics.html.

45. Fast Retailing Co., Ltd. (2010). *Fast Retailing UNIQLO Business: France.* Retrived from http://www.fastretailing.com/eng/group/strategy/france.html.

46. Fast Retailing Co., Ltd. (2010). *Fast Retailing UNIQLO Business: Signapore.* Retrieved from http://www.fastretailing.com/eng/group/strategy/singapore.html.

47. Ramchandani, Nisha. (December 3, 2009). Uniqlo sees Signapore as regional gateway. *The Business Times Signapore.* Retrieved on November 12, 2010 from Lexis Nexis Database.

48. Lwee, Melissa. (July 18, 2009). Fast and furious; In the battle for the shrinking consumer dollar, cheap chic is the name of the game and purveyors of fast fashion are the big winners. *The Business Times Signapore.* Retrieved on November 12, 2010 from Lexis Nexis Database.

49. Fast Retailing Co., Ltd. (2010) *Fast Retailing UNIQLO Business.* Retreived from http://www.fastretailing.com/eng/group/strategy/.

50. Kaiser, Amanda. (June 29, 2010). Uniqlo Prepares to Enter Malaysia. *Women's Wear Daily (Online).* Retrieved from http://www.wwd.com/business-news/uniqlo-prepares-to-enter-malaysia-3158933.

51. Wetherille, Kelly. (June 24, 2010). Uniqlo to Enter Taiwan This Fall. *Women's Wear Daily (Online).* Retrieved from http://www.wwd.com/markets-news/uniqlo-to-enter-taiwan-this-fall-3146653.

52. Foreman, Katya. (March 24, 2010). Uniqlo to Open in Moscow. *Women's Wear Daily (Online).* Retrieved from http://www.wwd.com/retail-news/uniqlo-to-open-in-moscow-3009973.

53. Fast Retailing Co., Ltd. (2010). *Fast Retailing UNIQLO Business: Malaysia.* Retrieved from http://www.fastretailing.com/eng/group/strategy/malaysia.html.

54. Wetherille, Kelly. (June 24, 2010). Uniqlo to Enter Taiwan This Fall. *Women's Wear Daily (Online).* Retrieved from http://www.wwd.com/markets-news/uniqlo-to-enter-taiwan-this-fall-3146653.

55. Chozick, Amy. (July 14, 2006). Style & Substance: Selling 'Japan-ness'; Japanese Retailers Try Trendier, Cheaper Approach as They Expand Into US. *Wall Street Journal (Eastern Edition)*, p. A9.

56. Bashford, Suzy. (November 22, 2001). Democratic dressing. *Marketing*, p. 22.

57. Bashford, Suzy. (November 22, 2001). Democratic dressing. *Marketing,* p. 22.

58. Mason, Tania. (September 13, 2001). Can Uniqlo win without logos? *Marketing,* p. 15.

59. Kaiser, Amanda. (April 29, 2010). Jil Sander Extends Uniqlo Deal. *Women's Wear Daily (Online).* Retrieved from http://www.wwd.com/retail-news/jil-sander-extends-uniqlo-deal-3054260/

60. Chozick, Amy. (July 14, 2006). Style & Substance: Selling 'Japan-ness'; Japanese Retailers Try Trendier, Cheaper Approach as They Expand Into US. *Wall Street Journal (Eastern Edition),* p. A9.

61. Uniqlo Co., Ltd. (2010). *Company Info Career Opportunities: Business Model.* Retrieved from http://www.uniqlo.com/us/employment/model/.

62. Uniqlo Co., Ltd. (2010). *Company Info Career Opportunities: Business Model.* Retrieved from http://www.uniqlo.com/us/employment/model/.

63. Uniqlo Co., Ltd. (2010). *Company Info About UNIQLO: Manufacturing.* Retrieved from http://www.uniqlo.com/us/corp/production/.

64. Alexander, Jan. (November 19, 2009). *Japan's Just-in-Time Clothes.* Retrieved from http://www.bnet.com/article/japans-just-in-time-clothes/366509.

65. Wetherille, Kelly. (July 22, 2010). Uniqlo Extends Partnership With Textile Manufacturer. *Women's Wear Daily,* 200(15), 13. Retreived on November 12, 2010 from ABI/Inform Database.

66. Sternquist, Brenda. (2007). *International Retailing.* (pp. 148-149). New York, New York: Fairchild Publications.

67. Alexander, Jan. (November 19, 2009). *Japan's Just-in-Time Clothes.* Retrieved from http://www.bnet.com/article/japans-just-in-time-clothes/366509.

68. Wetherille, Kelly. (July 22, 2010). Uniqlo Extends Partnership With Textile Manufacturer. *Women's Wear Daily,* 200(15), 13.

69. Takimoto, Daisuke. (August 2, 2010). Toray and Uniqlo—the Hidden Risks in a Successful Partnership. *Nikkei Business (Online).* Retreived from http://business.nikkeibp.co.jp/article/eng/20100802/215670/.

70. Uniqlo Co., Ltd. (2010). *Company Info About UNIQLO: Materials.* Retrieved from http://www.uniqlo.com/us/corp/material/.

71. Sternquist, Brenda. (2007). *International Retailing.* (pp. 79-80). New York, New York: Fairchild Publications.

72. Culture shock; Japanese firms in China. (July 10, 2010). *The Economist.* Retreived

on November 12, 2010 from Lexis Nexis Database.

73. Hori, Daisuke. (October 12, 2010). Japanese apparel makers exposed to China risks. *The Nikkei Weekly*. Retrieved on November 12, 2010 from Lexis Nexis Database.

74. WWD Staff. (January 14, 2010). Fashion Scoops: Tadashi Yanai Named Japan's Richest Man. *Women's Wear Daily (Online)*. Retrieved from http://www.wwd.com/fashion-news/fashion-scoops/in-the-money-2409220.

75. Sanchanta, Mariko. (February 11, 2010). Retailer Shops for Deals. *The Wall Street Journal*. Retrieved from http://online.wsj.com/article/SB10001424052748703382 904575058751388840486.html.

76. Sternquist, Brenda. (2007). *International Retailing*. (pp. 42). New York, New York: Fairchild Publications.

77. Fast Retailing Co., Ltd. (2010). *Investor Relations: CEO Message*. Retrieved from http://www.fastretailing.com/eng/ir/direction/message.html.

78. Kaiser, Amanda. (January 27, 2010). Fast Retailing's Uniqlo: The Year Ahead. *Women's Wear Daily (Online)*. Retrieved from http://www.wwd.com/retail-news/fast-retailings-uniqlo-the-year-ahead-2421007.

79. Sternquist, Brenda. (2007). *International Retailing*. (pp. 42). New York, New York: Fairchild Publications.

80. Sanchanta, Mariko. (February 11, 2010). Retailer Shops for Deals. *The Wall Street Journal*. Retrieved from http://online.wsj.com/article/SB10001424052748703382 904575058751388840486.html.

81. Fast Retailing Co., Ltd. (2010). *Investor Relations: M&A Strategy*. Retrieved from http://www.fastretailing.com/eng/ir/direction/manda.html.

82. Sternquist, Brenda. (2007). *International Retailing*. (pp. 139). New York, New York: Fairchild Publications.

83. Fast Retailing Co., Ltd. (2010). *Investor Relations: UNIQLO Business Strategy*. Retrieved from http://www.fastretailing.com/eng/ir/direction/tactics.html.

84. Sanchanta, Mariko. (February 11, 2010). Retailer Shops for Deals. *The Wall Street Journal*. Retrieved from http://online.wsj.com/article/SB10001424052748703382 904575058751388840486.html.

85. Fast Retailing Co., Ltd. (2010). *Investor Relations: CEO Message*. Retrieved from http://www.fastretailing.com/eng/ir/direction/message.html.

86. Chozick, Amy. (July 14, 2006). Style & Substance: Selling 'Japan-ness'; Japanese

Retailers Try Trendier, Cheaper Approach as They Expand Into US. *Wall Street Journal (Eastern Edition)*, p. A9.

87. Sternquist, Brenda. (2007). *International Retailing.* (pp. 53). New York, New York: Fairchild Publications.

88. Sternquist, Brenda. (2007). *International Retailing.* (pp. 55-57). New York, New York: Fairchild Publications.

89. Fast Retailing Co., Ltd. (2010). *Group Companies: UNIQLO Business.* Retrieved from http://www.fastretailing.com/eng/group/strategy/.

90. Sternquist, Brenda. (2007). *Internationl Retailing.* (pp. 52). New York, New York: Fairchild Publications.

91. Fast Retailing Co., Ltd. (2010). *Corporate Social Responsibility For Our Community: Initiatives at Local Franchise Stores.* Retrieved from http://www. fastretailing.com/eng/csr/community/franchise.html.

92. Mergent Online. (2010). *Fast Retailing Co., Ltd. Reports: Annual Reports.* Retrieved November 15, 2010 from Mergent Online Database.

93. Mergent Online. (2010). *Fast Retailing Co., Ltd. Reports: Annual Reports.* Retrieved November 15, 2010 from Mergent Online Database.

94. Mergent Online. (2010). *Fast Retailing Co., Ltd. Reports: Annual Reports.* Retrieved November 15, 2010 from Mergent Online Database.

95. Mergent Online. (2010). *Fast Retailing Co., Ltd. Reports: Annual Reports.* Retrieved November 15, 2010 from Mergent Online Database.

96. Fast Retailing Co., Ltd. (2010). *Investor Relations: Annual Reports FY 2009.* Retrieved from http://www.fastretailing.com/eng/ir/library/annual.html.

97. Fast Retailing Co., Ltd. (2010). *Fast Retailing Company Profile: Our Business.* Retrieved from http://www.fastretailing.com/eng/about/business/.

# Wal-Mart

*Mitchell Bowman, Ashton Cade, Brittney Jackson, Rashaad Mitchell, Kevin Deegan*

## Wal-Mart

Wal-Mart is the world's most successful retailer, with $405 billion in 2010 fiscal sales, expansion in 15 countries, and 2.1 million employees worldwide. Today Wal-Mart has nearly 9,000 stores and serves 176 million customers yearly. Wal-Mart is the number one discount retailer with its ability to adapt to various customer demographics and keep prices low with meticulous strategic planning. A leader in sustainability, corporate philanthropy, and employment opportunity, Wal-Mart ranked first among retailers in Fortune Magazine's 2010 most admired companies survey.[52]

## Flow Chart

|  |  | As of February 28, 2011 |  |
| Country | Year Entered | Number of Stores | Year Exited |
| --- | --- | --- | --- |
| Mexico | 1991 | 1739 | |
| Canada | 1994 | 325 | |
| Argentina | 1995 | 63 | |
| Brazil | 1995 | 480 | |
| Indonesia | 1995 | 2 | Exited 1998 |
| China | 1996 | 329 | |
| South Korea | 1998 | 16 | Exited 2006 |
| Germany | 1998 | 85 | Exited 2006 |
| United Kingdom | 1999 | 385 | |
| Japan | 2002 | 414 | |
| Costa Rica | 2005 | 181 | |
| El Salvador | 2005 | 78 | |
| Guatemala | 2005 | 176 | |
| Honduras | 2005 | 55 | |
| Nicaragua | 2005 | 61 | |
| Chile | 2009 | 282 | |
| India | 2009 | 5 | |

## Company History

Wal-Mart began making its imprint on the retail industry in 1962 when its first store opened in Rogers, Arkansas. The main objective of Sam Walton, the founder of Wal-Mart, was to save people money to help them live better. The company became incorporated October 31, 1969 and began trading in OTC markets. After just two years the stock, WMT, began trading on the New York Stock Exchange at a whopping $0.06 per share on August 31, 1972.3 A far cry from today's closing price of $52.13.3 By the end of the 70's, the retailer had grown to 276 stores in 11 states.[52]

Wal-Mart expanded its brand image in 1983 when it opened Sam's Membership Warehouse and in 1988 opened its first supercenter, which is now the company's dominant store format. Currently, these stores feature a complete grocery department and 36 departments of general merchandise with the purpose of keeping prices low every day. Supercenters appeal to customers who need a one stop shop location, where they can find all the goods for their family and household. In addition to the one stop shop, customers have also come to expect both quality national and private label brands at an affordable price.[52]

By 1989, there were 1,402 Wal-Mart stores and 123 Sam's Club locations, resulting in a tremendous increase of employment and awareness of Wal-Mart's presence in the retail industry. This surge in growth resulted in sales growing from $1 billion in 1980, to $26 billion by the end of the decade. In 1991, Wal-Mart acquired Western Merchandisers Inc. of Amarillo, Texas and introduced a private label brand Sam's American Choice. With most of the US market saturated Wal-Mart expanded internationally near Mexico City in 1991 with its first Sam's Club, where the company capitalized on the demand of the Mexican consumer and built relationships with Mexican retailers.[52]

## Competitive Advantage

### Grocery

As early as 1998, grocers around the United States were beginning to worry about what would happen if Wal-Mart was successful in their bid to become the nation's number one grocer, as it was doing with the retail sector, and for good reason.[96] Wal-Mart has surpassed Kroger and Food Lion in sales, while keeping their margins tight by applying the same techniques used to keep their price low on the non-food side of the store.[32] And not only has the introduction of a full-fledged grocery store within the retail store been a huge success, but customers who come for groceries are continuing their shopping on the non-food side of the store and vice versa.[18] Introducing the grocery department was a well planned and executed move, typical of the retail giant. And the distribution network that backs up the grocery side of the store is just as impressive with 40 Grocery Distribution Centers.[62] Most recently, Wal-Mart announced that it plans to use its clout to cut fruit and vegetable prices, a plan backed by First Lady Michelle Obama.[7]

### Cut Costs

Another way Wal-Mart is able to stay ahead of the competition is through its ever evolving cost cutting measures. One example is their lean inventory and just in time ordering systems.[2] Keeping just the bare minimum of products on the shelves to satisfy customer's immediate needs, and making sure there is only a day or two of stock left in the back rooms ensures that the absolute minimum amount of money is tied up with inventory.

## Efficient Supply Chain

Wal-Mart has the largest private delivery network in the United States.[63] There are also some interesting statistics to go along with that title such as: 7,600 Drivers, 6,650 Tractors, 54,000 Dry Van Trailers, 3,900 Reefer Trailers, 80,000 Associates in Logistics, 149 Distribution Centers, 757 Million Miles Driven in 2009, and 2.3 Million Total Store Deliveries Last Year.[63] And not only is the distribution system efficient, but it is also getting greener every year. Wal-Mart has invested a very significant amount of capital to ensure that its fleet is as efficient as possible. In doing so, it has made the fleet greener by reducing fuel consumption. Some of the changes to the fleet include fuel-efficient dual tires, aerodynamic tractor packages, installation of tag axels on trucks (axels that raise tires off the ground when they are not needed), and instead of keeping the engine running when the drivers are sleeping, fuel-sipping auxiliary power units have been installed.[47] With all of the improvements in their supply chain, and the continual innovation in advanced delivery methods, Wal-Mart is able to further reduce the end price to the consumer. Wal-Mart is even planning a trial of a home delivery service for its retail goods in California. The service is expected to compete with Amazon.com for the top spot as America's number one Internet retailer.[106] These same efficiencies are found throughout the company, including the distribution networks across the globe.

## EDLP Retail Goods

Every Day Low Pricing (EDLP), the rock bottom pricing strategy of Wal-Mart, begins with sourcing products for the absolute lowest price. From there it is on to its state of the art distribution network of 42 regional distribution centers where the goods will reach the stores in the most efficient means possible.[62] The EDLP strategy is in contrast to what other grocers and retailers may utilize, such as Kroger with its high-low pricing. Wal-Mart is constantly challenging its suppliers to become more efficient, thereby reducing the wholesale costs to Wal-Mart. Wal-Mart then is able to offer even lower prices than it had with its advanced supply chain.

## POS Technology

Since at least 1997, Wal-Mart has had POS sales data available to help plan and build predictive sales models. These models help Wal-Mart remain adequately stocked on the items that people are most likely to purchase during certain times or during certain events.[78] Being able to discover the seasonality of items like mouth wash and dog food has given Wal-Mart a powerful competitive advantage.[78] It is estimated that Wal-Mart has over 460 terabytes of information available for analysis.[24] A good example given by the Wall Street Journal is that the Internet, in its entirety, has only half as much at just 230 terabytes as of 2004.[24] When Hurricane Francis was threatening to strike Florida, Wal-Mart data miners discovered that an earlier hurricane had created a spike in demand for strawberry flavored Pop-Tarts and beer.[24] With this knowledge, the Wal-Mart executives were able to turn the predictive sales models into profits.

## Public Relations

Wal-Mart has had its share of successful entries into foreign market places, but the company has encountered some hardships. South Korea and Germany were both disastrous for Wal-Mart. Upon the announcement of Wal-Mart leaving South Korea and Germany, a generic statement was given about the ordeal. The statements were not identical but generally included ideas such as "it became increasingly clear that in South Korea's current environment it would be difficult for us to reach the scale we desired."[33] They announce complete withdrawal from South Korea. Legal matters are another front that Wal-Mart works hard to either keep quiet, or draw out in hopes of causing the other litigant into bankruptcy. A good example is a lawsuit brought in 2001, that claims that Wal-Mart pays women less than men, and the initial suit claims that Wal-Mart's expansive human resource database can even prove it. But after 10 years, Wal-Mart's lawyers have been able to stall the proceeding to the point that a judge has yet to hear the case.[42] Although Wal-Mart has more than its fair share of problems, the retail giant also donates thousands of dollars per store to the local community. The boards touting their contributions are posted near the entrance of each store.

## International Expansion

Wal-Mart is a multinational retailer. This means that their operations are decentralized and that they offer different products based on its geographic location, this expansion can be explained by the stages theory. The SIRE[2] theory poses that a company will initially expand into countries that are most similar to their home market. Mexico and Canada were the company's first moves in their international expansion strategy, as these countries are located within close proximity to the United States. This expansion can be seen as more of an internal move because of how it expanded in stages. These stages were focused on specific continents and then dramatic jumps to other continents. This demonstrates the idea of cultural proximity. Wal-Mart ensured that they saturated their home market before they actually expanded.[43][52]

The idea of cultural proximity states that retailers will expand into countries that are fairly similar to their own cultures. Wal-Mart followed this basic principle because the first countries they expanded to were Mexico in 1991 and Canada in 1994. Their cultures are similar and made the adjustment easier for Wal-Mart. This was followed by a jump to a new cultural envrionment when they expanded to China only two years after entering Canada. From China, Wal-Mart made another jump as it moved over to the United Kingdom and Germany. They made their way back East finally getting to South Korea and Japan.[43][52]

Pull factors are definitely considered when Wal-Mart moves into a country. Retailers like Wal-Mart will venture into countries that are less developed than the United States. "Markets with high growth in income can provide retailers with double digit growth".[43] Viewing Mexico's (the first country Wal-Mart expanded into) GDP growth in 1986(-3.8) and 1991(4.2) shows that there was significant growth in this five year period. Wal-Mart observed this growth and considered this business venture to be very advantageous for their company.[43][52]

## Mexico

Wal-Mart entered Mexico in 1991, originally as part of a joint venture with CIFRA, a Mexican food retailer. Since the cultural climate in Mexico is different than it is in the United States, it makes sense that Wal-Mart would enter into this joint venture. It allowed them to not only get a feel for how the business operated in Mexico, but they ultimately taught Wal-Mart how to merchandise and sell groceries. The main objective of this venture was to allow them to gain access and market share in a new country, while keeping the risk of failure. Keeping the risks low have allowed Wal-Mart to be extremely successful in Mexico, and in turn learned how to market produce in their stores across multiple countries.[26] [28][36][76] Since entering into Mexico, they have added 1,664 stores in over 265 cities. In addition to Wal-Mart Super Centers and Sam's Club Warehouses, it also has a stake in Bodega food discount stores, Superama supermarkets, as well as apparel stores and some restaurants. In 2001, Wal-Mart Stores decided to buy a majority stake in CIFRA, which ended up in Wal-Mart changing the name of their joint venture to Wal-Mart de México, S.A.B. de C.V., and have bought out their joint venture partner.

## Canada

Headquartered in Canada, Wal-Mart Canada was established in 1994 with the acquisition of the Woolco Canada chain of 122 stores. Wal-Mart Canada began as a discount store offering up to 80,000 products, including: apparel, household goods, toys, health and beauty items, food, and other merchandise. However, with the success of both Wal-Mart stores in Canada and Wal-Mart supercenters in the United States, the first supercenter arrived in Canada in 2006. Almost all Wal-Mart

Canada stores have a McDonald's located inside and in 2010 Wal-Mart opened its first bank, Wal-Mart Canada Bank. Wal-Mart Canada plans to open 15-20 stores each year. Wal-Mart Canada is expected to open 40 additional supercenters in 2011.[6][66]

## Argentina

Headquartered in Buenos Aires, Wal-Mart entered into Argentina in 1995 with the introduction of a Sam's Club. As of January 2010, Wal-Mart has amassed 63 stores in 4 different formats (Supercenters, Changomas, Changomas Express, and Mi Changomas. In 2007 Wal-Mart purchased a number of stores from Auchan, and converted stores in the towns of Avellaneda, Quilmes, and La Tablada into Wal-Mart Supercenters. In Argentina, the company uses a similar strategy as in Brazil due to the amount of competition in this country. As a Latin based country, Carrefour would have more of an advantage here, and actually has a greater market share, around 24.6%. Wal-mart relies on organic growth. Wal-Mart Argentina retains full control to take advantage of any changes in the market in this area.[1][28][64]

## Brazil

According to Hoovers, "Wal-Mart Brazil ranks as the third-largest retailer in the world's fifth-largest country." Wal-Mart Brazil is a wholly owned subsidiary of Wal-Mart Stores (WMB). When they entered Brazil in 1995, WMS only had two supercenters and three Sam's Club Warehouse stores. To help expand growth, they relied mainly on the acquisition of existing retailers in Brazil, including the purchase of 118 Bompreço stores in the North in 2004, and 140 supermarkets from Sonae, a Portuguese Retailer. In total, WMB has amassed 461 stores in Brazil, and has 79,800 employees. As a wholly owned subsidiary, Wal-Mart Brazil offers more control over the company in an international setting. To expand in this country, Wal-Mart relies on acquisitions to grow. This allows them to gain stores quickly, while implementing their style of business and their best ideas, without having to physically open new stores. This is partially due to the high level competition with retailers such as Carrefour and CBD, another Brazilian retailer. This allows them to compete by keeping costs low.[4][28][65]

## Indonesia

Wal-Mart entered into a licensing agreement with Indonesia Based Lippo Group in 1996.[22] This was the first time that Wal-Mart had attempted to license its operations overseas. The agreement ended after just two years. By that time, only two stores had been opened with the Wal-Mart name.[22] The end came about because a conflict arose after the Lippo Group bought a controlling stake in one of

Matahari's Mega M stores. Matahari's is a rival discounter and Wal-Mart feared the potential loss of sensitive competitive advantage due to what it saw as a violation of its non-competition clause in the franchise agreement.[22] There are reports that Wal-Mart is again attempting to break into this market. They purportedly are in a bidding war with South Korea's Lotte Shopping, French retailer Casino Guichard Perrachon SA, and the Lippo Group[45] to acquire Indonesia's Matahari Putra Prima hypermarket business. However, at final revision of this report, discussion has stalled.[44]

## China/ Hong Kong

Wal-Mart began their retail operations in China in 1996 with a supercenter and Sam's Club in Shenzen. In February 2007, Wal-Mart China invested in the hypermarket chain, Trust-Mart, which operates more than 100 retail units. Wal-Mart China strongly believes in local sourcing, over 95% of the merchandise in Wal-Mart China stores is sourced locally. Wal-Mart China is also committed to local talent development and diversity. The vast majority, 99.9%, of Wal-Mart China associates are Chinese nationals. Since many first-tier cities are becoming saturated, Wal-Mart will begin focusing on its expansion into second and third-tier cities through organic growth and small acquisitions.[9] [68]

## South Korea

In August 1998, Wal-Mart acquired four stores and six undeveloped sites from Makro, a chain of Netherlands-based membership clubs.[16] Three of the stores were located in South Korea's capital, Seoul, and the third was in Deajeon (Taejon), just to the south.[16] The man who led Makro's entrance into South Korea, was on board with Wal-Mart during the acquisition, as the International Division Senior VP and COO.[16] Wal-Mart may have assumed that the Asian stock market crisis of 1997 was the sole reason behind Makro's troubles. However, both companies had difficulty adjusting to the Korean consumer culture. On May 22, 2006, Wal-Mart announced that it would sell all of its interests in South Korea.[1] In profit and loss terms, Wal-Mart South Korea had lost around $10 million in 2005.[39] The failure in South Korea can be assumed to be due to location, failure to understand the Korean customer, the warehouse-style layout of the stores, and the lines of goods carried. The sale was made to South Korea's Shinsegae Company, who is the leading retailer with 79 E-Mart hypermarkets in the country.[51]

## Germany

Wal-Mart expanded into Germany in 1998, through the acquisition of the Wertkauf hypermarket chain.[50] The initial purchase was for 21 profitable, large-format Wertkauf stores.[46] But the acquisition may have been doomed from the beginning because Germany has restrictive policies on store hours and new development, difficult economic conditions, unfavorable demographics and intense price competition.[46] As if that was not enough, Wal-Mart went on to purchase 74 Interspar stores that were smaller and unprofitable.[46] The combination of entering a market where low prices were already expected of retailors, the purchase of unprofitable stores, and a strict German retail culture forced Wal-Mart to end operations in 2006. The exit was made by a sale of all stores to German retailor Metro AG, and while the exact details of the sale are unknown, Wal-Mart did acknowledge that even after the sale, they expected to see a loss of around $1 billion.[46]

## United Kingdom

Wal-Mart made ASDA, a chain of supermarkets in the United Kingdom, its subsidiary in 1999.[99] [100] ASDA is the United Kingdom's second largest retailer, after Tesco. It operates about 385 stores, including about 25 ASDA Living Stores, which mainly sell groceries and apparel. Since being bought by Wal-Mart in 1999, ASDA has set off a price war in the United Kingdom by implementing Wal-Mart's well known price roll back program.[77]

## Japan

Wal-Mart made its way into Japan in May of 2002. They acquired a 6.1% stake in Seiyu. Seiyu is an operator in Japan in charge of supermarkets, department stores, and shopping centers. Later in 2005 a majority interest in Seiyu was acquired. This made them a subsidiary of Wal-Mart. In 2007 their ownership stake of Seiyu increased by 44.2% from 50.9 to 95.1. Wal-Mart currently has 413 stores in Japan. Japan is a very fragmented market that consists of smaller retailers. These small "mom and pop" stores have completely saturated the market, which explains why Wal-Mart must proceed with acquisitions as opposed to growing organically.[28 31 74] Wal-Mart has experienced much difficulty adjusting into the Japanese culture as Seiyu reported losses for its first seven years of existence.[28 31 74]

## Costa Rica

Wal-Mart entered Costa Rica in 2005 when they acquired a 33% stake in Central American Retail Holding Company (CARHCO). They purchased their shares from a Dutch retailer named Royal Ahold NV. This allowed Wal-Mart to enter into the Central American countries of Guatemala, El Salvador, Honduras, Nicaragua, and of course Costa Rica. In the following year Wal-Mart gained over 50% of control in the company and changed the name to Wal-Mart Centroamérica, and as recently as 2009, Wal-Mart de México, S.A.B. de C.V. took over the Central America operations located in San Jose, Costa Rica. Although none of the stores are in a supercenter format, Wal-Mart has 9,918 associates in Costa Rica. Wal-Mart's success in Mexico has positioned them well for Costa Rica. are under one roof, there is probably not going to be many acquisitions in this area due to the little major competition that will be found in this country. Wal-Mart will use organic growth expansion because they do not have any competition.[10 28 69]

## El Salvador

In 2005 Wal-Mart was able to acquire more than 33 percent interest in Central American Retail Holding Company. A year later this interest increased to 51 percent. Along with this increase came a name change. This new name was Wal-Mart Centroamérica. This geographical region currently has 78 stores.[13 70]

## Guatemala

Also a part of the acquiring interest in CARCHO, Wal-Mart expanded into Guatemala. Guatemala is the second most penetrated Central American country with 176 Wal-Mart Centroamerica locations and 9440 employees. "Wal-Mart believes that their investment will add strength to the partnership by helping to keep prices low for consumers and will offer new opportunities to suppliers in the region for additional business development."[54] The majority of Guatemalan residents live in small highland villages and towns, which make up over half the population. The convenience store format is the primary format in this country.[20] The company operates under five different formats that appeal to a comprehensive range of consumers who have different needs and demands that vary by their geographical location.[71]

## Honduras

Wal-Mart was able to acquire more than 33 percent interest in Central American Retail Holding Company from the Dutch retailer Royal Ahold NV in September of 2005. In a year's time, Wal-Mart was able to increase its interest by 18%. With Wal-Mart being a majority owner, the CARHCO name was changed to Wal-Mart Centroamerica.[27 72]

## Nicaragua

In 2005 Wal-Mart entered the Nicaraguan market by acquiring 33% in CARHCO, Central America's leading supermarket and hypermarket chain.[49, 76] CARHCO understands the local consumer behavior and methods of doing business in Nicaragua. This helped Wal-Mart expand its business into its market. A year later, Wal-Mart's interest in the company increased to 51%, making it majority stakeholder, thus leading to the renaming of the company to Wal-Mart Centroamérica, operating 61 stores with 2,032 employees.[76]

## Chile

In 2009 Wal-Mart was able to acquire a majority stake in Distribución y Servicio D&S S.A., a food retailer located in Chile. This food retailer was a family owned business dating back to 1957. Wal-Mart's international presence in Chile is very commanding with 270 stores. It controls over 30% of total hypermarket, superstore, and warehouse store sales, according to the USDA Foreign Agricultural Service. Wal-Mart's focus to saturate the Chile market can be seen through the $300 million investment it plans to make in 2011.[8 28 67]

## India

Wal-Mart was one of the first western retailers to take advantage of the cash-and-carry format by signing a deal with Bharti Enterprises. The joint venture between Wal-Mart and Bharti Enterprises has expanded and now the two companies are looking for opportunities to expand into the South and the West. Earlier this year, Wal-Mart began working with farmers in India with direct farm programs in Punjab and Delhi, providing agricultural techniques and more efficient transportation. Wal-Mart's goal is to buy directly from 35,000 small and medium farmers by the end of 2015. The supply chain operation supports farmers and small manufacturers who have limited infrastructure and distribution strength and helps minimize wastage. A typical cash-and-carry store will measure between 50,000 and 100,000 square feet and sell a variety of fruits and vegetables, groceries, stationery, footwear, clothing, consumer durables, and other general merchandise.[29 73]

## Conclusion

The pattern of expansion shown by the preceding countries shows that Wal-Mart expands to countries that are culturally similar to its own before moving to countries with different cultures. This is the basis for cultural proximity. Wal-Mart also is decentralized in these countries and offers products tailored to the local shopping environment. This is typical of multinational retailers, such as Wal-Mart. And with Wal-Mart's recent bid for Massmart, in South Africa, we can see that Wal-Mart is again ready to make the jump to another country.

# Questions

**1.   Is the retailer classified as a global or a multinational retailer? Explain its pattern of expansion. What expansion strategy did/is the retailer use/using?**

*Wal-Mart is considered a multinational retailer because they decentralized. Their large-scale format prevents any type of codifying of their operations, which in turn prevents them from franchising. A multinational retailer will adjust the inventory in that country to the culture of that country. Wal-Mart has expanded internationally because they have saturated their current market in the United States. Their expansion is one that consists of internal moves as they expand in stages. Stages theory explains that a company will expand into countries with similar markets at first and then take on bigger risk later by expanding into countries that aren't as similar. Wal-Mart expanded to Mexico first followed by Canada.*[43]

**2.   Based on Dunning's Eclectic Theory, how do ownership, locational, and internalization factors play in your retailer's international expansion?**

*Many ownership advantages exist for Wal-Mart as a company. These consist of both asset-based and transaction-based advantages. Wal-Mart's 12 patents, sophisticated logistics system, and POS technology are all considered asset-based advantages. Its pricing strategies and exquisite customer service are examples of its transaction-based advantages. The decentralized management ensures better control of employees as different strategies can be employed in different countries. Pull factors and cultural proximity are locational factors that explain their expansion. When expanding it is observed that Wal-Mart will expand into developing countries. These countries are those who have growing GDP's and have the possibility to provide large profits. When Wal-Mart enters into less developed countries, their main focus is food. For example, this strategy was evident when Wal-Mart first expanded internationally to Mexico. Wal-Mart has very sophisticated systems that they use to operate their company very efficiently. Wal-Mart is very protective of these systems, and are careful not to leak any of their trade secrets. In the majority of their international expansion Wal-Mart has chosen not to license, which allows them to internalize their practices.*[62] *To help keep these trade secrets, Wal-Mart operates wholly owned subsidiaries in a large percentage of the countries.*

**3.   What role does cultural proximity and geographical proximity play in the retailers' international move?**

*Cultural proximity plays a key role in their expansion, expand into countries* with similar cultures. Wal-Mart was able to expand into Canada, a culture fairly similar to that of the United States. Wal-Mart will expand into countries and once in these countries they expand into those surrounding them. This is done because Wal-Mart wants to take advantage of the knowledge they now possess about the country's culture. An identifying attribute of a multinational retailer is the adjustment of their products they sell. This adjustment is based on the culture of that country. When a company has entered a country similar to their own culture, they have a significant advantage in selecting their product assortment. Incorrect selection of inventory will cause many issues financially. However, geographic proximity's role in their expansion is somewhat insignificant. Since Wal-Mart is a multinational retailer and operates with a decentralized management, their sourcing is mostly conducted within the country. It isn't necessary for their retailers to do much sourcing outside of the country.[43]

**4. Can you predict the retailer's future international expansion?**

Predicting Wal-Mart's future expansion is as easy as looking at a political map of the world and finding the locations where they currently do not have their feet on the ground. Wal-mart is considering moves back into some of those countries that they exited. In South Africa, Wal-Mart is currently the winning bidder for Massmart, which includes subsidiaries Game, Makro and Builders Warehouse. Wal-Mart made a move into the Indonesian market back in the late 90's that quickly unraveled. Now, Wal-Mart is back in the bidding process to purchase Indonesia's Matahari Putra Prima's hypermarket business. The next move for Wal-Mart would likely be north into countries that have high Muslim populations to build up its momentum towards moving into an Islamic state. A country like Egypt, Kuwait, or Saudi Arabia would be the most likely countries to be wooed by Wal-Mart after it spends some time getting acclimated to Africa. This move to the Middle East would only occur after the region recovers from the ongoing uprisings. Vietnam is also another contender according to a recent news article which also supports the eventual push into the Middle East.

## Propositions

**P1: The greater the ownership advantages for retailers, the less likely they will franchise or license.**

Wal-Mart has at least 12 patents and or applications for patents that give it specific rights to its method of doing business and intellectual property.[55][59] The patents and applications include RFID tags and methods for implementation, methods and systems to produce gourmet coffee, and for its database.[55][59] Wal-Mart also has obtained copyrights on various products.[57] Wal-Mart has also been very aggressive *in protecting its brand from outside sources by filing for 213 trademarks around the globe.[56][58][60] Wal-Mart has a great amount of ownership advantages; therefore this proposition is true for Wal-Mart.[23]*

**P2:  The greater the available organizational slack the greater the likelihood of expanding internationally.**

*Organizational slack for 1988-1990 are as followed: 1988(1.7), 1989(1.8), and 1990(1.7). Since the amount of excess cash seemed to be stagnant over three years, this proposition does not prove true for Wal-Mart.[48] They did have a large excess of liquid cash, but had not been seeing an increase.  A functional way of looking at this proposition is as follows:*

*Year 1 = (A), Year 2 = (B), Year 3 = (C)*

*A = 1.7, B = 1.8, C = 1.7*

*For this proposition to be true for Wal-Mart, A < B < C.  However, according to the research we conducted, A< B > C.  This does not support the proposition.*

**P3:The greater the recoverable slack the greater the likelihood of expanding internationally.**

*The recoverable slack for the following years are: 1988 (16.3%), 1989 (15.85%), 1990 (15.8%), 1991(15.8%). The lower the operating cost for a company, the more money this company will have to expand. This ratio determines what percent of net sales the expenses are. Since the ratios have decreased from 1989 to 1991, this means that Wal-Mart's expenses have increased over the 3-year period, and therefore does not fit the proposition above.[48]*

**P4:  The greater the potential slack the greater the likelihood of expanding internationally.**

*Ratio of Equity to Capital (3 year average before their first international expansion):[2][12]*

| Year | 1988 | 1989 | 1990 |
|---|---|---|---|
| Equity: | $2,257,267 | $3,007,900 | $3,965,561 |
| Working Capital: | $1,161,382 | $1,565,083 | $1,867,301 |
| Ratio: | 1.94 | 1.92 | 2.12 |

*Over the years Wal-Mart's organizational slack has been increasing and this is the three years prior to them expanding. Since they moved into Mexico in 1991 this information proves the proposition true to Wal-Mart's case.*[48]

**P5:Multinational retailers will move to countries with lower disposable income than their home country.**

*Below is a chart similar to the Flow Chart of International Expansion, but with only the first five countries Wal-Mart moved into. Finding consistent and reliable sources for the data from the early 1990's proved extremely difficult. In order to provide dependable disposable income numbers, we have found it necessary to use one source, Euro Monitor. The Euro Monitor has been conducting research in developing and emerging markets for 40 years. The single draw back to this is that we are only provided disposable income back to 2007.*

| Country | Year of Expansion | Country Disposable Income (USD Milliion) | Country Population | Per Person Disposable Income |
|---|---|---|---|---|
| Mexico[14] | 1991 | 732,414.4 | 110,755,000 | $6,612.92 |
| Canada[109] | 1994 | 968,665.8 | 34,371,000 | $28,182.65 |
| Argentina[108] | 1995 | 219,477.2 | 41,240,000 | $5,321.95 |
| Brazil[110] | 1995 | 1,335,404.6 | 192,988,000 | $6,919.63 |
| Indonesia[111] | 1995 | 436,623.3 | 236,199,000 | $1,848.54 |
| United States[107] | - | 10,581,641.3 | 311,957,000 | $33,920.19 |

*With the above chart we will assume between the 1990 and 2011 no country abruptly passed the United States in disposable income and then suffered an equally sudden and dramatic decrease in their economy. With that in mind, every country that Wal-Mart has moved to has had a lower disposable income. This proposition is true for both the country disposable income and per capita disposable income.*

**P6:Multinational retailers will move to countries that have a high positive change in GDP.**

*Since we are looking at the countries that Wal-Mart moved into, we need to look at least at the change in percent of GDP of Mexico and Canada, since those are their first two moves. According to World Bank Data, the GDP of Mexico from 1985-1991 are as follows:*

| 1985 | $184,473,097,296.041 |
|------|----------------------|
| 1986 | $129,440,191,340.197 |
| 1987 | $140,263,673,924.03 |
| 1988 | $183,144,276,294.09 |
| 1989 | $222,977,042,346.502 |
| 1990 | $262,709,785,592.711 |
| 1991 | $314,453,895,611.75279 |

$$\frac{(\$262,709,785,592.711 - \$184,473,097,296.041)}{\$262,709,785,592.711}$$

*The percentage comes out to be around 29.78% increase, making the proposition true for Wal-Mart in Mexico.*

*Next is Canada's GDP from 1989 to 1994.*

| 1989 | $555,513,513,513.514 |
|------|----------------------|
| 1990 | $582,722,831,676.38 |
| 1991 | $598,208,082,395.042 |
| 1992 | $579,531,728,303.136 |
| 1993 | $563,664,832,183.552 |
| 1994 | $564,493,995,313.415 |

$$\frac{(\$564,493,995,313.415 - \$555,513,513,513.514)}{\$564,493,995,313.415}$$

*This actually comes out to a 1.59% increase of the GDP of 1994 compared to the five years before that. So this proposition is true for Canada, Wal-Mart's second international move.*[102]

**P7:Multinational retailers will move to countries that have a high positive change in service-value added as % of GDP. The formula used to determine this proposition is shown below.**

**(Service % of GDP at the time of Expansion - Service% of GDP 5 years before expansion)/(Service% of GDP 5 years before expansion)**

*This proposition is true in relation to Wal-Mart's international expansion. The service percentage of GDP in Mexico in 1991 was 64.4%. The service percentages from 1986 to 1990 are as follows:*

| 1986 | 54.8% |
|------|--------|
| 1987 | 52.33% |
| 1988 | 59.99% |
| 1989 | 62.87% |
| 1990 | 63.73% |

*Over a five-year period the service percentage increased by 17.5% compared to the United States who only has increased 4.6%.*

*For Canada, the data is as follows for 1989 to 1994:*

| 1989 | 64.4% |
|------|--------|
| 1990 | 65.8% |
| 1991 | 68.0% |
| 1992 | 68.7% |
| 1993 | 68.3% |
| 1994 | 67.3% |

*Since there is an increase, albeit, a very small increase compared to the five year average data; this also proves true for Wal-Mart's expansion into Canada, although not as strong of a case as that of Mexico.[103]*

**P8:Multinational retailers will first move to countries that are culturally the most similar to their home country.**

*For this, Hofstede's cultural dimension indicators from the Cultural Dimension Theory will be used to describe the relationships for home country and host country. Wal-Mart's first move was to Mexico in 1991.[12] Mexico is similar to the United States. Mexico is more of a collectivist, the U.S. is more individualistic. At* the time of Wal-Mart's move to Mexico, uncertainty avoidance was relatively high. Power distance, American firms are often democratic, in Mexico, workers expect a boss or supervisor to give direction and guidance similar to India.[35] Given these reported indicators from 1996, just a few years after the international move, there are still some large differences in the cultures.

The next move that Wal-Mart made was to Canada. It is geographically close to the United States, as well as being close on Hofstede's demensions of difference. Both the United States and Canada are individualistic nations, focusing more on the self than the family or community as a whole. Also, Canada is similar in uncertainty avoidance as well, as it is below the world average on the Hofstede Scale. Because of this, Canadians are more likely to take risks, which is very similar to the United States. It is also a masculine nation, meaning that there are more gaps in the roles of males and females than that of countries that rank as feminine nations. They are also a low power distance country, meaning that Canada is fairly focused on equality, making them different from a country such as India, where there is clear differences between those with and without power, and a class system that is in place.[104] As mentioned in the above proposition, because Canada is culturally similar to the United States, this makes this proposition ture.

**P9:Multinational retailers will expand within the country and then will expand regionally within that area.**

Wal-Mart moved to Mexico in 1991, but did not expand further into Central and South America until 2005. The next move that Wal-Mart made was to Canada, moving into the northern portion of North America. Other than the first two moves, Wal-Mart started to "jump" to other locations. The third move that Wal-Mart made was to South America, where they expanded into Argentina and Brazil. After this expansion, they "jumped" to Asia, where they first expanded into Indonesia and China, as well as Korea a year later. Then they moved to Europe with stores located in Germany and the United Kingdom, before they moved back to Asia with stores in Japan. After Japan, they opened stores in five Central and South American locations including Guatemala and Nicaragua. The last two "jumps" Wal-Mart made were to Chile and India respectively. This proposition is true in the case of Wal-Mart.[52]

**P10: Periodically the multinational retailers will "jump" to a new geographic area and begin the stages form of expansion.**

Wal-Mart moved to Mexico in 1991, but did not expand further into Central and South America until 2005. After the first two moves into Mexico and Canada, Wal-Mart started to "jump" from area to area to expand internationally. After the company moved to Canada they then moved to Argentina and Brazil in 1995. Following expansion into South America, they "jumped" over international waters to Indonesia and China, followed by Korea. They next moved over to Europe by opening stores in Germany, and followed by the United Kingdom a year later in 1999. They "jumped" back to Asia in Japan, and then proceeded to jump back to Central and South America in 2005 with stores in Costa Rica, El Salvador, Guatemala, Nicaragua, and Honduras. They finally moved to Chile and India in 2009. Since Wal-Mart has the tendency to "jump" from place to place, this proposition is true in the case of Wal-Mart.[52]

**P11: Multinational retailers will move to countries that are geographically close to the home country initially, and then expand to more distant countries.**

Wal-Mart, being a U.S. based company, has two close neighbors: Mexico and Canada. Wal-Mart first moved to its neighbor to the south in Mexico in 1991, and for its first move it was a bordering country to the United States.[12] Wal-Mart's second international move was to Canada, the neighbor to the North in 1994.[5] This expansion to the North was also to a bordering country, and was the last one before "jumping" to a new area. The next move was to a more distant area, being South America, to Brazil, as well as Argentina, and up until 1995 it was the farthest move. Next they moved farther away to Asia, where they expanded into Indonesia, China and Korea. They continued to expand to these distant areas up until the final moves to Chile and India. Keeping up with this trend, there is talk of expanding Wal-Mart into South Africa, which would be one of the most distant moves for Wal-Mart to date. Since Wal-Mart did expand first to the neighboring countries of Canada and Mexico, this proposition proves true for Wal-Mart.

**P12: Multinational retailers will move to countries with large population bases.**

Since Wal-Mart first moved to Mexico and Canada, these will be the populations that we will be looking at. Also, since we are looking at populations as of 1991 of Mexico, and 1994 of Canada. According to the census taken during the beginning of 1990, in Mexico, the recorded population was 81.1 million. This recorded figure was a 2 percent increase from the previously conducted census in 1980.[97] This is a fairly large population so in the case of Wal-Mart moving into Mexico, the proposition is true.

The population of Canada also needs to be observed for this propostion. According to data from the Canadian Census of 1991, the population was at 28 million people, but since Wal-Mart did not move into Canada until 1994, we can assume that the population had grown some since 1991. This population is actually fairly *low, but well concentrated in the big cities of Canada such as Toronto, Montreal, and Vancouver, as some areas of Canada are very frigid and hard to live in. Since the population is rather low, it may not be true in Canada. After Canada, however you see moves into Brazil and China which are two of the highest populations in the world, so overall this proposition proves to be true in the case of Wal-Mart.*

## Endnotes

1.  Argentina fact sheet. (2011). Retrieved March 20, 2011, from Wal-Mart: About Us website: http://walmartstores.com/download/2222.pdf

2.  Bhatnagar, P. (2006, April 10). Wal-Mart puts the squeeze on vendors [Online article]. Retrieved February 24, 2011, from Cable News Network website: http://money.cnn.com/2006/04/10/news/companies/walmart_vendors/index.htm

3.  Bing.com. (2011, April 4). Wal-Mart Stores, Inc. Stock Information [Stock Information]. Retrieved April 4, 2011, from Microsoft website: http://www.bing.com/finance/     search?q=WMT&StockSubScenario=6&FORM=DTPFSA

4.  Wal-Mart Stores Inc. (2011, March 31). Brazil Fact Sheet [Fact Sheet]. Retrieved April 23, 2011, from Wal-Mart Stores Inc. website: http://walmartstores.com/download/1997.pdf

5.  Brent, P. (1994, March 22). Wal-Mart Meets The Press: Executives skirt major questions. The Financial Post (Toronto, Canada ). Retrieved on February, 25 2011. http://www.lexisnexis.com.proxy1.cl.msu.edu/hottopics/lnacademic/

6.  Canada fact sheet. (2011). Retrieved March 20, 2011, from Wal-Mart: About Us website: http://walmartstores.com/download/1998.pdf

7.  Cassidy, W. B. (2011). Wal-Mart orders $1 billion in supply chain savings. Journal of Commerce, pp. n/a. Retrieved April 25, 2011, from http://ezproxy.msu.edu/login?url=http://search. proquest.com/ docview/846757387?accountid=12598

8.  Chile fact sheet. (2011). Retrieved March 20, 2011, from Wal-Mart: About Us website: http://walmartstores.com/download/3718.pdf

9.  China fact sheet. (2011). Retrieved March 20, 2011, from Wal-Mart: About Us website: http://walmartstores.com/download/1999.pdf

10. Costa Rica fact sheet. (2011). Retrieved March 20, 2011, from Wal-Mart: About Us website: http://walmartstores.com/download/2000.pdf

11. Dow Jones & Company Inc. (2005, September 20). Wal-Mart Takes Control on Central America. Retrieved March 20, 2011, from http://money.cnn.com/2005/09/20/news/international/ walmart_centam.dj/index.htm

12. Eaton, T., & News, Mexico City Bureau of The Dallas Morning. (1993, October 24). A Shopper's; Heaven; Mexicans make Wal-Mart country's newest shrine. Retrieved April 25, 2011, from The Dallas Morning News. Website: http://www. lexisnexis.com.proxy2.cl.msu.edu/hottopics/lnacademic/

13. El Salvador fact sheet. (2011). Retrieved March 20, 2011, from Wal-Mart: About Us website: http://walmartstores.com/download/2001.pdf

14. Euromonitor. (2011). Mexico [Mexico Fact Sheet]. Retrieved April 1, 2011, from Euromonitor website: http://www.euromonitor.com/mexico/country-factfile

15. Euromonitor. (2011). USA [USA Fact Sheet]. Retrieved April 1, 2011, from Euromonitor website: http://www.euromonitor.com/usa/country-factfile

16. Gandolfi, F., Braun, M., Nanney, P., & Yoon, K. J. (2008, April). Colossal failure [Review of practices]. Retrieved February 3, 2011, from Regent Global Business Review website: http://www.regent.edu/acad/global/publications/rgbr/vol2iss1/2008%20April_Wal-mart_Gandolfi_et_al.pdf

17. Germany Data [Germany Data Sheet]. (2011). Retrieved February 3, 2011, from The World Bank Group website: http://data.worldbank.org/country/germany

18. Gogoi, P. (2008, March 7). Wal-Mart's Crossover Strategy Still Works [Online article]. Retrieved February 24, 2011, from Bloomberg L.P. website: http://www. businessweek.com/bwdaily/dnflash/content/mar2008/db2008036_169954.htm

19. Gomes, I. (2009, April 2). India attracts foreign players. Birmingham Post, pp. 40. Retrieved on February, 25 2011. http://www.lexisnexis.com.proxy1.cl.msu.edu/hottopics/lnacademic/

20. Guatemala. (2011). Retrieved March 20, 2011, from http://www.selectlatinamerica.co.uk /destinations/Guatemala/history

21. Guatemala fact sheet. (2011). Retrieved March 20, 2011, from Wal-Mart: About Us website: http://walmartstores.com/download/2002.pdf

22. Harbrecht, D. (1998, February 25). Out Of Indonesia: Wal-Mart Splits With Lippo. Retrieved February 3, 2011, from Business Week Online website: http://www. businessweek.com/bwdaily/dnflash/feb1998/nf80225b.htm

23. Hays, C. L. (2001, May 12). Wal-Mart to end practice of sharing sales data. The New York Times, pp. 1. Retrieved on February, 25 2011. http://www.lexisnexis. com.proxy1.cl.msu.edu/hottopics/lnacademic/

24. Hays, C. L. (2004, November 14). What Wal-Mart Knows About Customers' Habits [Online article]. Retrieved February 24, 2011, from The New York Times Company website: http://www.nytimes.com/2004/11/14/business/yourmoney/14wal.html

25. Hoovers. (2011). Wal-Mart Brazil [Hoovers Document Brazil]. Retrieved February 10, 2011, from Hoovers website: http://www.hoovers.com/company/Wal-Mart_Brazil/rhsxcji-1.html

26. Hoovers. (2011). Wal-Mart De México, S.A.B. de C.V. [Hoovers Document Mexico]. Retrieved February 10, 2011, from Hoovers website: http://www.hoovers.com/company/Wal-Mart_de_M%E9xico_SAB_de_CV/ctcrri-1.html

27. Honduras fact sheet. (2011). Retrieved March 20, 2011, from Wal-Mart: About Us website: http://walmartstores.com/download/2004.pdf

28. Hottovoy, R. J. (2011, January 26). Wal-Mart Looks Abroad For Growth: China, Brazil, India [Info On Strategies]. Retrieved March 31, 2011, from http://foundationge.com/perspectives/news/? p=139

29. India fact sheet. (2011). Retrieved March 20, 2011, from Wal-Mart: About Us website: http://walmartstores.com/download/1996.pdf

30. Indonesia Data [Indonesia Data Sheet]. (2011). Retrieved February 3, 2011, from The World Bank Group website: http://data.worldbank.org/country/indonesia

31. Japan fact sheet. (2011). Retrieved March 20, 2011, from Wal-Mart: About Us website: http://walmartstores.com/download/2005.pdf

32. Kapner, S. (2008, May 29). Wal-Mart puts the squeeze on food costs [Online article]. Retrieved February 24, 2011, from Fortune Magazine website: http://money.cnn.com/2008/05/28/magazines/fortune/kapner_walmart.fortune/index.htm

33. Katz, R., & Han, S. (2006, May 22). Wal-Mart Sells Korea Chain to Shinsegae for $869 Mln (Update9) [Online article]. Retrieved February 24, 2011, from BLOOMBERG L.P. website: http://www.bloomberg.com/apps/news?pid=news archive&sid=aIXz9HQqPUOA&refer=us

34. Korea, Rep. Data [Country Data]. (2011). Retrieved February 3, 2011, from The World Bank Group website: http://data.worldbank.org/country/korea-republic

35. Kunde, D. (1996, May 1). Acclimatizing to cultures; U.S. executives learning expectations in Mexico. The Dallas Morning News. Retrieved on February, 25 2011. http://www.lexisnexis.com.proxy1.cl.msu.edu/hottopics/lnacademic/

36. Mexico fact sheet. (2011). Retrieved March 20, 2011, from Wal-Mart: About Us website: http://walmartstores.com/download/2006.pd

37. News. (2011) Retrieved on February, 25 2011, from: http://www.lexisnexis.com.proxy1.cl.msu.edu/hottopics/lnacademic/

38. Nicaragua fact sheet. (2011). Retrieved March 20, 2011, from Wal-Mart: About Us

website: http://walmartstores.com/download/2007.pdf

39. Olsen, K. (2006, May 22). Wal-Mart pulls out of South Korea sells 16 stores [Article]. Retrieved February 3, 2011, from USA Today website: http://www. usatoday.com/money/industries/retail/2006-05-22-walmart-korea_x.htm?csp=34

40. Rvdirections.com (2011). [Map of Wal-Mart locations] [Internet only artwork]. Retrieved January 3, 2011,from http://www.rvdirections.com/Walmart___Sams_ Club_Map.gif

41. Services, etc., value added (% of GDP) Data Table [Service GDP]. (2011). Retrieved January 3, 2011, from The World Bank Group website: http://data.worldbank.org/ indicator/NV.SRV.TETC.ZS

42. Sherman, M. (2011). Court to look at huge Wal-Mart sex bias lawsuit. The Louisiana Weekly, pp. 11. Retrieved February 3, 2011, from http://ezproxy.msu.edu/ login?url=http://search.proquest.com/docview/ 840628835?accountid=12598

43. Sternquist, B. (2007). International Retailing (2nd ed.). New York: Fairchild Publications, Inc.    (Original work published 1998)

44. Suhartono, H., & Latul, J. (2011, January 10). Indonesia's Matahari scraps $1 billion Hypermart sale [Update to Indonesia Report]. Retrieved February 3, 2011, from Reuters website:    http://www.reuters.com/article/2011/01/10/us-matahari-idUSTRE70913I20110110

45. Thomas, Denny. (2010, November 4). UPDATE 2-Wal-Mart eyes bid for Indonesia Matahari units-sources [Report]. Retrieved February 3, 2011, from Reuters website: http://www.reuters.com/article/2010/11/04/matahari-walmart-idUSTOE6A304W20101104

46. Troy, Mike. (2006, August). Wal-Mart bids Auf Wiedersehen, ends nine-year grind in Germany. Retailing Today, 45(14), 1,41. Retrieved February 4, 2011, from ABI/INFORM Global. (Document ID: 1107358391).

47. Trucking Fleet [Online webpage]. (2011). Retrieved February 24, 2011, from Wal-Mart website: http://walmartstores.com/Sustainability/7674.aspx

48. Wal-Mart. (1990). Wal-Mart Annual Report 1990 [Financial Statements]. Retrieved March 10, 2011, from Wal-Mart website: http://www.walmartstores. com/Media/Investors/1990AR.pdf

49. Wal-Mart Announces Central American Investment. (2011). Retrieved March 30, 2011, from    http://www.prnewswire.com/news-releases/wal-mart-announces-central-american-investment-55043452.html

50. Wal-Mart Announces Sale of German Business; 85-Supercenter Chain to be Sold to Metro AG. (2006, 28 July). PR Newswire, 1.  Retrieved February 3, 2011, from

ABI/INFORM Dateline. (Document ID: 1084625691).

51. Wal-Mart Announces Sale of South Korean Business; 16-Supercenter Chain to be Sold to South Korean Retailer Shinsegae. (2006, 22 May). PR Newswire,1. Retrieved February 4, 2011, from ABI/INFORM Dateline. (Document ID: 1048250731).

52. Wal-Mart Corporation. (n.d.). About Us and History. Retrieved February 23, 2011, from http://walmartstores.com/AboutUs/

53. Wal-Mart Corporation. (n.d.). Nicaragua. Retrieved March 30, 2011, from http://walmartstores.com/AboutUs/9756.aspx

54. Wal-Mart International. (n.d.). Retrieved March 20, 2011, from http://money.cnn.com/ 2005/09/20/news/international/walmart_centam.dj/index.htm

55. Wal-Mart Stores Inc. Intellectual Property Information, Recent European Patents. (2011). Retrieved on February, 20 2011. Retrieved from http://www.lexisnexis.com.proxy2.cl.msu.edu/hottopics/lnacademic/

56. Wal-Mart Stores Inc. Intellectual Property Information, Recent International Trademarks. (2011). Retrieved on February, 20 2011. Retrieved from http://www.lexisnexis.com.proxy2.cl.msu.edu/hottopics/lnacademic/

57. Wal-Mart Stores Inc. Intellectual Property Information, Recent United States Copyrights. (2011). Retrieved on February, 20 2011. Retrieved from http://www.lexisnexis.com.proxy2.cl.msu.edu/hottopics/lnacademic/

58. Wal-Mart Stores Inc. Intellectual Property Information, Recent United States Federal Trademarks. (2011). Retrieved on February, 20 2011. Retrieved from http://www.lexisnexis.com.proxy2.cl.msu.edu/hottopics/lnacademic/

59. Wal-Mart Stores Inc. Intellectual Property Information, Recent United States Patents. (2011). Retrieved on February, 20 2011. Retrieved from http://www.lexisnexis.com.proxy2.cl.msu.edu/hottopics/lnacademic/

60. Wal-Mart Stores Inc. Intellectual Property Information. Recent United States States Trademarks. (2011). Retrieved on February, 20 2011. Retrieved from http://www.lexisnexis.com.proxy2.cl.msu.edu/hottopics/lnacademic/

61. Wal-Mart Stores Inc. (2011). International Map Widget [Interactive Map]. Retrieved April 4, 2011, from Wal-Mart Stores Inc. website: http://walmartstores.com/P/CountriesMap.aspx

62. Wal-Mart Transportation Network Maps [Supplychain maps]. (2011). Retrieved February 24, 2011, from Wal-Mart website: http://walmartprivatefleet.com/Services/NetworkMaps.aspx

63. Wal-Mart Transportation Statistics [Fleet statistics]. (2011). Retrieved February 24, 2011, from Wal-Mart website: http://walmartprivatefleet.com/CompetitiveAdvantage/Stats.aspx

64. Walmartstores.com: Argentina [Country Info]. Retrieved January 28, 2011, from Wal-Mart Stores Inc. website: http://walmartstores.com/AboutUs/243.aspx?p=246 (2010, December 31)

65. Walmartstores.com: Brazil [Country Info]. Retrieved January 28, 2011, from Wal-Mart Stores Inc. website: http://walmartstores.com/AboutUs/259.aspx?p=246 (2010, December 31)

66. Walmartstores.com: Canada [Country Info]. Retrieved January 28, 2011, from Wal-Mart Stores Inc. website: http://walmartstores.com/AboutUs/266.aspx?p=246 (2010, December 31)

67. Walmartstores.com: Chile [Country Info]. Retrieved January 28, 2011, from Wal-Mart Stores Inc. website: http://walmartstores.com/AboutUs/8935.aspx (2010, December 31)

68. Walmartstores.com: China [Country Info]. Retrieved January 28, 2011, from Wal-Mart Stores Inc. website: http://walmartstores.com/AboutUs/273.aspx?p=246 (2010, December 31)

69. Walmartstores.com: Costa Rica [Country Info]. Retrieved January 28, 2011, from Wal-Mart Stores Inc. website: http://walmartstores.com/AboutUs/9763.aspx (2010, December 31)

70. Walmartstores.com: El Salvador [Country Info]. Retrieved January 28, 2011, from Wal-Mart Stores Inc. website: http://walmartstores.com/AboutUs/9754.aspx (2010, December 31)

71. Walmartstores.com: Guatemala [Country Info]. Retrieved January 28, 2011, from Wal-Mart Stores Inc. website: http://walmartstores.com/AboutUs/9753.aspx (2010, December 31)

72. Walmartstores.com: Honduras [Country Info]. Retrieved January 28, 2011, from Wal-Mart Stores Inc. website: http://walmartstores.com/AboutUs/9755.aspx (2010, December 31)

73. Walmartstores.com: India [Country Info]. Retrieved January 28, 2011, from Wal-Mart Stores Inc. website: http://walmartstores.com/AboutUs/276.aspx?p=246 (2010, December 31)

74. Walmartstores.com: Japan [Country Info]. Retrieved January 28, 2011, from Wal-Mart Stores Inc. website: http://walmartstores.com/AboutUs/274.aspx?p=246 (2010, December 31)

75. Walmartstores.com: Mexico [Country Info]. Retrieved January 28, 2011, from Wal-Mart Stores Inc. website: http://walmartstores.com/AboutUs/277.aspx?p=246 (2010, December 31)

76. Walmartstores.com: Nicaragua [Country Info]. Retrieved January 28, 2011, from Wal-Mart Stores Inc. website: http://walmartstores.com/AboutUs/9756.aspx (2010, December 31)

77. Walmartstores.com: United Kingdom [Country Info]. Retrieved January 28, 2011, from Wal-Mart Stores Inc. website: http://walmartstores.com/AboutUs/275. aspx?p=246 (2010, December 31)

78. Walmartstores.com Wal-Mart Deploys Data Mining Software Into Its Production Support Environment [Online article]. (2011). Retrieved February 24, 2011, from Wal-Mart website: http://walmartstores.com/pressroom/news/4008.aspx

79. WDI and GDF. (2010). Services, etc., value added (% of GDP) [Spreadsheet]. Retrieved April 4, 2011, from Worldbank.org website: http://search.worldbank. org/quickview?name=%3Cem%3 EServices%2C%3C%2Fem%3E+%3Cem%3Eet c.%2C%3C%2Fem%3E+%3Cem%3Evalue%3C%2Fem%3E+%3C em%3Eadde d%3C%2Fem%3E+%3Cem%3E%28%25%3C%2Fem %3E+of+%3Cem%3EGDP %29%3C%2Fem%3E&id=NV.SRV.TETC.ZS&type=I ndicators&cube_no=2&qte rm=Services%2C+etc.%2C+value+added+%28%25+of+GDP%29+mexico+1991

80. Wheelock, B. (2004). Third quarter GDP grows at fastest rate since 1997. Retrieved on February, 25 2011. http://www.lexisnexis.com.proxy1.cl.msu.edu/hottopics/ lnacademic/

81. World Bank Argentina. (n.d.). Retrieved March 31, 2011, from Argentina GDP website: http://data.worldbank.org/country/argentina

82. World Bank Brazil. (n.d.). Retrieved March 31, 2011, from Brazil GDP website: http://data.worldbank.org/country/brazil

83. World Bank Canada. (n.d.). Retrieved March 31, 2011, from Canada GDP website: http://data.worldbank.org/country/canada

84. World Bank Chile. (n.d.). Retrieved March 31, 2011, from Chile GDP website: http://data.worldbank.org/country/chile

85. World Bank China. (n.d.). Retrieved March 31, 2011, from China GDP website: http://data.worldbank.org/country/china

86. World Bank Costa Rica. (n.d.). Retrieved March 31, 2011, from Costa Rica GDP website: http://data.worldbank.org/country/costa-rica

87. World Bank El Salvador. (n.d.). Retrieved March 31, 2011, from El Salvador GDP website: http://data.worldbank.org/country/el-salvador

88. World Bank Guatemala. (n.d.). Retrieved March 31, 2011, from Guatemala GDP website: http://data.worldbank.org/country/guatemala

89. World Bank Honduras. (n.d.). Retrieved March 31, 2011, from Honduras GDP website: http://data.worldbank.org/country/honduras

90. World Bank India. (n.d.). Retrieved March 31, 2011, from India GDP website: http://data.worldbank.org/country/india

91. World Bank Japan. (n.d.). Retrieved March 31, 2011, from Japan GDP website: http://data.worldbank.org/country/japan

92. World Bank Mexico. (n.d.). Retrieved March 31, 2011, from Mexico GDP website: http://data.worldbank.org/country/mexico

93. World Bank Mexico. (n.d.). Retrieved March 19, 2011, from GDP growth website: http://search.worldbank.org/quickview?name=%3Cem%3EGD P%3C%2Fem%3E+growth+ %28annual+%25%29&id=NY.GDP.MKTP. KD.ZG&type=Indicators&cube_no=2& qterm=mexico+GDP+1991

94. World Bank Nicaragua. (n.d.). Retrieved March 31, 2011, from Nicaragua GDP website: http://data.worldbank.org/country/nicaragua

95. World Bank United Kingdom. (n.d.). Retrieved March 31, 2011, from United Kingdom GDP website: http://data.worldbank.org/country/united-kingdom

96. World Bank Service GDP. (2011). Services, etc., value added (% of GDP) [Data Table]. Retrieved April 4, 2011, from The World Bank Group website: http://data. worldbank.org/ indicator/NV.SRV.TETC.ZS

97. Zellner, W. (1998, September 3). Look Out, Supermarkets Wal-Mart Is Hungry Experimental stores report]. Retrieved February 24, 2010, from Bloomberg L.P. website: http://www.businessweek.com/1998/37/b3595129.htm

98. Ordorica M. (1990). The population of Mexico in 1990 [Mexican Census]. Retrieved April 4, 2011, from National Center for Biotechnology Information website: http://www.ncbi.nlm.nih.gov/pubmed/12158096

99. Tyler, R. (2009, November 8). Wal-Mart 'sells' Asda for £6.9bn in group restructuring [Web article]. Retrieved April 23, 2011, from Telegraph Media Group Limited website: http://www.telegraph.co.uk/finance/newsbysector/ retailandconsumer/6527054/Wal-Mart-sells-Asda-for-6.9bn-in-group-restructuring.html

100. So Easily Online Limited. (2011). Corinth Investments Limited [Company Profile]. Retrieved April 23, 2011, from So Easily Online Limited website: http:// bizzy.co.uk/uk/02582550/corinth-services

101. United North America. (2010). Similarities & Differences Between Canada & United States [Chart and summary]. Retrieved April 24, 2011, from United North America website: http://www.unitednorthamerica.org/simdiff.htm

102. World Bank. (2011). Canada GDP 1994 [Canada GDP]. Retrieved April 24, 2011, from World Bank website: http://search.worldbank.org/data?qterm=Canada+gdp +1992&language= EN&format=html

103. World Bank. (2011). Service % GDP Canada 1994 [% Service GDP Canada]. Retrieved April 24, 2011, from World Bank website: http://search.worldbank.org/ data?qterm=service++ gdp+canada1994&language=EN&format=html

104. Itim International. (2011). Canada Geert Hofstede Explained [Hofstede Canada]. Retrieved April 24,2011, from Itim International website: http://www.geert-hofstede.com/ hofstede_canada.shtml

105. Canada. (2011). Canadians in Context — Population Size and Growth [Canada Population]. Retrieved April 24, 2011, from Human Resources and Skills Development Canada website: http://www4.hrsdc.gc.ca/.3ndic.1t.4r@-eng. jsp?iid=35

106. The Associated Press. (2011, April 24). Got groceries? Wal-Mart testing home delivery [News Article]. Retrieved April 24, 2011, from The Macomb Daily website: http://macombdaily.com/articles/2011/04/24/business/ doc4db340feaea08725835466.txt

107. Bureau of Economic Analysis. (2011, March 23). BEA SA50 Equals Disposable Personal Income [Chart]. Retrieved April 28, 2011, from U.S. Department of Commerce website: http://www.bea.gov/regional/spi/drill.cfm?selTable=SA50&s elLineCode=16&selYears =2007&rformat=Display

108. Euromonitor. (2011). Argentina [Argentina Fact Sheet]. Retrieved April 28, 2011, from Euromonitor website: http://www.euromonitor.com/argentina/country-factfile

109. Euromonitor. (2011). Canada [Canada Fact Sheet]. Retrieved April 28, 2011, from Euromonitor website: http://www.euromonitor.com/canada/country-factfile

110. Euromonitor. (2011). Brazil [Brazil Fact Sheet]. Retrieved April 28, 2011, from Euromonitor website: http://www.euromonitor.com/brazil/country-factfile

111. Euromonitor. (2011). Indonesia [Indonesia Fact Sheet]. Retrieved April 28, 2011, from Euromonitor website: http://www.euromonitor.com/Indonesia/country-factfile

Lightning Source UK Ltd.
Milton Keynes UK
UKOW051550071211

183269UK00001B/89/P